Fodor's

MADRID

Welcome to Madrid

The thud of a vermouth glass on an old zinc bar, the late-afternoon sun on worn cobblestones, the swoosh of a flamenco dancer's gown, the hush of a soaring museum hall—Madrid's sights and sounds pull you in from the moment you arrive. A few days in the Spanish capital will take you to the main sights—palaces, plazas, tapas bars, markets—all (for the most part) within walking distance from one another. Lengthier stints allow for deep dives into areas like Usera, Madrid's "secret" Chinatown across the river, and Lavapiés, a graffitied multicultural mecca, plus day trips to medieval cities with ancient monuments and gutsy Castilian cooking.

TOP REASONS TO GO

★ **Electric nightlife:** Let loose to bassy DJ sets, Latin jazz, or feisty flamenco.

★ **Artistic treasures:** Ponder prized Goyas, Picassos, El Grecos, and Velázquezes.

★ **Multiculturalism:** Senegalese lunch counters, Chinese hot pot, Venezuelan bars.

★ **Raucous festivals:** Feel the pulse at Madrid Pride, outdoor festivals, or a verbena (outdoor fair).

★ **Sporting events:** Bellow ¡gooooooool! like a Spaniard at a rollicking soccer match.

★ **Epic tapas crawls:** Embark on a gastronomical adventure.

Contents

Fodor's Features

MAPS

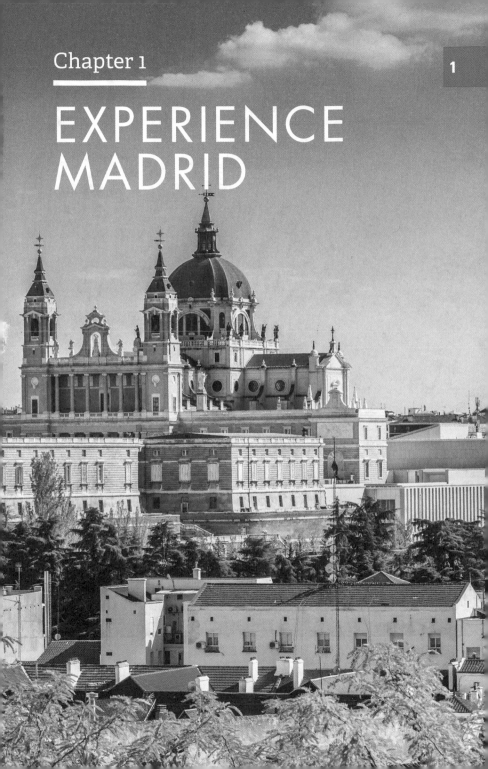

Chapter 1

EXPERIENCE MADRID

20 ULTIMATE EXPERIENCES

Madrid offers terrific experiences that should be on every traveler's list. Here are Fodor's top picks for a memorable trip.

1 | Parque del Buen Retiro

Leafy trails, outdoor cafés, and French gardens aren't just within reach of the city center—they're at the very heart of it in this park that spans nearly 300 acres in old Madrid. *(Ch. 7)*

2 Puerta del Sol

There's never a dull moment in this semicircular plaza, where friends gather, buskers perform, and bar crawls begin. *(Ch. 3)*

3 Museo Nacional Centro de Arte Reina Sofía

A towering sculpture by Roy Lichtenstein greets you at the door to Spain's preeminent modern art museum; beyond it, works like Picasso's *Guernica* await. *(Ch. 8)*

4 Museo del Prado

Spain's premier museum houses a treasure trove of 12th- to 19th-century European art and masterpieces by the Spanish greats including Velázquez, Goya, and El Greco. *(Ch. 7)*

5 Tapas

While there's still plenty of jamón to go around, tapas today are far more intriguing. Sample Madrileño standbys or eye-popping *nueva cocina* dishes in the city's many gastro-markets. *(Ch. 6, 8, 9)*

6 Botín

Guinness World Records calls this creaky local favorite the world's oldest restaurant, opened in 1725. Order the suckling pig, roasted in the original wood-burning oven. *(Ch. 8)*

7 Palacio de Liria

The stunning abode of the late Duchess of Alba finally opened to the public in 2019. It contains what some experts say is one of the finest private art collections in Spain. *(Ch. 5)*

8 Parque del Oeste

For a sunset stroll, there's no place like this charming park with a rose garden, fountains, dogs galore, and—drumroll—a transplanted 2,200-year-old Egyptian temple. *(Ch. 4)*

9 Plaza Mayor

Steeped in four centuries of history, Madrid's most famous square has Flemish-style spires, endless arcades, and busy sidewalk restaurants. *(Ch. 3)*

10 Food Markets

A curious new way to dine has emerged in Madrid in recent years with the transformation of old-school markets into experimental (and affordable) tapas emporiums. *(Chs. 3, 7, 8, 9)*

11 Museo Nacional Thyssen-Bornemisza

Bridging the gap between the classical Prado and modern Reina Sofía, this private collection presided over by a baroness spans seven centuries and countless artistic movements. *(Ch. 6)*

12 Shopping

Hand-sewn espadrilles, colorful painted ceramics, haute couture garments by avant-garde local designers—there's a souvenir for every type of traveler if you know where to look.

13 Real Madrid

In Spanish, *real* means "royal," and to the network of Real Madrid devotees around the world, the team is nothing short of that. Bow with locals at Estadio Santiago Bernabéu. *(Ch. 10)*

14 Flamenco

You don't have to go to Andalusia for traditional flamenco—Madrid is awash with outstanding performance venues that cater to all tastes and budgets.

15 Coffee Culture

The third-wave coffee revolution is sweeping the city, and there's no shortage of award-winning cafés serving complex brews alongside pastries and snacks.

16 Palacio Real

Welcome to the largest palace in Western Europe, nearly double the size of Versailles with 2,800 rooms. Visitors swoon over the only surviving Stradivarius quartet and the 18th-century Royal Kitchens. *(Ch. 4)*

17 Nightlife

As revelers around Europe tuck themselves into bed, the party in Madrid has barely begun. After a *primera copa* at a chic wine or cocktail bar, hit the *discoteca* and groove 'til the wee hours.

18 Churros at Chocolatería San Ginés

San Ginés is to Madrid what Café du Monde is to New Orleans: a national sensation that for generations has been frying spirals of piping-hot *churros* and *porras* (churros' larger cousins). *(Ch. 3)*

19 El Rastro

Merchants and shoppers have been congregating at this legendary open-air market every Sunday since 1740. Its 3,000-plus stalls brim with unique finds and tchotchkes. *(Ch.8)*

20 El Escorial

Take a day trip to Felipe II's imposing castle on a hill, a veritable labyrinth of gilded halls, grand frescoed chambers, and manicured Renaissance gardens. *(Ch. 12)*

WHAT'S WHERE

1 Sol. After a stroll through Plaza Mayor, settle in for some churros con chocolate at a legendary chocolatería or snap up handmade Spanish wares at a centuries-old crafts shop.

2 Palacio and Moncloa. Time-travel to Madrid's noble past in these districts defined by their palaces, French gardens, awe-inspiring religious sights, and stately plazas.

3 Chueca and Malasaña. Trendy tapas bars, packed nightclubs, fabulous vintage shops, and plenty of LGBTQ+ pride—the epicenter of Madrid's countercultural revolution of the 1980s hasn't lost its rakish edge, even if Airbnb and international chains are quickly encroaching.

4 Barrio de las Letras. Come nightfall, it doesn't get livelier than Letras, home to the pedestrianized Calle de las Huertas, Plaza de Santa Ana, and one of Europe's most coveted private art collections at the Museo Thyssen-Bornemisza.

5 Retiro and Salamanca. Taking in the sprawling El Retiro

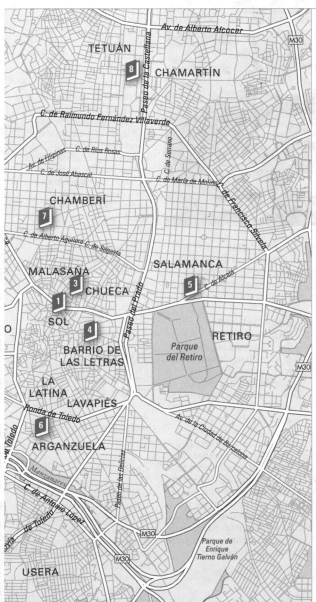

Park, unparalleled Prado Museum, and miles of boutique-lined side streets, these abutting barrios drip with old-world charm and panache.

6 La Latina, Lavapiés, and Arganzuela. Lavapiés, a graffitied multicultural hub with steep cobblestone streets and trendy restaurants, is a quick walk from the timeless taverns of La Latina and the rambunctious El Rastro flea market.

7 Chamberí. Once a sleepy residential neighborhood, Chamberí is a new culinary hot spot with gastro-markets and a pilgrimage-worthy tapas corridor, Calle de Ponzano.

8 Chamartín and Tetuán. Come for the *fútbol*—Real Madrid's home stadium is situated here—and stay for the down-home restaurants and locals-only nightclubs.

9 Carabanchel, Usera, and Latina. Explore a tourist-free side of Madrid's in these blue-collar barrios across the Manzanares that mix cutting-edge art studios with international restaurants, no-frills abuelo bars, and tranquil parks.

What to Eat and Drink in Madrid

TORRIJAS

Don't let locals hear you call it "Spanish French toast," but that's basically what *torrijas* are. A favorite treat during Holy Week, these deep-fried cinnamon-dusted pillows ooze like custardy bread pudding. The finest examples are plated fresh from the skillet and drizzled with warm honey.

BATTERED BACALAO

Salt cod has been a fixture on Spanish tables for more than half a millennium, so it's no surprise that locals are seasoned pros when it comes to cooking it just right. Though *bacalao* (salt cod) can take many forms—you might find it *al pil-pil* (in an emulsified garlic sauce), *a la vizcaína* (with melty peppers and onions), or in countless other newfangled variations—the classic Madrid rendition is battered and fried and served as a gloriously greasy *pincho*, a one-bite portion impaled with a toothpick.

BOCADILLO DE CALAMARES

Sure, a halved baguette filled with nothing but fried squid sounds like a dry, bland affair, but as with most of Madrid's celebrated dishes, the pleasure lies in its simplicity: rings of pristinely fresh squid are floured and flash-fried until juicy and tender and immediately piled into a cloud-soft hoagie. Enjoyed as is, the bocadillo could be the poster child of gastro-minimalism, but no one will give you grief for sprucing it up with some lemon juice or a dollop of aioli.

CALLOS A LA MADRILEÑA

Madrid-style tripe stew has long been a national sensation, both for its quality (you'll never perceive so much as a whiff of funk) and flavor, which is comfortingly smoky thanks to heaped spoonfuls of Spanish *pimentón* (paprika).

CHURROS

Unlike Mexican churros, which get a sprinkling of cinnamon sugar upon exiting the fryer, Spanish churros are always unsweetened, making them the perfect foil for the rich hot chocolate that's their requisite sidekick. In Madrid, they're often teardrop-shaped.

COCIDO MADRILEÑO

This soul-satisfying stew of chickpeas, vegetables, and various meats is the ultimate winter warmer. Traditionally it's presented in three courses, or *vuelcos*: the rich, gelatinous broth comes first, followed by the garbanzos and vegetables, and finally the fall-off-the-bone meats, which generally include beef shank, ham hocks, pork belly, and hen, plus sausages like *morcilla* (blood sausage) and chorizo.

CROQUETAS

The best Spanish-style croquettes have a shatteringly crisp exterior and a molten béchamel center flavored with whatever's handy: chopped ham ends, sautéed porcini mushrooms, flaked bacalao, leftover roast chicken—you name it. They're one of those hedonistically

Tortilla española

delicious "aha" tapas that you'll find yourself ordering at every opportunity.

GAMBAS AL AJILLO

Always a flamboyant spectacle, *gambas al ajillo* (garlicky shrimp) arrive sizzling in an abundance of olive oil. After fishing out each plump, briny morsel, indulge in the primal pleasure of dunking crusty bread into the garlic-and-chili-infused oil.

JAMÓN

Madrid's proximity to Spain's principal ham-producing regions, Andalusia and Extremadura, make it ground zero for some of the best porcine products money can buy. Sweet and subtle *jamón serrano*, the industry standard, is a gateway to the more complex—and expensive—stuff, *jamón ibérico de bellota* (acorn-fed Iberian ham).

PATATAS BRAVAS

Madrid's famous "angry potatoes" are fried in olive oil until crisp and blistered and blanketed in fiery chilivinegar sauce, making them an optimal bar food.

SPANISH GIN-TÓNIC

Order a gin and tonic (*gin-tónic* in Spanish) in Madrid and you'll be presented with a fishbowl-size goblet filled with ice, tonic, over-the-top garnishes (think cardamom, pink peppercorns, basil, or berries), and more gin than you'll care to remember the next morning. Traditionally, cocktail hour is after dinner, so don't be caught off guard when the waiter offers a round of *copas* upon clearing the dessert plates.

SPANISH WINE

You might know your Rioja from your Priorat and your cava from your Albariño, but Spain's most famous wines are a fraction of the enological treasures you can find in Madrid. Try a Manchegan Airén aged in *tinajas* (amphorae), a Rosé Txakoli from the Basque Country, or a local raspy red Garnacha or apricot-scented white Albillo from the Sierra de Gredos, an hour away from the city.

TORTILLA ESPAÑOLA

How can a simple omelet of potatoes, eggs, and onions taste so sublime? Buckets of fruity Spanish olive oil may have something to do with it. *Tortilla española* (Spanish tortilla, aka *tortilla de patata* or potato tortilla) is the most ubiquitous dish in Spain—Spanish kids grow up eating it at least once a week—and its joy lies in its countless variations.

Best Nightlife Spots in Madrid

CAFÉ CENTRAL
Madrid's best-known jazz venue hosts an enviable roster of international artists. Performances are usually 9–11 nightly, and tickets can be bought at the door or online (the latter is advisable if traveling around holiday time).

LA ALQUIMIA
Welcome to Madrid's newest hot spot for natural wine geeks. Pull up a stool in the snug bar area lined with shelves of wine bottles, and choose from an ever-changing selection of boutique bottles you won't find anywhere else.

CORRAL DE LA MORERÍA
Corral de la Morería is the ultimate soup-to-nuts *tablao* (flamenco cabaret) experience. Opt for an elegant meal in the main hall or at the adjacent four-table restaurant, which holds a Michelin star. The no-photography policy and whisper-quiet staff keep you focused on the passion-packed music.

CAFÉ BERLÍN
For a space so small and unassuming, Café Berlín packs quite the acoustic punch and draws an international eclectic crowd. Before midnight, catch nightly live music acts in a panoply of styles (flamenco, swing, soul, and more); from around 1 am on, drop in for the disco-inflected DJ sets that ooze good vibes until 6 am.

FABRIK
World-famous megaclub Fabrik is so far from the city center that you have to take a 30-minute charter bus to get there (€3; departures Friday and Saturday every 30 minutes from Plaza de España 11 pm–6 am). But those who make the trek—up to 7,000 people on a good night—are rewarded with euphoria-inducing DJ sets by big-name artists. You can thank the 44 Tecnare speakers for the ringing in your ears on the hazy ride back into town.

TEATRO KAPITAL
Perhaps Madrid's most legendary nightclub, Teatro Kapital has seven floors—each of which plays a different type of music spun by top local and international DJs—plus a small movie theater and rooftop terrace. Dress to impress for this one: no sneakers, shorts, or tank tops allowed. VIP tables overlooking the dance floor are a worthwhile splurge (from €140) if you can swing it.

MACERA TALLER BAR
The age-old technique of maceration rules at Macera, where bartenders treat spirits like blank canvases,

Café Berlin

imbuing them with surprising flavor combinations. Gin, for instance, is steeped with fresh cilantro, lime, and jalapeño until it achieves a grassy piquancy that shocks and pleases the palate all at once. After you've gotten your buzz on, head over to Macera Club (in Barrio de las Letras) for underground DJ sets 'til 6 am.

POSTUREO BAR
Tourists have yet to discover Chueca's buzziest gay bar, which opened just before the pandemic and caters to well-dressed creatives, trendy out-of-towners, models on their nights off, and everybody in between. Bartenders may not know what a Boulevardier is (even if they have all the requisite ingredients), but their sigh-worthy looks make them easy to forgive.

INDEPENDANCE CLUB
Next door to Kapital, Independance is a smaller club that draws a different crowd every night, thanks to its wide-reaching roster of DJs and performers that span afrobeats, grunge, K-pop, and nearly any dance genre you can think of. Of note is the MOOD party, often held on Thursday nights, which plays alternative, American-inflected pop and rap.

SALMON GURU
Regularly featured on best-of lists, Salmon Guru is Madrid's—and perhaps Spain's—most innovative *coctelería*. The nueva cocina tapas are almost as impressive as the eye-popping concoctions. Try the Chipotle Chillón, a crowd favorite made with mezcal, absinthe, and chipotle syrup.

What to Buy in Madrid

ESPADRILLES
Nothing screams summer in Spain like a pair of colorful rope-soled *alpargatas*, or espadrilles. Antigua Casa Crespo, in business since 1863, still makes them the old-fashioned way, using top-quality rope and hand-sewing the seams.

ÁBBATTE TEXTILES
The mother-and-daughter duo behind ÁBBATTE combines the former's hands-on expertise in textile construction with the latter's academic background in Spanish design history. The result? Plush, pillowy perfection with a nod to the past in every handmade piece, from blankets to bedspreads to cushions and rugs. All wares are woven in the Cistercian abbey of Santa María de la Sierra, an hour north of the city.

CAPES
Travelers who like their souvenirs on the zanier side should check out the merino wool capes at Seseña, the world's oldest cape maker. Seseña has outfitted the likes of Picasso, Hemingway, and Michael Jackson, and the fourth-generation owners are ever more experimental when it comes to newfangled fashions.

CERAMICS
The Moors brought exquisite ceramic craftsmanship to the Iberian Peninsula in the 8th century with their florid mosaics and *azulejos* (glazed tiles), and the art form reached its apogee in Spain during the Renaissance. Though you won't find specimens that old outside museums, the hand-painted jugs, bowls, and pitchers that grace the shelves of Cocol are a close approximation.

CUSTOM THREADS
Like many European cities, Madrid has a rich tradition of craftsmanship when it comes to custom-made apparel. Bespoke leather shoes, designer gowns, meticulously tailored suits—the art of individualized timeless couture is alive and well in Madrid; the only hitch is whether you can afford to shell out the euros for it. If so, make a beeline to Oteyza, whose expert tailors dress Madrid's upper crust with hand-stitched garments that fit like a glove.

FANS
Summer visitors are often surprised to see locals—mostly women—fanning themselves as if they stepped straight out of a Goya painting. But unlike during Spain's glory days, today's *abanicos* are seldom brandished for show—they're simpler in design, lightweight and practical and ideal for stuffing into a purse for use on the metro or restaurant terraces. Splurge on an attractive yet sturdy one at Casa de Diego, the legendary old-fashioned boutique at Puerta del Sol that makes each fan by hand.

GUITARS
Whether you're a seasoned *guitarrista* (guitar player) or are still wrapping your fingers around the main chords, you'll no doubt appreciate the artistry of a sleek handmade Spanish guitar. Try one on for size at Juan Álvarez, the luthier

Fans

made internationally famous by Eric Clapton in 1992, when the blues artist chose one of his guitars to play the now-mythical "Tears in Heaven" on MTV's *Unplugged*.

JAMÓN
No offense to Italy, but even the best prosciutto doesn't hold a candle to real-deal jamón ibérico de bellota, made from semi-wild black-hoofed pigs that roam the scrubby forests of southern Spain. To savor this delicacy at home—FDA regulations be damned—purchase vacuum-sealed envelopes of jamón at any traditional market (e.g., Mercado de la Paz, Mercado de la Cebada) or at specialty vendors like Cinco Jotas.

KITCHENWARE
To set yourself up for culinary success at home, you'll need (OK, want) some specialty cookware: earthenware *cazuelas*

(casserole dishes) come in all shapes and sizes; you'll use these for all-day stews and gratins. A paella pan is a must—you won't achieve optimal levels of *socarrat* (that blissfully burnt bottom layer of rice) without one. And then there's all the attractive dinnerware, from ceramic plates to olive-wood boards to glass *alcuzas* (oil dispensers). The lauded kitchen store Alambique carries all these items and more.

OLIVE OIL
Olive oil is the lifeblood of Spanish cooking, and even the standard supermarket stuff in Madrid is usually an echelon above what most Americans are used to. Spring for cold-pressed *aceite de oliva extra virgen* (extra-virgin olive oil) sold in opaque bottles—clear glass, though admittedly more attractive, exposes the oil to too much light, turning it rancid.

SOCCER SWAG
Even if you don't make it to the bleachers of Santiago Bernabéu Stadium, you can flaunt your Real Madrid spirit by sporting a jersey with the name of your favorite *futbolista* (football player) on the back. Avoid counterfeit merch by shopping at the stadium or at an official store in the city center.

WINE
Stock up on oddball varietals, limited-production releases, and cult natural wines at upmarket Lavinia (Salamanca), or the more alternative PASTORA (La Latina) or Bendito Vinos y Vinilos (Lavapiés). Fringe perk: you can sip while you shop, since all three stores double as wine bars.

Under-the-Radar Things to Do in Madrid

MADRID RÍO

Madrid Río, one the city's most ambitious urban planning initiatives in recent history, solved the space conundrum of Parque del Buen Retiro by laying nearly 30 km (18½ miles) of green space and bike-friendly paths along the Manzanares River.

CASA DE CAMPO

More than five times the size of Central Park, the Casa de Campo is Madrid's largest park and a nature-lover's paradise, complete with bike trails, lakeside restaurants, picnic tables, and pine forests. Strike out on a walk or jog and see how many hares, foxes, red squirrels, and hawks you can spot.

CHAMBERÍ FOOD SCENE

Fusion tapas spots, cheffy gastro-markets, timeless seafood restaurants, newfangled Basque pintxo bars—the district of Chamberí is Madrid's new culinary North Star. After grazing on international bites at Mercado de Vallehermoso, meander over to the bar-lined Calle de Ponzano for one of the city's most memorable tapas crawls.

CHINATOWN

Most visitors come and go without hearing so much as a murmur about Usera, one of Europe's most vibrant Chinatowns that established itself in the early 2000s. Situated across the Manzanares east of the Carabanchel district, its streets are lined with hot pot restaurants, dumpling stalls, dim sum parlors, and more—all punchy antidotes to the (sue us!) minimalist spiceless-ness of traditional Spanish cooking.

MATADERO MADRID

Once an industrial slaughterhouse complex, El Matadero is Madrid's most avant-garde creative arts and exhibition center. Thanks to its diverse roster of restaurants, bars, and day and evening events—which include plays, concerts, poetry readings, and movie screenings—the surrounding district of Arganzuela has gotten a new lease on life.

MUSEO DEL ROMANTICISMO

To catch a glimpse of how the Spanish bourgeoisie lived in the early 19th century, step into this marquis' palace decked out with ornate period furniture, evocative portraits, and other historical artifacts culled from the height of Spanish Romanticism. It's worth spending a few minutes admiring the flamboyantly decorated fans and backlit lithophanes. You only need an hour or two to take in the permanent collection, but don't rush out: the plant-filled interior patio is a gorgeous, tranquil place to enjoy tea and pastries.

NATURAL WINE BARS

You're never far from a *bodega* (wineshop) or *taberna* (pub or bar) in Madrid, but the wine served in these old-school haunts is almost always one-note, over-oaked plonk from industrial wine factories up north. To taste small-production Spanish wines that have personality and terroir for days, seek out natural wine bars like Bendito Vinos y Vinilos, La Caníbal, or—the newest

Matadero Madrid

arrivals on the scene—La Alquimia or Fun Fun.

NON-TOURISTY FLAMENCO

As any seasoned traveler to Spain will tell you, there's flamenco, and then there's *flamenco*. To experience the Andalusian art form at its purest and most vivacious, it pays to go where the tour-bus crowds don't. Consider Teatro Flamenco Madrid, a newcomer situated in Malasaña, which hosts concerts by professional dance troupes, or the more intimate La Quimera, conveniently located steps from Plaza Mayor.

RAYO VALLECANO

Most sports fans are familiar with Spain's powerhouse soccer team Real Madrid, but to enjoy a spirited match with locals and without the long lines and inflated price tag, step up to Rayo Vallecano's box office. The team's second-tier status doesn't make the games any less thrilling (think college basketball vs. NBA), especially when you catch them on their home turf, a short metro ride from the city center in the southeastern Madrid neighborhood of Vallecas. Known as Madrid's third team, *Los Franjirrojos* ("The Red Sashes") are a club with a great story and active, class-conscious supporters. They are also one of the last teams in Spain to represent a *barrio*, or neighborhood.

REGIONAL SPANISH CUISINE

Thanks to Madrid's diverse makeup, you don't have to catch a train to sample top regional specialties. Even the staunchest paella purists rave about Aynaelda's saffron-scented paella Valenciana, studded with *garrofón* (lima beans) and tender chunks of rabbit and chicken. For a culinary journey to Asturias in the mountainous north, head to Casa Mingo, a lively *sidrería* (cider house) that's been ladling *fabada* (bean soup) and splashing cider since 1888. Other regional restaurants worth marking on your map include El Rincón de Jaén, for Andalusian fare like *salmorejo* (cold tomato soup) and shrimp fritters; El Chacón, for hearty Galician octopus and smoked ham; and Gofio, for experimental Canarian tasting menus.

What to Watch and Read Before You Go to Spain

HOMAGE TO CATALONIA BY GEORGE ORWELL

Orwell's journals document his time at war in Catalonia, and his first-person narrative provides a view of war-torn Barcelona that today seems wholly foreign.

THE SHADOW OF THE WIND BY CARLOS RUIZ ZAFÓN

Daniel Sempere is 10 years old when his father, a bookseller in post–civil war Barcelona, takes him to a mysterious labyrinth filled with treasured but forgotten tomes and tells him to pick one that he will then dedicate his life to preserving. What follows is a tale of a young man who discovers a mysterious person—or perhaps creature—is destroying all remaining works of Julián Carax, the author whose book he now protects. The Shadow of the Wind's story of life, death, and history may be fictional, but its setting in a war-torn Spain is forceful, and the fact that it's sold more than 15 million copies hints at its compelling universe.

THE BEST THING THAT CAN HAPPEN TO A CROISSANT BY PABLO TUSSET

Pablo "Baloo" Miralles is the lazy, debaucherous scion of a well-to-do Spanish family. When his elder (and more accomplished) brother inexplicably disappears, Baloo suddenly finds himself pulled into the dealings of the family's powerful financial firm, a turn of events that inspires him to try to locate his missing sibling. Within this satirical quasi-detective story is a modern-day tale about the city of Barcelona.

FOR WHOM THE BELL TOLLS BY ERNEST HEMINGWAY

All the typical Hemingway elements are present in this fictional account of the Spanish Civil War: romance, bravado, glory, death, and tragedy. It's an incredibly evocative slice of historical fiction that's almost impossible to put down.

MARKS OF IDENTITY BY JUAN GOYTISOLO

A searing masterpiece from one of Spain's greatest novelists and poets describes the return of an exile to Barcelona. Goytisolo comes to the conclusion that every man carries his own exile with him, wherever he lives. The narrator (Goytisolo) rejects Spain itself and searches instead for poetry. This is a shocking and influential work and an affirmation of the ability of the individual to survive political tyranny. Marks of Identity was banned in Spain until after Franco's death.

MONSIGNOR QUIXOTE BY GRAHAM GREENE

This novel provides a wonderful journey through Spain in the company of Monsignor Quixote, an aging village priest, and his friend Sancho Panza, the communist ex-mayor. It's a contemporary reimagining of Miguel Cervantes's classic Don Quixote, set in Spain in the 1980s rather than the 1600s.

THE NEW SPANIARDS BY JOHN HOOPER

How was the transition from dictatorship to democracy accomplished so smoothly? How did a country noted for sexual repression find itself in the European vanguard in legalizing gay marriage? What's the deal with the Spanish royal family? This fascinating study is considered one of the clearest insights into the sociology and culture of modern Spain.

¡AY CARMELA! DIRECTED BY CARLOS SAURA

This 1990 film portrays the ethical and personal dilemmas a group of nomadic comedians faces during the Spanish Civil War. The film features a scene where Carmela, played by Carmen Maura, tries to teach a Polish prisoner, an International Brigadist, how to pronounce the /ñ/ sound in the word "España."

THE BEASTS (AS BESTAS) DIRECTED BY RODRIGO SOROGOYEN

A stark, deeply moving drama set deep in the Galician countryside, this award-winning 2022 film explores the claustrophobia and cruelty of rural life in Spain. The protagonists are a couple of French back-to-the-landers whose lives are unexpectedly upended by xenophobic neighbors out to make their lives a living hell.

ALL ABOUT MY MOTHER DIRECTED BY PEDRO ALMODÓVAR

After Manuela's 17-year-old son Esteban is killed before her eyes, she decides to move to Barcelona in order to find his father, a transvestite named Lola who doesn't know that Esteban exists. It's a brilliantly directed tale which sensitively examines a variety of complex topics such as bereavement, addiction, gender identity, and the impact of HIV. It earned director Pedro Almodóvar the Best Director award at the 1999 Cannes Film Festival and the Academy Award for Best Foreign Language Film in 2000.

PARALLEL MOTHERS DIRECTED BY PEDRO ALMODÓVAR

Penélope Cruz stars in this 2021 film set in Madrid that begins with a scene of two mothers giving birth. They don't know each other, but soon they will—as Almodóvar expertly weaves their stories together and explores themes related to the Spanish Civil War.

BELLE EPOQUE DIRECTED BY FERNANDO TRUEBA

It's 1931 and the Spanish monarchy is facing its final days. During this time of confusion and conflicting loyalties, Fernando, whose allegiance is to the army and goes on the run into the beautiful Spanish countryside. There he meets Manolo, a painter with the same political beliefs, and his four beautiful young daughters.

A GUN IN EACH HAND DIRECTED BY CESC GAY

Catalan director Cesc Gay recruited some top-notch Spanish actors and actresses for this comedy. Told through a series of vignettes, A Gun in Each Hand explores how changing gender roles in Spain affect modern relationships, how Spanish ideas about masculinity and relationships are evolving, and how that evolution can benefit women in Spain.

PAN'S LABYRINTH DIRECTED BY GUILLERMO DEL TORO

Set in the early years of Franco's dictatorship, this film follows an imaginative kid, Ofelia, who moves with her pregnant mother to her future stepfather's house. In her new home, she meets the faun, Pan, who tells her she might be the lost princess of an underground world. While she faces mythological creatures and terrifying beasts, rebellion is brewing in her stepfather's military post.

THE SILENCE OF OTHERS DIRECTED BY ALMUDENA CARRACEDO AND ROBERT BAHAR

This heartrending 2019 documentary follows an elderly woman's struggle to unearth her dead relatives, who were buried in a mass grave during the Spanish Civil War. Spain is second only to Cambodia in its number of mass graves, the result of an amnesty law put in place following Franco's dictatorship.

Madrid Today

"A breakwater of all the Spains" is how poet Antonio Machado described Madrid nearly a century ago, referring to its patchwork quilt of residents hailing from every corner of the Iberian Peninsula. Today, you could call Madrid a breakwater of the world. This, after all, is Europe's third-largest city—a place where, in the span of a single block, you might find a century-old tavern, a Senegalese textile supplier, a Sichuan hot pot restaurant, and a glitzy boutique hotel. In other words, the Madrid of Ernest Hemingway—of bullfights and *siestas* and sherry wine and frilly fans—has largely faded into the past. Expect instead a cosmopolitan, open-minded, modern metropolis with enough youth-driven verve to keep you on your toes but enough history and old-world charm to remind you that you're on vacation.

THE ARTS

The "Golden Triangle" of museums (Prado, Thyssen-Bornemisza, and Reina Sofía) play host to an ever-rotating repertoire of world-class exhibitions, so it's worth looking past the permanent collections. Up-and-coming local artists have found a new home across the river in scruffy Carabanchel, where converted industrial spaces come alive during ArtBanchel, an "open studio" festival held each May. Alternatively, you can get a taste of Carabanchel's cutting-edge art scene year-round at Sabrina Amrani Gallery.

Traditional Spanish artisanry is experiencing a renaissance, with locals finding new appreciation for the painted ceramics, woven baskets, blown glass, and handmade textiles of their forebears. Boutiques selling such "Made in Spain" treasures are popping up left and right; Cocol and Hijo de Epigmenio are two examples.

GASTRONOMY

In the last five years, Chamberí has become a new culinary nerve center, thanks to buzzy restaurant openings like Arima, Tripea, and Saddle and the sudden popularity of Mercado de Vallehermoso, a once-endangered market that lures trendsters with envelope-pushing tapas bars and international food stalls. Like any other international city, food fads here change on a dime: 2019 was the year of ramen and over-the-top burgers, 2020 and 2021 saw an uptick in upscale Italian and designer pizzerias, and 2022 and 2023 will go down as the years of restaurant pop-ups and natural wine.

NIGHTLIFE

Madrid has been synonymous with dusk-to-dawn nightlife for as long as dusk has turned to dawn. There's no excuse to head back to the hotel early, whether your definition of a great night out involves remixed reggaeton tracks (Oh My Club), live jazz (Sala Clamores), a live flamenco show (Teatro Flamenco Madrid), or simply a few vinos or cocktails at a hot spot like Macera, La Alquimia, or Viva Madrid.

TRANSPORTATION

The historic center is a low-emission zone (known as Madrid 360), meaning most rental cars aren't allowed entry. Beyond the dependable metro, there are ride-hailing apps (Uber, Bolt, and Cabify) plus dozens of public BiciMAD docks with electric-powered bikes for rent. The city is increasingly overrun with electric scooters and bikes available via apps such as Lime, Uber, and Bolt. A free (and emissions-free) bus service called Línea CERO (Line ZERO) connects Atocha railway station to Moncloa via Gran Vía. For trips farther afield, more and more Madrileños are ditching regional trains and buses for the more affordable BlaBlaCar ridesharing app.

Chapter 2

TRAVEL SMART

Updated by
Benjamin Kemper

POPULATION:
3.2 million

LANGUAGE:
Spanish

$ CURRENCY:
Euro

AREA CODE:
34

⚠ EMERGENCIES:
112

🚗 DRIVING:
On the right

⚡ ELECTRICITY:
220v/50 cycles; electrical plugs have two round prongs

⊗ TIME:
Six hours ahead of New York (except a couple weeks in spring and fall when it's five, due to a daylight savings discrepancy)

✈ AIRPORT:
MAD

⊕ WEB RESOURCES:
esmadrid.com/en
turismomadrid.es/en

FRANCE

Salamanca
Segovia
★ MADRID
PORTUGAL
Toledo

SPAIN

Córdoba

Seville   Granada

ALGERIA

MOROCCO

Know Before You Go

While you might get side-eye for ordering paella for dinner (rice is lunch here) or a *café con leche* in the evening (a *cortado*, or espresso with milk, is the standard afternoon pick-me-up), Madrid isn't big on hard-and-fast rules. Minor cultural foibles won't get you into serious trouble.

TAPAS TIPS

Tapas are Spanish bar snacks, and in Madrid, they can be complimentary or charged, depending on the establishment. Most traditional taverns will offer a free tapa—a handful of olives, a bit of cured sausage, or whatever the bartender feels like feeding you—with each drink. If you think you're due a tapa but it got lost in the shuffle, don't fret. Simply ask the (often flustered) bartender for *el aperitivo, por favor*. Note that many upscale bars and restaurants don't serve free tapas. If a tapa is a small aperitif geared toward individual barside consumption, a *ración* is a larger portion designed for sit-down sharing; these are always charged. Note to the less famished: *medias raciónes*, or half-portions, are often available even if they're not on the menu, so ask your waiter.

MANY MUSEUMS ARE FREE—IF YOU KNOW WHEN TO GO

The Prado, Madrid's most legendary museum, offers free entry from 6 pm to 8 pm Monday through Saturday and 5 pm to 7 pm Sunday, while the Museo Nacional Centro de Arte Reina Sofía, Spain's preeminent modern art museum, welcomes guests at no charge between 7 pm and 9 pm Monday and Wednesday–Saturday, and 12:30 to 2:30 Sunday. Many other museums and sights have complimentary days and times as well, and a number of smaller museums, such as Casa Museo Lope de Vega and the Madrid History Museum, are always free.

DRINK FROM THE TAP

The water quality is excellent in Madrid, but that doesn't keep bars and restaurants from trying to upsell the bottled stuff, particularly to unsuspecting tourists. If you want tap water, the term to remember is *agua del grifo* (as opposed to *agua mineral* for mineral water or *agua con gas* for sparkling water). Unlike in the United States, you always have to ask for it, and the default is sans ice. Most establishments will happily pour you a glass from the tap but, vexingly, aren't obligated to do so by law.

GETTING FROM A TO B

It's not worth renting a car in Madrid as the entire city center is a low-emission zone (called "Madrid 360"), off-limits to all but the greenest vehicles. Besides, Madrid is extremely walkable. The metro system, the most convenient and environmentally friendly way to get around, is exceptionally clean and reliable and runs 6 am–2 am. City buses are a fine alternative; night buses (locally known as *búhos*, "owls") run 2–6 am. Uber, Cabify, and Bolt are the most popular ride-hailing apps; Cabify is (marginally) better than competitors when it comes to workers' rights. Official taxis are ubiquitous (the green light up top means it's hailable) and not nearly as expensive as those in, say, Paris or Berlin. Unless you're accustomed to biking in traffic, skip the electric scooters, rentable city bikes, and BiciMAD (the local bikeshare system)—Madrid has a dearth of designated bike lanes.

NAVIGATION NOTE

Numbers in postal addresses come after street names (i.e., it's Calle de Fuencarral 10, not 10 Calle de Fuencarral), so that's how you should communicate where you're going, whether you're talking to a cabbie or using a navigation app.

"SPANISH TIME" IS A THING

Lunch at 3, dinner at 9— by American standards, Spain is on a pretty wacky mealtime schedule. Most restaurants don't take reservations before 2 and 8 for lunch and dinner, respectively, and the vast majority are closed Sunday night. Standard commercial hours are equally enigmatic: family-owned establishments often close from 2 to 5 pm for the *siesta* (afternoon "nap"), while others, especially international chains, operate straight through the day. Always check online or call ahead to ensure you don't wind up staring at a *cerrado* (closed) sign.

THERE'S A WRONG TIME (AND PLACE) FOR PAELLA
You're in Spain, so you want to eat paella—duh. Paella is one of Spain's most famous dishes, but it's native to Valencia and best sampled there or in neighboring Catalonia. That said, there *are* a few good paella spots in town (try Casa de Valencia, Aynaelda, or Cadaqués). Note: Paella is traditionally lunch fare, but don't think twice about ordering it for dinner.

SOME OF THE BEST FOOD ISN'T "SPANISH"
You didn't come all the way to Madrid to eat pad Thai and pizza, but visitors who limit themselves to Spanish food are missing some seriously thrilling bites. The city boasts one of Europe's best (and least-known) Chinatowns, Usera, where you can satisfy cravings for dim sum, wokked noodles, and *shao bing* (sesame flatbread). A sizable West African community translates into hearty, exuberantly spiced

dishes, perfect for when *jamón* fatigue sets in. And a recent influx of Venezuelans means hot and gooey *arepas* (stuffed cornmeal cakes), *tequeños* (cheese sticks), and *cachapas* (corn pancakes).

TIPPING ETIQUETTE
At upscale sit-down restaurants, tip up to 10% of the bill. At more casual spots, €1 per person is about right, though many Spaniards simply leave loose change or don't tip at all. It is always better to tip in cash, though most restaurants now allow you to tip with card if you request it. At bars and nightclubs, don't tip the bartender, even if you've ordered food—it's not a faux pas, but it's not common practice. In nice hotels, slip the bellhop a couple euros per bag and leave a few euros in the room each day for the housekeepers; €10–20 euros is about right for helpful concierges. In taxis, just round up the bill, unless you're schlepping particularly heavy (or numerous) bags, in which case a couple extra euros go a long way.

AVOID HOT TOPICS
Spain's politics are quite polarized at the moment, and you can never be sure about new acquaintances' sympathies. Hot-button topics best avoided (unless you're prepared for battle) include Catalan and Basque independence, the monarchy, bullfighting, Franco, and the Church. COVID denialism and the anti-vax movement are very fringe in Spain. Note that the Spanish flag

means different things to different people: for some it's a symbol of national unity, for others it's a link to Franco's dictatorship.

AVOID FINES
Drinking in public is prohibited, and if you're caught boozing in the street or on the metro, you could be hit with a €600 fine. Exceptions to this rule include designated outdoor dining areas and street fairs. That said, it's common to see locals flouting open container laws. Cannabis is illegal but decriminalized.

ALLOW TIME FOR SIDE TRIPS
Sandwiched between the two Castiles (Castile and León to the north and Castile-La Mancha to the south), Madrid is a fantastic jumping-off point for jaunts to those rugged historical regions. Toledo and Segovia are the most popular day-trip destinations from Madrid—with their stunning architectural monuments, soulful cooking, and fairy-tale churches and castles—but Cuenca, Salamanca, Sigüenza, and a number of other intriguing towns and cities are also well within reach. For more natural escapes, nearby mountain ranges such as the Sierra de Guadarrama and Sierra de Gredos have hidden mountain villages and well-marked trails for hiking.

Getting Here and Around

Air

Flying time from New York to Madrid is about seven hours; from London, it's just over two hours. Most flights from North America land in, or pass through, Madrid-Barajas Airport (MAD).

From North America, Air Europa, American Airlines, Delta, and Iberia Airlines fly to Madrid direct. Within Spain, Iberia is the main domestic airline and also operates low-cost flights through its budget airlines Iberia Express and Vueling. Air Europa and Ryanair offer inexpensive flights on most domestic routes.

Flying is an affordable, if somewhat impractical, way to travel between Madrid and Barcelona; the high-speed train is a better bet.

Bicycle

BiciMAD is Madrid's public bike-share service with 611 docks scattered around the city. The bikes are electric, meaning you hardly have to pedal, and are an alternative to the metro and buses, provided the weather is good and you're comfortable riding in traffic (separate bike lanes are virtually nonexistent). Occasional users can pay €2 per 30-minute ride, buying a ticket at each service station; avid urban cyclists staying for a month or more may wish to purchase a €25 yearly membership, which drastically lowers the cost of individual rides to €0.50 for up to 30 minutes. The bikes can be borrowed from and returned to any station in the system. ⚠ **Beware of mechanical issues (flat tires, dead batteries, etc.). If your bike doesn't work properly, return it (at no charge) at the same station and take out another.**

Bus

Within Spain, several private companies provide comfortable long-haul bus service, though the main one is Alsa. Fares are almost always lower than the corresponding train fares and service covers more towns, though buses are less frequent on weekends. Smaller towns don't usually have a central bus depot, so check routes carefully.

Alsa has a few premium options in addition to its regular seating; these include perks such as roomy leather seats, onboard à la carte meals, and a private waiting room. You also have the option of *asientos individuales*, individual seats (with no other seat on either side) that line one side of the bus.

At bus ticket counters, credit cards (except American Express) are generally accepted. If you buy your ticket on the bus (not recommended), it's cash only.

During peak travel times (Easter, August, and Christmas), it's a good idea to make a reservation at least a week in advance.

Car

American driver's licenses are valid in Spain but must be accompanied by an International Driving Permit (IDP). The IDP may facilitate car rental and help you avoid traffic fines—it translates your state-issued driver's license into 10 languages so officials can easily interpret the information on it. Permits are available from the American Automobile Association. ⚠ **Many U.S. travelers don't bother getting the IDP, but they risk higher fines if pulled over.**

Driving around Madrid isn't for the faint-hearted; access roads tend to be very congested, and in the center, strict

"Madrid 360" antipollution measures prohibit entry by private cars to many areas. Add to this the locals' impatience with drivers who don't know exactly where they're going plus the lack of parking lots and you have the potential for a stressful time behind the wheel.

Renting a car isn't necessary in the city center because there is excellent public transportation as well as taxi and ride-hailing app services. If you plan to explore beyond Madrid—to Andalusia, for example—you may wish to rent a car, particularly if you want to add side trips along the way. In this case, rent at the end of your stay in Madrid; some hired car companies will bring the vehicle to your hotel upon request.

Driving is the best (and sometimes only) way to see Spain's rural areas. The main cities are connected by a network of excellent four-lane divided highways (*autovías* and *autopistas*), which are designated by the letter *A* and have speed limits of 80 kph (50 mph) to 120 kph (75 mph). If the artery is a toll highway (*peaje*), it is designated *AP.* The letter *N* indicates a *carretera nacional*, a national or intercity route with local traffic, which may have four or two lanes. Smaller towns and villages are connected by a network of secondary roads with an alphabet soup of different letter designations.

CAR RENTALS

Alamo, Avis, Budget, Europcar, Hertz, and Enterprise have branches at major Spanish airports and in large cities. Smaller, regional companies and wholesalers offer lower rates. The online outfit Pepecar has been a big hit with travelers; in general, the earlier you book, the less you pay. Rates run as low as €15 per day, taxes included—but note that pickups at center-city locations are considerably cheaper than at the airports. All agencies have a range of models, but the bulk of rentals in Spain have manual transmission. Rates in Madrid begin at the equivalents of $60 per day and $190 per week including tax for an economy car with manual transmission and unlimited mileage. A small car is cheaper and prudent for the tiny roads and parking spaces in many parts of Spain.

Anyone 18 or older with a valid license can drive in Spain, but most rental agencies will not rent cars to drivers under 23.

DRIVING

Spain's highway system includes some 6,000 km (3,728 miles) of well-maintained superhighways. Still, you'll find some stretches of major national highways that are only two lanes wide, where traffic often backs up behind trucks. Autopista tolls are steep, but as a result these highways are often less crowded than the free ones. If you spring for the autopistas, you'll find that many of the rest stops are nicely landscaped and have decent (if overpriced) grub.

GASOLINE

Gas stations are plentiful in Madrid and in Spain. Most are self-service, and you pay after you fill up—except at night, when many pumps are prepay only. Gas can be twice as expensive per gallon as U.S. fuel. Before you fill up your rental car, check if it's gas or diesel, usually indicated on the car key or on the fuel cap itself.

PARKING

Madrid has private and public parking lots, where charges typically start at €2.50 an hour with lower rates for 24-hour stays. Street parking in the center is very limited and restricted to hourly rates. Most hotels offer parking, but it is rarely included in the room rate. Expect to pay at least €20 a day.

Getting Here and Around

RULES OF THE ROAD

Spaniards pass on the left, so stay in the right-hand lane when not passing. Children under 12 may not ride in the front seat, and seat belts are compulsory. Speed limits are 30 kph (19 mph) or 50 kph (31 mph) in cities, depending on the type of street; 90 kph (56 mph) on national highways; and 120 kph (75 mph) on the autopista or autovía. The use of cell phones by drivers, even on the side of the road, is illegal except with completely hands-free devices.

Severe fines are enforced throughout Spain for driving under the influence of alcohol. Spot Breathalyzer checks are often carried out, and you will be cited if the level of alcohol in your bloodstream is found to be 0.05% or above.

Spanish highway police are increasingly vigilant about speeding and illegal passing. Police can demand cash payment on the spot from non-Spanish drivers. Police disproportionately target rental-car drivers for speeding and illegal passing, so play it safe.

Ⓜ Public Transport

To ride the metro, you must buy a refillable *Tarjeta de Transporte Público* (Public Transportation Card), which costs €2.50 and can be obtained at ticketing machines inside any metro station. Each journey costs €1.50–€2, depending on how far you're traveling; you can also buy a 10-ride Metrobus ticket (€12.20). There are no free transfers between metro and bus systems. The *Abono Turístico* (Tourist Pass) allows unlimited use of public buses and the metro for one day (€8.40 for Zone A, €17 for Zone T) to seven days (€35.40 for Zone A, €70.80 for Zone T); buy it at tourist offices, metro stations, or select newsstands. The metro runs

6 am–1:30 am, though a few entrances close earlier.

Ⓢ Ridesharing

BlaBlaCar is Spain's leading intercity rideshare app. Its free platform allows you to book ahead using a credit card and message with the driver to set meeting and drop-off points. It's the most affordable way to travel to Madrid's outlying cities and beyond, as drivers aren't allowed to make a profit (you essentially help the driver offset the price of gas and tolls).

Ⓣ Taxi and Ride-Hailing Apps

Taxis work under several tariff schemes, and fraud is uncommon. Tariff 1 is for the city center 7 am–9 pm; meters start at €2.50. There is a fixed taxi fare of €30 to or from the airport from the city center. Tariff 2 is for the city center 9 pm–7 am on weekdays (and 7 am–9 pm on weekends and holidays); the meter starts at €3.15 and charges more per kilometer. You can reserve taxis by phone or through the MyTaxi mobile app, which works with local official taxi drivers. Uber, Cabify, and Bolt operate in Madrid as well.

Ⓣ Train

The chart here has information about popular train routes. Prices are for one-way fares (depending on seating and where purchased) and subject to change.

Slow trains run from Madrid to Lisbon (10 hours 30 minutes, overnight); by 2025, a new fast train should take 5 hours. There is a fast train from Barcelona to Paris (6 hours 20 minutes).

Train Travel Times

Madrid to Barcelona: €12–€185	High-speed trains make the trip in 2 hours 30 minutes (some stop in Lleida, Zaragoza, Figueres, and Girona)
Madrid to Bilbao: €36–€72	Semi-express Alvia train time is 4 hours 43 minutes
Madrid to Málaga: €42–€135	High-speed trains take 2 hours 25 minutes
Madrid to Córdoba: €20–€135	High-speed trains take 1 hour 44 minutes
Madrid to Seville: €31–€137	High-speed trains take 2 hours 20 minutes
Madrid to Granada: €42–€98	Fastest AVE trains take 3 hours 25 minutes
Madrid to Santander: €22–€78	Semi-express Alvia is 4 hours 5 minutes
Madrid to Valencia: €7–€91	High-speed trains make the trip in 1 hour 42 minutes (some stop in Cuenca and Requena-Utiel)
Madrid to Santiago de Compostela: €31–€104	Fastest time 3 hours

Spain's official high-speed train, the 290-kph (180-mph) AVE, connects Madrid with Alicante, Barcelona, Córdoba, Cuenca, Figueres, Granada, León, Lleida, Málaga, Murcia, Ourense, Segovia, Seville, Tarragona, Toledo, Valencia, Valladolid, and Zaragoza.

In the last three years, three budget high-speed competitors have arrived on the scene: **Avlo, Ouigo,** and **Iryo.** Avlo services destinations including Barcelona, Cuenca, Figueres, Girona, Tarragona, Valencia, and Zaragoza. Ouigo services Barcelona, Tarragona, Valencia, and Zaragoza. Iryo services Albacete, Alicante, Antequera, Barcelona, Córdoba, Cuenca, Málaga, Valencia, and Zaragoza.

Reservations for all the above can be made online; RENFE and AVE tickets can be purchased at ticket booths, but it's wiser to purchase online ahead of time. Book weeks in advance if you're traveling during Holy Week, on long holiday weekends, or in July and August. (RENFE's website is notoriously finicky; reservations can be made up to 62 days in advance, and some American credit cards do not work on the site.)

You cannot buy tickets online for certain regional lines or for commuter lines (cercanías).

DISCOUNTS

The best bargains on train travel are via Avlo, Iryo, and Ouigo; however, if you purchase a ticket on the RENFE website for the AVE or Alvia, there are still deals to be had: You can often get a discount of 20%–60%, depending on how far ahead you book and how you travel. Discounts on one-way tickets tend to be higher than on round-trips. The earliest opportunity to book is 62 days in advance of travel.

■ TIP→ If there are more than two of you traveling on the AVE, look for the word "mesa" in the fare column, quoting the price per person for four people traveling together and sitting at the same table. You have to buy all the tickets at the same time, but they're between 20% and 60% cheaper than regular tickets.

Essentials

🏃 Activities

The Spanish are keen sports fans, both as spectators and participants, and the national teams for soccer (football), basketball, and water polo rank among the best in the world. Madrid is home to two of the country's top soccer (Real Madrid and Atlético de Madrid) and basketball teams (Real Madrid and Estudiantes) and holds regular international championship games in several other sports, such as tennis and athletics.

Jogging is one of the most popular participant sports, and parks are packed on weekends with locals who also take an enthusiastic part in the city's many competitions, including the Madrid Marathon in late April. In winter, the mountain ranges to the north of the city receive thousands of visitors for decent (if crowded) downhill skiing and snowboarding, and pop-up skating rinks appear around Madrid at Christmas (weather permitting).

BASKETBALL

The Spanish are avid basketball fans and the country has several world-class players, many of whom play in the NBA, such as Pau and Marc Gasol and Ricky Rubio. The national men's team have won the World Championship twice (the latest in 2019) and the women's team took bronze position in 2018. In the last decade, Spain has won the highest number of FIBA basketball medals in the world. The Spanish league, ACB, runs from late September to early May and includes the Copa del Rey championship playoff. Madrid has three basketball teams: Real Madrid, Estudiantes, and Fuenlabrada. Real Madrid and Estudiantes rank among the best in Spain and play at their home stadium, the WiZink Center.

PARKS AND PLAYGROUNDS

Like most Spaniards, *Madrileños* spend a lot of time outdoors. Although central Madrid doesn't have many parks, the large number of squares and boulevards (often with designated children's areas) make up for the lack of green spaces. Locals flock to these on sunny days, particularly on weekends when the larger parks are packed to capacity. All parks have cafés and snack bars, usually open all year.

SKIING

In the winter, many locals head to the (increasingly artificial) snowy slopes in the three resorts north of the city. All are within an hour's journey of Madrid and offer skiing and snowboarding. The ski season runs from late December to late March when the resorts open daily.

SOCCER

Madrid is home to two big players in Spain's national obsession: "not a matter of life and death, but more important." Both Real Madrid and Atlético de Madrid regularly finish at the top or near it in the Spanish national soccer league (LaLiga) and play at the international level. They're also among the oldest teams in the country, founded in 1902 and 1903, respectively. The capital also has three other soccer teams, Getafe and Leganés (both in the top league) and Rayo Vallecano, in second division.

Real Madrid ranks among the world's best teams with an impressive list of accolades that include 14 European Championships, 7 Club World Cup wins, and 35 LaLiga titles. The team's home ground is the emblematic Estadio Santiago Bernabéu (Santiago Bernabéu Stadium), with capacity for more than 81,000 spectators and home to the club's trophies.

Real Madrid has an intense (yet mostly friendly) rivalry with Madrid's other top team, Atlético de Madrid, and locals fiercely support one or the other. Atlético de Madrid plays at Estadio Wanda Metropolitano (Metropolitano Stadium) with room for an audience of 68,000. Atlético regularly plays at the European level and holds several Cups.

LaLiga runs from mid-August to the end of May and all teams play each other twice during the season. Matches usually take place on weekends and tickets sell out fast. Those for the local "derby" matches between Real Madrid and Atlético de Madrid, twice a year, are the most expensive and you need to book as soon as sales open.

TENNIS

Since Manolo Santana won Wimbledon in 1966, Spanish tennis has gone from strength to strength and produced world-class players. Rafael Nadal is considered the greatest Spanish player of all time and one of the best in the world. Spain has produced several other world-number-one players, including Arantxa Sánchez Vicario, Garbiñe Muguruza, Carlos Moyá, and Juan Carlos Ferrero. Spain has one of the best, most comprehensive schedules of national junior, International Tennis Federation junior, and professional circuits of events of any country in the world. This cluster of high level junior and professional tournaments is a tremendous developmental advantage. Rising Spanish stars to look out for include Roberto Bautista Agut and teenager Carlos Alcaraz.

The Caja Mágica (Magic Box), designed by French architect Dominique Perrault, hosts the annual Madrid Open, part of the ATP Masters 1000 and Premier Mandatory, in May. The championship brings together the world's best players on its clay courts.

🍴 Dining

As Spain's most vibrant melting pot, Madrid is home to countless regional Spanish restaurants serving everything from Valencian paella to Basque *pintxos* (skewered snacks), but the most classic fare closely resembles that of Castile. International cuisines are well-represented, and dietary preferences (e.g., vegetarian, vegan, and gluten-free) are also widely accommodated. In Madrid you'll find the biggest variety of dining venues in the country, from upmarket Michelin-starred restaurants to "cheap and cheerful" *tascas*, or taverns, and just about everything in between. Americans will find Madrid dining to be a good value. Most restaurants are open six days a week for lunch and dinner (Monday is the most popular day to close) and many close all of August.

When it comes to traditional local fare, the climate described as *nueve meses de invierno y tres de infierno* (nine months of winter and three of hell) plays a major role, so most typical dishes are comfort food. Garlic soup, stewed chickpeas, and roast suckling pig and lamb are standbys. *Cocido madrileño* (a meat-packed winter stew) and *callos a la madrileña* (stewed tripe) are favored local specialties, although most restaurants also serve lighter dishes. Fish and seafood feature on most menus, and despite its inland location, Madrid has some of the best in Spain.

PAYING

Credit cards are widely accepted at restaurants in Madrid, with the exception of American Express. Tipping is not obligatory and locals tend to round up the price to the nearest euro or leave around 5% of the bill if the service is exceptional. Tips are rarely included in the bill.

Essentials

Most prices listed in menus are inclusive of 10% value-added tax (I.V.A.), but not all. If I.V.A. isn't included, it should read, " *10% I.V.A. no incluido en los precios* " at the bottom of the menu. Unless otherwise noted, the restaurants listed in this guide are open daily for lunch and dinner.

⇨ *Prices in the reviews are the average cost of a main course or equivalent combination of smaller dishes at dinner or, if dinner is not served, at lunch.*

RESERVATIONS AND DRESS

Reservations are advised at Madrid's most popular or exclusive venues daily, and on weekends and public holidays for all sit-down establishments. That said, if you arrive on the early side (1:30 for lunch and 8 for dinner), you should be able to snag a table. Like the rest of Spain, there's rarely a dress code for dining. Children are welcome at the vast majority of restaurants, though high chairs and booster seats are not a given.

MEALS AND MEALTIMES

Mealtimes in Madrid are later than elsewhere in Europe and even later than those in the rest of Spain. Lunch starts around 2:30 or 3, and dinnertime averages about 9 (or as late as 11 in the summer). Weekend eating times, especially dinner, can begin upward of an hour later. In areas with heavy tourist traffic, many restaurants have an all-day kitchen or open a bit earlier.

SMOKING

Smoking is banned in all restaurants and bars and, as of early 2023, is only permitted on outside, open terraces. A law banning smoking on terraces has been approved but is not yet enforced.

PRICES

What It Costs in Euros			
$	$$	$$$	$$$$
RESTAURANTS			
under €18	€18–€24	€25–€30	over €30

 ## Health

COVID-19

In the weeks leading up to travel, look out for symptoms including cough, fever, chills, trouble breathing, muscle pain, sore throat, and loss of smell or taste. It is recommended, but not obligatory, to take a COVID-19 test prior to traveling. It is no longer required to present a vaccination certificate upon arrival in Spain.

All travel restrictions and mask requirements in Spain have been eased as of early 2023, but Fodor's encourages travelers to continue wearing masks on airplanes, public transit, and in other crowded enclosed spaces. Not all travel insurance policies protect against pandemic-related cancelations, so always read the fine print. Medical facilities and some pharmacies still enforce mandatory masking.

 ## Lodging

The Spanish government classifies hotels as one to five stars, with an additional rating of five-star GL (*Gran Lujo*) indicating the highest quality; however, experience shows that these ratings often don't correspond to the overall feel of a hotel and should not be the sole factor in determining where to stay.

All hotel entrances are marked with a blue plaque bearing the letter *H* and the number of stars. The letter *R* (for *residencia*) after the letter *H* indicates an establishment with no meal service, with the possible exception of breakfast. The designations *fonda* (*F*), *pensión* (*P*), *casa de huéspedes* (*CH*), and *hostal* (*Hs*) indicate budget accommodations; these are no longer official categories, but you'll still find them in Madrid. In most cases, rooms in such buildings can be on the dreary side, so be sure to look at reviews and photos before committing.

Solo travelers might prefer to pay a bit extra for single occupancy of a double room (*habitación doble uso individual*). In lower-end hotels, request a double bed (*cama de matrimonio*) if you want one—if you don't, you may end up with two singles.

Spain has a wealth of small country hotels and *agroturismos*. Rusticae (⊕ www.rusticae.com) is a good resource for independently owned hotels in restored palaces, monasteries, mills, and estates—all generally in rural Spain.

Casas rurales (country houses similar to B&Bs) offer pastoral lodging, either in guest rooms or in self-catering cottages. You may also come across the term *finca*, or country estate house. Many *agroturismo* accommodations are fincas converted to upscale B&Bs.

PARADORES
The Spanish government operates nearly 100 *Paradores*—upscale hotels often in historic buildings or near significant sites. Rates vary depending on the location, and some offer better deals than others. Expect four- or five-star amenities and clean and well-furnished rooms, often with antiques or reproductions. Each Parador has a restaurant serving regional specialties, and you can stop in for a meal without spending the night. Some Paradores have not aged gracefully; be

sure to peruse photos and reviews prior to booking.

FACILITIES
Unless specified otherwise, all hotels in this guide have TVs, private bathrooms, phones, heat, Wi-Fi, and air-conditioning. Breakfast is noted only when it is included in the rate as it's not a typical perk. More and more hotels boast pools (both indoor and outdoor).

PARKING
Most large hotels in Madrid have dedicated parking lots or access to secure facilities within easy walking distance of the hotel. Hotels without parking will usually recommend the best place to leave your car. Expect to pay at least €20 a day (24 hours or less).

PRICES
By law, hotel prices in Madrid and the rest of Spain must be posted at the reception desk and should indicate whether the value-added tax (I.V.A. 10%) is included. Note that high-season rates prevail not only in summer but also during Holy Week and local *fiestas*. Breakfast is normally *not* included. As a general rule, you'll get a better room rate if you book via the hotel website directly rather than through a booking platform.

RESERVATIONS
Reservations are always a good idea and essential if you travel to Madrid during high season (spring, Easter, and Christmas). Weekends are usually busy at any time of year, especially during events such as World Pride and sporting events.

What It Costs in Euros			
$	$$	$$$	$$$$
HOTELS			
under €125	€125–€200	€201–300	over €300

Essentials

Nightlife

Unlike in other European cities, where partying is a young person's game, Madrid boasts plenty of bars and *discotecas* (nightclubs) with mixed-age crowds, and it's not uncommon for children to play on the sidewalks past midnight while multigenerational families and friends convene over coffee or cocktails at outdoor cafés.

For those who don't plan on staying out until sunrise, there are good lively bars along Cava Alta and Cava Baja, Calle de las Huertas near Plaza de Santa Ana, and Calle de Moratín near Antón Martín. Those who want to stay out 'til the wee hours have more options: Calle del Príncipe and Calle de la Cruz, with sardine-can bars lined with locals, and the scruffier streets that snake down toward Plaza de Lavapiés. Perhaps the neighborhood most synonymous with *la vida nocturna* is Malasaña, which has trendy hangouts along Calle de San Vicente Ferrer, Calle de la Palma, and all around Plaza del Dos de Mayo. Another major nightlife contender is Chueca, where tattoo parlors and street-chic boutiques sit between LGBT+ (yet hetero-friendly) bars, dance clubs, and after-hours clubs.

In general, cafés in Madrid can be classified into two groups: those that have been around for many years (e.g., La Pecera del Circulo de Bellas Artes, Café de Oriente), where writers, singers, poets, and discussion groups still meet and where conversations are usually more important than the coffee itself; and Nordic-style third-wave venues (HanSo Café, Toma Café, Hola Coffee, FOUR) tailored to hip and hurried urbanites that tend to have a wider product selection, modern interiors, and Wi-Fi.

Packing

Pack light. Although baggage carts are free and plentiful in most airports, they're rare in smaller train stations and most bus stations and you will not want to drag a big case around on side trips. Madrid has a continental climate and can be bitterly cold from late fall to early spring and searing hot in summer. It makes sense to wear casual, comfortable clothing and shoes for sightseeing, but you'll want to dress up a bit in the city for fine restaurants and nightlife. Bring masks for crowded enclosed spaces and for entering pharmacies.

Performing Arts

Madrid is a thriving center for performing arts and is home to Spain's most important venues and companies. The capital offers a year-round calendar of music, theater, and dance, indoor in the winter and open-air in the summer heat. You'll find entertainment for all tastes and genres, from baroque chamber music and Wagnerian opera to indie pop and flamenco fusion; classic Lope de Vega and Lorca theater to avant-garde Juan Mayorga and Laila Ripoll; traditional ballet to modern dance; plus concerts from the world's top artists and musicals.

Popular music festivals include Paraíso (electronic music), Primavera Sound (pop and electronic), Mad Cool (pop, rock, indie), Suma Flamenca (flamenco), and Festival Internacional de Jazz de Madrid.

💲 Tipping

Spaniards sometimes tip waiters and taxi drivers, but even then, only rarely and in small amounts. Taxi drivers do not expect tips, but they are welcome, especially if they help with your luggage. (Official supplements for luggage handling have been done away with.)

Tipping Guides for Madrid

Bartender	Not necessary
Bellhop	€1–€2 per bag, depending on the level of the hotel
Coat Check	Not necessary if paid; €1 otherwise
Hotel Concierge	€5–€20, depending on the service requested
Hotel Cleaner	€2–€5 per day, left in cash
Hotel Room Service Waiter	€1–€5 per delivery, even if a service charge has been added
Porter at Airport or Train Station	€1 per bag
Skycap at Airport	€1–€2 per checked bag
Spa Personnel, Barbers, Hairdressers	10%
Taxi and Ride-Hailing Drivers	Up to 10%; more for luggage assistance
Tour Guide	€2–€5 per person
Waiter	0–10%, preferably in cash; if tipping with card, must be communicated before tapping

🏛 U.S. Embassy/Consulate

All foreign governments have embassies in Madrid (some also have consular offices in other Spanish cities), and most offer consular services in the embassy building.

📍 Visitor Information

The largest tourist information office is on Plaza Mayor. There are two smaller offices located in Terminal 2 and Terminal 4 at the airport, as well as offices at Plaza del Callao, the Reina Sofía and Prado art museums, and the Royal Palace.

Helpful Phrases

BASICS

Hello	Hola	**oh**-lah
Yes/no	Sí/no	see/no
Please	Por favor	pore fah-**vore**
May I?	¿Me permite?	may pair-**mee**-tay
Thank you	Gracias	**Grah**-see-as
You're welcome	De nada	day **nah**-dah
I'm sorry	Lo siento	lo see-**en**-toh
Good morning!	¡Buenos días!	**bway**-nohs **dee**-ahs
Good evening!	¡Buenas tardes! (after 2pm)	**bway**-nahs-**tar**-dess
	¡Buenas noches! (after 8pm)	**bway**-nahs **no**-chess
Good-bye!	¡Adiós!/¡Hasta luego!	ah-dee-**ohss/ah** -stah **lwe**-go
Mr./Mrs.	Señor/Señora	sen-**yor**/ sen-**yohr**-ah
Miss	Señorita	sen-yo-**ree**-tah
Pleased to meet you	Mucho gusto	**moo**-cho **goose**-toh
How are you?	¿Que tal?	keh-tal

NUMBERS

one	un, uno	oon, **oo**-no
two	dos	dos
three	tres	tress
four	cuatro	**kwah**-tro
five	cinco	**sink**-oh
six	seis	saice
seven	siete	see-**et**-eh
eight	ocho	o-cho
nine	nueve	new-**eh**-vey
ten	diez	dee-**es**
eleven	once	**ohn**-seh
twelve	doce	**doh**-seh
thirteen	trece	**treh**-seh
fourteen	catorce	ka-**tohr**-seh
fifteen	quince	**keen**-seh
sixteen	dieciséis	dee-**es**-ee-**saice**
seventeen	diecisiete	dee-**es**-ee-see-**et**-eh
eighteen	dieciocho	dee-**es**-ee-o-cho
nineteen	diecinueve	dee-**es**-ee-new-**ev**-eh
twenty	veinte	**vain**-teh
twenty-one	veintiuno	**vain**-te-oo-noh
thirty	treinta	**train**-tah
forty	cuarenta	kwah-**ren**-tah
fifty	cincuenta	seen-**kwen**-tah
sixty	sesenta	sess-**en**-tah
seventy	setenta	set-**en**-tah
eighty	ochenta	oh-**chen**-tah
ninety	noventa	no-**ven**-tah
one hundred	cien	see-**en**
one thousand	mil	meel
one million	un millón	oon meel-**yohn**

COLORS

black	negro	**neh**-groh
blue	azul	ah-**sool**
brown	marrón	mah-**ron**
green	verde	**ver**-deh
orange	naranja	na-**rahn**-hah
red	rojo	**roh**-hoh
white	blanco	**blahn**-koh
yellow	amarillo	ah-mah-**ree**-yoh

DAYS OF THE WEEK

Sunday	domingo	doe-**meen**-goh
Monday	lunes	**loo**-ness
Tuesday	martes	**mahr**-tess
Wednesday	miércoles	me-**air**-koh-less
Thursday	jueves	hoo-**ev**-ess
Friday	viernes	vee-**air**-ness
Saturday	sábado	**sah**-bah-doh

MONTHS

January	enero	eh-**neh**-roh
February	febrero	feh-**breh**-roh
March	marzo	**mahr**-soh
April	abril	ah-**breel**
May	mayo	**my**-oh
June	junio	**hoo**-nee-oh
July	julio	**hoo**-lee-yoh
August	agosto	ah-**ghost**-toh
September	septiembre	sep-tee-**em**-breh
October	octubre	oak-**too**-breh
November	noviembre	no-vee-**em**-breh
December	diciembre	dee-see-**em**-breh

USEFUL WORDS AND PHRASES

Do you speak English?	¿Habla usted inglés?	ah-blah oos-**ted** in-**glehs**
I don't speak Spanish.	No hablo español	no **ah**-bloh es-**pahn**-**yol**
I don't understand.	No entiendo	no en-tee-**en**-doh
I understand.	Entiendo	en-tee-**en**-doh
I don't know.	No sé	no **seh**
I'm American.	Soy americano (americana)	soy ah-meh-**ree**-**kah**-no (ah-meh-ree-**kah**-nah)
What's your name?	¿Cómo se llama ?	koh-mo seh **yah**-mah
My name is . . .	Me llamo . . .	may **yah**-moh
What time is it?	¿Qué hora es?	keh **o**-rah es
How?	¿Cómo?	**koh**-mo
When?	¿Cuándo?	**kwahn**-doh
Yesterday	Ayer	ah-**yehr**
Today	hoy	oy
Tomorrow	mañana	mahn-**yah**-nah
Tonight	Esta noche	es-tah **no**-cheh
What?	¿Qué?	keh
What is it?	¿Qué es esto?	keh es **es**-toh

Why?	¿Por qué?	pore **keh**
Who?	¿Quién?	kee-**yen**
Where is ...	¿Dónde está ...	dohn-deh es-**tah**
...the train station?	la estación del tren?	la es-tah-see-**on** del trehn
...the subway station?	estación de metro	la es-ta-see-**on** del meh-tro
...the bus stop?	la parada del autobus?	la pah-**rah**-dah del ow-toh-**boos**
...the terminal? (airport)	el aeropuerto	el air-oh-**pwar**-toh
...the post office?	la oficina de correos?	la oh-fee-see- nah deh koh-**rreh**-os
...the bank?	el banco?	el **bahn**-koh
...the hotel?	el hotel?	el oh-**tel**
...the museum?	el museo?	el moo-**seh**-oh
...the hospital?	el hospital?	el ohss-pee-**tal**
...the elevator?	el ascensor?	el ah-sen-**sohr**
Where are the restrooms?	el baño?	el **bahn**-yoh
Here/there	Aquí/allí	ah-**key**/ah-**yee**
Open/closed	Abierto/cerrado	ah-bee-**er**-toh/ ser-**ah**-doh
Left/right	Izquierda/derecha	iss-key-**eh**-dah/ dare-**eh**-chah
Is it near?	¿Está cerca?	es-**tah sehr**-kah
Is it far?	¿Está lejos?	es-**tah leh**-hoss
I'd like ...	Quisiera ...	kee-see-**ehr**-ah
...a room	un cuarto/una habitación	oon **kwahr**-toh/**oo**-nah ah-bee-tah-see-**on**
...the key	la llave	lah yah-veh
...a newspaper	un periódico	oon pehr-ee-oh-**oh**-dee-koh
...a stamp	un sello de correo	oon **seh**-yo deh korr-**eh**-oh
I'd like to buy ...	Quisiera comprar ...	kee-see-**ehr**-ah kohm-**prahr**
...soap	jabón	hah-**bohn**
...suntan lotion	crema solar	**kreh**-mah soh-**lar**
...envelopes	sobres	so-brehs
...writing paper	papel	pah-**pel**
...a postcard	una tarjeta postal	**oon**-ah tar-**het**-ah post-**ahl**
...a ticket	un billete (travel)	oon bee-**yee**-teh
	una entrada (concert etc.)	**oona** en-**trah**-dah
How much is it?	¿Cuánto cuesta?	**kwahn**-toh **kwes**-tah
It's expensive/ cheap	Es caro/barato	es **kah**-roh/ bah-**rah**-toh
A little/a lot	Un poquito/mucho	oon poh-**kee**-toh/ **moo**-choh
More/less	Más/menos	mahss/**men**-ohss
Enough/too (much)	Suficiente/	soo-fee-see-**en**-teh/
I am ill/sick	Estoy enfermo(a)	es-**toy** en-**fehr**-moh(mah)
Call a doctor	Llame a un medico	ya-meh ah oon **med**-ee-koh

Help!	Socorro	soh-**koh**-roh
Stop!	Pare	pah-reh

DINING OUT

I'd like to reserve a table ...	Quisiera reservar una mesa ...	kee-**syeh**-rah rreh-sehr-**bahr** oo-nah meh-sah ...
...for two people.	para dos personas.	**pah**-rah dohs pehr-**soh**-nahs
...for this evening.	para esta noche.	**pah**-rah ehs-**tah** noh-cheh
...for 8 PM	para las ocho de la noche.	**pah**-rah lahs oh-choh deh lah noh-cheh
A bottle of ...	Una botella de ...	oo-nah bo-**teh**-yah deh
A cup of ...	Una taza de ...	oo-nah **tah**-sah deh
A glass of ...	Un vaso (water, soda, etc.) de...	oon **vah**-so deh
	Una copa (wine, spirits, etc.) de...	oona **coh**-pah deh
Bill/check	La cuenta	lah **kwen**-tah
Bread	El pan	el pahn
Breakfast	El desayuno	el deh-sah-**yoon**-oh
Butter	La mantequilla	lah man-teh-**kee**-yah
Coffee	Café	kah-**feh**
Dinner	La cena	lah **seh**-nah
Fork	El tenedor	el ten-eh-**dor**
I don't eat meat	No como carne	noh koh-moh **kahr**-neh
I cannot eat ...	No puedo comer ...	noh **pweh**-doh koh-**mehr**
I'd like to order ...	Quiero pedir ...	**kee**-yehr-oh peh-**deer**
I'd like ...	Me gustaría ...	Meh- goo-stah-ee-ah
I'm hungry/thirsty	Tengo hambre/sed	**Tehn**-goh **hahm**-breh/seth
Is service/the tip included?	¿Está incluida la propina?	es-**tah** in-cloo-ee-dah lah pro-**pee**-nah
Knife	El cuchillo	el koo-**chee**-yo
Lunch	La comida	lah koh-**mee**-dah
Menu	La carta, el menú	lah **cart**-ah, el meh-**noo**
Napkin	La servilleta	lah sehr-vee-**yet**-ah
Pepper	La pimienta	lah pee-mee-**en**-tah
Plate	plato	plato
Please give me ...	Por favor déme ...	pore fah-**vor deh**-meh
Salt	La sal	lah sahl
Spoon	Una cuchara	oo-nah koo-**chah**-rah
Sugar	El ázucar	el ah-**su**-kar
Tea	té	teh
Water	agua	ah-gwah
Wine	vino	**vee**-noh

Contacts

Air

**AIRPORT Granada Airport
(GRX).** ✉ *Granada* ⊕ *gra-
nadaairport.com.* **Seville
Airport (SVQ).** ✉ *Seville*
⊕ *www.sevilla-airport.
com/en/.*

AIRLINES Aena.
☎ *913/211000* ⊕ *www.
aena.es.* **Air Europa.**
☎ *911/401501* ⊕ *www.
aireuropa.com.* **Iberia.**
☎ *900/111500* ⊕ *www.
iberia.com.* **Iberia Express.**
☎ *919/046342* ⊕ *www.ibe-
riaexpress.com.* **Vueling.**
☎ *900/645000* ⊕ *www.
vueling.com.* **Transportation
Security Administration.**
⊕ *www.tsa.gov.*

 Bike

CONTACTS BiciMAD.
⊕ *www.bicimad.com.*

 Bus

CONTACTS Alsa.
☎ *91/020–7007* ⊕ *www.
alsa.es.* **Flixbus.** ⊕ *www.
flixbus.es.*

Ⓜ Public Transportation

**SUBWAY INFORMATION
Metro Madrid.** ☎ *90/044–
4404* ⊕ *www.metroma-
drid.es.*

�' Taxi

**TAXI SERVICES Radio Taxi
Gremial.** ☎ *91/447–3232,
91/447–5180* ⊕ *www.
radiotaxigremial.com.*
Radioteléfono Taxi.
☎ *91/547–8200* ⊕ *www.
radiotelefono-taxi.com.*
Telé-Taxi. ☎ *91/371–2131*
⊕ *www.tele-taxi.es.*

🚆 Train

CONTACTS RENFE.
☎ *912/320320* for tickets
and info ⊕ *www.renfe.
es.* **Rail Europe.** ⊕ *www.
raileurope.com.*

🏃 Activities

**PARKS AND PLAY-
GROUNDS Casa de Campo.**
Ⓜ *Casa de Campo.* **Madrid
Río.** Ⓜ *Puerta del Ángel.*
Parque del Buen Retiro.
Ⓜ *Retiro.* **Parque del Oeste.**
Ⓜ *Moncloa.*

SKIING La Pinilla. ✉ *Segovia* ⊕ *www.lapinilla.es.*
Puerto de Navacerrada.
✉ *Segovia* ⊕ *www.
puertonavacerrada.com.*
Valdesquí. ⊕ *www.valdes-
qui.es.*

**SOCCER Estadio Santiago
Bernabéu.** ✉ *Av. de Concha Espina 1, Chamartín*
⊕ *www.realmadrid.com/
en* Ⓜ *Santiago Bernabéu.*
**Estadio Wanda Metro-
politano.** ✉ *Av. de Luis
Aragonés 4* ⊕ *www.
atleticodemadrid.com*
Ⓜ *Estadio Metropolitano.*

TENNIS Caja Mágica.
✉ *Camino de Perales 23*
⊕ *www.madrid-open.com*
Ⓜ *San Fermín-Orcasur.*

🧭 Tours

BIKE BravoBike. ✉ *Calle
de Juan Álvarez
Mendizábal 19, Moncloa*
☎ *91/758–2945, 60/744–
8440 for WhatsApp*
⊕ *www.bravobike.com.*

**BIRD-WATCHING
Discovering Doñana.**
☎ *620/964369* ⊕ *www.
discoveringdonana.com.*

BUS Madrid City Tours.
☎ *91/369–2732* ⊕ *madrid.
city-tour.com.*

FOOD AND WINE Artisans of Leisure. ☎ *800/214–8144, 212/243–3239* ⊕ *www.artisansofleisure.com.* **Cellar Tours.** ☎ *911/436553 in Spain, 310/496–8061 in U.S.* ⊕ *www.cellartours.com.* **Devour Tours.** ☎ *91/902–5349 in Spain, 202/684–6916 in U.S.* ⊕ *www.devourtours.com.* **Walk and Eat Spain.** ☎ *91/215–8281* ⊕ *www.walkandeatspain.com* Ⓜ *Tribunal.*

HIKING Spain Adventures. ☎ *772/564–0330* ⊕ *www.spainadventures.com.*

LEARNING Go Abroad. ⊕ *www.goabroad.com.*

PERSONALIZED TOURS Madrid and Beyond. ☎ *91/758–0063 in Spain* ⊕ *www.madridandbeyond.com.* **Toma Tours.** ☎ *650/733116* ⊕ *tomaandcoe.com.*

WALKING TOURS Association of Official Tourist Guides of the Region of Madrid (APIT). ☎ *91/542–1214* ⊕ *www.apit.es.* **Carpetania Madrid.** ✉ *Calle de Jesús del Valle 11, Malasaña* ☎ *91/531–4018* ⊕ *www.carpetaniamadrid.com.*

⚠ Emergencies

FOREIGN EMBASSIES AND CONSULATES

U.S. Embassy. ✉ *Calle de Serrano 75, Madrid* ☎ *91/587–2200 for U.S.-citizen emergencies* ⊕ *es.usembassy.gov.*

🎭 Performing Arts

CONTACTS Auditorio Nacional de Música. ✉ *Calle del Príncipe de Vergara 146, Salamanca* ☎ *91/337–0140* ⊕ *www.auditorionacional.mcu.es* Ⓜ *Cruz del Rayo, Prosperidad.* **Círculo de Bellas Artes.** ✉ *Calle de Alcalá 42, Sol* ☎ *91/360–5400* ⊕ *www.circulobellasartes.com* Ⓜ *Banco de España.* **Teatro Real.** ✉ *Pl. de Isabel II s/n, Palacio* ☎ *91/516–0600* ⊕ *www.teatroreal.es* Ⓜ *Ópera.*

Great Itineraries

5 Days: Madrid Plus Granada or Seville and Side Trips

DAYS 1 AND 2: MADRID

Start the day with a visit to either the **Museo Prado**, the **Museo Thyssen-Borne-misza**, or the **Museo Nacional Centro de Arte Reina Sofía**. Then head to the elegant **Plaza Mayor**—a perfect jumping-off point for a tour of the Spanish capital. To the west, see the **Plaza de la Villa, Palacio Real, Teatro Real**, and the royal convents; to the south, wander around the maze of streets of **La Latina** and **El Rastro** and try some local tapas.

On Day 2, visit the sprawling **Barrio de las Letras**, centered on the Plaza de Santa Ana. This was the favorite neighborhood of writers during the Spanish Golden Age in the 17th century (Cervantes lies buried under a convent nearby), and it's still crammed with theaters, cafés, and good tapas bars. From here, you can pop to the Paseo del Prado to the east and visit any of the art museums in the area. After lunch, take an afternoon stroll in the **Parque del Buen Retiro** or wander in **Chueca** or **Malasaña**, the two funky hipster neighborhoods favored by young locals. From here, walk to the **Parque del Oeste** and the **Templo de Debod** to marvel at the city's sunset.

GRANADA

Getting Here: A few daily flights connect Granada with Madrid, and it's easy to get to the city from the airport by taxi, airport bus, or rental car. There are also several daily high-speed AVE trains from Madrid to Granada, and BlaBlaCar rideshares are plentiful.

Day 3: After arriving in Granada, visit the Catholic Monarchs' tomb at the **Capilla Real** (Royal Chapel) before exploring more Moorish monuments such as the **Palacio de la Madraza** (seminary) or **El Bañuelo** (bathhouse). Stroll around the Moorish **Albayzín** neighborhood for extraordinary views of Granada's highlight, the Alhambra, and the Sierra Nevada backdrop, extra special at sunset. Dine on the city's excellent tapas or take in a flamenco show.

Day 4: Granada's star of the show is, of course, the **Alhambra**, the most visited attraction in Spain. Its palace, fortress, patios, gardens, and museums alone merit the trip to Granada and need at least half a day to do them justice. Try to get an early-morning ticket to experience this wonder with fewer crowds. Note: reserve your ticket as far in advance as possible and show up at your ticketed time (preferably before) or you will not be allowed entry. Get lunch early before you pick up your hired car for a side trip excursion.

EVENING 4, DAY 5: SIDE TRIP OPTIONS

Option 1: Drive north to **Priego de Córdoba** (1¼ hours) to see one of the region's prettiest towns with a plethora of baroque churches, white facades decked with geraniums and stunning views. From here, drive to Córdoba and your hotel. Spend the next day exploring the **Mezquita-Catedral** (mosque-cathedral) and the **Jewish Quarter** and dine on the city's famous oxtail stew or *flamenquín* (pork fritter) washed down with local Montilla wine.

Option 2: Drive northeast to **Baeza** (1½ hours) and then to **Úbeda**, two jewels in Spain's Renaissance crown. Both are home to stunning architecture, seen in intricate facades on the many monuments; allow more time for Úbeda where you can visit the historic potter's quarter.

Option 3: Head south for the **Sierra Nevada** (1 hour) for a paradise of skiing in winter and trekking and climbing in summer. Or explore the **Alpujarra**, a unique mountain region dotted with picturesque Moorish villages set in stunning landscapes where time appears to stand still.

SEVILLE

Getting Here: Andalusia's second-largest airport, after Málaga, is in Seville and there are around four flights from Madrid a day. From Madrid, the best approach to Andalusia is via the high-speed AVE or low-cost Iryo. In just 2½ hours, the spectacular ride winds through the olive groves and rolling fields of Castile to Córdoba and on to Seville. From Seville's Santa Justa train station, get a cab (or rental car) to your hotel.

Day 3: Must-sees in the Andalusian capital include the **Cathedral** with its **La Giralda tower** and the **Reales Alcázares** (Royal Alcázars) Moorish palace. Between visits, explore the nearby **Barrio de Santa Cruz** neighborhood with its typical architecture, orange blossom trees, and tiny squares. Dine early on delicious tapas at one of the traditional *tavernas* (pubs) before an evening stroll along the banks of the Guadalquivir River.

Day 4: Start with a visit to one of the city's great private houses—**Palacio de las Dueñas**, **Casa de Pilatos** (Pilate's House), or **Palacio de la Condesa de Lebrija** (Palace of the Countess of Lebrija)—to see how the other half lived in the city. After lunch on tapas, admire the **Plaza de Toros de la Real Maestranza** (bullring) and stroll around the **Parque de María Luisa** before an aperitif in the bar at the Hotel Alfonso XIII. Then take in a flamenco show.

DAY 5: DAY TRIP OPTIONS

Seville is perfectly placed for several excellent side trips: taste the world-famous sherries of **Jerez de la Frontera** and admire the dancing horses before dining on Spain's freshest seafood at **Puerto de Santa María** or **Sanlúcar de Barrameda**; visit Spain's largest and one of its greatest Roman sites at **Itálica**, just outside Seville; drive to **Ronda**, one of Andalusia's most beautiful white towns, perched on a river gorge and the cradle of bullfighting; head for Europe's oldest city, the maritime **Cádiz**, and soak up the history in its narrow streets and along the fortress walls; or go to **Córdoba**, where the city's breathtaking **Mezquita-Catedral** (mosque-cathedral) and medieval **Jewish Quarter** await you. Don't miss the vibrant flower-packed patios while you're there.

Great Itineraries

10 Days: Madrid to the Alhambra

This trip takes in the best of vibrant Madrid and its world-class art museums and showcases some of Castile's historic gems before whisking you to the Moorish south, where Córdoba's majestic mosque, Seville's fragrant orange blossoms, and Granada's "heaven on earth" await.

DAYS 1–3: MADRID

Start the day with a visit to either the **Prado,** the **Thyssen-Bornemisza Museum,** or the **Queen Sofía National Museum Art Center.** Then head to the elegant **Plaza Mayor**—a perfect jumping-off point for a tour of the Spanish capital. To the west, see the **Plaza de la Villa, Palacio Real , Teatro Real ,** and the royal convents; to the south, wander around the maze of streets of **La Latina** and **El Rastro** and try some local tapas.

On Day 2, visit the sprawling **Barrio de las Letras,** centered on the **Plaza de Santa Ana.** This was the favorite neighborhood of writers during the Spanish Golden Age in the 17th century (Cervantes lies buried under a convent nearby), and it's still crammed with theaters, cafés, and good tapas bars. It borders the Paseo del Prado to the east, allowing you to comfortably walk to any of the art museums in the area. If the weather is pleasant, take an afternoon stroll in **E l Retiro Park.**

For your third day in the capital, wander around **Chueca** and **Malasaña,** the two funky hipster neighborhoods most favored by young Madrileños. **Fuencarral,** a landmark pedestrianized street that serves as the border between the two, is one of the city's trendiest shopping

enclaves. From there you can walk to the **Western Park** and the **Templo of Debod**—the best spot from which to see the city's sunset. Among the lesser-known museums, consider visiting the captivating **Museo Sorolla,** Goya's frescoes and tomb at the **Ermita de San Antonio de la Florida** (Chapel of San Antonio de la Florida), or the **Real Academia de Bellas Artes de San Fernando** (San Fernando Fine Art Royal Academy) for classic painting. People-watch at any of the terrace bars in either **Plaza de Chueca** or **Plaza del Dos de Mayo** in Malasaña.

Logistics: If you're traveling light, the subway (Metro Línea 8) or the bus (No. 203 during the day and N27 at night) will take you from the airport to the city for €5. The train costs €5 (including the supplement) and a taxi is a fixed price of €30. Once in the center consider walking or taking the subway rather than cabbing it in gridlock traffic.

DAYS 4 AND 5: CASTILIAN CITIES

There are several excellent options for half- or full-day side trips from Madrid to occupy Days 4 and 5. **Toledo** and **Segovia** are two of the oldest Castilian cities—both have delightful old quarters dating back to the Romans. There's also **El Escorial,** which houses the massive monastery built by Felipe II. Two other nearby towns also worth visiting are **Aranjuez** and **Alcalá de Henares.**

Logistics: Toledo and Segovia are stops on the high-speed train line (AVE), so you can get to either of them in a half hour from Madrid. To reach the old quarters of both cities, take a bus or cab from the train station or take the bus from Madrid. Buses and trains both go to El Escorial. Reach Aranjuez and Alcalá de Henares via the intercity train system (cercanías).

DAY 6: CORDOBA OR EXTREMADURA

Córdoba, the capital of both Roman and Moorish Spain, was the center of Western art and culture between the 8th and 11th centuries. The city's breathtaking **Mezquita**, which is now a cathedral, and the medieval **Jewish Quarter** bear witness to the city's brilliant past. From Madrid you could also rent a car and visit the lesser-known cities in the north of **Extremadura,** such as **Guadalupe** and **Trujillo,** and overnight in **Cáceres,** a UNESCO World Heritage Site, then return to Madrid the next day.

Logistics: The AVE and low-cost Iryo will take you to Córdoba from Madrid in less than two hours. One alternative is to stay in Toledo, also on the route heading south, and then head to Córdoba the next day, although you need to return to Madrid by train first. Once in Córdoba, take a taxi for a visit out to the summer palace at **Medina Azahara.**

DAYS 7 AND 8: SEVILLE

Seville's **cathedral,** with its tower La Giralda, **Plaza de Toros de la Real Maestranza,** and **Barrio de Santa Cruz** are visual feasts. Forty minutes south by train, you can sip the world-famous sherries of **Jerez de la Frontera,** then munch jumbo shrimp on the beach at **Sanlúcar de Barrameda.**

Logistics: From Seville's AVE station, take a taxi to your hotel. After that, walking and hailing the occasional taxi are the best ways to explore the city. A rental car is the best option to reach towns beyond Seville, except for Jerez de la Frontera, where the train station is an architectural gem in its own right.

DAYS 9 AND 10: GRANADA

The hilltop **Alhambra** palace, Spain's most visited attraction, was conceived by the Moorish caliphs as heaven on earth. Try any of the city's famous tapas bars and tea shops, and make sure to roam the magical steep streets of the **Albayzín,** the ancient Moorish quarter.

Logistics: Since 2019, you can travel from Madrid to Granada via AVE. Once down south, Sevilla and Córdoba make excellent add-ons. BlaBlaCar rideshares are also plentiful between Madrid and Granada.

Great Itineraries

Madrid Walking Tour

The Spanish have a term for their favorite pastime, *paseo,* which means a leisurely walk; in Madrid, it is a way of life. As clean, modern, and affordable as the Madrid metro is, walking really is the best way to get to know this vibrant city. Pack your practical shoes and make sure your paseo allows for impromptu stops for people-watching with cafés con leches and baskets of churros.

PLAZAS, PALACES, AND GARDENS

Start your tour at the Plaza Mayor, built in 1619 and one of the largest squares in Europe. Its almost 240 balconies have witnessed eclectic events from public executions, bullfights, and royal weddings to today's famous Christmas market. Don't miss the Mercado de San Miguel for a foodie feast.

From here, walk west to Plaza de la Villa, one of the oldest parts of the city whose jewel is the Casa de la Villa, built in the classic Madrid architectural style. Continue west to the Catedral de la Almudena, one of Europe's most modern cathedrals, although built in Madrid style and with a Gothic interior. Just next door is the imposing Palacio Real, an early-18th-century palace with 2,800 rooms and modeled on French royal residences. Nearby, you'll find Plaza de Oriente, with pleasant fountains and statues of Spanish monarchs; Jardines de Sabatini, gorgeous formal gardens; and the newly renovated and pedestrianized Plaza de España.

MADRID'S CHAMPS-ÉLYSÉES, SHOPPING, AND A MONASTERY

Head northwest to Gran Vía, Madrid's answer to the Parisian Champs-Élysées and flanked by designer shops and theaters housed in fine buildings in neoclassical and art deco styles. At Plaza del Callao, art lovers should make a side trip to the Monasterio de las Descalzas Reales (buy tickets ahead of time), a monastery whose bare facade hides a treasure trove of European artwork by Titian, Zurbarán, Brueghel the Elder, and Rubens, among others.

VIEWS, THE BIG THREE MUSEUMS, AND THE PARK

Continue on to Plaza del Sol, Madrid's bustling hub, which was gut-renovated in 2023. Enjoy the street performers and don't miss the iconic clock tower whose 12 chimes bring in the Spanish New Year. From here, take the elegant Calle de Alcalá, flanked on both sides by fine architecture. At the Círculo de Bellas Artes, head for the seventh floor where you'll find some of the best views in Madrid.

Back on ground level, make your way to the Paseo del Prado, also known as the Paseo del Arte as three of Europe's top art museums are nearby. Take your pick from the Museo Thyssen-Bornemisza, the Prado, or the Museo Nacional Centro de Arte Reina Sofía (your walk will be derailed if you try to see all three in the one afternoon). Enjoy a time-out from all the art and city bustle in El Retiro Park with more than 300 acres of gardens and parkland plus a boating lake. Plant lovers shouldn't miss the abutting Real Jardín Botánico (Royal Botanical Garden), home to an impressive range of botanical species.

Chapter 3

SOL

Updated by
Benjamin Kemper

◉ Sights	🍴 Restaurants	🛏 Hotels	🛍 Shopping	🍸 Nightlife
★★★★★	★★☆☆☆	★★★★★	★★★★★	★★★★★

NEIGHBORHOOD SNAPSHOT

TOP EXPERIENCES

■ **Chocolatería San Ginés:** Sample Spain's most legendary churros.

■ **La vida nocturna:** Kill the night Madrid-style at a bumping discoteca (nightclub).

■ **Rooftop-hopping:** Take in panoramic views from ritzy roof decks.

■ **Casa de Diego:** Snap up a hand-painted fan or umbrella.

■ **Puerta del Sol:** Get caught up in the mayhem of Madrid's busiest square.

GETTING HERE

All roads—and bike lanes and train tracks—lead to Sol, Spain's *kilómetro cero* (kilometer zero), the point from which the distances of all of Spain's official roads are measured. The Sol metro station (Líneas 1, 2, 3) is one of the busiest in the country as it is also a main hub for the commuter rail (*cercanías*). BiciMAD bike-share has docks on most blocks in this area. Sol lies within the "Madrid 360" low-emission zone and therefore cannot be accessed by most rental cars.

PLANNING YOUR TIME

Puerta del Sol and its surrounding streets and plazas are Madrid's cultural nerve center. Like Times Square in New York or Las Ramblas in Barcelona, Sol is eternally thronged with crowds both local and foreign—this is a place to watch your wallet, especially after dark. If it's your first time in Madrid, begin your sightseeing here. After checking out the curiosities of the semicircular "square" at Puerta del Sol (the "Kilómetro Cero" plaque; the equestrian statue of Carlos III; the sculpted bear in the *madroño* tree, Madrid's emblem), make your way to Plaza Mayor, the city's historical main square; then explore the cobblestone lanes east of the plaza in the direction of Plaza de Canalejas to wind up at Círculo de Bellas Artes, whose roof deck affords some of the city's most stunning views.

FUN FACT

For more than a century, Sol has been a nucleus of political activity. In the main square, see if you can spot the the restored 1756 French-neoclassical building with the clock tower. Today it houses the offices of the regional government, but during Franco's reign, it was the headquarters of his secret police and is still known colloquially as the Casa de los Gritos (House of Screams). Fast-forward to 2011, and Sol is where the 15-M movement would take shape. It began as a sleep-in against government austerity measures and blossomed into an organized revolution. The grassroots political party Podemos was created as a result. The 15-M demonstrations would go on to inspire Occupy Wall Street and other pro-democracy and anti-capitalist protests around the world.

This neighborhood, built in the 16th century around the Puerta del Sol, used to mark the city's geographic center, which today sits a tad to its east. Sol encompasses, among other sites, the monumental Plaza Mayor and popular pedestrian shopping area around Callao.

There's never a dull moment in Puerta del Sol, the bustling semicircular plaza where friends gather, buskers perform, and bar crawls begin. The *Puerta* ("gate") designation is a holdover from when this spot bore entry into the medieval city walls; *Sol* ("sun"), on the other hand, is a reference to a sun carving that adorned the gate. The clocktower atop the Real Casa de Correos (Royal House of the Post Office), the oldest building on the square, ushers Madrid into the New Year each December as onlookers partake in the Spanish tradition of eating 12 grapes in the last 12 seconds of the year.

◉ Sights

Mercado de San Miguel
MARKET | Adjacent to the Plaza Mayor, this gastronomic market is a feast for the senses. Its bustling interior—a mixture of tapas spots and grab-and-go counters— sits beneath a fin-de-siècle glass dome reinforced by elaborate wrought iron. Enjoy a glass of wine and maybe a snack here, but save your appetite: the market, as gorgeous as it may be, has become overpriced and underwhelming in recent years. There are two diamonds in the rough: Rocambolesc, with its futuristic ice creams by the Roca brothers, and Daniel Sorlut, a posh oyster bar. ✉ *Pl.*

de San Miguel s/n, Sol ⊕ mercadodesan-miguel.es Ⓜ Ópera.

★ Plaza Mayor
PLAZA/SQUARE | A symbol of Spain's imperial grandeur, this public square is often surprisingly quiet, perhaps since most locals wrote it off long ago as too touristy. The plaza was finished in 1619 under Felipe III, whose equestrian statue stands in the center, and is one of the largest in Europe, clocking in at 360 by 300 feet. It has seen it all: *autos-da-fé* ("trials of faith," or public burnings of heretics); the canonization of saints; criminal executions; royal marriages, such as that of Princess María and the king of Hungary in 1629; bullfights (until 1847); and masked balls.

The space was initially occupied by a city market, and many of the surrounding streets retain the charming names of the trades and foods once headquartered there. Nearby are Calle de Cuchilleros (Cutlers' Street), Calle de Lechuga (Lettuce Street), Calle de Fresa (Strawberry Street), and Calle de Botoneros (Button Makers' Street). The plaza's oldest building is the one with the brightly painted murals and gray spires, called Casa de la Panadería (Bakery House) in honor of the bread shop over which it was built; it is now the tourist office. Opposite is

the Casa de la Carnicería (Butcher Shop), now a rather underwhelming boutique hotel.

The plaza is closed to motorized traffic, making it a pleasant place for sidewalk sitting and coffee sipping as alfresco artists and street musicians put on impromptu shows. Sunday morning brings a stamp and coin market. Around Christmas the plaza fills with stalls selling trees, ornaments, and Nativity scenes. Whenever you visit, be sure to watch your phone and wallet. ⊠ *Sol* Ⓜ *Sol.*

★ Puerta del Sol

PLAZA/SQUARE | Crowded with locals, tourists, hawkers, and street performers, the Puerta del Sol is the nerve center of Madrid. It was renovated in 2023, and not all Madrileños are wild about its new, more austere look. A brass plaque in the sidewalk on the south side of the plaza marks Kilómetro Cero, the point from which all distances in Spain are measured. Across the square are two important statues: *El oso y el madroño* (a bear climbing a strawberry tree, Madrid's official symbol) and an equestrian statue of King and Mayor Carlos III. Watch your belongings when passing through, as the area is often packed with pedestrians. ⊠ *Sol* Ⓜ *Sol.*

Real Academia de Bellas Artes de San Fernando (*St. Ferdinand Royal Academy of Fine Arts*)

ART MUSEUM | Designed by José Benito de Churriguera in the waning baroque years of the early 18th century, this museum showcases 500 years of Spanish painting, from José Ribera and Bartolomé Esteban Murillo to Joaquín Sorolla and Ignacio Zuloaga. The tapestries along the stairways are stunning. The gallery displays paintings up to the 18th century, including some by Goya. Guided tours are usually available (check the website for times). The same building houses the Calcografía Nacional (National Prints Institute), which sells limited-edition prints from original plates engraved by

Spanish artists. There are often classical concerts and literary events in the small upstairs hall: tickets can be purchased on the website. ⊠ *Calle de Alcalá 13, Sol* ☎ *91/524–0864* ⊕ *www.realacademia-bellasartessanfernando.com* ✉ *€8 (free Wed.)* ⊗ *Closed Mon. and Aug.* Ⓜ *Sol.*

🍴 Restaurants

Gourmet Experience Callao

$ | **INTERNATIONAL** | On the rooftop of El Corte Inglés, Spain's largest department store, there's a gourmet food court with some of the best views in the city. Grab some tapas and a glass of wine here after perusing the shops around Callao. **Known for:** epicurean shopping; food court with something for everyone; stunning bird's-eye panoramas. $ *Average main: €15* ⊠ *Pl. de Callao 1, Sol* ✛ *Take 2nd entrance to El Corte Inglés as you're walking down Callao on Calle del Carmen and across from Fnac* ⊕ *www.elcorteingles.es* Ⓜ *Sol.*

La Casa del Abuelo

$$ | **TAPAS** | This rustic tapas hall is the oldest of three branches of a beloved local chain, and it has barely changed since it was founded in 1906. The tapa to try here is *gambas al ajillo*, shrimp sautéed with garlic. **Known for:** killer gambas al ajillo; bold proprietary Toro wines; traditional atmosphere. $ *Average main: €19* ⊠ *Calle de la Victoria 12, Sol* ☎ *91/521–2319* ⊕ *lacasadelabuelo.es* Ⓜ *Sol.*

La Pulpería de Victoria

$$ | **SPANISH** | **FAMILY** | A modern urban interpretation of a traditional Galician *pulpería* (octopus restaurant), this casual spot specializes in *polbo á feira*, boiled octopus cut into coins, drizzled with olive oil, and dusted with smoked paprika. Pair it with an icy glass of Albariño and a heap of blistered padrón peppers. **Known for:** Galician-style octopus; ocean-fresh shellfish; variety of Galician wines. $ *Average main: €20* ⊠ *Calle de la Victoria 2, Sol*

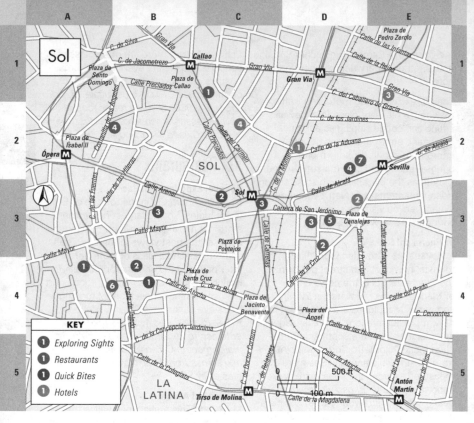

Sights ▼

1 Mercado de
San Miguel **A4**
2 Plaza Mayor **B4**
3 Puerta del Sol **C3**
4 Real Academia de
Bellas Artes de
San Fernando **D2**

Restaurants ▼

1 Gourmet Experience
Callao **C1**
2 La Casa del Abuelo **D3**
3 La Pulpería
de Victoria **D3**
4 Lambuzo **A2**
5 Lhardy **D3**
6 Mesón del
Champiñón **A4**
7 Paco Roncero
Restaurante **D2**

Quick Bites ▼

1 Bar La Campana **B4**
2 Casa Labra **C3**
3 Chocolatería
San Ginés **B3**

Hotels ▼

1 Ateneo Hotel **D2**
2 Four Seasons Hotel
Madrid **D3**
3 Iberostar Las Letras
Gran Vía **E1**
4 Liabeny **C2**

☎ 91/080–4929 ⊕ www.pulperiadevicto-ria.com Ⓜ Sol.

★ Lambuzo

$$ | **SPANISH** | **FAMILY** | This laid-back Andalusian barroom, one of three locations (the others are in Retiro and Chamberí), embodies the joyful spirit of that sunny region. Let the cheerful waitstaff guide you through the extensive menu, which includes fried seafood, unconventional croquetas (flecked with garlicky shrimp, for instance), and heftier shareables like creamy oxtail rice and seared Barbate tuna loin. **Known for:** carefree Andalusian vibe; a shoal's worth of seafood dishes; free marinated carrots with every drink. $ Average main: €22 ✉ Calle de las Conchas 9, Sol ☎ 91/143–4862 ⊕ www.barlambuzo.com ☻ Closed Mon. No dinner Sun. Ⓜ Ópera.

Lhardy

$$$$ | **SPANISH** | Opened in 1839, Lhardy—with its spiral staircase, varnished leather walls, gleaming chandeliers, and marble fireplaces—is one of Madrid's most treasured restaurants, and it maintains much of its original decor despite being acquired by a local restaurant group in 2021. Meals, as always, begin with hot consommé poured from a silver samovar and spiked with a chispín (sip) of sherry and continue with French-inflected dishes, ranging from duck à l'orange to sole in champagne sauce. **Known for:** freshest seafood; old-school Spanish and French dishes; veritable museum of local culinary history. $ Average main: €34 ✉ Carretera de San Jerónimo 8, Sol ☎ 91/521–3385 ⊕ lhardy.com ☻ No dinner Sun. Ⓜ Sol.

Mesón del Champiñón

$ | **TAPAS** | **FAMILY** | The scenic cobblestone street that winds down to La Latina from Mercado de San Miguel is lined with mediocre touristy tapas bars—this, however, isn't one of them. Inside the stone-walled tavern, locals and visitors alike chow down on the house specialty: griddled mushrooms with jamón (dry-cured ham) and garlic-parsley oil. **Known for:** next to the Plaza Mayor; mushroom mecca; just celebrated its 60th anniversary. $ Average main: €12 ✉ Cava de San Miguel 17, Sol ☎ 91/559–6790 ⊕ mesondelchampinon.com Ⓜ Sol, Ópera.

Paco Roncero Restaurante

$$$$ | **ECLECTIC** | In an aerie above one of Madrid's oldest, most exclusive gentlemen's clubs, the dining room and rooftop terrace of this tasting-menu-only restaurant (formerly known as La Terraza del Casino) are decorated with playful, almost circus-like elements such as bright blue pushcarts, checkered floors, and yellow velvet chairs. The cuisine is as thrilling and whimsical as the decor, with dishes ranging from crunchy sardines with ají romesco sauce to spicy ethereal pig ear fritters. **Known for:** Instagram-mable interiors; two Michelin stars; foams, jellies, and flamboyant flourishes. $ Average main: €120 ✉ Calle Alcalá 15, Sol ☎ 91/532–1275 ⊕ pacoroncerorestaurante.com ☻ Closed Sun. and Mon. ⌂ Jacket required Ⓜ Sol.

☕ Coffee and Quick Bites

Bar La Campana

$ | **SPANISH** | **FAMILY** | Scarfing down a hot calamari-filled baguette (bocadillo de calamares) while strolling through the Plaza Mayor is a Madrid tradition, and this bar's rendition is a cut above the rest. **Known for:** mix of tourists and locals; plaza-side dining; to-go hoagies. $ Average main: €7 ✉ Calle de Botoneras 6, Sol Ⓜ Sol.

Casa Labra

$ | **SPANISH** | **FAMILY** | The traditional tapa at this old-fashioned bar is battered salt cod fritters. Have a tajada de bacalao here, then meander over to Casa Revuelta (in La Latina), Madrid's other famous cod corner, and decide for yourself whose is better. **Known for:** open since 1860 (and hasn't changed much since); one-time

Enjoy tapas and a *clara* (half beer, half lemonade) at Mercado de San Miguel, one of the city's most popular covered food markets in the city center.

revolutionary hangout; legendary fried cod. $ *Average main: €6* ⊠ *Calle de Tetuán 12, Sol* ⊕ *www.casalabra.es* Ⓜ *Sol.*

Chocolatería San Ginés

$ | **CAFÉ** | **FAMILY** | San Ginés is to Madrid what Café du Monde is to New Orleans: a historical fried-dough mecca. For generations this 19th-century café has been frying spirals of piping-hot churros and *porras* (the churro's fatter, chewier cousin—try them) day and night. **Known for:** chocolate con churros; a local institution; central location. $ *Average main: €4* ⊠ *Pasadizo de San Ginés, Sol* ⊹ *Enter by Arenal 11* ☎ *91/365–6546* ⊕ *chocolateriasangines.com* Ⓜ *Sol.*

Hotels

Ateneo Hotel

$$ | **HOTEL** | **FAMILY** | This economical and somewhat dated property is set in an 18th-century building that once housed the Ateneo, a club founded in 1835 to promote freedom of thought. **Pros:** sizable rooms; triples and quadruples available; some rooms have skylights and balconies. **Cons:** major pedestrian artery; noisy area; uninspired decor. $ *Rooms from: €150* ⊠ *Calle de Montera 22, Sol* ☎ *91/521–2012* ⊕ *www.hotelateneo.es* ⇲ *44 rooms* ❍❙ *No Meals* Ⓜ *Gran Vía, Sol.*

Four Seasons Hotel Madrid

$$$$ | **HOTEL** | Everybody feels like a VIP stepping into the grand lobby—with its gilt-topped columns, enormous central skylight, and sleek spiral staircase—at this Four Seasons, which opened in 2020. **Pros:** above-and-beyond service touches; original artwork by emerging Spanish artists; celebrity-chef restaurant and outstanding breakfast. **Cons:** little sense of place; wildly expensive; situated above chain restaurants and boutiques. $ *Rooms from: €1,021* ⊠ *Calle de Sevilla 3, Sol* ☎ *91/088–3333* ⊕ *www. fourseasons.com* ⇲ *200 rooms* ❍❙ *Free Breakfast* Ⓜ *Sol.*

Iberostar Las Letras Gran Vía

$$$ | HOTEL | A modern, clubby hotel on the stately avenue of Gran Vía, Iberostar Las Letras is a welcoming oasis from the area's constant hubbub of tourists and shoppers. **Pros:** state-of-the-art gym; many rooms have balconies; happening rooftop bar. **Cons:** lackluster service and food in Gran Clavel; no spa; awkward bathroom design. Ⓢ *Rooms from: €235* ✉ *Calle Gran Vía 11, Sol* ☎ *91/523–7980* ⊕ *www.iberostar.com/en/hotels/madrid/iberostar-las-letras-gran-via* ⇌ *110 rooms* ⦿❙ *No Meals* Ⓜ *Banco de España.*

Liabeny

$$ | HOTEL | This reliable hotel situated between Gran Vía and Puerta del Sol was renovated in 2021 and has comfortable, Scandi-minimalist rooms awash with whites and grays as well as spacious bathrooms with marble walls. **Pros:** spacious bathrooms; near Callao shopping area; personable staff. **Cons:** small rooms; crowded noisy neighborhood; stairs to access public areas. Ⓢ *Rooms from: €191* ✉ *Calle de la Salud 3, Sol* ☎ *91/531–9000* ⊕ *www.liabeny.es* ⇌ *220 rooms* ⦿❙ *No Meals* Ⓜ *Sol.*

Nightlife

DANCE CLUBS

Cadavra Club

DANCE CLUBS | Opened in 2022, Cadavra is a bumping underground nightclub with something for every type of reveler, from live music lovers (Wednesday jam sessions and concerts Thursday–Saturday) to techno-heads (Thursday–Saturday starting around midnight). ✉ *Calle del Caballero de Gracia 10, Sol* ☎ *91/865–9389* ⊕ *cadavraclub.com* Ⓜ *Gran Vía, Sol.*

★ Sala Cocó

DANCE CLUBS | This club, with its wild color palette, huge dance floor, and better-than-average cocktails, is best known for its branded DJ nights, some of the most popular in the city. La Discoteca (formerly Chá Chá; tickets via ⊕ dice.fm) on Fridays and Mondo Disko (Thursdays and Saturdays) rage until dawn with house and electronic music often by international DJs. ✉ *Calle de Alcalá 20, Sol* ☎ *91/445–7938* ⊕ *www.mondodisko.es* ⊘ *Closed Mon.–Wed.* Ⓜ *Sevilla.*

Sala El Sol

DANCE CLUBS | Madrid's oldest discoteca continues to win over patrons with all-night dancing to live music (starting around midnight Thursday–Saturday) and DJ sets. Check the website to see what's on the docket, and prepurchase tickets for parties like Trueno, popular among techno-heads. ✉ *Calle de los Jardines 3, Sol* ☎ *91/522–4403* ⊕ *www.salaelsol.com* ⊘ *Closed Mon.* Ⓜ *Gran Vía.*

▣ Performing Arts

Círculo de Bellas Artes

CONCERTS | Concerts, theater, dance performances, art exhibitions, and other events are all part of the calendar at this performance and entertainment venue. There is also an extremely popular (and overpriced) café and rooftop restaurant-bar with breathtaking views of the city. ✉ *Calle de Alcalá 42, Sol* ☎ *91/360–5400* ⊕ *www.circulobellasartes.com* 🎟 *€5* Ⓜ *Banco de España.*

★ Flamenco La Quimera

FOLK/TRADITIONAL DANCE | FAMILY | Prepare for a soulful invigorating show at this old-school, not-too-kitschy flamenco tablao adjacent to the Plaza Mayor. The start times are 8 and 10 pm nightly, and the festivities spill over into a flamenco-fueled foot-stomping party that starts at midnight. ✉ *Calle de Cuchilleros 7, Sol* ☎ *91/356–9361* ⊕ *tablaolaquimera.com* 🎟 *€65 dinner package or €35 drink-only ticket* Ⓜ *Sol, Ópera.*

3

Sol

Shopping

CLOTHING

Capas Seseña

OTHER ACCESSORIES | Seseña is the oldest cape tailor in the world and one of Madrid's most emblematic shops. Since 1901, this family-run business has outfitted the likes of Picasso, Hemingway, and Michael Jackson in traditional merino wool and velvet capes, some lined with red satin. ⊠ *Calle de la Cruz 23, Sol* ☎ *91/531–6840* ⊕ *www.sesena. com* ⊘ *Closed Sun.* Ⓜ *Sol.*

CRAFTS AND DESIGN

Taller Puntera

CRAFTS | You can watch the artisans at work at this inviting atelier-boutique hybrid situated steps from Plaza Mayor. Regardless of what catches your eye—a leather cardholder, handbag, or perhaps a hand-bound notebook—you'll be pleasantly surprised by the prices. ⊠ *Pl. del Conde de Barajas 4, Sol* ☎ *91/364–2926* ⊕ *puntera.com* ⊘ *Closed Sun.* Ⓜ *Ópera, Tirso de Molina.*

FANS

★ Casa de Diego

OTHER SPECIALTY STORE | Established in 1823, Casa de Diego manufactures fans, umbrellas, and classic Spanish walking sticks with ornamented silver handles and also sells traditional Spanish ornamental combs, mantillas, and castanets. The British royal family buys autograph fans here for signing on special occasions. ⊠ *Puerta del Sol 12, Sol* ☎ *91/522–6643* ⊕ *casadediego.info* ⊘ *Closed Sun.* Ⓜ *Sol.*

HATS

Casa Yustas

HATS & GLOVES | Founded in 1894, Casa Yustas has headgear ranging from the three-corner hats of the Guardia Civil to Basque berets to Andalusian *sombreros de mayoral.* Designed as hands-free umbrellas for the rainy Cantabrian coast, Basque berets (sourced from legendary hatter Elosegui) are much wider than those worn by the French and make excellent gifts. ⊠ *Pl. Mayor 30, Sol* ☎ *91/366–5084* ⊕ *www.casayustas.com* Ⓜ *Sol.*

Activities

Hammam Al Ándalus

SPAS | Walk through a nondescript door off the noisy Plaza de Jacinto Benavente and suddenly you're in a serene Moorish-style bathhouse decorated with carved arches and Andalusian tile. Flickering candles light the way to a steam room, a relaxation area, shallow pools of varying temperatures, and a massage parlor where professional masseurs offer treatments ranging from 15 minutes to one hour. It's not an authentic hammam by any stretch, but it's the best-priced spa experience in town and a good rainy-day activity for adult travelers. ⊠ *Calle de Atocha 14, Sol* ☎ *91/429–9020* ⊕ *www. madrid.hammamalandalus.com* ☞ *From €37* Ⓜ *Sol.*

Chapter 4

PALACIO AND MONCLOA

4

Updated by
Benjamin Kemper

👁 Sights	🍴 Restaurants	🛏 Hotels	🛍 Shopping	🍸 Nightlife
★★★★★	★★★☆☆	★★★★★	★★★★☆	★★★★★

NEIGHBORHOOD SNAPSHOT

TOP EXPERIENCES

■ **Faro de Moncloa:** Ride the elevator to the observation deck of this defunct transmission tower for sweeping mountain and city views.

■ **Parque del Oeste:** Spot Civil War–era bunkers and a transplanted Egyptian temple on a walk through this stately park.

■ **Casa de Campo:** Hike, bike, or run in this 4,260-acre park that feels a world away from the city bustle.

■ **Museo Cerralbo:** Discover the secret riches of a discerning marquis.

■ **Ermita San Antonio de la Florida:** Visit Goya's tomb and savor frescoes painted by the master himself.

■ **Teleférico:** Dangle above the city skyline on a retro cable car.

PAUSE HERE

On Paseo del Pintor Rosales, the wide, leafy street that runs southeast to northeast along the top of Parque del Oeste, there's a hidden restaurant tucked just inside the park called La Perla de Rosales (No. 64). On a warm day, the patio surrounded by freshly cut grass beneath pine trees is a lovely place to sip a cold *caña* (half-pint) or nibble on fried calamari and *jamón* (dry-cured ham).

GETTING HERE AND AROUND

In Palacio, Ópera (Líneas 2, 5) is the closest metro stop to the Palacio Real (Royal Palace), while Callao (Líneas 3, 5) is shopping and dining central. The metro stops at Moncloa (Líneas 3, 6) and Argüelles (Líneas 3, 4, 6) are a fine jumping-off point to explore the urban corners of Moncloa, such as Calle de la Princesa (shopping, dining) and the district's historical sites, while Príncipe Pío (Líneas 6, 10) and Lago (Línea 10) are where to alight for adventures in Casa de Campo. Public bike-share service BiciMAD services all areas east of the Manzanares.

PLANNING YOUR TIME

Allot three hours for a brisk walk through the winding streets of these neighborhoods and Parque del Oeste (Western Park), which contains the Templo de Debod, Civil War bunkers, and a rose garden; budget additional time for touring the Palacio Real. Urban areas are safe at all hours of the day and night, but it's best to avoid parks after sunset.

On the western edge of the city center, Palacio and Moncloa are well-to-do districts packed with historical sites, palaces, parks, and restaurants suited to any budget. Palacio, named for the Palacio Real, is naturally a tourist magnet. Moncloa, developed centuries later, is more residential and expansive, taking in Casa de Campo and the Universidad Complutense de Madrid campus.

Palacio is a must on any travel itinerary given that it's Madrid's oldest neighborhood and contains Spain's Palacio Real, Europe's largest in terms of surface area. This is where Muhammad I established the city's first military post in the 9th century, essentially founding the city. Situated just west of Plaza Mayor, the neighborhood is a labyrinth of winding cobblestone streets lined with a mix of international chains and boutiques and timeworn Spanish holdouts.

Moncloa, by contrast, is more varied. Unurbanized in certain pockets and with student housing dominating others, it's less touristy. There are high-society communities like Aravaca and Puerta de Hierro, livelier urban areas like Argüelles (where college kids commandeer entire sidewalk cafés), and green lungs like the manicured Parque del Oeste, sections of the Madrid Río esplanade, and the more rugged Dehesa de la Villa and Casa de Campo.

Palacio
Sights

You can feel the history and grandeur of this noble district by simply tracing the palace's endless walls and wandering in and around Plaza de Oriente. Be sure to check out Plaza de España and the surrounding parks and pathways; the area was pedestrianized in 2022 in one of the biggest urban development projects the city has seen in years.

Catedral de la Almudena
CHURCH | The first stone of the cathedral, which faces the Palacio Real, was laid in 1883 by King Alfonso XII, and the resulting edifice was consecrated by Pope John Paul II in 1993. La Almudena is controversial due to its hodgepodge of architectural styles; it is playfully mocked by Madrileños, who sometimes call it *la fea* (the ugly one). Built on the site of the old church of Santa María de la Almudena (the city's main mosque during Arab

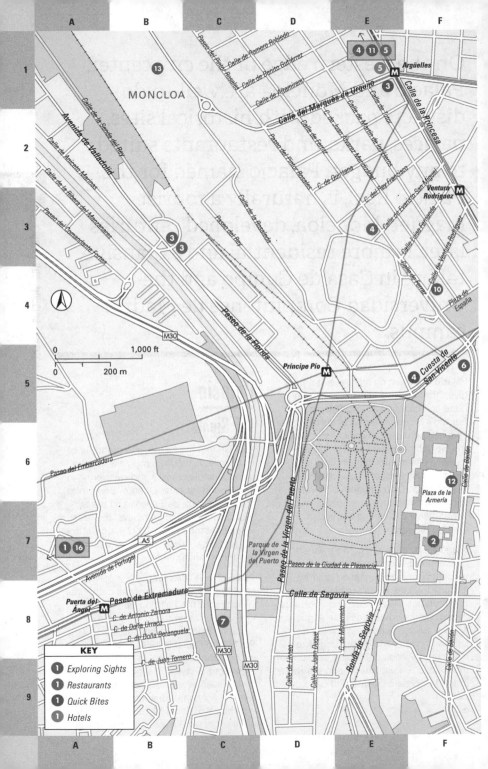

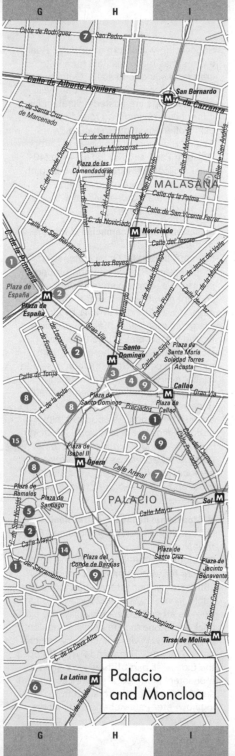

Palacio
and Moncloa

Sights ▼

1 Casa de Campo **A7**
2 Catedral de la
Almudena................. **F7**
3 Ermita de San Antonio
de la Florida **B3**
4 Faro de Moncloa......... **E1**
5 Iglesia de San Nicolás
de los Servitas **G7**
6 Jardines de Sabatini **F5**
7 Madrid Río................. **C8**
8 Monasterio de la
Encarnación............. **G5**
9 Monasterio de las
Descalzas Reales........ **I6**
10 Museo Cerralbo.......... **F4**
11 Museo del Traje.......... **E1**
12 Palacio Real.............. **F6**
13 Parque del Oeste **B1**
14 Plaza de la Villa **G7**
15 Plaza de Oriente **G6**
16 Teleférico **A7**

Restaurants ▼

1 Casa Ciriaco............. **G7**
2 Casa Lafu ....'....... **G5**
3 Casa Mingo.............. **B3**
4 Cuenllas................. **E3**
5 Desde 1911 .... **E1**
6 La Copita Asturiana **G9**
7 La Montaña.............. **H1**
8 Le Bistroman Atelier ... **G6**
9 Solito Taquería
Mexicana................ **H8**

Quick Bites ▼

1 Chocolatería Valor........ **I6**
2 Four........................ **G7**
3 Los Bocadillos **E1**
4 Tutti Frutti **F5**

Hotels ▼

1 Barceló Torre de
Madrid **G4**
2 Dear Hotel **G4**
3 Generator Madrid **H5**
4 Hotel Indigo Madrid –
Gran Vía.................. **H5**
5 Hotel Indigo Madrid –
Princesa,
an IHG Hotel.............. **E1**
6 Hotel Intur Palacio
San Martín............... **H6**
7 The Madrid Edition **I6**
8 Palacio de Los Duques
Gran Meliá............... **G5**
9 Room Mate
Macarena **H5**

rule), the cathedral has a wooden statue of Madrid's female patron saint, the Virgin of Almudena, allegedly discovered after being hidden by Christian devotees during the so-called Reconquest. The cathedral's name is derived from the place where the relic was found, within the wall of the old citadel (in Arabic, *al-mudayna*). ⊠ *Calle de Bailén 10, Palacio* ☎ *91/542–2200* ⊕ *catedraldelaalmudena.es* 🖾 *Free; museum and cupola €7* Ⓜ *Ópera.*

Iglesia de San Nicolás de los Servitas
(*Church of St. Nicholas of the Servites*)
RELIGIOUS BUILDING | There's some debate over whether this church, the oldest in central Madrid, once formed part of an Arab mosque. It was more likely built after the so-called Reconquest of Madrid in 1083, but the brickwork and horseshoe arches are evidence that it was crafted by either Mudejars (workers of Islamic origin) or Christian Spaniards well versed in the style. Inside, exhibits detail the Islamic history of early Madrid. ⊠ *Pl. de San Nicolás 6, Palacio* ☎ *91/559–4064* 🖾 *Suggested donation* Ⓜ *Ópera.*

Jardines de Sabatini (*Sabatini Gardens*)
GARDEN | The manicured gardens to the north of the Palacio Real, located where the royal stables once were, are a pleasant place to rest or watch the sun set. Renovated in 2022 as part of the Plaza de España overhaul, they are named for the prolific 18th-century architect who designed the Puerta de Alcalá, Royal Botanical Garden, and San Francisco el Grande convent, among other key sights. ⊠ *Calle Bailén s/n, Palacio* Ⓜ *Ópera.*

Madrid Río
CITY PARK | **FAMILY** | Madrid Río takes in some 32 km (20 miles) of green space and bike-friendly paths along the lazy, shallow Manzanares River, beginning at the Puente de los Franceses in the northwest and terminating at the Pasarela Legazpi in the southeast (though footpaths extend much farther south). A popular place to enter is Puente de Segovia, downhill from the Palacio Real; a Christmas market is held here with craft kiosks and food stalls. Outdoor concerts (check out the Veranos de la Villa series; lineups are posted online) and informal riverside dining round out the park's offerings. Note to nature lovers: Madrid Río connects to Casa de Campo, Western Park, and Madrid's 64-km (40-mile) Anillo Verde (Green Ring) bike path. ⊠ *Palacio* ⊕ *www.esmadrid.com/en/whats-on/veranos-de-la-villa* Ⓜ *Príncipe Pío, Pirámides, Legazpi.*

Monasterio de la Encarnación (*Monastery of the Incarnation*)
RELIGIOUS BUILDING | Once connected to the Palacio Real by an underground passageway, this cloistered Augustinian convent now houses fewer than a dozen nuns. It was founded in 1611 by Queen Margarita de Austria, the wife of Felipe III, and has several artistic treasures, including a reliquary where a vial with the dried blood of St. Pantaleón is said to liquefy every July 27. The ornate church has superb acoustics for medieval and Renaissance choral concerts. Tours are in Spanish only and take about 90 minutes. ⊠ *Pl. de la Encarnación 1, Palacio* ☎ *91/454–8803 for tourist office* ⊕ *www.patrimonionacional.es/en/visita/royal-monastery-la-encarnacion* 🖾 *€6 (free Wed. and Thurs. 4–6:30)* ⊗ *Closed Mon.* Ⓜ *Ópera.*

★ Monasterio de las Descalzas Reales
(*Monastery of the Royal Discalced/Barefoot Nuns*)
RELIGIOUS BUILDING | After a 20-month closure for renovations, this important 16th-century monastery reopened to the public in late 2021 with 200 new works from its art collection on display. The plain brick-and-stone facade belies an opulent interior strewn with paintings by Francisco de Zurbarán, Titian, and Pieter Bruegel the Elder—all part of the dowry of new monastery inductees—as well as a hall of sumptuous tapestries crafted from drawings by Peter Paul Rubens. Fifty works

from the collection were meticulously restored as part of the recent renovations. The convent was founded in 1559 by Juana of Austria, one of Felipe II's sisters, who ruled Spain while he was in England and the Netherlands. It houses 33 different chapels—the age of Christ when he died and the maximum number of nuns allowed to live at the monastery—with more than 120 immaculately preserved crucifixes among them. About a dozen nuns still live here and grow vegetables in the garden. ■TIP➜ **You must take a tour in order to visit the convent, and tickets must be bought online ahead of time (they sell out fast); those who don't speak Spanish can access an English guide through the app.** ⊠ *Pl. de las Descalzas s/n, Palacio* ☎ *91/454–8800* ⊕ *www.patrimonionacional.es/en/real-sitio/monasterio-de-las-descalzas-reales* ⊠ *€6* ⊘ *Closed Mon.* ⚲ *Reservations and pre-purchased tickets required* Ⓜ *Sol.*

★ **Palacio Real** (*Royal Palace*)
CASTLE/PALACE | The Palacio Real was built over Madrid's first defensive fortress, established by Berbers in the 9th century. It overwhelms with its sheer immensity against the city's silhouetted background. The palace was commissioned in the early 18th century by the first of Spain's Bourbon rulers, Felipe V. Outside, classical French architecture adorns the Patio de Armas: Felipe was obviously inspired by his childhood days at Versailles with his grandfather Louis XIV. Look for the stone statues of Inca prince Atahualpa and Aztec king Montezuma, perhaps the only tributes in Spain to these pre-Columbian American rulers. Notice how the steep bluff drops west to the Manzanares River—on a clear day, this vantage point commands a view of the mountain passes leading into Madrid from Old Castile. It's easy to see why Madrid's Berber rulers picked this spot for a fortress.

Inside, 2,800 rooms compete with one another for over-the-top opulence. A two-hour guided tour in English winds a mile-long path through the palace. Highlights include the Salón de Gasparini, King Carlos III's private apartments, with swirling inlaid floors and curlicued stucco wall and ceiling decoration, all glistening in the light of a two-ton crystal chandelier; the Salón del Trono, a grand throne room with the royal seats of King Felipe VI and Queen Letizia; and the banquet hall, the palace's largest room, which seats up to 140 people for state dinners. Despite being the official seat of the throne, no monarch has lived here since 1931, when Alfonso XIII was deposed after a Republican electoral victory. The current king and queen live in the far simpler Palacio de la Zarzuela on the outskirts of Madrid.

Also inside the palace are the Museo de Música (Music Museum), where five-stringed instruments by Antonio Stradivari form the world's largest such collection; the Painting Gallery, which displays works by Spanish, Flemish, and Italian artists from the 15th century on; the Armería Real (Royal Armory), with historic suits of armor and frightening medieval torture implements; the Real Oficina de Farmacia (Royal Pharmacy), with vials and flasks used to mix the king's medicines; and the Real Cocina, Europe's best-preserved royal kitchens, opened to the public for the first time in 2017 and whose framed handwritten menus, antediluvian wood-burning ovens, enormous copper cauldrons, wooden iceboxes, and nearly 3,000 antique kitchen utensils make it a must-stop for foodies. On Wednesday the Changing of the Guard takes place (every 30 minutes from 11–2) at the Puerta del Príncipe, across Plaza de Oriente, with a more solemn and lavish ceremony (with up to 100 guards and horses) the first Wednesday of each month at noon. ⊠ *Calle de Bailén s/n, Palacio* ☎ *91/454–8800* ⊕ *www.patrimonionacional.es/visita/palacio-real-de-madrid* ⊠ *From €12* Ⓜ *Ópera.*

With 3,748 rooms, Palacio Real is the largest palace in Western Europe.

Plaza de la Villa

PLAZA/SQUARE | Madrid's town council met in this medieval-looking complex from the Middle Ages until 2009, when it moved to the Palacio de Cibeles. It now houses municipal offices. The oldest building on the plaza is the Casa de los Lujanes, the one with the Mudejar tower. Built as a private home in the late 15th century, the house carries the Lujanes crest over the main doorway. Also on the plaza's east end is the brick-and-stone Casa de la Villa, built in 1629, a classic example of Dutch-influenced Madrid design with clean lines and spire-topped corner towers. Connected by an overhead walkway, the Casa de Cisneros was commissioned in 1537 by the nephew of Cardinal Cisneros. It's one of Madrid's rare examples of the flamboyant plateresque style, which has been likened to splashed water. Sadly, none of these landmarks are open to the public on a regular basis. ⊠ *Palacio* Ⓜ *Sol, Ópera.*

Plaza de Oriente

PLAZA/SQUARE | This stately semicircular plaza, sandwiched between the Palacio Real and the Teatro Real (Royal Theater), is flanked by massive statues of Spanish monarchs that were meant to be mounted atop the palace. Queen Isabel Farnesio, one of the first royals to live in the palace, had them removed because she was afraid their enormous weight would bring the roof down. (That's the official reason; according to local lore, the queen wanted the statues removed because her own likeness wouldn't have been placed front and center.) A Velázquez drawing of King Felipe IV is the inspiration for the statue in the plaza's center. It's the first equestrian bronze ever cast with a rearing horse. The sculptor, Italian artist Pietro Tacca, enlisted Galileo Galilei's help in configuring the statue's weight so it wouldn't tip over. The 2021 overhaul of Plaza de España eliminated all car traffic between Plaza de Oriente and Plaza de España and added pleasant footpaths and fountains. ⊠ *Palacio* Ⓜ *Ópera.*

🍴 Restaurants

Casa Ciriaco

$$ | SPANISH | Open for over a century, this Madrid institution is as famous for its *callos a la madrileña* (Madrid-style tripe) as it is for *gallina en pepitoria* , an old-school Spanish stew of wine-braised chicken thickened with hard-boiled yolks that's become increasingly hard to find. **Known for:** local comfort food; a neighborhood institution; fame in Spanish literature. [$] *Average main: €23* ✉ *Calle Mayor 84, Palacio* ☎ *91/548–0620* 🌐 *casaciriaco.es* 🕑 *No dinner Sun. and Mon.* [M] *Ópera.*

Casa Lafu

$$ | CHINESE | FAMILY | If you haven't tried Chinese food in Madrid, you're missing out—the city has some of the best Chinese restaurants in Europe thanks to a vibrant immigrant community. Casa Lafu, with its serene white-tablecloth dining room, stands out for its expertly prepared repertoire of regional dishes, from Sichuan-style *málà* (spicy) plates to Shanghainese wine-cooked meats and Cantonese dim sum. **Known for:** hot pot; upscale Chinese cuisine at affordable prices; rare regional specialties. [$] *Average main: €19* ✉ *Calle de la Flor Baja 1, Palacio* ☎ *91/548–7096* 🌐 *www.casalafu.com* [M] *Santo Domingo.*

★ La Copita Asturiana

$$ | SPANISH | FAMILY | In the heart of the tourist fray but blissfully under the radar, this teensy lunch-only restaurant with an old tin bar serves all the Asturian favorites, from *fabada* (bean stew) to *cachopo* (ham-and-cheese-stuffed cutlets) to creamy rice pudding. Asturian cider is the requisite beverage. **Known for:** northern Spanish comfort food; easy-on-the-wallet prices; kitsch decor. [$] *Average main: €18* ✉ *Calle de Tabernillas 13, Palacio* ☎ *91/365–1063* 🌐 *lacopitaasturiana.com* 🕑 *Closed Sat. No dinner* [M] *Tirso de Molina.*

Le Bistroman Atelier

$$$ | FRENCH | For a country that borders France, Spain has a surprising dearth of good French restaurants, which makes Le Bistroman all the more remarkable—not only is the food good by Spanish standards, it would be a hit in Paris with its homemade *everything*, from terrines to breads to pastries. Wild game (venison, squab) features prominently on the menu, and other highlights include an old-school cheese cart and throwback desserts like babas au rhum and vanilla bean soufflé. **Known for:** exquisite bouillabaisse (call in advance to order); varied French wine list; elevated bistro cooking. [$] *Average main: €29* ✉ *Calle de la Amnistia 10, Palacio* ☎ *91/447–2713* 🌐 *lebistroman.es/madrid* 🕑 *Closed Mon.* [M] *Ópera.*

Solito Taquería Mexicana

$$ | MEXICAN | FAMILY | Some of the best tacos you can gobble down in Madrid are found, improbably, in tourist central, just off Plaza Mayor. This inviting taquería, which opened in 2020, was an instant hit with locals thanks to pitch-perfect classics like *cochinita pibil* (slow-roasted marinated pork) chalupas, huitlacoche quesadillas, and pozole (choose from three types), as well as real-deal margaritas and *cajeta* (caramel) crepes. **Known for:** excellent margs and micheladas; unpretentious digs; central location. [$] *Average main: €20* ✉ *Calle de la Pasa 4, Palacio* ☎ *91/353–5822* 🌐 *solito-taqueria.com* 🕑 *Closed Mon.* [M] *Sol, Tirso de Molina.*

☕ Coffee and Quick Bites

Chocolatería Valor

$ | CAFÉ | FAMILY | Trace the western side of the Monasterio de las Descalzas Reales until you reach Chocolatería Valor, an ideal spot to indulge in piping-hot churros dipped in thick hot chocolate. Valor's churros are chewy, puffy, and snipped into batons, more akin to *porras* (churros' baking-soda-leavened sibling)

Teatro Real was one of the world's first opera houses to return to the stage after lockdown with a production of Verdi's *La Traviata*, tweaked to reflect life in the time of COVID-19.

than to standard crispy churros. **Known for:** one of the best chocolaterías in town; family-friendly atmosphere; outdoor seating. $ *Average main: €6* ⊠ *Calle del Postigo de San Martín 7, Palacio* ☎ *91/522–9288* ⊕ *www.valor.es* Ⓜ *Callao.*

★ Four

$ | **CAFÉ** | **FAMILY** | Expertly pulled espressos, natural wines, and unexpectedly outstanding food—think velvety scrambled eggs, flavorful quiches, and homemade cakes and pastries—have made this café on Plaza del Biombo an instant hit with locals and expats, many of whom treat the roomy communal table like a coworking space (just be considerate and order more than a coffee if you plan on staying awhile). **Known for:** industrial-chic decor plus sunny patio seating; genial bilingual staff; €15 weekday prix fixe. $ *Average main: €10* ⊠ *Calle de Calderón de la Barca 8, Palacio* ☎ *62/257–1608* ⊕ *www. fourmadrid.com* ⊗ *Closed Tues.* Ⓜ *Ópera.*

 ## Hotels

Generator Madrid

$$ | **HOTEL** | Generator Madrid might be a budget hotel with shared (up to eight-person) rooms, but it runs circles around most of the city's big-name hotels in the design department, and guests can't get enough of the rooftop bar, plush towels, and Instagram-ready interiors. **Pros:** bubbly staff and fellow guests; PlayStation in the lobby; buzzy rooftop bar. **Cons:** towels (€5 rental) not included in the rate; storing luggage in lockers costs €2 per hour; no laundry facilities or kitchen. $ *Rooms from: €173* ⊠ *Calle de Silva 1, Palacio* ☎ *91/047–9800* ⊕ *www. staygenerator.com/hostels/madrid* ⇗ *129 rooms* ⦿ *No Meals* Ⓜ *Callao.*

Hotel Indigo Madrid – Gran Vía

$$ | **HOTEL** | A colorful and casual hotel off the bustling Gran Vía thoroughfare, Indigo is best known for its rooftop lounge and outdoor infinity pool, rare features in Madrid. **Pros:** sceney rooftop infinity

pool; restaurant that punches above its weight; well-equipped gym. **Cons:** interior rooms get little natural light; loses vitality in cold-weather months; dated decor. [$] *Rooms from: €200* ✉ *Calle de Silva 6, Palacio* ☎ *91/200–8585* 🌐 *www.indigo-madrid.com* 🛏 *85 rooms* 🍴 *No Meals* [M] *Santo Domingo.*

Hotel Intur Palacio San Martín

$$ | **HOTEL** | In an unbeatable location across from Monasterio de las Descalzas Reales, this hotel—once the U.S. embassy and later a luxurious residential building crowded with noblemen—has the architectural bones of a turn-of-the-century mansion with its hand-carved ceilings, marble foyers, and intricate iron balconies. **Pros:** good variety at breakfast; spacious rooms; lobby with glass-domed atrium. **Cons:** bland interiors; bare-bones gym; church bells in the morning. [$] *Rooms from: €174* ✉ *Pl. de San Martín 5, Palacio* ☎ *91/701–5000* 🌐 *www.intur.com/hotel-palacio-san-martin-madrid* 🛏 *103 rooms* 🍴 *No Meals* [M] *Ópera, Callao.*

★ The Madrid Edition

$$$$ | **HOTEL** | Ian Schrager, the visionary hotelier best known for creating Studio 54, is the brains behind one of Madrid's most buzzed-about hotel openings in recent memory. **Pros:** exquisite Mexican breakfasts; across from Las Descalzas Reales convent; serene Natura Bissé spa and spacious gym with the latest Technogym equipment. **Cons:** minor service foibles; overlooks a scruffy unkempt square; photo-snapping influencers left and right. [$] *Rooms from: €532* ✉ *Pl. de Celenque 2, Palacio* ☎ *91/954–5420* 🌐 *www.editionhotels.com/madrid* 🛏 *200 rooms* 🍴 *No Meals* [M] *Sol, Ópera.*

Palacio de Los Duques Gran Meliá

$$$$ | **HOTEL** | In this luxurious urban oasis with an expansive courtyard tucked behind Gran Vía, reproductions of famous Diego Velázquez paintings feature in every room. **Pros:** Dos Cielos, one of the city's best hotel restaurants; underfloor heating and deep-soak tubs; rooftop bar and splash pool. **Cons:** rooms are less attractive than public areas; rooftop often off-limits because of private events; no great views from rooms. [$] *Rooms from: €437* ✉ *Cuesta de Santo Domingo 5 y 7, Palacio* ☎ *91/541–6700* 🌐 *www.melia.com/en/hotels/spain/madrid/palacio-de-los-duques-gran-melia* 🛏 *180 rooms* 🍴 *No Meals* [M] *Santo Domingo.*

Room Mate Macarena

$$$ | **HOTEL** | A newer addition to the Room Mate chain, Macarena opened in 2020 smack on the Gran Vía thoroughfare. **Pros:** photogenic and flamboyant design; rooftop open until 2 am on weekends; gleaming new property. **Cons:** pool looks bigger in photos than in person; breakfasts more befitting of a youth hostel; loud interiors. [$] *Rooms from: €242* ✉ *Calle Gran Vía 43, Palacio* ☎ *91/116–1191* 🌐 *room-matehotels.com/es/macarena-gran-via* 🛏 *130 rooms* 🍴 *No Meals* [M] *Santo Domingo, Callao.*

🍸 Nightlife

BARS

Fun Fun

WINE BARS | Cozily furnished with vintage sofas, baroque mirrors, and low tables, this dimly lit hideaway is where locals go to catch up over Spanish natural wine. Keep an eye on their Instagram (@funfunmadrid) for pop-up dinners and events. ✉ *Calle de Don Pedro 20, Palacio* ☎ *69/144–5481* 🌐 *funfunmadrid.com* [M] *La Latina, Tirso de Molina.*

DANCE CLUBS

Cool

DANCE CLUBS | This gritty, Berlin-style underground club hosts techno-driven dance parties on weekend nights. The most popular parties are the mixed-crowd Stardust (Fridays), with mostly techno music, and the LGBTQ+-focused Yass Club (Saturdays), with a mix of pop, house, and hip-hop. ✉ *Calle de Isabel*

la Católica 6, Palacio ☎ *63/459–6212*
⊕ *www.salacoolmadrid.com* ⊗ *Closed Sun.–Wed.* Ⓜ *Santo Domingo.*

Velvet

DANCE CLUBS | Trippy and chameleonlike, thanks to colorful LED lights and the undulating shapes of the columns and walls, this is the place to go if you want a late-night drink without the thunder of a full-blown DJ. ⊠ *Calle de Jacometrezo 6, Palacio* ☎ *63/341–4887* ⊕ *www.velvetdisco.es* ⊗ *Closed Mon.–Wed.* Ⓜ *Callao.*

MUSIC CLUBS

★ Café Berlín

LIVE MUSIC | For a space so small, Café Berlín packs a huge acoustic punch and draws an international eclectic crowd. Before midnight, catch nightly live music acts in a panoply of styles (flamenco, swing, soul, and more); from around 1 am on, drop in for the disco-inflected DJ sets that ooze good vibes until 6 am. ⊠ *Costanilla de los Ángeles 20, Palacio* ☎ *91/559–7429* ⊕ *berlincafe.es* Ⓜ *Santo Domingo.*

El Amante

DANCE CLUBS | With two winding floors filled with nooks hosting the city's best-heeled crowds, this might be the closest thing you'll find in Madrid to a posh private New York club. Music is usually bass-heavy electronic or house. The door is tough, so be sure to dress to impress (no sneakers allowed). Get here before 1:30 am or be ready to wait in line. ⊠ *Calle de Santiago 3, Palacio* ☎ *91/755–4460* Ⓜ *Ópera.*

🎭 Performing Arts

Teatro Real

OPERA | This resplendent neoclassical theater is the city's premier venue for opera and dance performances. Built in 1850, it fell into disuse from 1925 to 1966 because of political upheaval. A major restoration project endowed it with golden balconies, plush seats, and state-of-the-art stage equipment. Opera buffs rave about the choir, said to be one of the best in the world. The theater sometimes hosts flamenco on Friday evenings in the smaller auditorium. ⊠ *Pl. de Isabel II s/n, Palacio* ☎ *91/516–0600* ⊕ *www.teatroreal.es* Ⓜ *Ópera.*

FLAMENCO

Corral de la Morería

FOLK/TRADITIONAL DANCE | A Michelin-starred dinner followed by a world-class flamenco performance in the same building sounds too good to be true, but at Corral de la Morería the food (Basque with an Andalusian twist) is as invigorating as the twirling and stomping *bailaoras*. Opt for an elegant, market-driven prix fixe to be enjoyed during the show or splurge on an exclusive tasting experience at the four-table Gastronómico restaurant that earned the venue its coveted star. Wine pairings, which hinge on rare back-vintage sherries and other *vinos generosos* (fortified wines), are well worth the extra euros. ⊠ *Calle de la Morería 17, Palacio* ☎ *91/365–8446* ⊕ *www.corraldelamoreria.com* Ⓜ *La Latina.*

🛍 Shopping

CERAMICS

★ Antigua Casa Talavera

CRAFTS | Opened in 1904, this is the best of Madrid's many ceramics vendors. Despite the name, the finest wares sold here are from Manises, near Valencia, but the blue-and-yellow Talavera ceramics are also excellent. All pieces are hand-painted and bear traditional Spanish motifs that have been used for centuries. ⊠ *Calle de Isabel la Católica 2, Palacio* ☎ *91/547–3417* ⊕ *www.antiguacasatalavera.com* ⊗ *Closed Sun.* Ⓜ *Santo Domingo.*

SPECIALTY STORES

Alambique

OTHER SPECIALTY STORE | Amateur and professional cooks will love this terrific little shop (est. 1978) that sells everything

The city's cable car, Teleférico, connects Parque del Oeste and Casa de Campo and offers views of the top attractions, including the Palacio Real.

from paella pans to earthenware *cazuelas* (casserole dishes) to olive-wood cheese boards. Cooking classes in Spanish are also available. ⊠ *Pl. de la Encarnación 2, Palacio* ☎ *91/547–4220* ⊕ *www. alambique.com* ⊘ *Closed Sun.*

Moncloa

Sights

★ Casa de Campo

CITY PARK | FAMILY | Over five times the size of New York's Central Park, Casa de Campo is Madrid's largest park and a nature-lover's paradise, complete with bike trails, picnic tables, pine forests, lakeside restaurants (seek out Villa Verbena, run by the folks behind Triciclo in Barrio de las Letras), and a public outdoor pool (€5 entry). See if you can spot wildlife like hawks, foxes, hares, and red squirrels—and, from November to May, a flock of sheep cared for by a real-deal shepherd. The park's name ("country

house") is a holdover from when the grounds were the royal family's hunting estate. It became public property in May 1931 with the arrival of the Spanish Second Republic, which dissolved royal landholdings. ⊠ *Moncloa* Ⓜ *Casa de Campo, Lago, Batán.*

Ermita de San Antonio de la Florida
(*Goya's Tomb*)

CHURCH | Built between 1792 and 1798 by Italian architect Francisco Fontana, this neoclassical chapel was financed by King Carlos IV, who also commissioned Goya to paint the vaults and the main dome. Goya depicted events of the 13th century (such as St. Anthony of Padua resurrecting a dead man) as if they had happened in his own time five centuries later, with naturalistic images never used before to paint religious scenes. Opposite the image of the frightening dead man on the main dome, Goya painted himself as a man covered with a black cloak. Goya, who died in Bordeaux in 1828, is buried here (without his head, which was stolen in France) under an unadorned

Yes, it's a little odd to find an ancient Egyptian temple in downtown Madrid, but rest (or, pose) easy; it was a gift from the Egyptian government.

gravestone. ⊠ *Glorieta de San Antonio de la Florida 5, Moncloa* ☎ *91/542–0722* ⊕ *www.sanantoniodelaflorida.es* 🖃 *Free* ⊙ *Closed Mon.* Ⓜ *Príncipe Pío.*

Faro de Moncloa

VIEWPOINT | FAMILY | This UFO-like tower is 360 feet tall and an excellent viewpoint from which to gaze at some of the city's most outstanding buildings including the Palacio Real, Palacio de Cibeles (City Hall), the four skyscrapers to the north, and up to 50 landmarks for which you'll find descriptions in English and Spanish. ⊠ *Av. de la Memoria 2, Moncloa* 🖃 *€4* ⊙ *Closed Mon.* Ⓜ *Moncloa.*

Museo Cerralbo

ART MUSEUM | One of Madrid's most captivatingly opulent museums is also one of its least known. This former palace, built in 1893 by the marquis of the same name, preserves the nobleman's art collection including works by El Greco, Tintoretto, Van Dyck, and Zurbarán. These hang in gilded and frescoed halls appointed with ornate period furniture. ⊠ *Calle de Ventura Rodríguez 17, Moncloa* ☎ *91/547–3646* ⊕ *www.culturaydeporte. gob.es/mcerralbo/en/home.html* 🖃 *€3. Free Thurs. 5–8 pm and Sun.* ⊙ *Closed Mon.* Ⓜ *Ventura Rodríguez.*

Museo del Traje (*Costume Museum*)
OTHER MUSEUM | Trace the evolution of dress in Spain here, from rare old royal burial garments to French fashion pieces of Felipe V's reign and the haute couture creations of Balenciaga and Pertegaz. Explanatory notes are in English, and the museum has a superb modern Spanish restaurant, Café de Oriente, overlooking the gardens. ⊠ *Av. de Juan de Herrera 2, Moncloa* ☎ *91/550–4700* ⊕ *www. culturaydeporte.gob.es/mtraje/inicio. html* 🖃 *€3. Free Sat. after 2:30 and Sun.* ⊙ *Closed Mon.* Ⓜ *Ciudad Universitaria.*

★ Parque del Oeste

CITY PARK | FAMILY | This is many Madrileños' favorite park for its pristine yet unmobbed paths and well-pruned lawns and flower beds. From dawn to dusk, expect to see dogs cavorting off-leash, couples sprawled out beneath the trees, and groups of friends playing frisbee and fútbol. From Paseo del Pintor Rosales, meander downhill toward Avenida de Valladolid, crossing the train tracks, and you'll hit Madrid Río; walk southwest and you'll find Temple of Debod and, beyond, the newly pedestrianized Plaza de España. This park also contains the city's only cable car (see "Teleférico") and, 100 yards beneath it, a rose garden (Rosaleda ⬛ free entry) containing some 20,000 specimens of more than 650 rose varieties that reach their peak in May. In the quieter northern section of the park (along Avenida de Séneca), you'll happen upon Civil War–era bunkers interspersed among plane-tree-lined promenades, a sobering reminder that Parque del Oeste was the western front of Madrid's resistance against Franco's armies. ✉ *Paseo del Pintor Rosales s/n, Moncloa* Ⓜ *Argüelles, Moncloa, Ventura Rodríguez, Pl. de España.*

Teleférico

AMUSEMENT RIDE | FAMILY | Kids and adults alike appreciate the sweeping views from this retro cable car, which swoops you 2.5 km (1.6 miles) from the Rosaleda gardens (in Parque del Oeste) to the center of Casa de Campo in about 10 minutes. If you're feeling active, take a (very) long hike to the top and ride back into the city, or pause in Casa de Campo for primo picnicking.

■ **TIP→ This is not the best way to get to the zoo and theme park, located approximately 2 km (1 mile) from the drop-off point in Casa de Campo. You're better off riding the Teleférico out and back, then taking the bus to the zoo.** ✉ *Estación Terminal Teleférico, Paseo de Pintor Rosales s/n, at Calle del Marqués de Urquijo, Moncloa* ☎ *91/406–8810* ⊕ *teleferico.emtmadrid. es* ⬛ *€6* Ⓜ *Argüelles.*

🍴 Restaurants

Casa Mingo

$ | SPANISH | FAMILY | Madrid's oldest *sidrería* (cider house) is a grand cathedral-like hall with barrel-lined walls, double-height ceilings, and creaky wooden chairs. The star menu item is roast chicken, hacked up unceremoniously and served in a puddle of cider jus—old-school bar food at its finest (the other dishes are nothing to write home about). **Known for:** Asturian cider; roast chicken; a Madrid institution. Ⓢ *Average main: €17* ✉ *Paseo de la Florida 34, Moncloa* ☎ *91/547–7918* ⊕ *www.casamingo.es* Ⓜ *Príncipe Pío.*

Cuenllas

$$$ | SPANISH | Epitomizing old-world luxury, Cuenllas (KWEN-yas) is Moncloa's most venerable dining establishment, in business since 1939. After sitting down at the bar or in the dining room for a meal of Spanish bistro fare (think warm salt-cod brandade, Santoña anchovy canapés, and marinated partridge) accompanied by reserva wines, peruse the adjoining Ultramarinos gourmet shop for edible souvenirs including caviar, cheeses, wines, and homemade charcuterie. **Known for:** standout traditional wine list; French-inflected Spanish dining; charmingly old-fashioned waiters. Ⓢ *Average main: €27* ✉ *Calle de Ferraz 5, Moncloa* ☎ *91/559–1705* ⊕ *www.cuenllas.es* ☾ *Closed Sun.* Ⓜ *Ventura Rodríguez.*

★ Desde 1911

$$$$ | SEAFOOD | One of the buzziest restaurants in Madrid, this modern seafood mecca—with sleek wooden tables and floor-to-ceiling windows—serves rare delicacies from the country's top fishing fleets. On the ever-changing menu, you might find *quisquillas de Motril* (sweet white shrimp with bright blue roe), precious little elvers, or Basque lobster stew—all accompanied by wines selected by Sergio Otero, of DiverXO fame. **Known for:** twee old-school cheese cart; uber-trendy hot spot; finest seafood in Madrid. $ Average main: €51 ⊠ Calle del Vivero 3, Moncloa ☎ 91/545–7286 ⊕ desde1911.es ⊗ Closed Sun. and Mon. No dinner Tues. and Wed. Ⓜ Guzmán el Bueno, Cuatro Caminos.

La Montaña

$ | **SPANISH** | **FAMILY** | The average customer age in this time-warpy tavern is pushing 70, which is always a good sign—Madrid's abuelos and abuelas never settle for subpar Spanish cooking. In the snug tile-walled dining room, tuck into disappearing classics like braised baby squid in ink sauce and stewed baby fava beans (verdinas) with prawns; then satisfy your sweet tooth with a custardy fried torrija (Spanish "French" toast). **Known for:** kitschy Spanish décor; lots of local clientele; dependable down-home cooking. $ Average main: €17 ⊠ Calle del Rey Francisco 28, Moncloa ☎ 91/547–3111 ⊗ Closed Mon. No dinner Sun. Ⓜ Ventura Rodríguez.

 Coffee and Quick Bites

Los Bocadillos

$ | **SANDWICHES** | **FAMILY** | Unhinge your jaw and devour a bocadillo de calamares, the classic Madrid sub overstuffed with fried calamari, at the most popular outpost of this local chain; ask for lemon and aioli to zhuzh it up. **Known for:** near Parque del Oeste; cheap cañas (half-pints of Mahou); classic Spanish-style hoagies. $ Average main: €6 ⊠ Calle del Marqués de Urquijo 1, Moncloa.

Tutti Frutti

$ | **ICE CREAM** | **FAMILY** | Ice cream made on the premises with fresh fruit, top-quality chocolate, and all sorts of other add-ins make this corner heladería a neighborhood favorite come summer. **Known for:** unconventional flavors; favorite local ice cream spot; all-natural ingredients. $ Average main: €4 ⊠ Cuesta de San Vicente 22, Moncloa ☎ 91/541–1074 ⊕ www.heladeriatuttifrutti.com ⊗ Closed Nov.–Feb. Ⓜ Príncipe Pío.

Hotels

Barceló Torre de Madrid

$$$ | **HOTEL** | A jewel box of glowing lights, harlequin furniture, and gilded mirrors, the soaring Barceló Torre de Madrid opened in 2017 and remains one of the trendiest hotels in town. **Pros:** cutting-edge design by local artists; sleek pool and spa area; excellent Somos restaurant. **Cons:** feels understaffed; limited pool hours; confusing elevators. $ Rooms from: €240 ⊠ Pl. de España 18, Moncloa ☎ 91/524–2339 ⊕ www. barcelo.com/en-us/barcelo-torre-de-madrid 🛏 256 rooms ﹖◯﹗ No Meals Ⓜ Pl. de España.

Dear Hotel

$$$ | **HOTEL** | Catty-corner to Plaza de España, Dear Hotel is a sleek urban property with an exclusive feel. **Pros:** all rooms face out; swanky rooftop bar with 360-degree views; Scandi-chic furnishings. **Cons:** tiny pool; no gym or spa; cramped lobby. $ Rooms from: €249 ⊠ Calle Gran Vía 80, Moncloa ☎ 91/412–3200 ⊕ www.dearhotelmadrid. com 🛏 162 rooms ﹖◯﹗ No Meals Ⓜ Pl. de España.

Hotel Indigo Madrid – Princesa, an IHG Hotel

$$ | **HOTEL** | This bright budget option opened in 2019 in the heart of residential Argüelles, steps from the bustling shopping street Calle de la Princesa. **Pros:** five-minute walk from Parque del Oeste; cheery decor; rain showers. **Cons:** poor soundproofing; so-so breakfast; basic bathrooms. $ Rooms from: €148 ⊠ Calle del Marqués de Urquijo 4, Moncloa ☎ 91/548–1900 ⊕ www.ihg.com/ hotelindigo/hotels/us/en/madrid/madpc/ hoteldetail 🛏 101 rooms ﹖◯﹗ No Meals Ⓜ Argüelles.

Chapter 5

CHUECA AND MALASAÑA

Updated by
Benjamin Kemper

👁 **Sights**
★★☆☆☆

🍴 **Restaurants**
★★★★☆

🛏 **Hotels**
★★☆☆☆

🛍 **Shopping**
★★★★★

🍸 **Nightlife**
★★★★★

SECRETS OF LIRIA PALACE AND THE DUCHESS OF ALBA

If you wanted to visit the seat of the late Duchess of Alba, Liria Palace, before it opened to the public in 2019, you made a formal request and waited—for approximately three years. Why the extreme exclusivity? And what lay beyond the palace walls that people would willingly wait so many years to see?

The House of Alba owns the greatest private art collection in Spain, and the aristocratic family's highlight reel is on display in the halls of Liria Palace. Rooms loosely organized by artistic movement drip with paintings by Spanish greats like El Greco, Goya, Zurbarán, Zuloaga, and Velázquez, and there's a surprisingly deep assemblage of Italian Renaissance works as well by Perugino, Sanzio, and Fra Bartolomeo, among others. In the library, you'll find Columbus's handwritten logbooks, Fernando II's original will, and a weathered first edition of *Don Quixote*. The opulently decorated rooms appointed with period furniture are art pieces in themselves.

DETAILS

☎ 915/908454

⊕ www.palaciodeliria. com

🎫 €15 (includes tour)

Group tours start every 30 minutes and last 65 minutes. Your ticket has an assigned tour time.

■ TIP→ Visits are by tour only. Buy tickets in advance online. If tours are sold out for the date in question, try your luck as a walk-in 15 minutes before the tour is set to depart.

WHAT IS THE HOUSE OF ALBA?

Meet one of Spain's most powerful dukedoms—past, present, and (if history is any indication) future. Tracing its origins to 14th-century Castile, the family is worth an estimated $3.8 billion today and owns approximately 130 square miles of land across the Iberian Peninsula. Of the twentysome castles and palaces it presides over, most notable are the Palacio de Las Dueñas in Seville, Castillo de Coca in Segovia, and Palacio Monterrey (Monterrey Palace) in Salamanca.

THE LATE, GREAT DUCHESS

No one has made more of a splash in Liria Palace's 254-year history than Duchess of Alba Cayetana Fitz-James Stuart, who died in 2014. Bearing more officially recognized titles than any royal on earth, according to Guinness World Records, she was baptized in Madrid's Palacio Real and was related to Christopher Columbus, Winston Churchill, and Queen Elizabeth II. But a prim-and-proper aristocrat she was not—during Franco's reign, she hosted racy fashion shows (famously for Yves Saint-Laurent) and was known to break out in gutsy flamenco dance.

The Salón Goya

A FRAUGHT LEGACY

For the better part of a century, members of the House of Alba have graced the front pages of tabloids—Cayetana for her outlandish remarks and scandalous relationships (she wedded a possibly closeted ex-Jesuit priest and later a suitor 30 years her junior), and her children for infighting, drugs, and sex. On the other hand, the late duchess was a great defender of the Roma in Seville and even built a church for them. The family has done an admirable job of preserving some of Spain's finest artistic treasures; indeed, Liria Palace was reconstructed virtually in its entirety after the Spanish Civil War. But the power that dynasties like the House of Alba continue to wield in Spain is unpalatable to many modern Spaniards.

OTHER PALACES WORTH VISITING IN MADRID

Museo Cerralbo, within walking distance of Liria, is a nobleman's 19th-century abode that is now a sumptuous art museum. In Parque del Buen Retiro, you'll find the Palacio de Cristal, or "Glass Palace," a soaring turn-of-the-century greenhouse that now holds modern art exhibitions. The Palacio Real, the official residence of the Spanish monarchs, is nearly double the size of Versailles with 2,800 rooms.

The Salón Italiano

NEIGHBORHOOD SNAPSHOT

TOP EXPERIENCES

- **"La hora del vermú":** Happy hour is synonymous with vermouth and tapas in this part of Madrid.

- **Palacio de Liria:** Tour the dazzling abode of the late Duchess of Alba.

- **LGBT+ nightlife:** Party the night away in Madrid's "gayborhood."

- **Espadrille shopping:** Snap up colorful rope-soled sandals at a 158-year-old artisan shop.

- **Cocktails:** Sip the latest trends in European mixology.

- **Plaza-hopping:** Stroll among picturesque plazas: San Ildefonso, Dos de Mayo, Juan Pujol, Chueca, and Pedro Zerolo, to name a few.

GETTING HERE

Chueca and Malasaña, compact side-by-side neighborhoods, are bounded by Calle de Alberto Aguilera and Calle de Sagasta to the north and Gran Vía and Calle de Alcalá to the south. Malasaña is to the west of Calle de Fuencarral, Chueca to the east. The western and eastern borders of the combined neighborhoods are Calle de la Princesa and Paseo de la Castellana, respectively.

Malasaña is serviced by metro stations around its perimeter; clockwise from the neighborhood's northwest corner, these are: Argüelles (Líneas 3, 4, 6), San Bernardo (Líneas 2, 4), Bilbao (Líneas 1, 4), Tribunal (Líneas 1, 10), Gran Vía (Líneas 1, 5), Callao (Líneas 3, 5), Ventura Rodríguez (Línea 3), and Plaza de España (Líneas 3, 10). Noviciado (Línea 2) is roughly in Malasaña's center.

Chueca is also serviced by metro stations on its periphery; clockwise from the neighborhood's northwest corner, these are: Bilbao, Alonso Martínez (Líneas 4, 5, 10), Banco de España (Línea 2), Gran Vía, and Tribunal. Chueca (Línea 5) is located in the heart of the neighborhood.

There are BiciMAD bike-share docks throughout both neighborhoods.

PLANNING YOUR TIME

Allot a few hours to explore these neighborhoods on foot, or more if you plan on making pit stops to wine, dine, and people-watch. Tapas and cocktail bars are particularly mobbed on weekend nights.

PAUSE HERE

Plaza del Dos de Mayo is the nerve center of Malasaña—bustling, picturesque, and unapologetically gritty. Let your gaze wander to the center of the square, to the brick gate framing a white statue. That archway is all that remains of the 17th-century Palacio de Monteleón, the abode of Hernán Cortés's monied grandchildren. It was converted into a barracks before being razed by Napoleon's army in the early 19th century. The statue, *Daoiz and Velarde* by sculptor Antonio Solá, dates to 1822 and commemorates two locally famous rebels who defended Madrid against the French.

Chueca and Malasaña were ground zero for Madrid's countercultural revolution called the *Movida Madrileña*, a political and artistic reawakening that followed Franco's death in 1975. The movement's motto *"Madrid nunca duerme"* ("Madrid never sleeps") still rings true in Chueca, Spain's favorite "gayborhood," and in Malasaña, a bastion of nonconformist nightlife.

Chueca, a subsection of Justicia district, is named after the Plaza de Chueca, which in turn is named after Federico Chueca, author and composer of *zarzuelas* (short musical plays). Today the neighborhood is Spain's most iconic LGBT+ quarter, and it has held that unofficial title since the 1980s, when the first gay bars arrived on the scene. Nowadays most young LGBT+ Madrileños live and party elsewhere because of the barrio's soaring rents, tourist crowds, and more mature clientele, but for a fun, carefree, and rowdy night out, Chueca never disappoints, regardless of age or orientation. The downside of Chueca's reputation as a gay district is that its myriad other attractions—ranging from museums to pretty plazas to fantastic galleries and restaurants—are often overshadowed.

Malasaña has a youthful, off-beat pulse rivaled only, perhaps, by Lavapiés, its more multicultural counterpart. Formerly called Barrio de las Maravillas, the neighborhood is centered on Plaza de Dos de Mayo, which commemorates the May 2 uprising against French occupation in 1808. Manuela Malasaña, for whom

the barrio is named, was a martyr in the conflict. At the end of the 20th century, Malasaña emerged as an emblem of the Movida Madrileña, its rough-and-ready streets featuring prominently in music and cinema thanks to emerging talents like Alaska, Mecano, Hombres G, and film director Pedro Almodóvar. These days the neighborhood is far cleaner and less rambunctious than it was in its cultural heyday, thanks to massive waves of gentrification in the early 2000s and 2010s, but its rebellious spirit lives on—head to Plaza de Dos de Mayo any weekend night and you'll see crowds of locals flouting open container laws.

Chueca

 Sights

Mercado de San Antón
MARKET | Chueca's neighborhood market has been reborn. In 2022, the three-floor complex underwent a massive renovation that gutted and revamped the second floor entirely and added 16 new

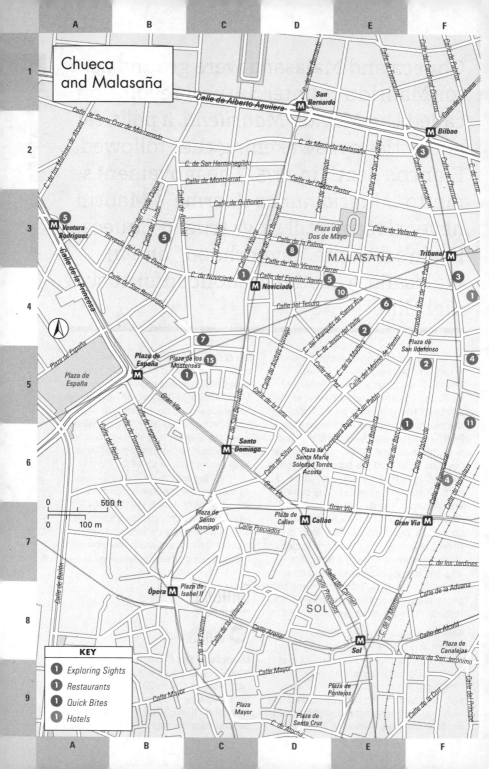

Sights ▼

1 Mercado de Los Mostenses C5
2 Mercado de San Antón........... H6
3 Museo de Historia de Madrid F4
4 Museo del Romanticismo......... G3
5 Palacio de Liria A3

Restaurants ▼

1 Bar La Gloria C4
2 Bodega de la Ardosa............... F5
3 Café Comercial..................... F2
4 Casa Hortensia
   Restaurante y Sidrería F5
5 Casa Macareno................... D4
6 Casa Salvador..................... G6
7 Celso y Manolo H7
8 DSpeak............................. H4
9 El Señor Martín I3
10 La Colmada.......................... E4
11 La Tita Rivera....................... F5
12 Lettera Trattoria Moderna G7
13 Mercado de la Reina.............. G7
14 Roostiq............................. H6
15 Selva C5
16 Trattoria Pulcinella H4

Quick Bites ▼

1 Café de la Luz E6
2 Casa Julio E4
3 Faraday H5
4 Golda............................... I3
5 La Carbonera....................... B3
6 Lolina Vintage Café................. E4
7 Misión Café.......................... C4
8 Toma Café 1 .... D3

Hotels ▼

1 Bastardo Hostel..................... F4
2 Only YOU Boutique Hotel H6
3 The Principal Madrid.............. H7
4 7 Islas Hotel F6
5 URSO Hotel & Spa................. G3

stalls including an offshoot of the centennial Café Comercial. After browsing the more traditional grocery stalls on the ground floor, take the escalator up to the second for a rollicking *tapeo* (tapas crawl) or go up one additional floor to imbibe at 11 Nudos, a sceney rooftop restaurant and bar owned by Spanish craft gin Nordés. ✉ *Calle de Augusto Figueroa 24, Chueca* ☎ *91/330–0730* 🌐 *www.mercadosananton.com* [M] *Chueca.*

Museo de Historia de Madrid (*Madrid History Museum*)
HISTORY MUSEUM | FAMILY | The intricate, over-the-top 18th-century doorway to this museum, formerly a hospice, is one of the finest pieces of baroque civil architecture in Spain, so it's a wonder that what lies beyond it flies under the radar of most tourists. Painted fans, period clothing, gleaming china and porcelain, and an exhibit on the Dos de Mayo Uprising are the main attractions, and there are usually a few paintings on loan from the Prado as well. ✉ *Calle de Fuencarral 78, Chueca* ☎ *91/701–1863* ⏲ *Closed Mon.* [M] *Tribunal.*

Museo del Romanticismo (*Museum of Romanticism*)
HISTORY MUSEUM | To catch a glimpse of how the Spanish bourgeoisie lived in the early 19th century, step into this former palace of a marquis. Each room sparkles with ornate period furniture, evocative portraits, and other historical artifacts culled from the height of Spanish Romanticism. It's worth spending a few minutes admiring the flamboyantly decorated fans and backlit lithophanes. The museum can be seen in an hour or two, but don't rush out: the plant-filled interior patio is a lovely, tranquil place to enjoy tea and pastries. ✉ *Calle de San Mateo 13, Chueca* ☎ *91/448–1045* 🌐 *www.culturaydeporte.gob.es/mromanticismo/en/inicio.html* 🎟 *€3. Free Sat. after 2 pm* ⏲ *Closed Mon.* [M] *Tribunal.*

🍴 Restaurants

★ Casa Hortensia Restaurante y Sidrería
$$ | SPANISH | FAMILY | Approximate a vacation to northern Spain by dining at this true-blue Asturian restaurant (or at the more casual sidrería in the bar area), where that region's unsung comfort-food dishes—such as *fabada* (pork-and-bean stew), Cabrales cheese, and *cachopo* (cheese-stuffed beef cutlets)—take center stage. The obligatory tipple is *sidra,* bone-dry Asturian cider that's aerated using a battery-powered gadget designed for this task. **Known for:** authentic fabada; cider bottles with fun DIY aerators; local crowd. [$] *Average main: €20* ✉ *Calle de la Farmacia 2, 2nd and 3rd fl., Chueca* ☎ *91/539–0090* 🌐 *www.casahortensia.com* ⏲ *Closed Mon. No dinner Sun.* [M] *Chueca.*

★ Casa Salvador
$$ | SPANISH | Whether you approve of bullfighting or not, the culinary excellence of Casa Salvador—a checkered-tablecloth, taurine-themed restaurant that opened in 1941—isn't up for debate. Sit down to generous servings of featherlight fried hake, hearty oxtail stew, and other stodgy (in the best way) Spanish classics, all served by hale old-school waiters clad in white jackets. **Known for:** time-warpy decor; walls packed with bullfighting paraphernalia; cloud-light fried hake and stewed oxtail. [$] *Average main: €23* ✉ *Calle de Barbieri 12, Chueca* ☎ *91/521–4524* 🌐 *www.casasalvadormadrid.com* ⏲ *Closed Sun. No dinner Mon.* [M] *Chueca.*

Celso y Manolo
$$ | TAPAS | This hip neighborhood favorite has around a dozen tables and an extensive eclectic menu geared toward sharing that features game meats, seafood, and cheeses from the mountainous northern region of Cantabria. Organic wines sourced from around the country make for spot-on pairings. **Known for:** market-driven cuisine; Cantabrian

specialties; varied menu. $ *Average main: €19* ✉ *Calle de la Libertad 1, Chueca* ☎ *91/531–8079* ⊕ *www.celsoymanolo.es* Ⓜ *Chueca.*

DSpeak

$$$ | SPANISH | Diego Guerrero, the punk-rock chef of two-Michelin-star Dstage, also runs this more casual outpost. The menu turns classic Spanish dishes—for example, monkfish in salsa verde, Canarian wrinkly potatoes, stewed *verdinas* (baby favas)—on their heads by adding unorthodox ingredients like seaweed, kimchi, whey, and liquid-nitrogen-frozen fruit, and the result is thrilling. **Known for:** experimental Spanish dining; big-name chef; buzzy subterranean cocktail bar. $ *Average main: €27* ✉ *Calle de Fernando VI 6, Chueca* ☎ *91/319–5435* ⊕ *www.dstageconcept.com* ⊗ *Closed Mon. No dinner Sun.* Ⓜ *Tribunal, Alonso Martínez.*

El Señor Martín

$$$$ | SEAFOOD | Pristine fish, salt, roaring open flame—these are the main ingredients at El Señor Martín, a white-table seafood restaurant beloved by local food critics that makes a great venue for romantic dinners and special occasions. Consider springing for a gloriously obscure fish you've never heard of, like Mediterranean sand eel, wreckfish, plaice, or alfonsino—all meticulously filleted and grilled to juicy perfection. **Known for:** secret gourmet hangout; fantastic fish and seafood; Basque chef who grills with panache. $ *Average main: €49* ✉ *Calle del General Castaños 13, Chueca* ☎ *91/795–7170* ⊕ *www.srmartin.es* ⊗ *Closed Sun. and Mon.* Ⓜ *Alonso Martínez, Colón.*

La Tita Rivera

$ | TAPAS | This budget-friendly bar—specializing in hot stuffed bread rolls (called *casis*) and flavored hard cider—has an industrial vibe, thanks to exposed pipes, high ceilings, and a semi-open kitchen. The best part, however, is the under-the-radar courtyard with room for spreading out. **Known for:** stuffed bread rolls; hidden interior patio; flavored draft ciders. $ *Average main: €12* ✉ *Calle de Pérez Galdós 4, Chueca* ☎ *91/522–1890* ⊕ *www.latitarivera.com* Ⓜ *Chueca.*

Lettera Trattoria Moderna

$$ | ITALIAN | Sicilian chef Francesco Ingargiola recreates the bold flavors of his childhood—with plenty of fine-dining flourishes—at this inviting ultramodern trattoria one block from the Gran Vía thoroughfare. Start with an order of crispy artichokes, flavored with lardo and topped with Italian foie gras, before moving on to homemade pastas like linguini with shrimp or Madrid's best carbonara. **Known for:** regional Italian cooking; unusual homemade pastas; romantic dining room. $ *Average main: €22* ✉ *Calle de la Reina 20, Chueca* ☎ *91/805–3342* ⊕ *www.letteramadrid.com* ⊗ *Closed Tues.* Ⓜ *Gran Vía, Chueca.*

Mercado de la Reina

$$ | TAPAS | Perhaps the only worthwhile tapas restaurant on Gran Vía, Madrid's main commercial artery, Mercado de la Reina serves everything from croquetas to grilled vegetables to tossed salads. Enjoy them in the casual bar area, in the slightly more formal dining room, or on the outdoor patio. **Known for:** inexpensive eats; convenient location; lounge bar downstairs. $ *Average main: €20* ✉ *Calle Gran Vía 12, Chueca* ☎ *91/521–3198* ⊕ *www.grupomercadodelareina.com* Ⓜ *Banco de España, Gran Vía.*

★ Roostiq

$$$ | EUROPEAN | Fire is the secret ingredient at Roostiq, where pizzas sizzle and puff in a wood-burning oven and meat, fish, and vegetables char until tender over white-hot embers. Even the cheesecake is of the Basque "burnt" variety, brown and caramel-y on the outside and gooey within. **Known for:** open-hearth roasts and pizzas; 150 champagnes to choose from; trendy industrial digs. $ *Average main: €27* ✉ *Calle de Augusto Figueroa 47, Chueca* ☎ *91/853–2434* ⊕ *www.roostiqmadrid.com* Ⓜ *Chueca.*

Trattoria Pulcinella

$$ | **ITALIAN** | **FAMILY** | When Enrico Bosco arrived in Madrid from Italy in the early '90s, he couldn't find a decent Italian restaurant, so he decided to open one. Always bustling and frequented by families and young couples, this trattoria seems like a direct transplant from Naples with its superb fresh pastas, pizzas, and focaccias. **Known for:** affordable down-home Italian fare; family friendly; excellent fresh pastas. [$] *Average main: €19* ✉ *Calle de Regueros 7, Chueca* ☎ *91/319–7363* 🌐 *www.pulcinellamadrid.com* [M] *Chueca.*

Coffee and Quick Bites

Faraday

$ | **CAFÉ** | Faraday is a chic little café known for its meticulously roasted beans, mathematically precise baristas, and gorgeous midcentury modern furniture. Laptops are allowed. **Known for:** great music; closed 2–4 pm; excellent coffee. [$] *Average main: €5* ✉ *Calle de San Lucas 9, Chueca* 🌐 *faraday-cafeteria.negocio.site* 🕒 *Closed Mon.* [M] *Alonso Martínez, Chueca.*

★ Golda

$ | **CAFÉ** | This cheery yellow-tiled café serving Middle Eastern-inflected sandwiches and pastries is packed from breakfast to lunch, when neighborhood-dwellers show up for falafel, shakshuka, and spinach pie. At 8:30 pm, Golda morphs into "Golfa," its boozier late-night alter ego serving tapas and natural wine. **Known for:** homemade salads and sweet and savory pastries; expertly pulled espresso drinks; laptop-friendly. [$] *Average main: €12* ✉ *Calle de Orellana 19, Chueca* ☎ *91/069–1070* 🌐 *www.goldacafe.com* [M] *Alonso Martínez, Colón.*

Hotels

★ Bastardo Hostel

$$ | **HOTEL** | Whether you're a solo traveler looking to make friends or a cash-strapped couple (or group of friends) trying to do Madrid on a budget, consider holing up at Bastardo, a designer hostel with communal and private rooms that doubles as a cool-kid hangout. **Pros:** pulsing rooftop bar; buzzy young vibe; tours, activities, concerts, and more. **Cons:** windows don't open (and the AC is weak in some rooms); rooms near the rooftop are noisy at night; not always squeaky clean. [$] *Rooms from: €195* ✉ *Calle de San Mateo 3, Chueca* ☎ *68/251–9535* 🌐 *bastardohostel.com* 🛏 *57 rooms* 🍴 *No Meals* [M] *Tribunal.*

★ Only YOU Boutique Hotel

$$$$ | **HOTEL** | The Ibizan owners of this hotel bring that island's mix of glamour, energy, and cutting-edge music and design to one of Madrid's most happening neighborhoods. **Pros:** outstanding tapas at Padrino bar; double-paned glass blocks out street noise; all-day breakfast. **Cons:** breakfast lacks quality and variety; rooms overlooking Calle del Barquillo can be pricey; no bathtubs in some upgraded rooms. [$] *Rooms from: €355* ✉ *Calle del Barquillo 21, Chueca* ☎ *91/005–2222* 🌐 *www.onlyyouhotels.com* 🛏 *125 rooms* 🍴 *No Meals* [M] *Chueca.*

The Principal Madrid

$$$$ | **HOTEL** | Dozens of hotels flank Gran Vía, Madrid's main artery, but the five-star Principal rises above the fray—and not just on account of its swanky rooftop cocktail bar. **Pros:** outdoor breakfasts and rooftop with 360-degree views; Ramón Freixa–helmed restaurant; luxurious feel with personal touches. **Cons:** rooms not fully soundproofed; rooftop pool is tiny; middling breakfast. [$] *Rooms from: €461* ✉ *Calle del Marqués de Valdeiglesias 1, Chueca* ☎ *91/521–8743* 🌐 *www.theprincipalmadridhotel.com* 🛏 *76 rooms* 🍴 *No Meals* [M] *Chueca.*

URSO Hotel & Spa

$$$$ | **HOTEL** | In a neoclassical building so stunning it was featured in Almodóvar's 2021 film *Parallel Mothers*, URSO boasts old-world comfort and avant-garde design

The heart of Madrid's LGBTQ+ community is centered around a neighborhood named after Spanish composer and author Federico Chueca.

to satisfy alternative types and jet-setters alike. **Pros:** stunning facade; Natura Bissé spa with seven-meter hydromassage pool; calming rooms. **Cons:** overpriced; entry-level rooms are dark and cramped; smallish gym and chilly pool. $ *Rooms from: €400* ✉ *Calle de Mejía Lequerica 8, Chueca* ☎ *91/444–4458* ⊕ *www. hotelurso.com* ➷ *78 rooms* ⦿ *No Meals* Ⓜ *Alonso Martínez, Tribunal.*

Nightlife

Chueca's LGBT+-oriented venues— including all of those listed below—are welcoming to customers of all genders and sexual orientations.

BARS

Bar Cock

COCKTAIL LOUNGES | This classic—if hilariously named—bar (est. 1921) resembles a gentlemen's club with dark-wood interiors and cathedral-like ceilings. It serves a variety of cocktails to an older, business-y crowd. ✉ *Calle de la Reina 16, Chueca* ☎ *91/532–2826* ⊙ *Closed Sun. and Mon.* Ⓜ *Gran Vía.*

Café Belén

CAFÉS | The handful of tables at this rootsy bar are rarely empty on weekends, thanks to the cozy candlelit atmosphere and picture windows that open in summer. Expect a young, mixed crowd. Weeknights are more mellow. ✉ *Calle de Belén 5, Chueca* ☎ *91/308–2747* ⊕ *www.elcafebelen.com* ⊙ *Closed Mon.* Ⓜ *Chueca.*

Del Diego

COCKTAIL LOUNGES | There are no fripperies of modern mixology to be found at Del Diego, and that's just how the dyed-in-the-wool regulars like it. This legendary bar has been pouring flawless classic cocktails like dirty martinis and white Russians since the late 1990s, and amigos, you'd better believe they're all that and a bag of chips. ✉ *Calle de la Reina 12, Chueca* ☎ *91/523–3106* ⊕ *www.deldiego.com* ⊙ *Closed Sun.* Ⓜ *Gran Vía.*

La Kama

DANCE CLUBS | If you feel like dancing but don't want to commit to all-out clubbing, pop into La Kama for a garishly garnished *gin-tónic* and endless pop and reggaeton sing-alongs. ⊠ *Calle de Gravina 4, Chueca* ☎ *91/522–3226* ⊕ *grupolakama.com/la-kama-bar* Ⓜ *Chueca.*

★ Macera Taller Bar

COCKTAIL LOUNGES | The age-old technique of maceration rules at Macera, where bartenders treat spirits like blank canvases, imbuing them with surprising flavor combinations. Gin is steeped with fresh cilantro, lime, and jalapeño until it achieves a zippy grassy piquancy. Whiskey might be infused with almonds, fresh cherries, mint, or vanilla bean. There's a second, clubbier outpost on Calle de Ventura de la Vega 7 in Barrio de Las Letras. ⊠ *Calle de San Mateo 21, Chueca* ☎ *91/011–5810* ⊕ *www.maceradrinks.com* ⊗ *Closed Mon.* Ⓜ *Alonso Martínez, Tribunal.*

Vinoteca Vides

WINE BARS | This dressed-down wine bar is a great spot to sample classically styled Spanish wines at a terrific price. There's a particularly deep selection of grippy *M onastrells*, a dark high-alcohol grape ubiquitous in southern Spain. ⊠ *Calle de la Libertad 12, Chueca* ☎ *91/531–8444* ⊕ *vinotecavides.es* Ⓜ *Chueca.*

DANCE CLUBS

DLRO Live

DANCE CLUBS | This unpretentious, unapologetically campy bar attracts a motley crew of LGBTQ+ (but primarily gay male) revelers of all ages and nationalities with its pop and reggaeton music. It's a Chueca standby. ⊠ *Calle de Pelayo 59, Chueca* ☎ *91/319–5302* ⊕ *deliriochueca.com* Ⓜ *Chueca.*

Fulanita de Tal

DANCE CLUBS | Chueca's favorite lesbian bar hosts popular concerts and dusk-to-3:30 am dance parties in an intimate, unpretentious space. The music varies night to night and mixes pop, oldies, reggaeton, and electro. ⊠ *Calle de Regueros 9, Chueca* ☎ *91/319–5069* ⊕ *www.fulanitadetal.es* ⊗ *Closed Mon.– Wed.* Ⓜ *Alonso Martínez, Chueca.*

Postureo Bar

BARS | One of Chueca's buzziest gay bars, Postureo caters to well-dressed creatives, selfie-snapping influencers, and models on their nights off. The bartenders may not know what a Negroni is—even if they have all the requisite ingredients—but you come for the scene, not for the mixology. ⊠ *Calle de Belén 9, Chueca* ☎ *64/019–3165* ⊗ *Closed Mon.– Wed.* Ⓜ *Chueca.*

MUSIC CLUBS

Café Libertad 8

LIVE MUSIC | Almost every classic Madrileño songwriter, musician, and poet has passed through this timeworn hangout, which opens at 3:30 pm (entertainment generally starts at 9). Acoustic guitar concerts priced at less than €10 a head are fantastic—and virtually devoid of tourists. Many shows are free (check the website for details). ⊠ *Calle de la Libertad 8, Chueca* ☎ *91/532–1150* ⊕ *www.libertad8cafe.com* Ⓜ *Chueca.*

Intruso Bar

LIVE MUSIC | Easy to miss (it's tucked inside a building just a block off Fuencarral), this is one of Chueca's best lounge bars, and it's open past 5 am nightly. There are live DJs and funk and jazz bands starting around 9; expect a mixed-age crowd. ⊠ *Calle de Augusto Figueroa 3, Chueca* ⊕ *www.intrusobar.com* Ⓜ *Chueca.*

Museo Chicote

LIVE MUSIC | This landmark cocktail bar–lounge is said to have been one of Hemingway's haunts. Much of the interior can be traced to the 1930s, but modern elements (like the in-house DJ and hordes of international visitors) keep this spot firmly in the present. ⊠ *Calle Gran Vía 12, Chueca* ☎ *91/532–6737* ⊕ *www. museochicote.com* Ⓜ *Gran Vía.*

🛍 Shopping

BOUTIQUES AND FASHION
Mans Concept
MEN'S CLOTHING | Owned by Andalusian fashion wunderkind Jaime Álvarez, this is Madrid's most cutting-edge made-to-measure menswear boutique. Ready-made clothes are also available in the shop and online. ⊠ *Calle de San Bernardino 15, Chueca* ⊕ *www.manscon-ceptmenswear.com* ⌚ *Closed weekends* Ⓜ *Alonso Martínez, Chueca.*

Nac
WOMEN'S CLOTHING | You'll find a broad selection of European designer brands (e.g., Bergamot, Forte Forte, Pomandère, Babo) at Nac. The store on Calle de Génova is the biggest of the four in Madrid. ⊠ *Calle de Génova 18* ☎ *91/310–6050* ⊕ *www.nac.es* Ⓜ *Colón, Alonso Martínez.*

Oteyza
MIXED CLOTHING | Every garment sold at master tailor Oteyza takes at least two months to make, and the classic craftsmanship shows in the immaculate suits, jackets, and shirts. Get fitted while you're in Madrid and pony up the euros for shipping—you won't regret it. ⊠ *Calle del Conde de Xiquena 11, Chueca* ☎ *91/448–8623* ⊕ *deoteyza.com* ⌚ *Closed Sun.* Ⓜ *Chueca.*

★ Pez
WOMEN'S CLOTHING | A favorite among local fashionistas, this store has two branches—one dedicated to high-end women's wear and another to furniture and decor—on the same street. ⊠ *Calle de Regueros 2 and 15, Chueca* ☎ *91/310–6677* ⊕ *www.pez-pez.es* ⌚ *Closed Sun.* Ⓜ *Chueca.*

Próxima Parada
WOMEN'S CLOTHING | The bubbly owner of this women's-wear store culls daring, colorful garments from Spanish designers for her devoted (mostly 40-and-above) clientele. ⊠ *Calle del Conde de Xiquena 9, Chueca* ☎ *91/523–1929* ⊕ *www.facebook.com/tiendaproxi-maparada* ⌚ *Closed Sun.* Ⓜ *Chueca.*

CERAMICS
Guille García-Hoz
CERAMICS | This renowned ceramicist is known for painted plates and gleaming white urns decorated with animal motifs. ⊠ *Calle de Génova 4, 5th fl., Chueca* ☎ *91/308–3149* ⊕ *www.guillegarciahoz. com* ⌚ *Closed weekends* Ⓜ *Chueca.*

FOOD AND WINE
La Productería
FOOD | You'll find organic local cheeses, gourmet tinned food, charcuterie, and natural wine at this pocket-size shop. ⊠ *Calle de Barbieri 21, Chueca* ☎ *60/835–7175* ⊕ *www.laproducteria. com* ⌚ *Closed Sun. and Mon.* Ⓜ *Chueca.*

Malasaña

👁 Sights

Mercado de Los Mostenses
MARKET | **FAMILY** | Forget the architectural fruit displays and polished tapas stalls of Mercado de San Miguel or Mercado de la Paz—this market's allure is its rough-and-ready atmosphere, neighborhood crowd, and rock-bottom prices. In the morning and late afternoon, you'll spot locals filling their shopping carts with always-fresh meat and produce; from 1:30 to 3 pm, all three floors teem with families and workers on their lunch break scoping out *menú del día* (set meal) options. ⊠ *Pl. de Los Mostenses 1, Malasaña* ☎ *91/542–5838* ⌚ *Closed Sun.* Ⓜ *Pl. de España, Noviciado.*

Palacio de Liria (*Liria Palace*)

HISTORIC HOME | In 2019, this working palace belonging to the House of Alba, one of Spain's most powerful noble families, formally opened to the public. Its sumptuous halls and creaky passages are hung with works selected from what many consider to be Spain's finest private art collection—you'll spot Titians, Rubens, Velázquezes, and other instantly recognizable paintings. In the library, Columbus's diaries from his voyage to the New World are on display as well as the first Spanish-language Bible and other priceless official documents. The neoclassical palace was built in the 18th century but was bombed during the Spanish Civil War (only the facade survived); its collection of works thankfully were safeguarded during the conflict. The Duchess of Alba oversaw the reconstruction of the palace to its precise original specifications. ■ **TIP→ Visits are by tour only, but if online tickets are sold out, try your luck as a walk-in.** ✉ *Calle de la Princesa 20, Malasaña* ☎ *91/590–8454* 🌐 *www.palaciodeliria.com* 🎫 *€15 (includes tour)* [M] *Ventura Rodríguez.*

🍴 Restaurants

Bar La Gloria

$ | **SPANISH** | **FAMILY** | Your reward for overlooking the soulless IKEA furnishings of this family-run dinette is honest home-cooked food served at exceptionally reasonable prices for the neighborhood. Try Cordoban-style *flamenquines* (ham-and-cheese-stuffed pork), salmon tartare, or (on Sunday) a crave-worthy paella Valenciana. **Known for:** budget weekday prix fixes; Sunday paella; local crowd. [$] *Average main: €16* ✉ *Calle del Noviciado 2, Malasaña* ☎ *91/083–1401* 🌐 *www.barlagloria.es* 🕒 *Closed Mon. No dinner Sun.* [M] *Noviciado.*

★ Bodega de la Ardosa

$$ | **SPANISH** | A 19th-century *bodega* (wine vendor), with barrel tables and dusty gewgaws hanging from the walls, Bodega de la Ardosa is a welcome anachronism in modern Malasaña and a tourist magnet for good reason. The bar's claim to fame—and the dish Madrileños make special trips for—is its award-winning *tortilla española,* or Spanish omelet, always warm with a runny center. **Known for:** 100-plus years of history; tortilla española; draft vermú and unfiltered sherry "en rama". [$] *Average main: €18* ✉ *Calle de Colón 13, Malasaña* ☎ *91/521–4979* 🌐 *www.laardosa.es* [M] *Tribunal.*

Café Comercial

$$ | **SPANISH** | When this centenary café—one of the oldest in Madrid—shuttered in 2015, ostensibly for good, the public outcry was so great that it inspired a local restaurant group to buy the property and give it a much-needed revamp. In a dining room that combines original elements (huge mirrors, carved wooden columns) with new high-design fixtures, feast on a menu that's a dance between Café Comercial classics, including ham croquetas and tuna-topped *ensaladilla rusa* (potato salad), and novel creations by chef Pepe Roch. **Known for:** one of Madrid's first literary cafés; modern menus by Pepe Roch; outstanding seafood rice. [$] *Average main: €22* ✉ *Glorieta de Bilbao 7, Malasaña* ☎ *91/088–2525* 🌐 *www.cafecomercialmadrid.com* [M] *Bilbao.*

★ Casa Macareno

$$ | **TAPAS** | **FAMILY** | Whether you pull up a stool at at the marble bar or sit down for a soup-to-nuts feast in the azulejo-lined dining room, you're in for some of Madrid's finest traditional tapas with a twist here. Madrileños come from far and wide to share heaped plates of ensaladilla rusa, a house specialty, as well as textbook-perfect croquetas and hefty steaks served with sherry gravy and house-cut fries. **Known for:** hidden gem in Malasaña; dependably exceptional old-school tapas; over-and-above service. [$] *Average main: €20* ✉ *Calle de San Vicente Ferrer 44, Malasaña*

☎ 658/596572 ⊕ www.casamacareno.com Ⓜ Tribunal, Noviciado.

La Colmada

$ | TAPAS | The first thing you'll notice about this teeny seafood-centric tapas bar is its bright blue walls, a nod to the sea. Sure, you could cobble together a full meal from the menu of delectable cheeses, cured sausages, hams, and *conservas* (canned seafood; seek out La Pureza and Ana María brands), but La Colmada is better suited to casual, booze-fueled snacking. **Known for:** top-quality canned delicacies; affordable Spanish wines; jovial atmosphere. $ *Average main: €12* ✉ *Calle del Espíritu Santo 19, Malasaña* ☎ *91/017–6579* ⊕ *www.lacolmada.com* ⊗ *Closed Sun.* Ⓜ *Tribunal.*

Selva

$ | SPANISH | At this secret local hangout tucked behind Gran Vía and Mercado de los Mostenses, €12 gets you an appetizer, entrée, dessert, and drink—and a free cordial if the old-school waiters take a liking to you. The menu is a highlight reel of Spanish soul food including *cocido madrileño* (meat and garbanzo stew; served on Wednesdays when it's cold out), *salmorejo* (chilled tomato-garlic soup), sherried kidneys, Asturian fabada, and *huevos rotos* (lacy fried eggs and potatoes). **Known for:** affordable Spanish soul food; old-school atmosphere; hidden gem off Gran Vía. $ *Average main: €12* ✉ *Pl. de los Mostenses 7, Malasaña* ☎ *91/542–5516* ▱ *No credit cards* ⊗ *Closed Sun. and Mon.* Ⓜ *Noviciado, Pl. de España.*

☕ Coffee and Quick Bites

Café de la Luz

$ | CAFÉ | The grandmotherly upholstery, fringed lampshades, plush wingback chairs, and wooden bookshelves make Café de la Luz a cozy spot to curl up with a book, catch up with friends, or get some work done. Coffees will run you about €2 apiece, and if you're peckish, there's a good variety of sweets and open-faced sandwiches to sate your appetite. **Known for:** cheap and cheerful coffees and sandwiches; homey digs; laptops allowed. $ *Average main: €10* ✉ *Calle de la Puebla 8, Malasaña* ☎ *91/523–1199* Ⓜ *Gran Vía, Tribunal.*

Casa Julio

$ | TAPAS | Ooey-gooey oversize croquetas stuffed with hot béchamel and any range of fixings (start with the classic jamón) are the tapa to order at this snug neighborhood hangout. **Known for:** cozy hole-in-the-wall; legendary croquettes and affordable Spanish snacks; Malasaña tapas crawl staple. $ *Average main: €11* ✉ *Calle de la Madera 37, Malasaña* ☎ *91/522–7274* ⊗ *Closed Sun.* Ⓜ *Noviciado.*

La Carbonera

$$ | SPANISH | Cheese geeks unite at this pocket queso bar with enough Manchego, Idiazabal, Mahón, and other delectable national varieties to make you an armchair expert on Spanish cheeses. There's another, newer, location in Barrio Salamanca at ✉ **Known for:** excellent cheeses; intimate, romantic dining room; tasty Spanish fusion dishes. $ *Average main: €21* ✉ *Calle de Bernardo López García 11, Malasaña* ☎ *91/110–0669* ⊕ *www.lacarboneramadrid.com* ⊗ *Closed Sun. and Mon.* Ⓜ *Noviciado.*

Lolina Vintage Café

$ | CAFÉ | Diverging in spirit from the stuffier baroque-style cafés of the neighborhood, this cozy spot with mismatched vintage furniture attracts an artsy crowd. **Known for:** cheap and cheerful; Malasaña hideaway; assortment of teas, booze, and baked goods. $ *Average main: €9* ✉ *Calle del Espíritu Santo 9, Malasaña* ☎ *91/523–5859* ⊕ *lolinacafe.com* Ⓜ *Tribunal.*

★ Misión Café

$ | **CAFÉ** | From the owners of Hola Coffee, Madrid's preeminent third-wave coffee shop, comes this über-trendy roomier outpost two blocks from Gran Vía. Beyond the single-origin espressos and other classics made from roasted-in-house beans, there are warming chai lattes, shrubs, and (seasonal) cold brew. **Known for:** complex brews made with roasted-in-Madrid beans; killer pastries; cool-kid hangout. [$] *Average main: €14* ✉ *Calle de los Reyes 5, Malasaña* ☎ *91/064–0059* 🌐 *www.mision.cafe* [M] *Noviciado, Pl. de España.*

Toma Café 1

$ | **CAFÉ** | The originator of Madrid's third-wave coffee revolution, Toma—with two other locations in Chamberí (Toma Café Olavide and Proper Sound)—is a favorite among expats and local coffee geeks. After satisfying your cold brew, flat white, or pour-over cravings in the newly renovated digs, indulge in any of the delicious open-face tostas. **Known for:** excellent coffee selection; always busy; major expat hangout. [$] *Average main: €11* ✉ *Calle de la Palma 49, Malasaña* ☎ *91/704–9344* 🌐 *toma.cafe/en* [M] *Noviciado.*

Hotels

★ 7 Islas Hotel

$$ | **HOTEL** | Minimalist industrial design—think polished concrete floors, Edison bulbs, and workbench stools—mixes with eye-popping original art at this independently owned hotel one block north of Gran Vía. **Pros:** sleek updated rooms; worthwhile downstairs bar; good value. **Cons:** no gym, pool, or sauna; overly spartan furnishings; so-so soundproofing. [$] *Rooms from: €186* ✉ *Calle de Valverde 14, Malasaña* ☎ *91/523–4688* 🌐 *www.7islashotel.com* 🛏 *79 rooms* 🍴 *No Meals* [M] *Gran Vía.*

Nightlife

BARS

Casa Camacho

BARS | An essential Malasaña experience is gulping down a few ice-cold "yayos"—vermouth, gin, seltzer, lemon slice—at the tin bar alongside free no-nonsense tapas like olives and stewed chickpeas. ✉ *Calle de San Andrés 4, Malasaña* ☎ *91/531–3598* 🕒 *Closed Tues. and Wed.* [M] *Tribunal, Noviciado.*

Cazador

BARS | You may as well be in Williamsburg or Kreuzberg at this popular and un-campy (mostly) gay bar where an artsy clientele sips *cañas* (half-pints) and dangerously cheap cocktails before heading out to the discoteca. ✉ *Calle Pozas 7, Malasaña* ☎ *63/997–0916* 🌐 *www.facebook.com/cazadorbar* 🕒 *Closed Sun. and Mon.* [M] *Noviciado.*

De Vinos

WINE BARS | A snug, casual wine bar in the quieter Conde Duque area of Malasaña, De Vinos pours hard-to-find wines from regions like Bierzo, Somontano, and—of course—Madrid. Cured sausages and Spanish cheeses make fine accompaniments. ✉ *Calle de la Palma 76, Malasaña* ☎ *91/182–3499* 🕒 *Closed Sun. and Mon.* [M] *Noviciado.*

1862 Dry Bar

COCKTAIL LOUNGES | One of Madrid's swankiest and most skilled coctelerías, 1862 Dry Bar shakes and stirs immaculately prepared cocktails that incorporate sherries and unconventional aromatics. The only snag? On busy nights, drinks take forever to arrive. ✉ *Calle del Pez 27, Malasaña* ☎ *60/953–1151* 🌐 *www.1862drybar.com* [M] *Noviciado.*

Fábrica Maravillas

BREWPUBS | At Madrid's only city-center brewpub, you can taste fun and funky beers that a zany French brewmaster ferments in his "beer lab" a few feet from your barstool. ✉ *Calle de Valverde*

29, Malasaña ☎ 91/521–8753 ⊕ www.fmaravillas.com Ⓜ Gran Vía.

Santamaría Coctelería
COCKTAIL LOUNGES | This cocktail bar mixes vintage design with artsy touches and caters to a laid-back bohemian crowd. Choose from a variety of not-too-fussy cocktails including one bearing the club's name, made with mixed-berry juice and vodka or gin. ✉ Calle de la Ballesta 6, Malasaña ☎ 91/034–1811 ⊕ santamariacocteleria.com Ⓜ Gran Vía.

DANCE CLUBS
★ BarCo
DANCE CLUBS | One of Malasaña's most popular nightclubs, for both its live shows (funk, jazz, and more) and late-night DJ sets, BarCo is a guaranteed good time. Acoustics here are a rung above the competition's. ✉ Calle del Barco 34, Malasaña ☎ 91/531–7754 ⊕ www.salabarco.com ⊘ Closed Sun.–Wed. Ⓜ Tribunal.

Café La Palma
DANCE CLUBS | This feel-good nightclub with a bar, chill-out area, and medium-size dance floor draws a mixed-age, LGBTQ+-friendly crowd with live performances and DJ sets that rage until 6 am. ✉ Calle de la Palma 62, Malasaña ☎ 91/522–5031 ⊕ www.cafelapalma.com Ⓜ Noviciado.

Ocho y Medio
DANCE CLUBS | Not for the faint of heart, the booze-fueled pop and techno parties here are a favorite of the younger set and peak at 4 am. Arrive before 1 am to avoid slow, snaking lines. ✉ Calle de Barceló 11, Malasaña ☎ 91/541–3500 ⊕ ochoymedioclub.com ⊘ Closed Sun.–Thurs. Ⓜ Tribunal.

Siroco
DANCE CLUBS | A small, under-the-radar club that brings in local electronic DJs and a mostly Madrileño crowd, Siroco is a fun place to end a night of Malasaña mischief. ✉ Calle de San Dimas 3, Malasaña ☎ 91/593–3070 ⊕ siroco.es ⊘ Closed Sun.–Wed. Ⓜ Noviciado.

MUSIC CLUBS
Tupper Ware
DANCE CLUBS | Throw on a graphic tee and a pair of ripped jeans and fist-pump the night away at this alternative rock and indie bar that blasts throwback cult classics till 3 am daily. ✉ Corre. Alta de San Pablo 26, Malasaña ☎ 91/446–4204 Ⓜ Tribunal.

🎭 Performing Arts

Centro Cultural de Conde Duque
CONCERTS | This venue taking up an entire city block is best known for its summer live music concerts (flamenco, jazz, pop) and has free exhibitions, lectures, and theater performances. The quiet, well-lit library is a good place for studying or working. The wing at the southern end of the complex is dedicated to contemporary art. ✉ Calle del Conde Duque 11, Malasaña ☎ 91/588–5834 ⊕ www.condeduquemadrid.es Ⓜ Ventura Rodríguez.

FLAMENCO
★ Teatro Flamenco
FOLK/TRADITIONAL DANCE | FAMILY | Less a traditional tablao and more a modern performance venue, Teatro Flamenco hosts a variety of classical and modern interpretations of flamenco dance and song. ✉ Calle del Pez 10, Malasaña ☎ 91/159–2005 ⊕ teatroflamencomadrid.com Ⓜ Noviciado.

🛍 Shopping

ART AND DESIGN
★ Hijo de Epigmenio
CRAFTS | Owners Juanma and Rigas travel from village to village to source the stunning artisan ceramics, fabrics, glass, and more on display at this sunlight-filled boutique. Don't miss the Níjar ceramics with their cheery colorful splotches and the Caribbean-blue vases of hand-blown Mallorcan glass. ✉ Calle de la Puebla 13, Malasaña ☎ 91/066–7019 ⊕ hijodeepigmenio.com ⊘ Closed Sun. Ⓜ Gran Vía, Callao.

La Fiambrera

ART GALLERIES | The polar opposite of your standard stuffy gallery, La Fiambrera sells colorful pop art at affordable prices. There's also a small bookshop and café. ⊠ *Calle del Pez 7, Malasaña* ☎ *91/704–6030* ⊕ *www.lafiambrera.net* ⊗ *Closed Sun. and Mon.* Ⓜ *Noviciado, Santo Domingo.*

BOOKS

J&J Books and Coffee

BOOKS | A block off San Bernardo, this is a charming café and bookstore with a good selection of used books in English. They sell bagels, too—a rarity in Madrid. ⊠ *Calle del Espíritu Santo 47, Malasaña* ☎ *91/521–8576* ⊕ *jandjbooksandcoffee. weebly.com* Ⓜ *Noviciado.*

BOUTIQUES AND FASHION

★ Antigua Casa Crespo

SHOES | *Alpargatas*, or espadrilles, grace the feet of chic beachgoers from Nantucket to Nevis, but Madrileños have been rocking these rope-soled sandals (in some form or another) for at least six centuries. Antigua Casa Crespo opened in 1863 on what was then the outskirts of town, and it remains the city's most legendary *alpargatería*, thanks to the breadth of styles, colors, and patterns on offer. Their wares are still made by hand from esparto grass in Spain. ⊠ *Calle del Divino Pastor 29, Malasaña* ☎ *91/521– 5654* ⊕ *www.antiguacasacrespo.com* ⊗ *Closed Sun.* Ⓜ *San Bernardo.*

★ Aramayo

MIXED CLOTHING | A well-curated selection of vintage threads keeps this boutique packed with cool kids. There's a particularly wide selection of billowy patterned shirts and worn-in Levis. There's another location by Sol at Plaza de Herradores 8. ■TIP➜ **As in all vintage stores, be sure to check garments for stains, tears, and missing buttons before buying.** ⊠ *Corredera Alta de San Pablo 2, Malasaña* ☎ *91/013– 4753* ⊕ *aramayo.es* Ⓜ *Tribunal.*

Magpie Vintage

MIXED CLOTHING | A fashion temple that screams "Movida Madrileña," the '80s countercultural movement that ushered Madrid into the modern era, this vintage store is decked out with wildly patterned skirts and dresses and fluorescent track jackets. ⊠ *Calle de Velarde 3, Malasaña* ☎ *91/448–3104* ⊕ *www.magpie.es* ⊗ *Closed Sun.* Ⓜ *Bilbao.*

Sportivo

MEN'S CLOTHING | Time to bust out the big bucks—Sportivo is one of the best menswear boutiques in the city, with two floors of hand-picked garments by the buzziest designers out of Spain, France, Japan, and beyond. ⊠ *Calle del Conde Duque 20, Malasaña* ☎ *91/542–5661* ⊕ *www.sportivostore.com* Ⓜ *Ventura Rodríguez.*

FOOD

★ Quesería Cultivo

FOOD | This sleek cheese shop with on-site "caves" for aging is a cheese lover's paradise. Seek out rare treasures like Torrejón, a raw ashed-rind sheep's cheese from Castile, and snap up a bottle of organic Spanish wine while you're at it. There's a second location in La Latina on Carrera de San Francisco 14. ⊠ *Calle del Conde Duque 15, Malasaña* ☎ *91/0000–300* ⊕ *www.queseriacultivo. com* ⊗ *Closed Sun.* Ⓜ *San Bernardo.*

Chapter 6

BARRIO DE LAS LETRAS

6

Updated by
Benjamin Kemper

 Sights
★★☆☆☆

 Restaurants
★★★★★

 Hotels
★★★★★

 Shopping
★★★★☆

 Nightlife
★★★★★

NEIGHBORHOOD SNAPSHOT

TOP EXPERIENCES

■ **Tapas:** Strike out on a tapas crawl in this buzzy, bar-lined neighborhood.

■ **Museo Thyssen-Bornemisza:** Time-travel to different eras of European art through some of the Continent's most prized works.

■ **Plaza de Santa Ana:** Claim a bench or outdoor table on this quintessentially Spanish square.

■ **Nightlife:** Dance until your legs are jelly at a trendy discoteca.

■ **Crafts:** Shop for one-of-a-kind artisan wares.

GETTING HERE

Letras is such a small neighborhood that no metro stop falls within its limits, but Sol (Líneas 1, 2, 3), Antón Martín (Línea 1), and Sevilla (Línea 2) are each less than a five-minute walk away. BiciMAD bike-share services the area with docks scattered throughout. Letras falls within the Madrid 360 low-emission zone, so check with your car rental agency to see if your particular vehicle is allowed entry.

PLANNING YOUR TIME

Evenings are particularly magical in Letras: traffic-free streets teem with groups of well-dressed Madrileños out for tapas and drinks, outdoor *terrazas* (terraces) overflow onto cobblestone plazas, and historical buildings are lit up to reveal dramatic facades. As the night wears on, restaurants close shop and cocktail bars and nightclubs become the center of the action. Dining and nightlife are Letras's main attractions, but don't let that dissuade you from wandering the area by day, when streets are comparatively tranquil, museums like the Thyssen-Bornemisza are open, and restaurants and cafés aren't short on tables.

FUN FACT

What's in a name? Before Letras was Letras, the barrio was called Huertas del Prado, or "Orchards of the Prado." Indeed, the name Calle de las Huertas ("Street of the Orchards"), the neighborhood's main artery, harks back to a time when the road ran between fruit trees and vegetable gardens.

Barrio de las Letras (just "Letras" to locals) is known for its charming balconied buildings and electric restaurant and bar scene. Once a *castizo* (Madrid jargon for "authentic") part of town, Letras is now packed with well-to-do tourists and Madrid's nouveau riche. In short, it's a *scene.*

Letras is a historical (read: unofficial) neighborhood that technically belongs to the district of Cortes, but Madrileños use its colloquial name, celebrating the writers and playwrights of the Spanish Golden Age who lived here. At the heart of the barrio is Plaza de Santa Ana with its noble buildings, iconic theater, and crowded tapas bars, though you'll see more locals wining and dining on and around the pedestrianized Calle de las Huertas. As you explore, remember to look down—sidewalks here bear quotes in bronze from the neighborhood's one-time denizens—Quevedo, Góngora, Lope de Vega, and Cervantes, to name a few.

◉ Sights

CaixaForum

ART MUSEUM | Swiss architects Jacques Herzog and Pierre de Meuron (who designed London's Tate Modern) converted an early-20th-century power station into a stunning arts complex that arguably turns Madrid's "Golden Triangle" of art museums into a quadrilateral. Belonging to one of the country's wealthiest foundations (La Caixa bank), the structure seems to float above the sloped public plaza, with a tall vertical garden designed by French botanist Patrick Blanc on its northern side contrasting with a geometric rust-color roof. Inside, the soaring exhibition halls display ancient as well as contemporary art including pieces from La Caixa's proprietary collection. ⊠ *Paseo del Prado 36, Barrio de las Letras* ☎ *91/330–7300* ⊕ *caixaforum.org/es/madrid* ⊠ *€6* Ⓜ *Estación del Arte.*

Casa Museo Lope de Vega

HISTORIC HOME | A contemporary and adversary of Cervantes, Lope de Vega (1562–1635) wrote some 1,800 plays and enjoyed great success during his lifetime. His former home is now a museum with an intimate look into a bygone era: everything from the whale-oil lamps and candles to the well in the tiny garden and the pans used to warm the bedsheets brings you closer to the great dramatist. Thirty-five-minute guided tours in English are by reservation only (either by phone or email) and run through the playwright's professional and personal life—including his lurid love life—while touching on 17th-century traditions. ⊠ *Calle de Cervantes 11, Barrio de las Letras* ☎ *91/429–9216* ✎ *casamuseolopedevega@madrid.org* ⊕ *www.casamuseolopedevega.org* ⊠ *Free* ⊙ *Closed Mon.* ☞ *Advance booking required* Ⓜ *Antón Martín, Sol.*

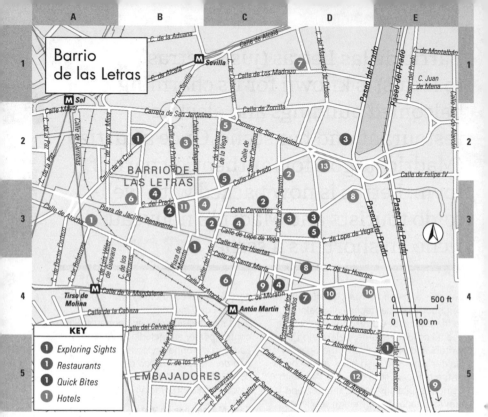

Barrio de las Letras

The vertical outdoor garden is a stunning element of the CaixaForum cultural center. The sculpture in front of the building is changed periodically.

★ Museo Thyssen-Bornemisza

ART MUSEUM | The far-reaching collection of the Thyssen's almost 1,000 paintings traces the history of Western art with examples from every important movement, from 13th-century Italian Gothic through 20th-century American pop art. The works were gathered from the 1920s to the 1980s by Swiss industrialist Baron Hans Heinrich Thyssen-Bornemisza and his father; the museum, inaugurated in 1992, occupies the light-filled galleries of the late-18th-century *Palacio de Villahermosa*. Critics have described the museum's paintings as the minor works of major artists and the major works of minor artists, and the collection traces the development of Western humanism as no other in the world.

One highlight is Hans Holbein's *Portrait of Henry VIII*. American artists are also well represented; look for the Gilbert Stuart portrait of Impressionists and Post–Impressionists including Camille Pissarro, Pierre-Auguste Renoir, Claude Monet, Edgar Degas, Vincent van Gogh,

and Paul Cézanne. Track down Pissarro's *Rue Saint-Honoré in the Afternoon, Effect of Rain* for a jolt of mortality, or Renoir's *Woman with a Parasol in a Garden* for a sense of bucolic beauty lost.

Within 20th-century art, the collection is strong on dynamic German Expressionism and works by Georgia O'Keeffe, Andrew Wyeth, Edward Hopper, Francis Bacon, Robert Rauschenberg, and Roy Lichtenstein. The temporary exhibits can be fascinating and in summer are sometimes open until 11 pm. In summer, the rooftop terrace (closed Mondays; accessible via a separate entrance on Calle de Zorrilla) is an appealing place to kick back with a coffee or cocktail. You can buy tickets to the museum in advance online. ✉ *Paseo del Prado 8, Barrio de las Letras* ☎ *91/791–1370* ⊕ *www.museothyssen. org* ✉ *€13. Free Mon. with online reservation* Ⓜ *Banco de España.*

Plaza de Santa Ana

PLAZA/SQUARE | This plaza was the heart of the theater district in the 17th century—the Golden Age of Spanish literature—and is now one of Madrid's most happening nightlife centers. A statue of 17th-century playwright Pedro Calderón de la Barca faces the Teatro Español, where other literary legends such as Lope de Vega, Tirso de Molina, and Ramón María del Valle-Inclán released some of their world-renowned plays. Opposite the theater, beside the ME by Meliá hotel, is the diminutive Plaza del Ángel, with one of Madrid's best jazz clubs, Café Central. Cervecería Alemana, a favorite haunt of Hemingway, is on the southeast corner and makes phenomenally tender fried calamari. ⊠ *Barrio de las Letras* Ⓜ *Sol, Sevilla.*

 Restaurants

Amano
$$ | TAPAS | *A mano* means "by hand" in Spanish, and lest this experimental white-walled tapas and wine bar come across as pretentious, there's an entire section of the menu devoted to finger food. Whet your appetite with one-bite wonders like fried eggplant drizzled with honey and garlicky *salmorejo* (a cold tomato soup), then settle in for heftier plates like stewed oxtail, which basically melts on fork impact. **Known for:** innovative vegetable-driven tapas; varied wine list with French selections; stylish minimalist interiors. Ⓢ *Average main: €24* ⊠ *Pl. de Matute 4, Barrio de las Letras* ☎ *91/527–7970* ⊕ *amanorest. com* ☺ *Closed Mon. and Tues.* Ⓜ *Antón Martín.*

★ Casa González
$ | SPANISH | This gourmet shop (est. 1931) doubles as a cozy bar where you can sample most of the stuff on the shelves, including canned asparagus, charcuterie, anchovies, and a varied well-priced selection of Spanish cheeses and wines. It also serves good inexpensive breakfasts. **Known for:** regional wines and cheeses; delectable sobrassada-honey toast; quaint setting. Ⓢ *Average main:*

€11 ⊠ *Calle del León 12, Barrio de las Letras* ☎ *91/429–5618* ⊕ *www.casagonzalez.es* Ⓜ *Antón Martín.*

El Barril de las Letras
$$$ | SEAFOOD | Seafood lovers shouldn't miss this modern, Ibiza-chic *marisquería* (seafood restaurant) with original wrought-iron columns, white tablecloths, and ample alfresco seating. The griddled prawns from Dénia are always a treat, as are the cloudlike roasted sole and any number of rice dishes. **Known for:** romantic ambience; impeccable seafood; outdoor dining. Ⓢ *Average main: €29* ⊠ *Calle de Cervantes 28, Barrio de las Letras* ☎ *91/186–3632* ⊕ *barrildelasletras. com* Ⓜ *Antón Martín.*

Gofio
$$$$ | FUSION | Savor a rare taste of Canary Island cuisine—with quite a few twists—at this envelope-pushing, Michelin-starred restaurant helmed by Tenerife-born chef Safe Cruz. Expect foaming, smoking concoctions that incorporate traditional Canarian specialties like green mojo, Gomero goat cheese, and—of course—*gofio* (stone-ground corn flour). **Known for:** Canarian fine dining at a value; smoky volcanic wines; gorgeous uncontrived plating. Ⓢ *Average main: €65* ⊠ *Calle de Lope de Vega 9, Barrio de las Letras* ☎ *91/599–4404* ⊕ *gofiorestaurant. com* ☺ *Closed Mon. and Tues.* Ⓜ *Antón Martín.*

La Huerta de Tudela
$$ | SPANISH | Real talk: it can be hard to find a vegetable in Madrid. But in Navarra, the region this restaurant looks to for inspiration, there's never a shortage of asparagus, artichokes, cardoons, piquillo peppers, and other seasonal delicacies. **Known for:** vegetarian- and celiac-friendly cuisine; many bottles of wine under €20; delectable crispy artichokes. Ⓢ *Average main: €24* ⊠ *Calle del Prado 15, Barrio de las Letras* ☎ *91/420–4418* ⊕ *www.lahuertadetudela.com* Ⓜ *Antón Martín.*

While exploring the side streets that branch off Plaza de Santa Ana, keep an eye out for the various tapas restaurants, art galleries, bookstores, and boutiques that make this neighborhood so authentic.

La Sanabresa

$ | SPANISH | FAMILY | Most budget prix fixes in Madrid are limited to lunch, but La Sanabresa offers a budget three-course dinner as well. Choose from over 20 appetizers and 40 entrées that comprise a highlight reel of grandmotherly Spanish cuisine: gazpacho, ensaladilla rusa, fried anchovies, chicken cutlets, and on and on. **Known for:** prix fixes are a steal; traditional holdout in a gentrified area; satisfying soups and stews. Ⓢ *Average main: €14* ✉ *Calle del Amor de Dios 12, Barrio de las Letras* ☎ *91/429–0338* ☉ *Closed Sun.* Ⓜ *Antón Martín.*

Sua by Triciclo

$$$$ | STEAKHOUSE | Madrid's best modern steak house, Sua ("fire" in Basque) is dedicated to meats and wild-caught fish cooked over open flame. Occupying a stunning circular indoor courtyard, the restaurant has an ample list of Champagnes, cavas, and bold Spanish reds, fittingly luxurious sidekicks to a 40-day dry-aged sirloin from Galicia or roasted scarlet shrimp plucked from Andalusia's Atlantic coast. **Known for:** flame-licked steaks and seafood; impressive cathedral-like dining room; attentive service. Ⓢ *Average main: €32* ✉ *Calle de Moratín 22, Barrio de las Letras* ☎ *91/527–7165* ⊕ *www.suabytriciclo.com/en* ▭ *No credit cards* ☉ *Closed Tues.* Ⓜ *Antón Martín.*

★ Taberna La Elisa

$$ | TAPAS | The old-fashioned *azulejo* (glazed tile) walls, painted red facade, and squat wooden barstools might fool you into thinking this newcomer is any old tavern, but behind the swinging door, cooks are busy plating novel takes on tapas that you didn't know needed improving. Take the crispy pig ear, doused in the usual spicy brava sauce—it gets an unorthodox hit of freshness from tarragon-packed mojo verde. **Known for:** flavor-bomb tapas; Andalusian-style decor; trendy crowd. Ⓢ *Average main: €23* ✉ *Calle de Santa María 42, Barrio de las Letras* ☎ *91/421–6409* ⊕ *www. tabernalaelisa.com* Ⓜ *Antón Martín.*

★ Triciclo

$$$ | TAPAS | Triciclo serves inventive Spanish-style bistronomie—think baby Asturian favas with mushrooms and seaweed-and-spot-prawn ravioli with saffron and borage. R *aciones* (sharing dishes), in one-third portions as well as half and full ones, are ideal for creating your own tasting menu whether at the bar or in the dining room. **Known for:** tapas with a modern twist; time-honored institution; excellent service. Ⓢ *Average main: €27* ✉ *Calle de Santa María 28, Barrio de las Letras* ☎ *91/024–4798* ⊕ *www.restaurantetriciclo.com* ☾ *Closed Sun.* Ⓜ *Antón Martín.*

Vinoteca Moratín

$$ | SPANISH | You'd be hard-pressed to find a more romantic restaurant than this snug wine bar with a rotating menu of a dozen or so dishes and eclectic Spanish wines. Antique wooden tables are tucked among bookshelves and wine cabinets, and fresh flowers grace the entryway and wait stations. **Known for:** Spanish wine list with quirky small-production bottles; seasonal bistro fare; intimate ambience. Ⓢ *Average main: €19* ✉ *Calle de Moratín 36, Barrio de las Letras* ☎ *91/127–6085* ⊕ *www.vinotecamoratin.com* ☾ *Closed Sun. and Mon.* Ⓜ *Antón Martín.*

☕ Coffee and Quick Bites

Casa Toni

$ | TAPAS | The tapas are offal-y good at this pocket-size bar specializing in variety meats like pig ear (served crackly with spicy brava sauce) and *zarajos* (lamb intestines wrapped around a stick and fried until crisp, an old-school Madrid snack). **Known for:** terrific offal tapas; shockingly affordable; legendary greasy spoon. Ⓢ *Average main: €12* ✉ *Calle de la Cruz 14, Barrio de las Letras* ☾ *Closed Tues.* Ⓜ *Sol, Antón Martín.*

Cervecería Alemana

$ | TAPAS | Fried calamari *a la romana* , made with fresh, ultra-tender squid as opposed to the standard frozen stuff, is the star tapa at this 117-year-old Hemingway hangout that's confusingly not *Alemana* (German) in the slightest. **Known for:** top-notch calamari; white-suited waiters with big personalities; historical digs. Ⓢ *Average main: €14* ✉ *Pl. de Santa Ana 6, Barrio de las Letras* ☎ *91/429–7033* ⊕ *www.cerveceriaalemana.com* Ⓜ *Sol, Antón Martín.*

Cervecería Cervantes

$ | TAPAS | Cervecería Cervantes is improbably down-to-earth for such a posh, tourist-oriented neighborhood—the kind of place where you throw your olive pits right onto the floor. Most patrons come for the ice-cold *cañas* (half-pints), but there are traditional tapas of varying quality. **Known for:** free tapa with beer; diamond in the touristy rough; perfect for a drink after the Prado. Ⓢ *Average main: €15* ✉ *Pl. de Jesús 7, Barrio de las Letras* ☎ *91/429–6093* ☾ *No dinner Sun.* Ⓜ *Antón Martín.*

★ Chocolat Madrid

$ | CAFÉ | FAMILY | Always crisp and never greasy—that's the mark of a well-made churro, and Madrid Chocolat's piping-hot baskets of fried dough always hit the spot. **Known for:** comfortable dining area; city's best churros; terrific grilled ham-and-cheese sandwiches. Ⓢ *Average main: €6* ✉ *Calle de Santa María 30, Barrio de las Letras* ☎ *91/429–4565* ⊕ *chocolatmadrid.com* Ⓜ *Antón Martín.*

La Dolores

$ | TAPAS | A lively corner bar with a colorful trencadís-tiled facade, this is a solid spot for a cold beer and a nosh after visiting the nearby museums. Try the *matrimonio* ("marriage") tapa, which weds one pickled and one cured anchovy on a slice of crusty baguette. **Known for:** affordable no-nonsense tapas; refreshing cañas; mixed crowd of foreigners and locals. Ⓢ *Average main: €12* ✉ *Pl. de Jesús 4, Barrio de las Letras* ☎ *91/429–2243* Ⓜ *Antón Martín.*

Hotels

Catalonia Puerta del Sol
$$ | **HOTEL** | The regal cobblestone corridor leading to the reception desk, the atrium with granite ashlar walls, and the magnificent wooden staircase (presided over by a lion statue) reveal this building's 18th-century origins. **Pros:** grand quiet building; spacious rooms; generous breakfast bar. **Cons:** rather uncharming street; rooms are slightly dated; smoking permitted in the courtyard. *[$] Rooms from: €190 ✉ Calle de Atocha 23, Barrio de las Letras ☎ 91/369–7171 🌐 www.cataloniahotels.com/en/hotel/catalonia-puerta-del-sol 🛏 63 rooms 🍴 No Meals [M] Tirso de Molina.*

DoubleTree by Hilton Madrid-Prado
$$$ | **HOTEL** | This DoubleTree may appear corporate, but any stuffiness is mitigated by a warm staff eager to help with every need. **Pros:** relaxing earth-tone accents; excellent in-room amenities; one of the city's best Japanese restaurants. **Cons:** no valet parking; dull bar; no sense of place. *[$] Rooms from: €291 ✉ Calle de San Agustín 3, Barrio de las Letras ☎ 91/360–0820 🌐 www.hilton.com/en/hotels/madprdi-doubletree-madrid-prado/ 🛏 61 rooms 🍴 No Meals [M] Antón Martín.*

Gran Hotel Inglés
$$$$ | **HOTEL** | This legendary hotel, inaugurated in 1853, is the oldest in Madrid—and after a painstaking renovation by Rockwell Group, it reopened in 2018 to great fanfare. **Pros:** one of the city's most iconic hotels; magazine-cover-worthy design; made-to-order breakfasts featuring artisanal Spanish products. **Cons:** disappointing Casa Lobo restaurant; phenomenally expensive; street noise. *[$] Rooms from: €586 ✉ Calle de Echegaray 8, Barrio de las Letras ☎ 91/360–0001 🌐 www.granhotelingles.com 🛏 48 rooms 🍴 No Meals [M] Sevilla.*

Hotel Catalonia Las Cortes
$$$ | **HOTEL** | In a late-18th-century palace formerly owned by the Duke of Noblejas, this hotel, a few yards from Plaza de Santa Ana, still bears traces of opulence and grandeur. **Pros:** blissfully underpriced; big walk-in showers; gorgeous architectural details. **Cons:** common areas are rather dull; no gym, pool, or spa; no bar. *[$] Rooms from: €220 ✉ Calle del Prado 6, Barrio de las Letras ☎ 91/389–6051 🌐 www.cataloniahotels.com/en/hotel/catalonia-las-cortes 🛏 74 rooms 🍴 No Meals [M] Sevilla, Antón Martín.*

Hotel Urban
$$$$ | **HOTEL** | A five-minute walk from Puerta del Sol and Parque del Buen Retiro (El Retiro Park), Hotel Urban blends buttoned-up business aesthetics with tropical accents in the form of Papua New Guinean artifacts and other rare museum-grade works. **Pros:** stellar à la carte breakfasts; roof deck that's a destination in itself; celebrity chef restaurant. **Cons:** smallish rooms with so-so soundproofing; tiny gym with no treadmill; early-aughts interiors in desperate need of renovation. *[$] Rooms from: €309 ✉ Carrera de San Jerónimo 34, Barrio de las Letras ☎ 91/787–7770 🌐 www.hotelurban.com 🛏 103 rooms 🍴 No Meals [M] Sevilla.*

★ ME Madrid Reina Victoria
$$$$ | **HOTEL** | In an unbeatable location, this historic hotel used to play host to visiting bullfighters (hence the bulls' heads hanging in the lounge), but it's decidedly more hip these days under the management of Meliá's youthful subdivision, ME. **Pros:** cool clubby vibe; unbeatable location; rooftop bar with great views of city. **Cons:** some rooms are cramped; plaza-facing rooms can be noisy; key cards demagnetize easily. *[$] Rooms from: €312 ✉ Pl. de Santa Ana 14, Barrio de las Letras ☎ 91/701–6000 🌐 www.melia.com/en/hotels/spain/madrid/me-madrid-reina-victoria 🛏 192 rooms 🍴 No Meals [M] Sol.*

NH Collection Madrid Suecia
$$$$ | **HOTEL** | The building housing the NH Collection Madrid Suecia was once home

to Ernest Hemingway and Che Guevara; today's guests are decidedly tamer, but the retro aesthetic lives on in the hotel's brown velvet couches, towering tropical plants, and suave concierges. **Pros:** renovated rooms; rooftop bar with great views; nine-minute walk from the Prado. **Cons:** robes and slippers not provided in entry-level rooms; windowless gym; overpriced restaurant. $ *Rooms from: €309* ⊠ *Calle del Marqués de Casa Riera 4, Barrio de las Letras* ☎ *91/200–0570* ⊕ *www.nh-hotels.com/hotel/nh-collection-madrid-suecia* ⇨ *123 rooms* ⦿ *No Meals* Ⓜ *Banco de España.*

NH Collection Paseo del Prado

$$$ | HOTEL | In a turn-of-the-20th-century palace overlooking Plaza de Neptuno, this hotel preserves the building's erstwhile grandeur with wooden headboards, gold-framed mirrors, tufted sofas, and wing chairs. **Pros:** within the Golden Triangle of museums; gym with panoramic views; "lazy Sunday checkout" at 3 pm. **Cons:** need to upgrade to get good views; inconsistent food at Estado Puro; uninspiring interiors. $ *Rooms from: €298* ⊠ *Pl. Cánovas del Castillo 4, Barrio de las Letras* ☎ *91/330–2400* ⊕ *www.nh-hotels.com/hotel/nh-collection-madrid-paseo-del-prado* ⇨ *115 rooms* ⦿ *No Meals* Ⓜ *Banco de España.*

Only YOU Hotel Atocha

$$$ | HOTEL | One of the trendiest, most youthful hotels in town, Only YOU Atocha has a swanky high-design lobby, rooftop restaurant, spacious gym, and industrial-chic accommodations. **Pros:** gorgeous designer furniture; intriguing pop-ups and events; cloud-soft beds. **Cons:** exterior-facing rooms are very noisy; food quality falls short; looks out over major intersection. $ *Rooms from: €215* ⊠ *Paseo de la Infanta Isabel 13, Barrio de las Letras* ☎ *91/409–7876* ⊕ *www.onlyyouhotels.com/hoteles/only-you-hotel-atocha* ⇨ *205 rooms* ⦿ *No Meals* Ⓜ *Estación del Arte.*

Radisson Blu Hotel, Madrid Prado

$$$$ | HOTEL | Surprisingly boutique-y for a Radisson, this hotel has a streamlined urban feel that suits its middle-of-it-all location. **Pros:** pool and spa; room service; breakfast from 6:30 am. **Cons:** some standard rooms are rather small; pricey breakfast; middling restaurant. $ *Rooms from: €310* ⊠ *Calle de Moratín 52, Barrio de las Letras* ☎ *91/524–2626* ⊕ *www.radissonhotels.com/en-us/hotels/radisson-blu-madrid-prado* ⇨ *54 rooms* ⦿ *No Meals* Ⓜ *Estación del Arte.*

Room Mate Alicia

$$$ | HOTEL | Room Mate Alicia's all-white lobby with curving walls, backlit ceiling panels, and gilded columns oozes early 2000s, but its prime location and competitive rates make up for the passé aesthetics. **Pros:** central location; brightly colored rooms; laid-back atmosphere. **Cons:** standard rooms are small; underwhelming breakfast; no restaurant or gym. $ *Rooms from: €265* ⊠ *Calle del Prado 2, Barrio de las Letras* ☎ *91/389–6095* ⊕ *room-matehotels.com/en/alicia/* ⇨ *34 rooms* ⦿ *No Meals* Ⓜ *Sevilla.*

URBANSEA Atocha 113

$$ | HOTEL | A metropolitan outpost of the Blue Sea resort chain, URBANSEA Atocha 113 is a basic 36-room hotel just north of the eponymous railway station. **Pros:** equidistant between Barrio de las Letras and Lavapiés; complimentary 24-hour coffee in lobby; single rooms ideal for solo travelers. **Cons:** bare-bones services and somewhat deteriorated facilities; in-room sinks and bathrooms with no doors in some rooms; exterior rooms facing Calle de Atocha are noisy and pricey. $ *Rooms from: €145* ⊠ *Calle de Atocha 113, Barrio de las Letras* ☎ *91/369–2895* ⊕ *www.blueseahotels.com/en/hoteles/destinos/madrid/madrid-centro/urbansea-atocha-113* ⇨ *36 rooms* ⦿ *No Meals* Ⓜ *Estación del Arte.*

Westin Palace

$$$$ | HOTEL | Situated inside the "Golden Triangle," the Westin Palace is known for

its unbeatable location, stately facade, and classical decor. **Pros:** historic grand hotel; 24-hour gym with adjoining roof deck; rooms have USB ports and antifog mirrors. **Cons:** standard rooms face a backstreet; overpriced; won't meet design lovers' expectations. [$] *Rooms from: €378* ✉ *Pl. de las Cortés 7, Barrio de las Letras* ☎ *91/360–8000* 🌐 *www.palacemadrid.com* 🛏 *467 rooms* 🍴 *No Meals* [M] *Banco de España, Sevilla.*

Nightlife

BARS

Bocanada

WINE BARS | Blink and you could miss this tiny, dimly lit wine bar presided over by a trained sommelier with a predilection for oddball bottles. Go on a weeknight, when you're more likely to snag a stool, and don't miss the modern tapas, which punch above their weight. ✉ *Calle del León 5, Barrio de las Letras* ☎ *60/665–6083* 🕒 *Closed Mon. and Tues.* [M] *Sevilla, Antón Martín.*

Casa Alberto

BARS | This 194-year-old bar will transport you to a typical Spanish tavern of yore. The banged-up tin washbasin, the baroque cash register, the wooden bar shelves and low tables with wooden stools—these details haven't changed in over a century. The house vermouth is the tipple to try; elbow your way to the onyx-topped bar and sip it with a handful of olives or cheese (skip the underwhelming food). ✉ *Calle de las Huertas 18, Barrio de las Letras* ☎ *91/429–9356* 🌐 *www.casaalberto.es* 🕒 *Closed Mon.* [M] *Antón Martín.*

La Venencia

WINE BARS | This dusty sherry-only bar hasn't changed a lick since the Spanish Civil War, from its no-tipping policy to its salty waiters to its chalked bar tabs. The establishment is named for the tool used to extract sherry through the bunghole of a barrel. ✉ *Calle de Echegaray 7, Barrio de las Letras* ☎ *91/429–7313* 🌐 *www.lavenencia.com* [M] *Sol.*

RADIO

COCKTAIL LOUNGES | This sceney bar in the ME Madrid Reina Victoria is split between a bottom-floor lounge and a more exclusive rooftop terrace with 360-degree views—a boon to chic summer revelers both local and international. The doorman planted outside means you shouldn't dress too casual. ✉ *ME Madrid Reina Victoria, Pl. de Santa Ana 14, Barrio de las Letras* ☎ *91/445–6886* 🌐 *radiomemadrid.com* [M] *Antón Martín.*

Salmon Guru

COCKTAIL LOUNGES | Regularly featured on best-of lists, Salmon Guru is Madrid's—and perhaps Spain's—most innovative coctelería. Come here to impress and geek out over eye-popping concoctions like the Chipotle Chillón, made with mezcal, absinthe, and chipotle syrup. The *nueva cocina* tapas are almost as impressive as the drinks. ✉ *Calle de Echegaray 21, Barrio de las Letras* ☎ *91/000–6185* 🌐 *www.salmonguru.es* [M] *Antón Martín.*

★ **Viva Madrid**

COCKTAIL LOUNGES | The Argentine celebrity mixologist behind Salmon Guru has converted one of Madrid's oldest tabernas, built in 1856, into a see-and-be-seen cocktail hot spot. The building's architectural bones remain, from the carved-wood bar to the arched doorways to the tiled walls, but the rest, particularly the flamboyantly garnished drinks and well-dressed crowd, feels distinctly current. ✉ *Calle de Manuel Fernández y González 7, Barrio de las Letras* ☎ *91/605–9774* 🌐 *vivamadrid1856.com* 🕒 *Closed Mon.* [M] *Sevilla, Antón Martín.*

DANCE CLUBS

Discoteca Azúcar

DANCE CLUBS | Salsa dancing is a fixture of Madrid nightlife. Even if you don't have the guts to twirl and shake with the pros on the dance floor, you'll be almost as entertained sipping a mojito on the sidelines. Entry with two cocktail vouchers costs €12. ⊠ *Calle de Atocha 107, Barrio de las Letras* 🕾 *91/429–6208* ⊕ *azucarsalsadisco.com* ⊗ *Closed Sun.– Wed.* Ⓜ *Estación del Arte.*

Independance Club

DANCE CLUBS | Your favorite underground European artist has likely played at this perennially packed venue with a large subterranean dance floor and good sound and lights. ⊠ *Calle de Atocha 125, Barrio de las Letras* 🕾 *68/351–6474* ⊕ *indepandanceclub.com* ⊗ *Closed Sun.–Tues.* Ⓜ *Estación del Arte.*

★ Teatro Kapital

DANCE CLUBS | Madrid's most famous nightclub, Kapital has seven floors—each of which plays a different type of music (spun by top local and international DJs, of course)—and room for 2,000 partiers, plus a small movie theater and rooftop terrace. Dress to impress: no sneakers, shorts, or tanks allowed. VIP tables overlooking the dance floor (approximately €200 for four people) are a worthwhile splurge if you can swing it. ⊠ *Calle de Atocha 125, Barrio de las Letras* 🕾 *91/420–2906* ⊕ *www.grupo-kapital. com* ⊗ *Closed Mon. and Tues.* Ⓜ *Estación del Arte.*

MUSIC CLUBS

★ Café Central

LIVE MUSIC | Madrid's best-known jazz venue is swanky, and the musicians are often internationally known. Performances are usually 9–11 nightly, and tickets can be bought at the door or online. ⊠ *Pl. de Ángel 10, Barrio de las Letras* 🕾 *91/369–4143* ⊕ *www.cafecentralmadrid.com* Ⓜ *Antón Martín.*

FLAMENCO

★ Cardamomo Tablao Flamenco

THEMED ENTERTAINMENT | Ask a local flamenco aficionado where to catch a rollicking, foot-stomping show and they're likely to recommend this brick-walled *tablao*, which is intimate enough that everybody feels like they're in the front row. A handful of Spanish dishes are available, but suffice to say, flamenco is Cardamomo's forte. ⊠ *Calle de Echegaray 15, Barrio de las Letras* 🕾 *91/805–1038* ⊕ *cardamomo.com* Ⓜ *Sol, Antón Martín.*

Shopping

BOUTIQUES AND FASHION

★ ANDRESGALLARDO

JEWELRY & WATCHES | Madrid's porcelain whisperer, Gallardo fashions second-hand shards and custom-made porcelain elements into runway-ready jewelry and accessories. ⊠ *Calle de San Pedro 8, Barrio de las Letras* 🕾 *91/053–5352* ⊕ *andresgallardo.com* ⊗ *Closed Sun.* Ⓜ *Antón Martín.*

Elisa & Eduardo Rivera

MIXED CLOTHING | This is the flagship store of two young Spanish designers with clothes and accessories for both men and women. All garments are handmade in an atelier north of Madrid. Other stores can be found on ⊠ *Calle de Sagasta 4* and ⊠ *Calle del Clavel 4.* ⊠ *Pl. del Ángel 4, Barrio de las Letras* 🕾 *91/521–5145* ⊕ *www.eduardorivera.es* Ⓜ *Sol.*

Peseta

JEWELRY & WATCHES | Shop made-in-Spain handbags, backpacks, clutches, totes, and more at this boutique by Asturian seamstress and fashion designer Laura Martínez. Expect splashy, wild patterns in every hue. ⊠ *Calle de las Huertas 37, Barrio de las Letras* 🕾 *91/052–5971* ⊕ *www. peseta.org* Ⓜ *Antón Martín.*

Santacana

OTHER SPECIALTY STORE | Keep your hands warm—and stylish—during Madrid's chilly winters with a pair of custom hand-made gloves by Santacana, a family-run glover that's been open since 1896. ⊠ *Calle de las Huertas 1, Barrio de las Letras* 🕾 *91/704–9670* ⊕ *santacana.es* Ⓜ *Antón Martín.*

Chapter 7

RETIRO AND SALAMANCA

Updated by
Benjamin Kemper

👁 Sights	🍴 Restaurants	🛏 Hotels	💼 Shopping	🍸 Nightlife
★★★★☆	★★★★☆	★★★★★	★★★★★	★★★☆☆

NEIGHBORHOOD SNAPSHOT

TOP EXPERIENCES

■ **Parque del Buen Retiro:** Walk, jog, or rent a rowboat and bob around the carp-filled *estanque* (pool).

■ **Museo del Prado:** Feast your eyes on some of the world's most iconic and recognizable paintings.

■ **Tapas:** Hop around the bar-lined streets of Ibiza neighborhood and feast on rave-worthy upmarket tapas.

■ **Calle de Serrano:** Swipe your way down this high-end shopping street brimming with boutiques.

■ **Palacio de Cibeles:** Take the elevator to the observation deck for breathtaking views at sunset.

GETTING HERE

The Retiro district takes in such disparate neighborhoods as the noble Paseo del Arte (metro: Banco de España, Línea 2), containing the Prado and Real Jardín Botánico (Royal Botanical Garden); the well-to-do Ibiza (metro: Ibiza, Línea 9), popular for its tapas bars; the blue-collar, up-and-coming Pacífico (metro: Pacífico, Líneas 1, 6), home to the royal tapestry factory; and humbler residential barrios like Estrella and Adelfas (not included in this guide).

Directly above Parque del Buen Retiro (El Retiro Park) lies Salamanca, a famously posh district whose restaurants and boutiques are concentrated around the following metro stops: Retiro (Línea 2), Serrano (Línea 4), and Velázquez (Línea 4).

Retiro and Salamanca are serviced by the BiciMAD bike-share network and lie outside the "Madrid 360" low-emission zone, meaning all vehicles may enter. Parking lots dot both districts, a welcome convenience as street parking can be difficult to find on evenings and weekends.

PLANNING YOUR TIME

Take the better part of a day to explore, starting at the Prado (allot at least two hours) and continuing on to El Retiro Park, where a two-hour stroll is enough time to both see the main attractions—the central pond, Palacio de Cristal (Crystal Palace), and manicured gardens near the Felipe IV Gate—and unwind on a bench. Cross to the park's eastern edge and you're in the Ibiza neighborhood, an ideal spot for tapas; head north to Calle de Alcalá and you're in Salamanca, where clothing and jewelry shops intermingle with restaurants both classic and modern.

FUN FACT

In the northeast corner of El Retiro Park, a few steps in from Avenida de Menéndez Pelayo, you'll stumble upon the remains of the Ermita de San Pelayo y San Isidro (San Pelayo and San Isidoro Hermitage). The structure is one of Madrid's only examples of Romanesque architecture, dating to at least 1270. Curiously the ruins are from Ávila and were installed in the park in 1896 as a cultural site. Visible are the portal and apse.

Straighten your tie and zhuzh your hair—you've arrived in Madrid's equivalent of New York's Upper East Side or London's Kensington: a charming, tree-lined playground for the rich complete with luxury apartments, Michelin-starred restaurants, and one of Europe's most scenic parks, El Retiro Park.

But get off the main shopping streets and you'll see that these districts are not all glitz and glam. East and south of the park, in Retiro, you'll find upper-middle-class neighborhoods like Ibiza and Pacífico, with their fair share of modest apartments and mom-and-pop bars and restaurants. In addition to the eponymous park, the Retiro district holds the prestigious Prado, an essential stop on any Madrid itinerary. The sliver of Retiro real estate called Paseo del Arte (the Art Walk), sandwiched between the western side of the park and the Paseo del Prado, is where you'll find some of the city's most exclusive and expensive homes.

Salamanca was part of the 19th-century city expansion program called the Ensanche, which removed the city walls and created new, gridded neighborhoods. The area was originally intended to provide shelter for the working class, but because of its desirable parkside location, it swiftly became a hot spot for the well-to-do, a legacy that remains as the district contains the most expensive homes per square foot in the country.

Retiro

 Sights

Cuesta de Moyano
PEDESTRIAN MALL | Home to Europe's most expansive permanent book fair since 1925, this pedestrian avenue has around 30 wooden stalls filled with new and secondhand books. In addition to being a pleasant street to stroll—it connects Paseo del Prado with El Retiro Park—this is also a good place to find collectible and first-edition books. The tourist information kiosk hands out free English-language maps and brochures. ⊠ *Cuesta de Moyano s/n, Retiro* ⊕ *www. cuestamoyano.es.*

Estación de Atocha
TRAIN/TRAIN STATION | Madrid's main train station is a steel-and-glass hangar built in the late 19th century by Alberto de Palacio y Elissague, who became famous for his work with Ricardo Velázquez on the Palacio de Cristal in El Retiro Park. It was the site of one of the 2004 Al-Qaeda train bombings that collectively killed 193 and injured over 2,000, the topic of the 2022 Netflix documentary *11M: Terror in Madrid.* Today, following renovations

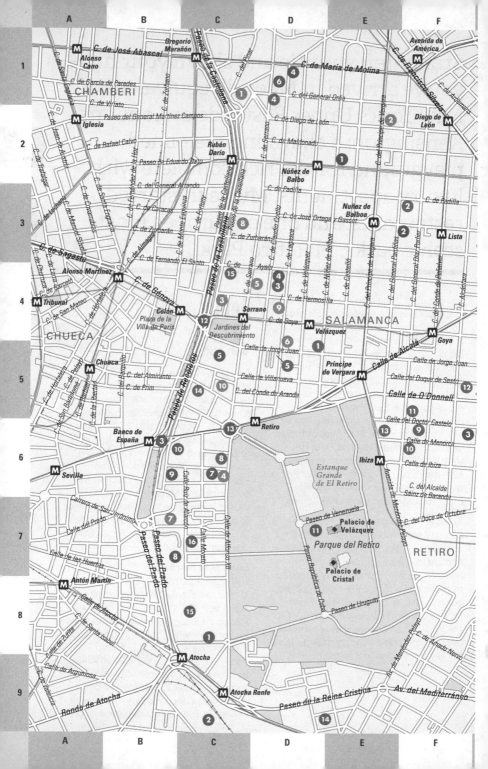

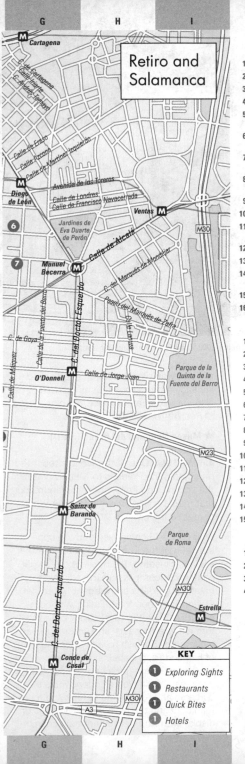

Retiro and Salamanca

KEY

1 Exploring Sights
1 Restaurants
1 Quick Bites
1 Hotels

Estación de Atocha's covered tropical garden contains 7,000 plants from more than 260 species.

by architect Rafael Moneo, the station's main hall resembles a greenhouse; it's filled with tropical trees and contains a busy turtle pool, a magnet for kids. ⚠ **Beware of detours and delays through 2024. In 2022, the city green-lit a €69 million renovation that will reroute the station's main entrance through the iconic wrought-iron façade facing Calle de Atocha.** ✉ *Paseo de Atocha s/n, Retiro* ☎ *91/243–2323* Ⓜ *Estación del Arte, Atocha RENFE.*

Fuente de Cibeles (*Cybele Fountain*)
FOUNTAIN | The Plaza de Cibeles, where three of Madrid's most affluent districts (Centro, Retiro, and Salamanca) intersect, is both an epicenter of municipal grandeur and a crash course in Spanish architecture. Two palaces, Buenavista and Linares (baroque and baroque revival, respectively), sit on the northern corners of the plaza and are dwarfed by the ornate Palacio de Cibeles. In the center of the plaza stands one of Madrid's most defining symbols, Cybele Fountain, a depiction of the Roman goddess of the Earth driving a lion-drawn chariot. During

the civil war, patriotic Madrileños risked life and limb to sandbag it as Franco's Nationalist aircraft bombed the city. ✉ *Retiro* Ⓜ *Banco de España.*

★ **Museo Nacional del Prado** (*Prado Museum*)
ART MUSEUM | One of the world's top museums, the Prado is to Madrid what the Louvre is to Paris: an iconic landmark that merits a visit by every traveler who comes to the city.

King Carlos III commissioned the construction of the Prado in 1785 as a natural science museum, the nucleus of a larger complex encompassing the adjoining botanical gardens and elegant Paseo del Prado. But when the building was completed in 1819, the royal family opted to turn it into a museum showcasing the art gathered by Spanish royalty since the time of Fernando and Isabel. In the 21st century the museum got a new building and wing resurrecting long-hidden works by Zurbarán and Antonio de Pereda and more than doubling the number of paintings on display from the permanent collection.

The Prado's jewels are by the nation's three great masters, Goya, Velázquez, and El Greco, though the museum also holds masterpieces by Flemish, Dutch, German, French, and Italian artists, collected when their lands were part of the Spanish Empire. The museum benefited greatly from the anticlerical laws of 1836, which forced monasteries, convents, and churches to forfeit many of their artworks for public display.

Enter the Prado via the Goya entrance, with steps opposite the Mandarin Oriental Ritz hotel. The layout varies (grab a floor plan), but the first halls on the left coming from the Goya entrance (Rooms 7A–11 on the second floor) are usually devoted to 17th-century Flemish painters, including Peter Paul Rubens (1577–1640), Jacob Jordaens (1593–1678), and Anthony van Dyck (1599–1641).

Room 12 introduces you to the meticulous brushwork of Velázquez (1599–1660) in his numerous portraits of kings and queens. Look for *Las Hilanderas* (*The Spinners*), evidence of the artist's talent for painting light. The Prado's most famous canvas, Velázquez's *Las Meninas* (*The Maids of Honor*), combines a self-portrait of the artist at work with a mirror reflection of the king and queen in a revolutionary interplay of space and perspectives. Picasso was obsessed with this work and painted several copies of it—now on display in the Picasso Museum in Barcelona—in his own abstract style.

The south ends of the second and top floors (*primera planta* and *segunda planta*) are reserved for Goya (1746–1828), whose works range from the bucolic to the horrific in tone. Among his early masterpieces are portraits of the family of King Carlos IV, for whom he was court painter. One glance at their unflattering and imbecilic expressions, especially in *The Family of Carlos IV,* reveals the loathing Goya developed for these self-indulgent, reactionary rulers. His famous

side-by-side canvases, *The Clothed Maja* and *The Nude Maja,* may represent the young Duchess of Alba, whom Goya adored and frequently painted. No one knows whether she ever returned his affection. The adjacent rooms house a series of idyllic scenes of Spaniards at play, painted as designs for tapestries.

Goya's paintings grew political around 1808, when Madrid rose up against occupying French troops. *The 2nd of May* portrays the insurrection at the Puerta del Sol, and its even more terrifying companion piece, *The 3rd of May,* depicts the nighttime executions of patriots who had rebelled the day before. The garish light in this work typifies the romantic style, which favors drama over detail, and makes it one of the most powerful indictments of violence ever committed to canvas. Goya's "Black Paintings" are dark, disturbing works, completed late in his life, that reflect his inner turmoil after losing his hearing and his embitterment over the bloody War of Independence. These are copies of the enormous, hallucinatory paintings Goya made with marvelously free brushstrokes on the walls of his house (known as La Quinta del Sordo: "the Deaf One's Villa"), situated near the Manzanares River. Don't miss the terrifying *Saturn Devouring One of His Sons* (which Goya displayed in his dining room!), a painting that communicates the ravages of age and time.

The Prado's ground floor (*planta baja*) is filled with 15th- and 16th-century Flemish paintings, including the bizarre proto-surrealist masterpiece *Garden of Earthly Delights* by Hieronymus Bosch (circa 1450–1516). In Rooms 60A, 61A, and 62A, contemplate the passionately spiritual works of El Greco (Doménikos Theotokópoulos, 1541–1614), the Greek-born artist who lived and worked in Toledo, known for his mystical elongated forms and faces—a style that was

Continued on page 119

EL PRADO:
MADRID'S BRUSH WITH GREATNESS

One of the world's top museums, the Prado is to Madrid what the Louvre is to Paris, or the Uffizi to Florence: a majestic city landmark and premier art institution that merits the attention of every traveler who visits the city.

The Prado celebrated its 200th anniversary in 2019, and its unparalleled collection of Spanish paintings (from the Romanesque period to the 19th century—don't expect to find Picassos here) makes it one of the most visited museums in the world. Foreign artists are also well represented—the collection includes masterpieces of European painting such as Hieronymus Bosch's *Garden of Earthly Delights*, *The Annunciation* by Fra Angelico, *Christ Washing the Disciples' Feet* by Tintoretto, and *The Three Graces* by Rubens—but the Prado is best known as home to more paintings by Diego Velázquez and Francisco de Goya than anywhere else.

Originally meant by King Charles III to become a museum of natural history, the Prado nevertheless opened, in 1819, as a sculpture and painting museum under the patronage of his grandchild, King Philip VII. For the first bewildered *madrileños* who crossed the museum's entrance back then, there were only about 300 paintings on display. Today there are more than 3 million visitors a year and 2,000-plus paintings are on display (the whole collection is estimated at about 8,000 canvases, plus 1,000 sculptures).

WHEN TO GO
The best time to visit the Prado is during lunch time, from 1-3, to beat the rush.

HUNGRY?
If your stomach rumbles during your visit, check out the café/restaurant in the foyer of the new building.

CONTACT INFORMATION
✉ Paseo del Prado s/n, 28014 Madrid
☎ (34) 91 330 2800.
⊕ www.museodelprado.es
Ⓜ Banco de España, Estacíon del Arte

HOURS OF OPERATION
🕐 Mon.–Sat. 10 AM–8 PM, Sun. 10 AM–7 PM, Closed New Year's Day, Fiesta del Trabajo (May 1), and Christmas.

ADMISSION
💶 €15. Free Mon. to Sat. 6 PM–8 PM, Sun. 5 PM-7 PM. To avoid lines, buy tickets in advance online.

The Trinity by El Greco, 1577. Oil on canvas.

THREE GREAT MASTERS

FRANCISCO DE GOYA 1746–1828

Goya's work spans a staggering range of tone, from bucolic to horrific, his idyllic paintings of Spaniards at play and portraits of the family of King Carlos IV contrasting with his dark, disturbing "black paintings." Goya's attraction to the macabre assured him a place in posterity, an ironic statement at the end of a long career in which he served as the official court painter to a succession of Spanish kings, bringing the art of royal portraiture to unknown heights.

Francisco de Goya

Goya found fame in his day as a portraitist, but he is admired by modern audiences for his depictions of the bizarre and the morbid. Beginning as a painter of decorative Rococo figures, he evolved into an artist of great depth in the employ of King Charles IV. The push-pull between Goya's love for his country and his disdain for the enemies of Spain yielded such masterpieces as *Third of May 1808*, painted after the French occupation ended. In the early 19th century, Goya's scandalous *The Naked Maja* brought him before the Spanish Inquisition, whose judgment was to end his tenure as a court painter.

DIEGO VELÁZQUEZ 1599–1660

A native of Seville, Velázquez gained fame at age 24 as court painter to King Philip IV. He developed a lifelike approach to religious art in which both saints and sinners were specific people rather than generic types. The supple brushwork of his ambitious history paintings and portraits was unsurpassed. Several visits to Rome, and his friendship with Rubens, made him the quintessential baroque painter with an international purview.

Diego Velázquez

DOMENIKOS THEOTOKOPOULOS
(AKA "EL GRECO") 1541–1614

El Greco's art was one of rapture and devotion, but beyond that his style is almost impossible to categorize. "The Greek" found his way from his native Crete to Spain through Venice; he spent most of his life in Toledo. His twisted, elongated figures imbue both his religious subjects and portraits with a sense of otherworldliness. While his palette and brushstrokes were inspired by Italian Mannerism, his approach to painting was uniquely his own. His inimitable style left few followers.

Domenikos Theotokopoulos

SIX PAINTINGS TO SEE

SATURN DEVOURING ONE OF HIS SONS (1819)
FRANCISCO DE GOYA Y LUCIENTES

In one of fourteen nightmarish "black paintings" executed by Goya to decorate the walls of his home in the later years of his life, the mythological God Kronos, or Saturn, cannibalizes one of his children in order to derail a prophecy that one of them would take over his throne. *Mural transferred to canvas.*

Saturn Devouring One of His Sons

THE GARDEN OF EARTHLY DELIGHTS OR LA PINTURA DEL MADROÑO (1500)
HIËRONYMUS BOSCH

Very little about the small-town environment of the Low Countries where the Roman Catholic Bosch lived in the late Middle Ages can explain his thought-provoking, and downright bizarre, paintings. His depictions of mankind's sins and virtues, and the heavenly rewards or demonic punishments that await us all, have fascinated many generations of viewers. The devout painter has been called a "heretic," and compared to Salvador Dalí for his disturbingly twisted renderings. In this three-panel painting, Adam and Evė are created, mankind celebrates its humanity, and hell awaits the wicked, all within a journey of 152 inches! *Wooden Triptych.*

The Garden of Earthly Delights

LAS MENINAS (THE MAIDS OF HONOR) (1656-57)
DIEGO VELÁZQUEZ DE SILVA

Velázquez's masterpiece of spatial perspective occupies pride-of-place in the center of the Spanish baroque galleries. In this complex visual game, *you* are the king and queen of Spain, reflected in a distant hazy mirror as the court painter (Velázquez) pauses in front of his easel to observe your features. The actual subject is the Princess Margarita, heir to the throne in 1656. *Oil on canvas.*

Las Meninas

STILL LIFE (17th Century; no date)
FRANCISCO DE ZURBARÁN

Best known as a painter of contemplative saints, Zurbarán, a native of Extremadura who found success working with Velázquez in Seville, was a peerless observer of beauty in the everyday. His rendering of the surfaces of these homely objects elevates them to the stature of holy relics, urging the viewer to touch them. But the overriding mood is one of serenity and order. *Oil on canvas.*

Still Life

DAVID VICTORIOUS OVER GOLIATH (1599)
MICHELANGELO MERISI (CARAVAGGIO)

Caravaggio used intense contrasts between his dark and light passages (called *chiaroscuro* in Italian) to create drama in his bold baroque paintings. Here, a surprisingly childlike David calmly ties up the severed head of the giant Philistine Goliath, gruesomely featured in the foreground plane of the picture. The astonishing realism of the Italian painter, who was as well known for his tempestuous personal life as for his deftness with a paint brush, had a profound influence on 17th century Spanish art. *Oil on canvas.*

David Victorious over Goliath

THE TRINITY (1577)
DOMENIKOS THEOTOKOPOULOS (EL GRECO)

Soon after arriving in Spain, Domenikos Theotokopoulos created this view of Christ ascending into heaven supported by angels, God the Father, and the Holy Spirit. It was commissioned for the altar of a convent in Toledo. The acid colors recall the Mannerist paintings of Venice, where El Greco was trained, and the distortions of the upward-floating bodies show more gracefulness than the anatomical contortions that characterize his later works. *Oil on canvas.*

The Trinity

PICASSO AND THE PRADO

The Prado contains no modern art, but one of the greatest artists of the 20th century had an important history with the museum. **Pablo Picasso** (1891–1973) served as the director of the Prado during the Spanish civil war, from 1936 to 1939. The Prado was a "phantom museum" in that period, Picasso once noted, since it was closed for most of the war and its collections hidden elsewhere for safety.

Picasso with his wife
Jacqueline Roque

Later that century, the abstract artist's enormous *Guernica* hung briefly on the Prado's walls, returning to Spain from the Museum of Modern Art in 1981. Picasso had stipulated that MoMA give up his anti-war masterpiece after the death of fascist dictator Francisco Franco, and it was displayed at the Prado and the Casón del Buen Retiro until the nearby Reina Sofía was built to house it in 1992.

Picasso in his atelier

shocking to a public accustomed to strictly representational images. Two of his greatest paintings, *The Resurrection* and *The Adoration of the Shepherds,* are on view here. Before you leave, stop in the 14th- to 16th-century Italian rooms to see Titian's *Portrait of Emperor Charles V* and Raphael's *Portrait of a Cardinal.*

Buy tickets in advance online; to save a few bucks on an audio guide, download the Prado Museum Visitor Guide app ahead of your visit. ⊠ *Paseo del Prado s/n, Retiro* ☎ *91/330–2800* ⊕ *www. museodelprado.es* 🖾 *€15, permanent collection free Mon.–Sat. 6–8 pm and Sun. 5–7 pm* Ⓜ *Banco de España, Estación del Arte.*

Museo Nacional de Artes Decorativas

ART MUSEUM | This palatial building show-cases 70,000 items including textiles, furniture, jewelry, ceramics, glass, crystal, and metalwork. The collection starts with medieval and Renaissance items on the first floor and ends with 18th- and 19th-century pieces on the top floor. The ground floor rotates temporary exhibitions and avant-garde works. This museum can be seen as part of the *Abono Cinco Palacios,* a €12 pass that grants access to five mansion-museums over a 10-day period. ⊠ *Calle de Montalbán 12, Retiro* ☎ *91/532–6499* ⊕ *www. culturaydeporte.gob.es/mnartesdecorativas/portada.html* 🖾 *€3, free Thurs. after 5 and Sun.* ☉ *Closed Mon.* Ⓜ *Retiro.*

Museo Naval

HISTORY MUSEUM | History buffs interested in old vessels and warships shouldn't miss the 500 years of Spanish naval history displayed in this newly renovated museum. The collection, which includes documents, maps, weaponry, paintings, and hundreds of ship models of different sizes, now features English-language placards and is fully wheelchair-accessible. Beginning with Queen Isabel and King Fernando's reign and the expeditions led by Christopher Columbus and the conquistadores, exhibits also

reveal how Spain built a naval empire that battled Turkish, Algerian, French, Portuguese, and English armies and commanded the oceans and shipping routes for a century and a half. Moving to the present day, the museum covers Spain's more recent shipyard and naval construction accomplishments. ⊠ *Paseo del Prado 3, Retiro* ☎ *91/523–8789* ⊕ *armada.mde.es/museonaval* 🖾 *€3 suggested donation* ☉ *Closed Mon.* Ⓜ *Banco de España.*

Palacio de Cibeles (*Cybele Palace*)

VIEWPOINT | This ornate building on the southeast side of Plaza de la Cibeles, built at the start of the 20th century and formerly called Palacio de Comunicaciones, is a massive stone compound bearing French, Viennese, and traditional Spanish influences. It first served as the city's main post office and, after renovations, is now an administrative building housing the mayor's office, a cultural center called CentroCentro (a pleasant place to study or work), several exhibition halls, dining options (on the second and sixth floors), and a rooftop lookout. ⊠ *Pl.*

¡A correr!

Jogging is a great way to explore Madrid, but be prepared for hills. The best running spots are El Retiro Park—where the main path circles the park (approximately 2½ miles) and others weave under trees and through gardens—and the Parque del Oeste (Western Park), which has more uneven terrain and fewer people. Casa de Campo, a bit farther afield, is crisscrossed by hilly trails and ideal for distance runners (bring your phone so you don't get lost); same goes for the Madrid Río esplanade and much longer Anillo Verde ("Green Ring"), which you can access by crossing a bridge at the northwest corner of Western Park.

Paseo del Prado

Any visit to Madrid should include a stroll along the museum-lined Paseo del Prado, which became a UNESCO World Heritage Site along with El Retiro Park in 2021. You can tour the area in about two hours (longer, of course, if you visit the Prado).

■TIP→ The Paseo del Arte pass allows you to visit the Prado, the Museo Nacional Centro de Arte Reina Sofía, and the Museo Thyssen-Bornemisza for €32. You can buy it at any of the three museums and don't have to visit all on the same day.

The Paseo del Prado stretches from Plaza de Cibeles to Plaza del Emperador Carlos V (also known as Plaza de Atocha) and is home to Madrid's three main art museums—the Prado, Reina Sofía, and Thyssen-Bornemisza—as well as the CaixaForum, an art institution with fabulous temporary exhibitions. In earlier times the Paseo marked the eastern boundary of the city, and in the 17th century it was given a cleaner neoclassical look. A century later, King Carlos III designed a leafy nature walk with glorious fountains and a botanical garden to provide respite to Madrileños during the scorching summers.

Start your walk on Plaza Cánovas del Castillo, with its Fuente de Neptuno (Fountain of Neptune); on the northwestern corner is **the Thyssen-Bornemisza**. To your left, across from the plaza, is the elegant, just-renovated Mandarin Oriental Ritz, which abuts the colonnaded Palacio de la Bolsa (historical stock exchange); across from it on the right is **the Prado**, the best example of neoclassical architecture in the city and one of the world's best-known museums. It was enlarged in 2007 with the addition of what's widely known as "Moneo's cube," architect Rafael Moneo's steel-and-glass building that encloses the cloister of Monasterio de los Jerónimos. This monastery, the oldest original building in this part of town (built in 1503), is dwarfed by the museum. It once sat at the core of the **El Retiro Park**, which stretched as far as the Paseo del Prado until the 19th century, when Queen Isabel II sold a third of its terrain to the state. Always bustling, it is a great place to unwind after sightseeing.

To the right of the Prado, across from Murillo Gate, is the **Jardín Real Botánico**, also a wonderful place to relax with a book or sketch in the shade of an exotic tree. Across the street is a sloping plaza that leads to **CaixaForum**.

The Paseo del Prado ends at the **Estación de Atocha**, a grand old train station resembling the overturned hull of a ship. To its west, across from Calle Atocha, lies **the Reina Sofía**, Madrid's modern art museum and the home of Picasso's *Guernica*.

The grand Palacio de Cibeles was opened to the public in 2011, so you can now enjoy drinks or dinner with a view on the eighth floor terrace or just chill in the Centro Cultural on the ground floor.

de Cibeles 1, Retiro ☎ 91/480–0008 ⊕ *www.centrocentro.org* ✉ *Free, Mirador Madrid €3* ⊙ *Closed Mon.* Ⓜ *Banco de España.*

★ Parque del Buen Retiro (*El Retiro*)

CITY PARK | FAMILY | Once the private playground of royalty, Madrid's main park—which was granted World Heritage status in 2021 by UNESCO—is a 316-acre expanse of formal gardens, fountains, lakes, exhibition halls, children's play areas, and outdoor cafés. There is a puppet theater featuring slapstick routines that even non-Spanish-speakers will enjoy; shows are free and generally take place on weekends at 12:30 pm. The park is especially lively on weekends, when it fills with buskers, jugglers, and other street performers as well as hundreds of Spaniards out for exercise. There are occasional concerts in summer. From the entrance at Puerta de Alcalá, head to the park's center, where you'll find the estanque (pond), presided over by a grandiose equestrian statue of King Alfonso XII erected by his mother.'

The 19th-century Palacio de Cristal, southeast of the estanque, was built as a steel-and-glass greenhouse for exotic plants—and, horrifically, tribesmen displayed in a "human zoo"—from the Philippines, a Spanish colony at the time, and is now a free-admission art exhibition space. Next door is a small lake with ducks, swans, and gnarled swamp trees. Along the Paseo del Uruguay at the park's south end is the Rosaleda (Rose Garden), an explosion of color and heady aromas. West of the Rosaleda, look for a statue called the *Ángel Caído* (*Fallen Angel*), a rare depiction of the Prince of Darkness falling from grace. In February 2023, the *Montaña Artificial* ("Man-Made Mountain") at the northeast corner of the park reopened after nearly 20 years of neglect. Built in 1817, the pink building with a vaulted ceiling was a folly of Ferdinand VII and has a waterfall and cats galore. ✉ *Puerta de Alcalá s/n, Retiro* Ⓜ *Retiro.*

The Puerta de Alcalá (Door of Alcalá) was once one of the five doors used to enter the walled city of Madrid when travelers visited from France, Aragón, and Catalonia.

Puerta de Alcalá

NOTABLE BUILDING | This triumphal arch, today a popular backdrop for photos, was built by Carlos III in 1778 to mark the site of one of the ancient city gates. You can still see numerous bullet and cannonball holes on its exterior, left intentionally as a reminder of Madrid's tumultuous past. ⊠ *Calle de Alcalá s/n, Retiro* Ⓜ *Retiro.*

Real Fábrica de Tapices

FACTORY | Tired of previous monarchs' dependency on Belgian and Flemish thread mills and craftsmen, King Felipe V decided to establish the Royal Tapestry Factory in Madrid in 1721. It was originally housed near Alonso Martínez and moved to its current location in 1889. Some of Europe's best artists collaborated on the factory's tapestry designs, the most famous of whom was Goya, who produced a number of works on display at the Prado. The factory, the most renowned of its kind in Europe, is still in operation—you can tour the workshop floor and watch weavers at work. They apply traditional weaving techniques from the 18th and 19th centuries to modern and classic designs—including Goya's. Prebooking online is required, and all visitors get a tour (English tours usually begin at 12:30 pm weekdays). ⊠ *Calle de Fuenterrabía 2, Retiro* ☎ *91/434–0550* ⊕ *www.realfabricadetapices.com* 🖾 *€5* 🕙 *Closed weekends and Aug.* ♿ *Reservation required* Ⓜ *Menéndez Pelayo, Estación del Arte.*

Real Jardín Botánico (*Royal Botanical Garden*)

GARDEN | **FAMILY** | You don't have to be a horticulturalist to appreciate the breadth of the exotic plant collection here. Opened in 1781 and emblematic of the Age of Enlightenment, this lush Eden of bonsais, orchids, cacti, and more houses more than 5,000 species of living plants and trees in just 20 acres. Its dried specimens number over a million, and many were brought back from exploratory voyages to the Americas. ⊠ *Pl. de Murillo 2, Retiro* ☎ *91/420–3017* ⊕ *rjb.csic.es* 🖾 *€6* Ⓜ *Estación del Arte.*

San Jerónimo el Real

RELIGIOUS BUILDING | Ferdinand and Isabella used this church and cloister behind the Prado as a *retiro,* or place of respite—hence the name of the adjacent park. The building, one of the oldest in the city (built in the early 16th century), was devastated in the Napoleonic Wars and rebuilt in the late 19th century. ✉ *Calle de Moreto 4, Retiro* ☎ *91/420–3078* 🌐 *www.parroquiasanjeronimoelreal.es* 🎫 *Free* [M] *Banco de España, Estación del Arte.*

🍴 Restaurants

Horcher

$$$$ | **GERMAN** | A beacon of old-world Spanish hospitality, Horcher is a Madrid classic with German influences. Wild game—boar, venison, partridge, and duck—is the centerpiece of the menu, which also includes comfort-food classics like ox stroganoff with a Pommery mustard sauce and pork chops with sauerkraut. **Known for:** wild game dishes; German-inflected wine list; to-die-for baumkuchen (a German-style spit cake). [$] *Average main: €37* ✉ *Calle de Alfonso XII 6, Retiro* ☎ *91/522–0731* 🌐 *restaurantehorcher.com* 🕓 *Closed Sun. No lunch Sat.* 👔 *Jacket required (tie optional)* [M] *Retiro.*

La Castela

$$ | **TAPAS** | **FAMILY** | Traditional taverns with tin-top bars, vermouth on tap, and no-nonsense waiters are a dying breed in Madrid, but this one, just a couple of blocks from El Retiro Park, has stood the test of time. It's always busy with locals clamoring over plates of sautéed wild mushrooms, tuna ventresca and roasted pepper salad, and stewed chickpeas with langoustines. **Known for:** colorfully plated tapas; friendly staff; neighborhood crowd. [$] *Average main: €21* ✉ *Calle del Doctor Castelo 22, Retiro* ☎ *91/574–0015* 🌐 *restaurantelacastela.com* 🕓 *Closed Sun.* [M] *Ibiza.*

★ La Catapa

$$$ | **SPANISH** | La Catapa's tapas are classic but never old hat, inventive but never pretentious. The burst-in-your-mouth *croquetas* (croquettes) and garlicky razor clams may lure the crowds, but the hidden gems are in the vegetable section: it's hard to decide between the artichoke menestra with crisped *jamón* (dry-cured ham), ultra-creamy *salmorejo* (gazpacho's richer, more garlicky sibling), and umami-packed seared mushrooms. **Known for:** elevated tapas; decadent cream-filled pastry "cigars"; a Retiro institution. [$] *Average main: €25* ✉ *Calle de Menorca 14, Retiro* ☎ *68/614–3823* 🌐 *tabernalacatapa.eatbu.com* 🕓 *Closed Sun. and Mon.* [M] *Ibiza.*

La Raquetista

$$ | **FUSION** | Shaking up Retiro's traditional tapas scene, La Raquetista is known for *nueva cocina* dishes that vary from night to night, including tuna "pastrami," uni with potato cream, and cider-marinated wild boar tenderloin, all served bar-side or in a snug five-table dining room. **Known for:** eye-popping fusion tapas; to-die-for torreznos (fried pork rinds); unusual Spanish wines. [$] *Average main: €21* ✉ *Calle del Doctor Castelo 19, Retiro* ☎ *91/831–1842* 🌐 *laraquetista.com* 🕓 *No dinner Sun.* [M] *Ibiza.*

Martín Bar

$ | **SPANISH** | This hole-in-the-wall opened in 1940 serves no-frills Castilian classics like *patatas revolconas* (mashed potatoes with paprika and pork rinds), ham croquettes, and meatballs so good they're often gone before the dinner rush. Don't expect to find a seat unless you go at off hours. **Known for:** affordable Spanish bar food; crowds on weekends; outdoor parkside dining. [$] *Average main: €12* ✉ *Av. de Menéndez Pelayo 17, Retiro* ☎ *91/573–1167* 🕓 *Closed Mon.* [M] *Ibiza.*

Hotels

Hotel Palacio del Retiro, Autograph Collection

$$$$ | **HOTEL** | An early-20th-century palace built for a noble family with extravagant habits (the elevator carried their horses up and down from the rooftop exercise ring), this hotel mixes old-world elegance with modern bells and whistles. **Pros:** spacious elegant rooms; walking distance from the Prado; bathrooms stocked with all sorts of complimentary products. **Cons:** pricey breakfast; lower rooms facing the park can get noisy; cumbersome room keys. [$] *Rooms from: €416* ✉ *Calle de Alfonso XII 14, Retiro* ☎ *91/523–7460* 🌐 *www.marriott.com/en-us/hotels/madre-hotel-palacio-del-retiro-autograph-collection/overview* 🛏 *50 rooms* 🍴 *No Meals* [M] *Retiro.*

★ **Mandarin Oriental Ritz, Madrid**

$$$$ | **HOTEL** | A €99 million renovation by Mandarin Oriental completed in 2021 breathed new life to this grande dame overlooking the Prado, replacing mustard-colored drapes, dim sconces, and faded carpets with bright whites, gold accents, and stunning contemporary art. **Pros:** celebrity-chef restaurant Deessa; new fitness center and chandelier-lighted pool; the epitome of modern luxury. **Cons:** many museum-grade antiques were auctioned off in the revamp; inconsistent El Jardín restaurant; priced too high for the vast majority of travelers. [$] *Rooms from: €1,195* ✉ *Pl. de la Lealtad 5, Retiro* ☎ *91/701–6767* 🌐 *www.mandarinoriental.com* 🛏 *153 rooms* 🍴 *No Meals* [M] *Banco de España.*

Nightlife

BARS

Florida Park

GATHERING PLACES | El Retiro Park is now a nightlife destination, thanks to Florida Park, the see-and-be-seen leisure complex with six venues: El Pabellón, a white-tablecloth restaurant; La Galería, an informal tapas bar; La Terraza, a chic rooftop terrace; Los Kioscos, an indoor-outdoor bar with live music; La Cúpula, a cocktail bar open late; and La Sala, a tony nightclub that heats up on weekends. ✉ *Parque del Buen Retiro, Paseo de la República Dominicana 1, Retiro* ☎ *91/827–5275* 🌐 *floridapark.es* [M] *Ibiza.*

Shopping

Qava

FOOD | Featuring exclusively Spanish cheeses from small producers, Qava doesn't just source and sell killer cheeses that make great gifts—it also ages each wheel to perfection in on-site "caves." Sample them in an eight-table tasting area alongside carefully selected wines. The 11 pm closing time means you can work Qava into a tapas crawl or—if you're feeling European—make it a final dessert stop. ✉ *Calle del Doctor Castelo 34, Retiro* ☎ *91/853–2853* 🌐 *www.qavadequesos.com* 🕒 *Closed Sun.* [M] *Ibiza, O'Donnell.*

Salamanca

Sights

★ **Mercado de la Paz**

MARKET | Salamanca's gleaming main market is a hangarlike food emporium selling everything from wild game to softball-size Calanda peaches to sashimi-grade tuna to the country's finest jamón and canned seafood. Standout restaurants here include Casa Dani (arguably the city's best Spanish omelet; see separate entry) and Matteo Cucina Italiana (osteria-style pastas and risotto). ✉ *Calle de Ayala 28, Salamanca* ☎ *91/435–0743* 🌐 *www.mercadodelapaz.com* 🕒 *Closed Sun., Sat. after 2 pm* [M] *Serrano.*

Museo Arqueológico Nacional (*National Archaeological Museum*)

HISTORY MUSEUM | **FAMILY** | This museum boasts three large floors filled with

Spanish relics, artifacts, and treasures ranging from ancient history to the 19th century. Among the highlights are *La Dama de Elche*, the bust of a wealthy 5th-century-BC Iberian woman (notice that her headgear vaguely resembles the mantillas and hair combs still associated with traditional Spanish dress); the ancient Visigothic votive crowns discovered in 1859 near Toledo, believed to date back to the 7th century; and the medieval ivory crucifix of Ferdinand and Sancha. There is also a replica of the early cave paintings in Altamira (access to the real thing, in Cantabria Province, is highly restricted).

■ TIP➜ **Consider getting the multimedia guide offering select itineraries to make your visit more manageable.** ⊠ *Calle de Serrano 13, Salamanca* ☎ *91/577–7912* ⊕ *www.man.es* ⊠ *€3, free Sat. after 2 and Sun. before 2* ⊙ *Closed Mon.* Ⓜ *Colón, Serrano.*

Museo Lázaro Galdiano

HISTORIC HOME | This stately mansion of writer and editor José Lázaro Galdiano (1862–1947) is a 10-minute walk across the Castellana from Museo Sorolla. Its remarkable collection spans five centuries of Spanish, Flemish, English, and Italian art. Bosch's *St. John the Baptist* and a number of Goyas are highlights, with El Greco's *San Francisco de Assisi* and Zurbarán's *San Diego de Alcalá* close behind. This museum can be seen as part of the Abono Cinco Palacios, a €12 pass that grants access to five local mansion-museums. ⊠ *Calle de Serrano 122, Salamanca* ☎ *91/561–6084* ⊕ *www. flg.es* ⊠ *€7 (free last hr)* ⊙ *Closed Mon.* Ⓜ *Gregorio Marañón.*

Plaza de Colón

PLAZA/SQUARE | Named for Christopher Columbus, this plaza surrounds a statue of the explorer (identical to the one in Barcelona's port) looking west from a high tower. Beyond Plaza de Colón is **Calle de Serrano,** the city's premier shopping street (think Gucci, Prada,

and Loewe). Stroll in either direction on Serrano for some window-shopping. ⊠ *Salamanca* Ⓜ *Colón.*

🍴 Restaurants

★ Cadaqués

$$$$ | CATALAN | Never has an open kitchen in Madrid been so mesmerizing: at Cadaqués, black-clad cooks tend to rows of paella pans sizzling over pluming orange wood embers and flip Flintstones-worthy steaks and whole fish licked by open flame. It feels like the type of rustic experience you'd encounter at the Mediterranean seaside, but Cadaqués sits squarely on Jorge Juan, Madrid's poshest street. **Known for:** best rice dishes in town; a slice of the Levant in Madrid; refined Mediterranean decor with well-heeled clientele to match. Ⓢ *Average main: €55* ⊠ *Calle de Jorge Juan 35, Salamanca* ☎ *91/360–9053* ⊕ *restaurantecadaques. com* Ⓜ *Velázquez.*

Casa Carola

$$$$ | SPANISH | *Cocido madrileño,* Madrid's quintessential boiled dinner of rich consommé, butter-soft chickpeas, and some half-dozen cuts of meat, is the must-order item at this Salamanca institution, especially in the winter, when temperatures plummet. The wooden straight-back chairs, kitschy cotton bibs, and walls hung with black-and-white photos belie the fact that this lunch-only restaurant opened just two decades ago, but one taste of its famous cocido, and you might as well be at an *abuela*'s kitchen table. **Known for:** cocido madrileño served in three courses; old-timey interiors; warm service. Ⓢ *Average main: €33* ⊠ *Calle de Padilla 54, Salamanca* ☎ *91/401–9408* ⊕ *www.casacarola.com* ▤ *No credit cards* ⊙ *No dinner* Ⓜ *Lista.*

★ Casa Dani

$ | SPANISH | Casa Dani is a legendary bar in Mercado de la Paz whose *tortilla de patata* (potato omelet) is easily the best in town, and perhaps the country (if first place in the National Spanish Omelet Championship of 2019 is any indication). Each hefty wedge is packed with caramelized onions and served hot and slightly runny. **Known for:** possibly world's best tortilla española; value prix-fixe lunch; long lines that are worth the wait. [$] *Average main: €13* ✉ *Mercado de la Paz, Calle de Ayala 28 (also Calle de Lagasca 49), Salamanca* ✣ *Back right corner* ☎ *91/575–5925* 🌐 *www.casadani.es* 🕒 *Closed Sun. No dinner* [M] *Serrano.*

Cinco Jotas Serrano

$$$ | **TAPAS** | Cinco Jotas ibérico ham is a sight to behold: translucent and shimmering like shards of red stained glass, a shade darker than prosciutto and twice as fragrant. That's because this famous producer uses only 100% purebred, acorn-fed Iberian hogs. **Known for:** the Rolls Royce of jamón; tranquil and elegant patio; Ibérico pork dishes beyond just ham. [$] *Average main: €28* ✉ *Calle de Serrano 118, Salamanca* ☎ *91/563–2710* 🌐 *www.cincojotas.es* [M] *Rubén Darío, Gregorio Marañón.*

★ El Paraguas

$$$$ | **SPANISH** | This low-ceiling dining room filled with plush armchairs, starched white tablecloths, and colorful bouquets is a welcoming spot to feast on refined Asturian dishes like sea urchin gratin, morels stuffed with truffled foie gras, pheasant with braised green beans, and suckling lamb confit. Weather permitting, you can request a patio table to watch Madrid's one percent parade down Calle de Jorge Juan. **Known for:** haute Asturian cuisine; romantic dining room and terrace; fantastic seafood. [$] *Average main: €34* ✉ *Calle de Jorge Juan 16, Salamanca* ☎ *91/431–5950* 🌐 *www.elparaguas.com* [M] *Serrano.*

El Pescador

$$$ | **SEAFOOD** | Owned by the proprietors of one the best fish markets in town, Pescaderías Coruñesas, this seafood restaurant with a warm modern interior welcomes guests with an impressive window display of fresh seafood—red and white prawns, Kumamoto oysters, goose barnacles, and the renowned Galician Carril clams are just some of what you might see. Fish (including turbot, sole, grouper, and sea bass) is cooked to your liking in the oven, on the grill, in a pan with garlic, or battered and fried. **Known for:** extravagant seafood displays; dayboat fish; crisp Galician wines. [$] *Average main: €27* ✉ *Calle de José Ortega y Gasset 75, Salamanca* ☎ *91/402–1290* 🌐 *www.marisqueriaelpescador.net* 🕒 *Closed Sun.* [M] *Lista, Núñez de Balboa.*

El Rincón de Jaén

$$ | **SPANISH** | **FAMILY** | This Andalusian taberna evokes the raucous energy and down-home cuisine of that sunny region. Start with *pescaíto frito,* a mix of seafood that's lightly fried and served with lemon halves, before moving on to more substantial dishes like the peeled tomato salad topped with oil-cured tuna belly (easily one of the best salads in town) and whole roasted fish and braised meats. **Known for:** Andalusian joie de vivre; tomato and tuna salad; complimentary tapas with drinks. [$] *Average main: €24* ✉ *Calle de Don Ramón de la Cruz 88, Salamanca* ☎ *91/401–6334* 🌐 *elrincondejaen.com* [M] *Lista.*

La Tasquería

$$ | **TAPAS** | La Tasquería draws restaurant industry pros and food writers with its bold menu revolving around off-cuts like liver, kidneys, tripe, and tongue—onetime staples of the Spanish diet that fell out of favor but are now getting a modern makeover. Even the squeamish should consider ordering delectable dishes like ravioli filled with lamb sweetbreads, and cod tripe *fideuà* (pasta "paella"). **Known for:** offal everything; good-value €55 tasting menu; craft beers and sherries. [$] *Average main: €24* ✉ *Calle del Duque de Sesto 48, Salamanca* ☎ *91/451–1000* 🌐 *latasqueria.com* 🕒 *Closed Mon. No dinner Sun.* [M] *Príncipe de Vergara.*

Noi

$$$ | MODERN ITALIAN | Hand-rolled pastas, craveable vegetable dishes, and reimagined Italian classics keep Salamanca prepsters pouring in night after night. Wow your date, boss—or simply your hungry self—with dishes like leeks and cockles swimming in saffron cream, tagliatelle tossed in arugula ragù, and crunchy broccoli and beef lasagna. **Known for:** inventive Italian cooking; Salamanca hot spot; colorful Instagram-ready interiors. Ⓢ *Average main: €27* ⊠ *Calle de Recoletos 6, Salamanca* ☎ *91/069–4007* ⊕ *restaurantenoi.com* ⊟ *No credit cards* ⊗ *Closed Sun. and Mon.* Ⓜ *Banco de España, Retiro.*

Ten Con Ten

$$$ | SPANISH | This "gin bar" helped start the Spanish *gin-tónic* craze of the late 1980s, and though perhaps not as avant-garde as it once was, the quality of food and drinks is consistently fantastic. Grab a cocktail at one of the wooden high-tops in the bar area, or sit down for a soup-to-nuts dinner in the classy dining room at the back—just remember to book a table weeks, if not months, in advance. **Known for:** expertly made gin-tónics; memorable gastro-bar fare; hand-cut jamón ibérico. Ⓢ *Average main: €29* ⊠ *Calle de Ayala 6, Salamanca* ☎ *91/515–4332* ⊕ *restaurantetenconten. com* Ⓜ *Serrano.*

☕ Coffee and Quick Bites

Confitería Rialto

$ | BAKERY | Rialto's famous *moscovitas*, slightly salty almond-toffee wafers coated in chocolate, are one of Madrid's most delectable confections. Moscovitas are also sold at some El Corte Inglés locations. **Known for:** traditional Spanish pastries; retro feel; famous toffee cookies. Ⓢ *Average main: €9* ⊠ *Calle de Núñez de Balboa 86, Salamanca* ☎ *91/426–3777* ⊕ *moscovitas.com* ⊗ *Closed Sun.* Ⓜ *Núñez de Balboa.*

Oriol Balaguer

$ | BAKERY | Catalan chef Oriol Balaguer takes chocolates and croissants to new heights at this ritzy *bombonería ,* whose attractive treats make phenomenal gifts—or afternoon pick-me-ups. **Known for:** chocolate lover's dream; chichi clientele; ultra-flaky croissants. Ⓢ *Average main: €10* ⊠ *Calle de José Ortega y Gasset 44, Salamanca* ☎ *91/401–6463* ⊕ *www.oriolbalaguershop.com* Ⓜ *Lista.*

★ Panem

$ | BAKERY | Of all the marvelous bakeries in Madrid, Panem (take-out only) is the most technically skilled, churning out impeccable croissants, baguettes, and a wide range of Spanish and French pastries including Kouign-ammans, *roscones* (Three Kings cakes), and *torrijas* (Spanish "French" toast). **Known for:** three blocks from El Retiro; sourdough breads made from specialty flours; ultra-flaky French pastries. Ⓢ *Average main: €7* ⊠ *Calle de Fernán González 42, Salamanca* ☎ *91/795–9107* ⊗ *Closed Sun. and Mon.* Ⓜ *Ibiza, O'Donnell.*

Religion Specialty Coffee

$ | CAFÉ | After browsing the art collection at the Lázaro Galdiano, walk north a block to reach this charming café suited to both working and schmoozing. There are sandwiches, chia bowls, smoothies, and pastries on the menu, in addition to teas and the usual coffee drinks. **Known for:** affordable brunch; well-made coffee and tea; laptop-friendly. Ⓢ *Average main: €9* ⊠ *Calle de María de Molina 24, Salamanca* ☎ *91/069–8221* ⊕ *religioncoffee. es* Ⓜ *Gregorio Marañón.*

🛏 Hotels

Barceló Emperatriz

$$$ | HOTEL | Worthy of an empress, as its name implies, this sumptuous property on a tree-shaded block offers knowledgeable concierge services, healthy breakfast options, an updated gym, and an extensive pillow menu. **Pros:** good value for luxury; king-size beds and in-room hot tubs; solid little gym. **Cons:** cramped lobby; 10-minute taxi from center of town; small pool and gym. [$] *Rooms from: €250* ✉ *Calle de López de Hoyos 4, Salamanca* ☎ *91/342–2490* 🌐 *www.barcelo.com/en-us/barcelo-emperatriz* 🛏 *146 rooms* 🍴 *No Meals* [M] *Núñez de Balboa.*

Hotel Fénix Gran Meliá

$$$$ | HOTEL | A Madrid institution that has played host to the likes of the Beatles, Cary Grant, and Rita Hayworth, this hotel has an impressive lobby with marble floors, antique furniture, and a stained-glass dome ceiling. **Pros:** celebrity hangout Hortensio restaurant; great breakfast buffet; above-and-beyond service. **Cons:** small bathrooms; guest rooms show some wear; VIP policy excludes standard-room guests from certain areas. [$] *Rooms from: €450* ✉ *Calle de Hermosilla 2, Salamanca* ☎ *91/431–6700* 🌐 *www.melia.com/en/hotels/spain/madrid/fenix-gran-melia* 🛏 *225 rooms* 🍴 *No Meals* [M] *Colón.*

Heritage Madrid Hotel

$$$$ | HOTEL | Hotel Orfila's newer stylish sibling, the Relais & Château–approved Heritage lies north of Salamanca's commercial hubbub in a stately residential area. **Pros:** standout old-meets-new furnishings; "secret" rooftop bar and terrace; plush towels and robes. **Cons:** far from most sights; no gym, pool, or sauna; unpolished staff. [$] *Rooms from: €433* ✉ *Calle de Diego de León 43, Salamanca* ☎ *91/088–7070* 🌐 *www.heritagemadridhotel.com* 🛏 *46 rooms* 🍴 *No Meals* [M] *Av. de América.*

ICON Embassy

$$$ | HOTEL | This airy, playfully decorated hotel with larger-than-average rooms occupies a converted palace on Calle de Serrano, Salamanca's main shopping corridor. **Pros:** sleek modern design; steps from high-fashion boutiques; health-focused dining at Florafina restaurant. **Cons:** so-so soundproofing; inconsistent breakfast quality; four-person room is cramped. [$] *Rooms from: €266* ✉ *Calle de Serrano 46, Salamanca* ☎ *91/431–3060* 🌐 *www.iconembassy.com* 💳 *No credit cards* 🛏 *75 rooms* 🍴 *Free Breakfast* [M] *Serrano.*

ICON Wipton

$$$$ | HOTEL | Whites, grays, and dark woods define this boutique hotel on Salamanca's most opulent street, Jorge Juan. **Pros:** calming atmosphere; location on main dining and nightlife street; standout breakfasts. **Cons:** entry-level rooms are a tight fit; noise travels from ground-floor bar; small desks in guest rooms. [$] *Rooms from: €314* ✉ *Calle de Jorge Juan 17, Salamanca* ☎ *91/435–5411* 🌐 *www.iconwipton.com* 🛏 *61 rooms* 🍴 *No Meals* [M] *Serrano, Velázquez.*

★ **Rosewood Villa Magna**

$$$$ | HOTEL | Barrio de Salamanca's most distinctive hotel, which reopened in late 2021 under the Rosewood umbrella after a yearlong eight-figure renovation, is now one of the swankiest properties in Spain. **Pros:** inviting spa and public areas with fireplaces and cushy sofas; Madrid's best hotel breakfast and high tea; impeccable service. **Cons:** Amós restaurant still getting its footing; big-city surroundings lack charm; unrenovated bathrooms feel old-fashioned. [$] *Rooms from: €982* ✉ *Paseo de la Castellana 22, Salamanca* ☎ *91/587–1234* 🌐 *www.rosewoodhotels.com/en/villa-magna* 🛏 *154 rooms* 🍴 *No Meals* [M] *Rubén Darío, Colón.*

Tótem Madrid

$$$ | HOTEL | Tótem checks all the boxes for a solid boutique hotel: genial service, streamlined design, sought-after location, and good food and cocktails. **Pros:** charming tree-lined block; excellent cocktail bar and restaurant; bubbly service. **Cons:** many attractions not within walking distance; disappointing breakfast; interior rooms not as pleasant. [$] *Rooms from: €217* ✉ *Calle Hermosilla 23, Salamanca* ☎ *91/426–0035* 🌐 *www.totem-madrid.com* 🛏 *64 rooms* 🍴 *No Meals* [M] *Serrano.*

Barrio de Salamanca is Madrid's most stylish district, with gorgeous buildings housing the usual designer suspects like Chanel and Hermes as well as High Street standbys like Muji and Zara.

VP Jardín de Recoletos

$$$ | **HOTEL** | **FAMILY** | This high-end apartment-hotel offers great value on a quiet street just a couple of blocks from El Retiro Park, the Prado, and shopping areas. **Pros:** spacious rooms with kitchens; good restaurant; good value with periodic deals via website. **Cons:** the garden closes at midnight and can be noisy; could use a redesign; breakfast not served in the garden. $ *Rooms from: €225* ✉ *Calle de Gil de Santivañes 6, Salamanca* ☎ *91/781–1640* ⊕ *www.recoletos-hotel. com* ⇆ *43 rooms* ¶○¶ *No Meals* Ⓜ *Colón.*

Nightlife

DANCE CLUBS

Bling Bling

DANCE CLUBS | This glitzy ever-crowded nightclub attracts a well-heeled local crowd with house, reggaeton, and remixed pop tracks. Dress to impress: this isn't an easy door. ✉ *Calle de Génova 28, Salamanca* ☎ *91/064–4479* ۞ *Closed Sun. and Mon.* Ⓜ *Colón.*

Goya Social Club

LIVE MUSIC | The Funktion One sound system blasts techno and house music till the wee hours at this improbably unpretentious Salamanca hot spot. Expect long lines after 1 am. The cover is around €15 and you must be 21 or over to enter. ✉ *Calle de Goya 43, Salamanca* ☎ *68/165–0040* ⊕ *www.goyasocialclub. com* ۞ *Closed Sun.–Thurs.* Ⓜ *Serrano.*

WINE BARS

La Alquimia

WINE BARS | Welcome to Madrid's newest hot spot for natural wine geeks. Pull up a stool in the snug bar area and choose from an ever-changing selection of boutique bottles you won't find anywhere else. ✉ *Calle de Amador de los Rios 1, Salamanca.*

 Performing Arts

Auditorio Nacional de Música

CONCERTS | Madrid's main concert hall has spaces for both symphonic and chamber music. ✉ *Calle del Príncipe de Vergara*

146, Salamanca ☎ *91/337–0140* ⊕ *www. auditorionacional.mcu.es* Ⓜ *Cruz del Rayo, Prosperidad.*

Shopping

BOUTIQUES AND FASHION

Salamanca is Madrid's quintessential shopping district with a high concentration of shops and boutiques on Calles de Claudio Coello, Lagasca, and the first few blocks of Serrano.

Adolfo Domínguez

MIXED CLOTHING | This popular Galician designer creates simple, elegant lines for men and women. Of the numerous locations around the city, this flagship is the most varied and cutting-edge. ✉ *Calle de Serrano 40, Salamanca* ☎ *91/727–1749* ⊕ *www.adolfodominguez.com* Ⓜ *Serrano.*

Loewe

LEATHER GOODS | Luxury Spanish fashion house Loewe (Lo-EH-veh), which is having a moment among trendy young Spaniards, carries designer purses, accessories, and clothing made of butter-soft leather in gorgeous jewel tones. That voluminous red dress Rihanna flaunted at the 2023 Super Bowl? A Loewe masterpiece. The store at Serrano 26 displays the women's collection; men's items are a block away at Serrano 34. ✉ *Calle de Serrano 26 and 34, Salamanca* ☎ *91/577–6056* ⊕ *www.loewe.com* Ⓜ *Serrano.*

Pedro del Hierro

MIXED CLOTHING | This Madrileño designer has a solid reputation for his casual preppy clothes for both sexes. The boutique is chic and inviting with walnut and marble furnishings and a section devoted to garments by sister company Cortefiel. ✉ *Calle de Serrano 29, Salamanca* ☎ *91/575–6906* ⊕ *pedrodelhierro.com* Ⓜ *Serrano.*

Purificación García

HANDBAGS | For women and men searching for elegant all-day wear, this store offers some standout pieces, particularly handbags. ✉ *Calle de Serrano 28, Salamanca* ☎ *91/435–8013* ⊕ *purificaciongarcia.com* Ⓜ *Serrano.*

JEWELRY

Coolook

JEWELRY & WATCHES | Spanish jeweler Mar Aldeguer sells nature-inspired jewelry made from precious and semiprecious metals and stones at this welcoming boutique. ✉ *Calle de Serrano 84, Salamanca* ☎ *91/626–3920* ⊕ *www.coolook.es* ⊙ *Closed Sun.* Ⓜ *Rubén Darío, Núñez de Balboa.*

FOOD AND WINE

Lavinia

WINE/SPIRITS | Every attendant is a trained sommelier at this sprawling wine store. Beyond the 4,000-plus bottles from nearly every viticultural region imaginable, there are books, glasses, and bar accessories on sale. A Spanish restaurant on-site pours some 50 wines by the glass and has outdoor seating (skip the food; it's overpriced and underwhelming). ✉ *Calle de José Ortega y Gasset 16, Salamanca* ☎ *91/426–0604* ⊕ *www.lavinia.es* ⊙ *Closed Sun.* Ⓜ *Núñez de Balboa.*

Mantequerías Bravo

WINE/SPIRITS | Stock up on Spanish wines, olive oils, cheeses, and hams at this old-timer that's been around since 1931. ✉ *Calle de Ayala 24, Salamanca* ☎ *91/575–8072* ⊕ *www.mantequerias-bravo.com* ⊙ *Closed Sun.* Ⓜ *Serrano.*

TEXTILES

★ Ábbatte

FABRICS | Every blanket, tablecloth, throw, and rug sold at this deservedly pricey textile shop is woven by hand using the finest natural fibers in the Cistercian abbey of Santa María de la Sierra in Segovia. ✉ *Calle de Villanueva 27, Salamanca* ☎ *91/622–5530* ⊕ *www.abbatte.com* ⊙ *Closed weekends* Ⓜ *Príncipe de Vergara.*

Chapter 8

LA LATINA, LAVAPIÉS, AND ARGANZUELA

8

Updated by
Benjamin Kemper

👁 Sights	🍴 Restaurants	🏨 Hotels	👜 Shopping	🍸 Nightlife
★★★★☆	★★★★★	★★☆☆☆	★★★★☆	★★★★★

NEIGHBORHOOD SNAPSHOT

TOP EXPERIENCES

■ **El Rastro:** Snap up eclectic antiques, clothes, and tchotchkes at this epic Sunday flea market.

■ **Traditional markets:** Rub shoulders with a local crowd while grazing on tapas, charcuterie, and natural wine.

■ **International food:** When jamón fatigue sets in, branch out in Lavapiés with dishes from Senegal, Cuba, Italy, and beyond.

■ **People-watching:** Lavapiés offers a vibrant cross-section of Madrid that other barrios lack.

■ **Matadero Madrid:** There's always a cutting-edge exhibit on in this converted abattoir.

■ **Museo Nacional Centro de Arte Reina Sofía:** Ponder Picasso's *Guernica* here.

PLANNING YOUR TIME

Spend most of your time in the endlessly intriguing neighborhoods of Lavapiés and La Latina, and venture down to the less-colorful Arganzuela district if you enjoy alternative art, in which case the Matadero is a must-see. Expect crowds and chaos in La Latina on Sundays as the area turns into flea market central. La Latina and Lavapiés are rather deserted during the day on weekdays (there aren't many offices in the area) but come to life evenings and weekends, when their many—*many*—bars and restaurants fling open their doors. The high concentration of family-run establishments here means restaurants and shops often shut for the afternoon siesta, usually 2–5 pm (restaurants 4–8 pm).

GETTING HERE

Explore Lavapiés and La Latina from their eponymous metro stops (Línea 3 and Línea 5, respectively), or get off at Embajadores (Líneas 3, 5) or Estación de Arte (Línea 1) and weave up Lavapiés to end in La Latina.

Arganzuela is serviced by three stops on Línea 3. Finding parking is tricky in Lavapiés and La Latina, especially on weekends. BiciMAD bike-share services all three neighborhoods.

FUN FACT

When exploring La Latina, architecture buffs should keep an eye out for *casas a la malicia,* illegally constructed apartments from the 16th to 18th century recognizable by their asymmetrical, randomly placed windows. Their confusing floor plans were intended to dupe the municipal authorities into believing they contained fewer dwellings (allowing landlords to evade property taxes), one of many examples of this neighborhood's unruly character.

One of Madrid's most eccentric, fashionable, and fast-changing areas, the combined neighborhoods of La Latina, Lavapiés, and Arganzuela offer dining, sightseeing, and art to keep you busy for days. Snag a patio table on a neighborhood plaza and watch the world go by. You might see teenagers kicking around a soccer ball, *abuelos* playing dominoes in the shade, or expats catching up over sudsy *cañas* (half-pints) at an outdoor café.

La Latina is perhaps Madrid's most *castizo* (loosely, "authentic") neighborhood with its deep-rooted history and hardscrabble spirit. Its layout has changed little since medieval times, with sinuous cobblestone streets emptying onto wide plazas, but its demographic makeup has in the last decade due to soaring rents and the arrival of Airbnb. Though its mom-and-pop businesses preserve the old-world aesthetic of La Latina of yore, the neighborhood doesn't have the same pleasingly gritty edge it once did. But that doesn't keep Madrileños from flocking here every chance they get, especially around August 15, when the neighborhood's famous Verbena de la Paloma street fair unfolds to the oompah of the chotis.

Cross Calle de Toledo, La Latina's eastern border, and you're in **Lavapiés,** another swiftly gentrifying barrio with steeper narrower streets. First constructed as a poor settlement outside the city walls, today it's one of Madrid's most diverse and sought-after neighborhoods for expats and artsy types, a patchwork quilt of old-timey Spanish establishments intermingled with Chinese convenience stores, Indian restaurants, and North and West African jewelry shops. It's partly due to this cosmopolitan pulse that Lavapiés has overtaken Malasaña and La Latina as Madrid's trendiest district. The buzz is a double-edged sword as chain hotels go up and immigrants and longtime denizens are priced out of their apartments. Relics of the barrio's storied past are never far away: like La Latina, Lavapiés has its own architecture hallmark, the *corrala,* a shared-living residence with communal bathrooms and a central patio that became popular in the 17th century as the neighborhood expanded.

Stretching south and west of La Latina and Lavapiés all the way to the banks of the Manzanares, **Arganzuela** is a working-class district with relatively few historical sights and places of import to the average traveler. Its prime attraction is Matadero Madrid, an arts and culture center occupying a defunct slaughterhouse; snug neighborhood restaurants; and long swaths of the Madrid Río esplanade.

La Latina

Officially part of the Palacio neighborhood, this bustling area surrounding the eponymous metro stop is bordered by Calle de Segovia to the north, Calle de Toledo to the east, Puerta de Toledo to the south, and Calle de Bailén, with its imposing Basílica de San Francisco El Grande, to the west. It houses some of the city's oldest buildings, plenty of sloping streets, and an array of unmissable tapas spots—especially on Cava Baja and Cava Alta, and in the area around Plaza de la Paja.

Sights

Basílica de San Francisco El Grande

CHURCH | In 1760 Carlos III built this basilica on the site of a Franciscan convent, allegedly founded by St. Francis of Assisi in 1217. The dome, 108 feet in diameter, is the largest in Spain, even larger than that of St. Paul's in London. The seven main doors, of American walnut, were carved by Casa Juan Guas. Three chapels adjoin the circular church, the most famous being that of San Bernardino de Siena containing a Goya masterpiece depicting a preaching San Bernardino. The figure standing on the right, not looking up, is a self-portrait of Goya. The 16th-century Gothic choir stalls came from La Cartuja del Paular in rural Segovia province. ⊠ *Calle Gran Vía de San Francisco 19, La Latina* ☎ *91/365–3800* ⊠ *€5 guided tour (in Spanish); free self-guided Sat.* ☉ *Closed Sun. and Mon.* Ⓜ *Puerta de Toledo, La Latina.*

Cava Baja

STREET | Madrid's most popular tapas street is crowded with excellent (if arguably overpriced) tapas bars and traditional *tabernas* (pubs). Its lively, and rather international, atmosphere spills over onto nearby streets and squares including Almendro, Cava Alta, Plaza del Humilladero, and Plaza de la Paja. Expect full houses and long wait times on weekend nights. ⊠ *La Latina* Ⓜ *La Latina.*

Jardín del Príncipe de Anglona (*Garden of the Prince of Anglona*)

CITY PARK | Enter Madrid's "secret garden" through a swinging wrought-iron gate at the north end of Plaza de la Paja. Hiding in plain sight, the 18th-century grounds are a little-known oasis with a burbling fountain, mampuesto stone paths, low-cut boxwood hedges, and a small arbor. Shaded benches around the perimeter feel a world away from the bustling plaza mere steps from where you sit. ⊠ *Pl. de la Paja 6, La Latina* Ⓜ *La Latina.*

Mercado de la Cebada

MARKET | FAMILY | An unrenovated building and budget-friendly tapas and groceries make this market a local favorite for both shopping and snacking. The hangar-like space is at its busiest on Saturday from noon to 3 pm, when seafood stalls transform into makeshift fish and shellfish restaurants, frying, steaming, and boiling their freshest wares and serving them on plastic plates alongside jugs of unlabeled table wine—quite the party. ⊠ *Pl. de la Cebada s/n, La Latina* ☎ *91/366–6966* ⊕ *www.mercadodelacebada.com* ☉ *Closed Sun.* Ⓜ *La Latina.*

★ Plaza de la Paja

PLAZA/SQUARE | At the top of a hill, on Costanilla de San Andrés, sits the most important square of medieval Madrid. It predates the Plaza Mayor by at least two centuries. The sloped plaza's jewel is the Capilla del Obispo (Bishop's Chapel), built between 1520 and 1530, where peasants deposited their tithes, called

You can't leave Madrid without tasting the famous huevos estrellados (eggs with ham and fries) of Casa Lucio on Madrid's most famous tapas street, Cava Baja.

diezmas—one-tenth of their crop. Architecturally the chapel traces the transition from the blocky Gothic period, which gave the structure its basic shape, to the Renaissance, the source of its decorations. It houses a polychrome altarpiece with scenes from the New Testament and a carved alabaster cenotaph by Francisco Giralte that art historians fawn over. Seven cloistered nuns live in the building and hold Mass in the chapel on Sundays at 6:30 pm and at several other times during the week (check the schedule on the door or call for details). To visit the chapel it is imperative to reserve in advance; tours are in Spanish only. The chapel is part of the complex of the domed Iglesia de San Andrés (Church of San Andrés), one of Madrid's oldest. ✉ *La Latina* ☎ *91/559–2874* ✉ *reservascapilladelobispo@archimadrid.es* 🎟 *€4 (Capilla del Obispo)* 🕒 *Chapel tours Tues. 9:30–12:30 and Thurs. 4–5:30* ✍ *Reservation required to visit chapel* [M] *La Latina.*

🍴 Restaurants

Casa Botín

$$$ | SPANISH | Botín, established in 1725, is the world's oldest restaurant (according to Guinness World Records) and was a favorite of Ernest Hemingway—the final scene of *The Sun Also Rises* is set in this very place. The *cochinillo asado* (roast suckling pig), stuffed with aromatics, doused with wine, and crisped in the original wood-burning oven, is a must. **Known for:** world's oldest restaurant; roast lamb and suckling pig; roving music ensembles. [$] *Average main: €27* ✉ *Calle de Cuchilleros 17, La Latina* ☎ *91/366–4217* 🌐 *botin.es* [M] *Tirso de Molina.*

★ Casa Gerardo

$ | TAPAS | *Tinajas*, huge clay vessels once filled to the brim with bulk wine (but now defunct), sit behind the bar at this raucous no-frills bodega specializing in Spanish cheese and charcuterie. Ask the waiters what they've been drinking and eating lately, and order precisely that. **Known for:** unforgettable old-world

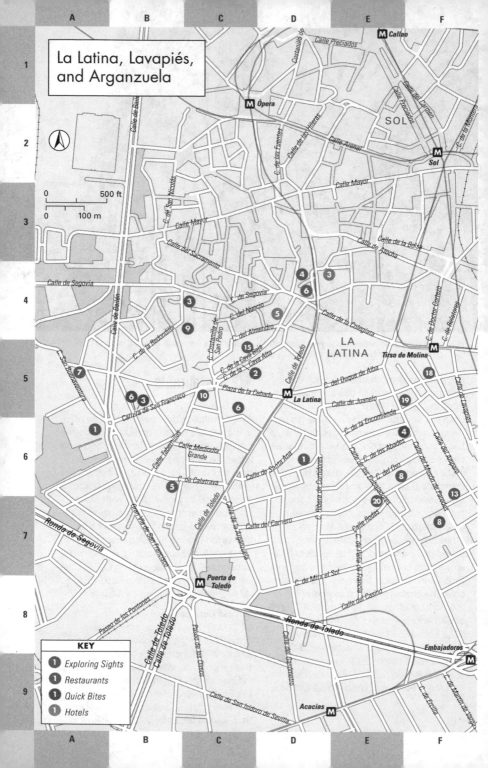

Sights ▼

Restaurants ▼

Quick Bites ▼

Hotels ▼

atmosphere; wide selection of wines and charcuterie; frazzled yet friendly staff. $ Average main: €11 ⊠ Calle de Calatrava 21, La Latina ☎ 91/221–9660 ⊙ Closed Mon. Ⓜ La Latina, Puerta de Toledo.

★ Casa Revuelta

$ | SPANISH | Many tapas bars serve pincho de bacalao (battered cod, an old-school standby), but the fan favorite is Revuelta's rendition, which is crisp, featherlight, and not too salty. Elbow your way to the 1930s-era bar and ask for a pincho de bacalao and a glass of Valdepeñas, a Manchegan red that comes chilled in tiny stemless glasses—just like the olden days. **Known for:** battered salt cod canapés; midmorning vermú (vermouth) rush; time-warp decor. $ Average main: €8 ⊠ Calle de Latoneros 3, La Latina ☎ 91/366–3332 ⊕ www.casarevuelta. com ⊙ Closed Mon. No dinner Sun. Ⓜ La Latina.

El Landó

$$$ | SPANISH | This old-timey restaurant, with dark wood-paneled walls lined with bottles of wine, serves classic Spanish food like huevos estrellados, grilled meats, and fish (sea bass, haddock, grouper, and more) in various preparations. Check out the pictures of famous celebrities who've eaten at this typically noisy landmark; they line the staircase that leads to the main dining area. **Known for:** castizo ambience; huevos estrellados and top-shelf Extremaduran ham; impeccably cooked seafood. $ Average main: €26 ⊠ Pl. de Gabriel Miró 8, La Latina ☎ 91/366–7681 ⊙ No dinner Sun. Ⓜ La Latina.

★ Juana La Loca

$$$ | TAPAS | This tony gastro bar serves newfangled tapas that are well worth their higher-than-usual price tag. Spring for the tempura soft-shell crab bao with chive mayonnaise, garlicky artichoke flatbread, or any other tapa del día, but whatever you do, order the famous tortilla de patata, irresistible with its molten core and handfuls of caramelized onions.

Known for: nueva cocina tapas done right; earth-shatteringly good tortilla de patata; cheek-by-jowl crowds. $ Average main: €25 ⊠ Pl. de Puerta de Moros 4, La Latina ☎ 91/366–5500 ⊕ juanalaloca.es ⊙ Closed Mon. Ⓜ La Latina.

Los Huevos de Lucio

$$ | SPANISH | Don't let the crowds dissuade you from entering this Cava Baja stalwart—tables and barstools open up fast. The nonnegotiable dish to try here is huevos estrellados, "bashed" fried eggs tucked between olive-oil-fried potatoes and topped with optional add-ons like jamón, chistorra sausage, and pisto (Spanish ratatouille). **Known for:** fried egg nirvana; great salads and vegetable dishes; uproarious atmosphere. $ Average main: €19 ⊠ Calle de Cava Baja 32, La Latina ☎ 91/366–2984 ⊕ loshuevosdelucio.com Ⓜ La Latina.

🍴 Coffee and Quick Bites

★ Pastora

$ | CAFÉ | At this sun-drenched two-table coffee shop, grab a café con leche before perusing the shelves, which are stocked with Spanish conservas (preserved foods), natural wines, and other culinary gems that make great gifts or picnic fare. **Known for:** local trendster hangout; natural wine for sale (and by the glass, if you ask); small-production Colombian coffee. $ Average main: €5 ⊠ Carrera de San Francisco 12, La Latina Ⓜ La Latina, Puerta de Toledo.

★ Taberna Sanlúcar

$ | TAPAS | This cozy tiled bar will teleport you to the coastal Andalusian city of the same name with briny olives, bone-dry Manzanilla sherries, and shatteringly crisp tortillitas de camarón (shrimp fritters). **Known for:** bubbly helpful waitstaff; outstanding conservas and fried seafood; Andalusian tavern ambience. $ Average main: €13 ⊠ Calle de San Isidro Labrador 14, La Latina ☎ 91/354–0052 ⊕ tabernasanlucar.com ⊙ Closed Mon. Ⓜ La Latina.

A Good Walk: Old Madrid

Wander around Puerta del Sol for a look at Madrid's oldest buildings, bustling taverns, and cobblestone alleys. Allow about two hours, or more if you visit the Palacio Real or Real Monasterio de la Encarnación.

Begin at the freshly remodeled **Puerta del Sol**, the center of Madrid and a major social and transportation hub, then take Calle Mayor to **Plaza Mayor**. Inaugurated in 1620 on the site of a street market, this is Madrid's historical main square, where you'll find the Casa de la Panadería (Bakery House)— an imposing building with mythological figures painted on its facade, home of the main tourism office.

Exit Plaza Mayor through the "Cutler's Arch" (Arco de Cuchilleros) and go down the stairs: to the right is Calle de Cava de San Miguel—an ancient-looking stretch of colorful taverns that inches uphill to the posh Mercado de San Miguel and Calle Mayor; to the left is Calle de Cuchilleros ("Cutlers' Street"), which leads to the Plaza de Puerta Cerrada, or "Closed Gate." The mural up to your right reads "*Fui sobre agua edificada; mis muros de fuego son*" ("I was built on water; my walls are made of fire"), a reference to the city's origins as a fortress with abundant springs and flint ramparts. Cross the street to **Calle de Cava Baja** , packed with taverns and restaurants. At Plaza del Humilladero, walk past Plaza de San Andrés and take Costanilla de San Andrés from Plaza de Puerta de Moros, down to **Plaza de la Paja**, which was renovated in 2022. The **Capilla del Obispo**, on the south edge of the plaza, completed in 1535, houses one of Spain's most magnificent Renaissance altarpieces. Look right on narrow Calle del Príncipe

de Anglona—at its end you'll see a tall redbrick Mudejar tower, the only original element belonging to San Pedro el Real (St. Peter the Royal), one of Madrid's oldest churches.

Cross Calle de Segovia to Plaza de la Cruz Verde, take the stairs (Calle del Rollo) to your right, go straight to Calle del Cordón, then turn left. Walk up the stairs and cross the Plaza del Cordón and Calle del Sacramento to get to **Plaza de la Villa**; noteworthy buildings here are (west) the former city hall main office, finished in 1692; (east) the Casa and Torre de los Lujanes, the oldest civil building in Madrid, dating to the mid-15th century; and (south) the Casa de Cisneros, from the 16th century. Turn left on Calle Mayor and walk to Calle de San Nicolás; on the corner is the Palacio del Duque de Uceda, a residential building from the 17th century now used as a military headquarters. Turn right onto Calle de San Nicolás (San Nicolás de los Servitas is Madrid's oldest standing church, with a Mudejar tower dating to the 17th century) and walk to Plaza de Ramales, where you'll find a display of a ruined section of the foundation of the medieval Iglesia de San Juan (Church of San Juan), demolished in the 19th century. Take Calle de San Nicolas until it becomes Calle de Lepanto, which leads to the **Plaza de Oriente**. The equestrian statue of Felipe IV was sculpted from a drawing by Velázquez, who worked and died in what is now a residential building on the east side of the plaza. Take a breather in the plaza, then visit the **Palacio Real**, the adjacent **Jardines de Sabatini**, or the nearby **Monastery of the Incarnation**.

Hotels

★ The Hat

$ | **HOTEL** | The Hat epitomizes the fast-growing category of "designer hostels," affordable properties geared toward the younger set with sleek multiperson (and some private) rooms, bumping weekend events, and generous breakfasts. **Pros:** rooftop bar; steps from Plaza Mayor; bountiful breakfasts. **Cons:** hotel guests not prioritized on rooftop, which fills up fast; some rooms are dark; location means tourists are everywhere. *[$] Rooms from: €74 ✉ Calle Imperial 9, La Latina ☎ 91/772–8572 🌐 thehatmadrid.com 🛏 42 rooms 🍴 Free Breakfast [M] Tirso de Molina.*

Posada del León de Oro

$$$ | **HOTEL** | More like a modern village inn than a metropolitan hotel, this refurbished late-19th-century property was built atop the remains of a stone wall that encircled the city in the 12th century, which you can see through glass floor panels at the hotel entrance and in the casual restaurant. **Pros:** located in tapas central; restaurant with more than 300 Spanish wines; high ceilings with exposed wood beams. **Cons:** interior-facing rooms are small; late-night noise; cramped entry-level rooms. *[$] Rooms from: €247 ✉ Calle de Cava Baja 12, La Latina ☎ 91/119–1494 🌐 www.posadadelleondeoro.com 🛏 27 rooms 🍴 No Meals [M] La Latina.*

Nightlife

BARS

Delic

CAFÉS | This warm, inviting café-bar is an all-hours hangout. Homesick travelers will find comfort in Delic's carrot cake, brownies, and pumpkin pie (seasonal), while low-key revelers will appreciate the bar's coziness and late hours (open until 1:30 am on weekends). *✉ Pl. de la Paja, Costanilla de San Andrés 14, La Latina ☎ 91/364–5450 🌐 delic.es 🕓 Closed Mon. [M] La Latina.*

El Viajero

BARS | You can find fine modern raciones here (the ultracreamy burrata stands out), but this place is better known for its middle-floor bar, which fills up with a cocktail-drinking after-work crowd, and rooftop terrace decorated with potted plants. Beware of the 10% surcharge that comes with outdoor dining, and expect so-so service. *✉ Pl. de la Cebada 11, La Latina ☎ 91/366–9064 🌐 www.elviajero-madrid.com 🕓 Closed Mon. [M] La Latina.*

★ Sala Equis

CABARET | This trendy cinema-bar hybrid occupies a former adult-film theater. The first floor is a high-ceilinged bar with bleacher seating, deck chairs, cushy sofas, and an ivy-covered wall. Upstairs, there's a quieter lounge with velvet walls and warm neon lights; continue to the top floor and you've reached the main attraction, a 55-seat cinema with cocktail service that plays art-house films (buy tickets online in advance). The Spanish movies don't have subtitles, but there are frequent screenings of undubbed English films. *✉ Calle del Duque de Alba 4, La Latina ☎ 91/429–6686 🌐 salaequis.es [M] Tirso de Molina.*

Shopping

CRAFTS AND DESIGN

★ Cocol

CRAFTS | There's no better shop in Madrid for top-quality Spanish artisan wares. The shelves in this tiny independently owned boutique off Plaza de la Paja are lined with everything from exquisite Andalusian pottery to hand-sewn blankets, antique esparto baskets, and leather soccer balls. *✉ Costanilla de San Andrés 18, La Latina ☎ 91/919–6770 🌐 cocolmadrid.es [M] La Latina.*

FOOD

Madrid & Darracott

WINE/SPIRITS | More than just a neighborhood wine shop with a well-curated cellar, Madrid & Darracott hosts daily

Summer Terraces

Madrid is blazing hot from late spring to early fall, but locals can't resist being outdoors. So they make do with some 2,000 bars and restaurants with alfresco spaces (some fashioned with mist systems) for enjoying the cool nighttime air. These were social lifelines during the pandemic, when indoor dining was limited and often ill-advised.

For classy alfresco food and drink, we recommend hotel restaurants with gardens or quiet rooftop patios such as El Jardín de Orfila (at Hotel Orfila), Heritage Madrid, El Paraguas, and Paco Roncero.

Two midrange restaurants with good terraces are Sacha and Cinco Jotas Jorge Juan, the latter run by the famous jamón house. More casual full-service dining options include El Viajero (La Latina) and Casa Lafu (Palacio).

If you just want a glass of wine and a tapa or two, scope out La Latina neighborhood, especially Plaza de la Paja or Plaza de San Andrés, or the terraces at Plaza de Olavide in Chamberí. Calle de Argumosa in Lavapiés is another famous street for *terraceo* (terrace-hopping), but don't expect anything too gastronomical.

Among the younger, alternative set, go-to plazas include Plaza de Chueca in the eponymous barrio (and the nearby Plaza de Vázquez de Mella), Plaza de Agustín Lara, Plaza del Dos de Mayo, and Plaza de las Comendadoras, whose top hangout is Federal Café.

There's wonderful (and more chichi) seating along Paseo de la Castellana, above the Mercado de San Antón in Chueca, at the Círculo de Bellas Artes rooftop, and at a variety of hotel rooftops that have become hot spots in the last few years: Hotel Urban, ME Madrid, The Principal, Iberostar Las Letras, Gran Meliá Palacio de los Duques, Room Mate Macarena, and Room Mate Óscar, to name a few.

8

La Latina, Lavapiés, and Arganzuela LAVAPIÉS

---

wine tastings in English. Wondering about the difference between Rioja and Ribera del Duero or what makes Cava sparkle? Reserve your spot online and show up sober—the pours are generous. ✉ *Calle del Duque de Rivas 8, La Latina* ☎ *91/219–1975* ⊕ *www.madriddarracott. com* ⊗ *Closed Sun.* Ⓜ *Tirso de Molina.*

Lavapiés

Lavapiés, technically part of the Embajadores neighborhood, spokes out from Plaza de Lavapiés. Its perimeter is roughly delineated by the following metro stops: La Latina, Tirso de Molina, and Antón Martín to the north; Estación de Arte (formerly Atocha) to the east; and Embajadores to the south. Calle de Argumosa has one of Spain's highest concentration of bars, and its sidewalks teem with outdoor diners come summer. Calle del Doctor Fourquet is lined with art galleries and studios. Plaza de Nelson Mandela, Plaza de Agustín Lara, and Plaza de Lavapiés are the main social hubs.

 Sights

★ Museo Nacional Centro de Arte Reina Sofía

ART MUSEUM | Spain's national museum of contemporary art houses works by all the major 20th-century Spanish painters and sculptors. Its collection breaks

The bustling Rastro flea market takes place every Sunday 10–2; you never know what kind of treasures you might find.

from tradition by grouping works of the great modern masters—Picasso, Miró, and Salvador Dalí—by historical context as opposed to artistic movement. So, Goya's *Disasters of War* engravings (a precursor of the avant-garde movements of the 20th century) sits beside one of the first movies ever made, *Employees Leaving the Lumière Factory* by the Lumière brothers. Picassos and Dalís are not displayed together but are rather scattered around the 38 rooms. The museum also displays important works by Juan Gris, Jorge Oteiza, Pablo Gargallo, Julio González, Eduardo Chillida, and Antoni Tàpies.

The crown jewel is Picasso's *Guernica*. The sprawling black-and-white canvas depicts the horror of the Nazi bombing of innocent civilians in the ancient Basque town of Gernika in 1937 during the Spanish Civil War. The work was commissioned by the Republican government for the Spanish pavilion at the 1937 World's Fair in an attempt to garner sympathy for the Republican cause. Rooms adjacent

to *Guernica* reconstruct the artistic significance of Spain's participation in the World's Fair with works by Miró, Josep Maria Sert, Alexander Calder, and others. *Guernica* did not reach Madrid until 1981, as Picasso had stipulated in his will that the painting return to Spain only after democracy was restored.

The fourth floor in the Sabatini Building is devoted to art created after World War II, and the Nouvel Annex displays paintings, sculptures, photos, videos, and installations from the last quarter of the 20th century.

The museum was once a hospital, but the austerity of the space is somewhat relieved (or ruined, depending on your point of view) by the playful pair of glass elevator shafts on its facade. Three separate buildings joined by a common vault were added to the original complex in 2005—the first contains an art bookshop and a public library, the second a center for contemporary exhibitions, and the third an auditorium and restaurant. The latter, which got a face-lift in 2017, is a colorful, space-age spot to enjoy a café con leche—or a cocktail—and an eye-catching tapa or two. ✉ *Calle de Santa Isabel 52, Lavapiés* ☎ *91/774–1000* 🌐 *www.museoreinasofia.es* 🎟 *From €12 (free Mon. and Wed.–Sat. after 7 pm, Sun. 12:30–2:30)* 🕒 *Closed Tues.* [M] *Estación del Arte.*

★ Mercado de Antón Martín

MARKET | Go on an international tapas crawl here—nibbling on tacos (at Cutzamala), sushi (at Yokaloka), homemade croissants (at Cafés Tornasol), and more—without so much as stepping outside. Doppelgänger, an eclectic tasting-menu-only cubbyhole headed by a young Somali–Spanish chef, is currently all the rage. ✉ *Calle de Santa Isabel 5, Lavapiés* ☎ *91/369–0620* 🌐 *www.mercadoantonmartin.com* 🕒 *Closed Sun.* ☞ *Some businesses are also closed Mon.* [M] *Antón Martín.*

Plaza de Agustín Lara (*House of Sombrerete*)

PLAZA/SQUARE | The historical 19th-century residence Corrala de Sombrerete, which overlooks this lively square from the southeast corner, is one of Madrid's few remaining *corralas*, tenement houses distinguished by timber frames and a central patio. It is closed to the public but still worth a walk-by. Beyond it is a brick building with a hollow cupola dominating the square: the Escolapios de San Fernando, one of several churches and parochial schools razed due to anti-Catholic sentiments during the Spanish Civil War. It is one of Madrid's only unrepaired Civil War ruins. Though partially refurbished by the Universidad Nacional de Educación a Distancia (UNED), which turned one section into a library, the building is closed to the public. ✉ *Calle del Sombrerete 13, Lavapiés* [M] *Lavapiés.*

Plaza de Lavapiés

PLAZA/SQUARE | This oblong plaza is Lavapiés's nerve center. To the east is Calle de la Fe (Street of Faith), named for the church of **San Lorenzo**. ✉ *Lavapiés* [M] *Lavapiés.*

🍴 Restaurants

Bar Santurce

$ | **TAPAS** | This take-no-prisoners abuelo bar near the top of El Rastro is famous for griddled sardines, served hot and greasy in an odiferous heap with nothing but a flick of crunchy salt. Beware, super-smellers: eau de sardine is a potent perfume. **Known for:** sardine mecca; inexpensive and unfussy; busy on Sunday. [$] *Average main: €10* ✉ *Pl. del General Vara del Rey 14, Lavapiés* ☎ *64/623–8303* 🌐 *www.barsanturce.com* 🕒 *Closed Mon.* [M] *La Latina.*

El Rincón de Marco

$ | **CUBAN** | **FAMILY** | Step straight into Havana at this hidden Cuban bar and restaurant where rumbas and *sones* flow from the speakers and regulars burst into impromptu dance parties. Whatever you end up eating—a €7 *ropa vieja* (cumin-scented beef stew), or perhaps the heftier €10 *picapollo* (fried chicken)—be sure to nab an order or two of fried plantains for the table. **Known for:** home-cooked Cuban food; kitschy decor; music that makes you want to dance. [$] *Average main: €10* ✉ *Calle de los Cabestreros 10, Lavapiés* ☎ *91/210–7500* 🕒 *Closed Mon.* [M] *Lavapiés.*

La Burlona

$$ | **TAPAS** | Indulge in some self-pampering or impress a special someone at this sunlight-flooded gastro-tavern with minimalist decor that serves creatively plated dishes that taste as good as they look (think porcini and foie fideuà or Cantonese-style Iberian pork ribs). Burlona's clandestine coctelería, El Trilero, is downstairs in the arcaded brick basement if you fancy a cocktail after your meal. **Known for:** eye-popping modern tapas; more than 30 small-production wines by the bottle; secret bar below. [$] *Average main: €21* ✉ *Calle de Santa Isabel 40, Lavapiés* ☎ *91/018–0018* 🌐 *www.laburlona.com* 🕒 *Closed Mon. and Tues.* [M] *Lavapiés.*

La Oveja Negra

$ | **VEGETARIAN** | Traveling as a vegan in Madrid is becoming easier thanks to affordable inviting restaurants with palate-popping food like Oveja Negra. Try vegan takes on Spanish classics like sidra-braised soy chorizo, leek-and-squash croquetas, and meatless pâtés. **Known for:** tasty vegan cuisine; laid-back vibe; punk atmosphere. [$] *Average main: €14* ✉ *Calle de Buenavista 42, Lavapiés* ☎ *66/585–7363* 🌐 *ovejavegana.com* [M] *Lavapiés.*

★ La Teranga

$ | **AFRICAN** | **FAMILY** | To get a literal taste of Lavapiés's vibrant West African community, step into this family-run Senegalese hole-in-the-wall that serves the neighborhood's best *mafé* (meat-and-peanut stew), *samousas* (spicy meat-filled turnovers), and *thieboudienne* (Senegal's national dish, made with fish and vegetables)—at exceptionally affordable prices. **Known for:** almost exclusively West African clientele; warm and welcoming staff; Senegalese home cooking. [$] *Average main: €10* ✉ *Calle de Caravaca 12, Lavapiés* ☎ *60/214–1016* [M] *Lavapiés.*

Los Chuchis

$$ | **BRITISH** | For groups larger than two, reservations are a must at this cozy neighborhood bar decorated with books, colorful knickknacks, and fresh flowers. You can count on British chef Scott Preston to provide craveable pub food like craggy-crispy potato skins and oozy baked feta, plus healthier, more Mediterranean options like curried vegetable couscous and flake-apart hake with clams and salsa verde. **Known for:** British pub food; u-shape bar; cozy vibe. [$] *Average main: €18* ✉ *Calle del Amparo 82, Lavapiés* ☎ *91/127–6606* 🌐 *www.facebook.com/LosChuchisBar* ⏲ *Closed Mon. and Tues.* [M] *Embajadores.*

★ Melo's

$ | **SPANISH** | This beloved old Galician bar changed hands in 2021—it's now run by three twentysomething Madrid natives who couldn't bear to see their favorite neighborhood hangout disappear—but the menu of eight infallible dishes has miraculously stayed the same (save for the addition of battered cod, a secret family recipe of one of the new business partners). Come for the jamón-flecked croquetas, blistered Padrón peppers, and griddled football-size *zapatilla* sandwiches; stay for the dressed-down conviviality and the *cuncos* (ceramic bowls) overflowing with slatey Albariño.✉ **Known for:** old-school Galician bar food; oversize ham croquetas; battered cod grandfathered in from Casa Revuelta. [$] *Average main: €11* ✉ *Calle del Ave María 44, Lavapiés* ☎ *91/527–5054* [M] *Lavapiés.*

Restaurante Badila

$$ | **SPANISH** | **FAMILY** | This mom-and-pop lunch-only staple has paper tablecloths, walls hung with ceramic plates, and a chalked menu. The ever-rotating prix fixe menu is the move here—for €15 (or €18 on weekends), choose from, say, rustic bean stew, a huge T-bone steak, or a wild-mushroom scramble, followed by homemade chocolate cake. **Known for:** great-value prix fixe; lovingly made modern Spanish food; bubbly staff. [$] *Average main: €18* ✉ *Calle de San Pedro Mártir 6, Lavapiés* ☎ *91/429–7651* ⏲ *No dinner* [M] *Tirso de Molina.*

Taberna de Antonio Sánchez

$$ | **SPANISH** | A Lavapiés landmark opened in 1786, this taberna's regulars have included realist painter Ignacio Zuloaga, countless champion bullfighters, and King Alfonso XIII. Sip on a sudsy caña in the creaky, characterful bar area along with a free tapa or two and then scram—there's much better food to be had in this barrio. **Known for:** centuries-old decor; museum-grade bullfighting paraphernalia; cold cañas poured from an ancient pewter tap. [$] *Average main: €18* ✉ *Calle del Mesón de Paredes, Lavapiés* ☎ *91/539–7826* 🌐 *www.tabernaantoniosanchez.com* ⏲ *No dinner Sun.* [M] *Lavapiés.*

Tasca Barea

$ | TAPAS | Floor-to-ceiling windows, an intimate corner bar, and throwback tapas keep this "tasca moderna" packed with neighborhood dwellers night after night. Particularly addictive are the *gildas* (anchovy skewers) and *marineras murcianas*, loopy crackers topped with potato salad and draped with an anchovy. **Known for:** fun, breezy ambience; pet-friendly; traditional tapas in danger of disappearing. $ *Average main: €14* ✉ *Calle de Rodas 2, Lavapiés* ⊕ *tascabarea.wixsite. com/tascabarea* Ⓜ *Lavapiés.*

☕ Coffee and Quick Bites

Bar El Boquerón

$ | SEAFOOD | Step back in time in this pocket-size seafood restaurant specializing in boquerones en vinagre, freshly shucked oysters, and prawns *a la plancha*. **Known for:** true-blue neighborhood spot; fresh seafood; charming hole-in-the-wall. $ *Average main: €14* ✉ *Calle de Valencia 14, Lavapiés* ⊘ *Closed Wed. No dinner Sun.* Ⓜ *Lavapiés.*

Hola Coffee

$ | CAFÉ | Spaniards love their morning cafés con leche and afternoon *cortados* (espresso with steamed milk), but until a few years ago, it was hard to find a truly great cup of joe in Madrid. Enter Hola Coffee, whose multilayered third-wave espressos and cold brews are made with beans the company roasts itself. **Known for:** third-wave coffees made with house-roasted beans; multilingual expat staff and clientele; alternative music and atmosphere. $ *Average main: €9* ✉ *Calle del Doctor Fourquet 33, Lavapiés* ☎ *91/056–8263* ⊕ *hola.coffee* Ⓜ *Lavapiés.*

Plántate Café

$ | CAFÉ | This coffee shop with exposed-brick walls is an adorable breakfast nook worth seeking out for its single-origin brews and well-priced plant-based brunches. **Known for:** plenty of vegan options; open till 7:30 pm; popular with

expats. $ *Average main: €13* ✉ *Calle del Mesón de Paredes 28, Lavapiés* ☎ *91/023–0291* ⊕ *www.facebook.com/ plantatecafe* Ⓜ *Lavapiés.*

Pum Pum Café

$ | CAFÉ | FAMILY | Get your brunch fix here with killer homemade pastries, eggs Benedict, and single-origin coffees. **Known for:** fantastic baked goods; local crowd; best brunch in Lavapiés. $ *Average main: €9* ✉ *Calle de Tribulete 6, La Latina* ⊕ *www.pumpumcafe.com* Ⓜ *Lavapiés.*

Hotels

Artrip

$$$ | HOTEL | A stone's throw from Madrid's "Golden Triangle" of museums, Artrip is a little-known gem of a hotel ideally suited to art-loving travelers. **Pros:** non-touristy area; independently owned; youthful design touches. **Cons:** street noise; small showers; no parking. $ *Rooms from: €212* ✉ *Calle de Valencia 11, Lavapiés* ☎ *91/539–3282* ⊕ *www. artriphotel.com* ⤴ *17 rooms* ⦿ *No Meals* Ⓜ *Embajadores.*

CoolRooms Palacio de Atocha

$$$$ | HOTEL | The splashiest hotel in this part of town, CoolRooms is situated five minutes on foot from both Sol and Antón Martín market. **Pros:** spacious rooms; neon signs and clubby young atmosphere; fresh flowers and plants galore. **Cons:** no gym; overeager and occasionally harried staff; unheated shallow pool. $ *Rooms from: €317* ✉ *Calle de Atocha 34, Lavapiés* ☎ *91/088–7780* ⊕ *cool-rooms.com/palaciodeatocha* ⤴ *35 rooms* ⦿ *No Meals* Ⓜ *Antón Martín, Sol.*

Hotel Freedom

$$ | HOTEL | FAMILY | Rooms in this inexpensive and cheerful hotel overlooking Plaza de Antón Martín have turquoise walls, crimson sofas, and multicolor headboards. **Pros:** independently owned; trendy location; immaculately clean. **Cons:** lobby-adjacent room is noisy; no restaurant, bar, gym, or room service; no breakfast. $ *Rooms from: €160* ⊠ *Calle de Santa Isabel 4, Lavapiés* ☏ *91/073–6271* ⊕ *hotelfreedom.com* ⋑ *21 rooms* ‖⊙‖ *No Meals* Ⓜ *Antón Martín.*

Nightlife

BARS

★ Bendito Vinos y Vinilos

WINE BARS | This unassuming stall inside Mercado de San Fernando is a wine-industry hangout—one of the city's top spots for sampling hard-to-find natural and biodynamic wines. Pair whatever wine the bartenders are drinking lately with Bendito's well-priced cheeses and charcuterie such as *mojama* (cured tuna) from Andalusia and ribbons of smoky *cecina* (beef "ham") from León. ⊠ *Mercado de San Fernando, Calle de Embajadores 42, Lavapiés* ☏ *66/175–0061* ⊕ *www.benditovino.com* ⊙ *Closed Mon.* Ⓜ *Lavapiés.*

La Caníbal

WINE BARS | At this newly expanded wine-and-tapas hot spot with communal tables ideally suited to large groups, you can pull up a stool and choose from dozens of boutique bottles or some 15 small-production Spanish wines on tap. ⊠ *Calle de Argumosa 28, Lavapiés* ☏ *91/539–6057* ⊕ *lacanibal.com* Ⓜ *Estación del Arte.*

La Fisna Vinos

WINE BARS | This romantic wine bar pours more than 50 wines by the glass and serves a delectable menu of market-driven tapas. You'd be hard pressed to find a more impressive roster of French wines anywhere in the city. ⊠ *Calle del Amparo 91, Lavapiés* ☏ *91/539–5615* ⊙ *Closed weekends* Ⓜ *Lavapiés.*

Savas

BARS | Lavapiés upped its cocktail game with Savas, a pocket-size bar that has quickly become a cult hangout for mixology geeks and neighborhood scenesters. The classic cocktails are expertly made—think White Russians and Tom Collinses at about €11 apiece—and local craft beers by La Virgen are on offer. ⊠ *Calle de la Sombrerería 3, Lavapiés* ⊙ *Closed Tues.* Ⓜ *Lavapiés.*

MUSIC AND DANCE CLUBS

Club 33

DANCE CLUBS | This intimate nightclub caters to a local alternative crowd and is a favorite stop on the lesbian party circuit, though revelers of all orientations flock here in droves. ⊠ *Calle de la Cabeza 33, Lavapiés* ☏ *91/369–3302* ⊕ *www.club33madrid.es* ⊙ *Closed Sun.–Wed.* Ⓜ *Lavapiés.*

Performing Arts

FILM

Cine Doré (*Filmoteca*)

FILM | A rare example of Art Nouveau architecture in Madrid, the alternative Cine Doré shows movies from the Spanish National Film Archives and eclectic foreign films, often at budget rates (and you frequently get a short film or two in addition to a feature). The pink neon-trimmed lobby has a sleek café-bar and a bookshop. ⊠ *Calle de Santa Isabel 3, Lavapiés* ☏ *91/369–1125* ⊕ *www.culturaydeporte.gob.es/cultura/areas/cine/mc/fe/cine-dore* Ⓜ *Antón Martín.*

La Casa Encendida

CONCERTS | Film festivals, alternative art shows, dance performances, and events for children (in Spanish) are held here. In summer, there are outdoor concerts on the rooftop, which is open to the public and a pleasant place to unwind with a book when nothing is on. ⊠ *Ronda de Valencia 2, Lavapiés* ☏ *91/506–2180* ⊕ *www.lacasaencendida.es* ⊠ *Free* Ⓜ *Embajadores, Lavapiés.*

⬤ Shopping

ART

Swinton & Grant

ART GALLERIES | Equal parts gallery, bookshop, and café, this art space sells works by contemporary names both Spanish and international, including Augustine Kofie, Olga de Dios, and David de la Mano. Less pricey purchases can be made in the bookshop, which sells curious 'zines and hard-to-find art anthologies. ☒ Calle de Miguel Servet 21, Lavapiés ☎ 91/449–6128 ⊕ swintongallery.com ⊗ Closed Sun. and Mon. Ⓜ Embajadores.

BOOKS

La Casquería

BOOKS | Buy (mostly Spanish) used books by the pound at this stall occupying a former casquería (offal shop). ☒ Mercado de San Fernando, Calle de Embajadores 41, Lavapiés ☎ 91/527–2512 ⊕ lacasqueria.com Ⓜ Lavapiés.

CRAFTS

★ Yolanda Andrés

CRAFTS | These are not your grandma's embroideries! Yolanda Andrés's thought-provoking "paintings with thread" interpret the centuries-old technique through a modern-day lens—with stunning results. Beyond the framed artwork (don't miss the technicolor "Artichoke" line), there are embroidered pillowcases, totes, and more. ☒ Calle de la Encomienda 15, Lavapiés ☎ 91/026–0742 ⊕ yolandaandres.com ⊗ Closed Tues. and Sun. Ⓜ Tirso de Molina.

FLEA MARKETS

★ El Rastro

MARKET | FAMILY | On Sunday morning, Calle de la Ribera de Curtidores is closed to traffic and jammed with outdoor booths selling everything under the sun. Find everything from antique furniture to rare vinyl of flamenco music and keychains emblazoned with "CNT," Spain's old anarchist trade union. Practice your Spanish by bargaining with vendors over paintings, heraldic iron gates, new and used clothes, and even hashish pipes. Plaza del General Vara del Rey has some of El Rastro's best antiques, and the streets beyond—Calles de Mira el Río Alta and Mira el Río Baja—boast all sorts of miscellany. The market shuts down shortly after 2 pm, in time for a street

party to start in the area known as La Latina at and around the bar El Viajero in Plaza del Humilladero.

■TIP→ Off the Ribera are two galerías, courtyards with higher-quality higher-priced antiques shops. ☒ Calle de la Ribera de Curtidores s/n, La Latina ⊗ Closed Mon.–Sat. Ⓜ La Latina.

MUSIC

Percusión Campos

MUSIC | This percussion shop and workshop—where Canarian Pedro Navarro crafts his own cajones flamencos, or flamenco box drums—is hard to find, but his pieces are greatly appreciated among professionals. Prices run €90–€220 and vary according to the quality of woods used. ☒ Calle del Olivar 36, Lavapiés ☎ 91/539–2178 ⊕ www.percusioncampos.com ⊗ Closed Sun. Ⓜ Lavapiés.

Arganzuela

Arganzuela is such a huge district that a born-and-bred Madrileño would never say, "let's meet in Arganzuela." Locals instead speak in terms of the neighborhood's subdistricts: Imperial, Legazpi, Las Delicias, Palos de Moguer, La Chopera, Las Acacias, and Atocha. The lack of historical sights—with the notable exception of Matadero Madrid—keeps this blue-collar area largely off tourists' radar.

◉ Sights

★ Matadero Madrid

ARTS CENTER | What was once Madrid's largest slaughterhouse is now one of its most vibrant arts and culture centers. The Matadero Municipal de Legazpi was in operation from 1925 to 1996; at its peak, it comprised 64 buildings and processed over 500 cattle and 5,000 sheep per day. The complex is a stunning example of Spanish fin-de-siècle civil architecture, all stone-and-redbrick facades punctuated by wide doorways and arched windows. Today its bays are thronged with families, tourists, and plenty of pierced-and-tattooed artists. Events range from film screenings to poetry slams to art exhibits and design fairs. La Cantina, the restaurant on the premises, is pleasant for a drink, though the food is nothing special. ✉ *Pl. de Legazpi 8, Arganzuela* ☎ *91/318–4670* 🌐 *www.mataderomadrid.org* 🎟 *Free* [M] *Legazpi.*

🍴 Restaurants

Bar Toboggan

$ | INTERNATIONAL | Thanks to independently owned gems like Toboggan, La Chopera neighborhood is beginning to attract a younger, cooler crowd. This corner bar with outdoor seating serves mouthwatering international tapas ranging from tacos to tortilla to homemade hummus in a sunlit space. **Known for:** local La Virgen beer; open late nights; good-vibes-only atmosphere. [$] *Average main: €13* ✉ *Pl. de Rutilio Gacís 2, Local 1, Arganzuela* ☎ *91/245–6432* 🌐 *www.bartoboggan.com* [M] *Legazpi.*

★ Bodega Salvaje

$ | SPANISH | If you can't make it to the windmill-dotted planes of *Don Quixote*'s La Mancha, you can at least get a taste of that region's flavorful, rib-sticking cuisine at this beloved neighborhood bar within walking distance from the Matadero. Beyond the Manchegan classics—*atascaburras* (potato-bacalao mash), *machacón* (mashed fresh tomato-pepper salad), and *asadillo* (cumin-scented roasted red peppers)—there's a long ever-changing list of Spanish craft beers. **Known for:** pleasant patio; Madrid's best Manchegan restaurant; cheerful waitstaff. [$] *Average main: €13* ✉ *Calle de Jaime el Conquistador 25, Arganzuela* 🕒 *No dinner Sun.* [M] *Legazpi.*

Habesha

$ | ETHIOPIAN | Chili fiends are often disappointed that Spanish food is seldom spicy, but at this mom-and-pop Ethiopian restaurant, you'll find plenty of fiery stews and sauces. Vegans and vegetarians flock here for fresh crunchy slaws, lentil *sambusas* (stuffed pastries), and slow-cooked greens, while omnivores come for the *doro wat* (spiced chicken). **Known for:** home-cooked Ethiopian cuisine; bountiful vegetarian and vegan options; cheery service. [$] *Average main: €14* ✉ *Paseo de Santa María de la Cabeza 16, Arganzuela* ☎ *63/256–0112* 🕒 *Closed Mon.* [M] *Estación de Arte.*

Piantao Legazpi

$$$ | ARGENTINE | This upmarket Argentine *asador* (steak house) hits all the high notes with its daintily crimped empanadas, regional breads, gutsy South American wines, and flame-licked vegetables and steaks airlifted in from La Pampa with just the right amount of char. In 2023, another location, Piantao Chamberí, opened by the Alonso Martínez metro station. **Known for:** industrial yet refined digs; attentive and knowledgeable service; gooey dulce de leche cheesecake. [$] *Average main: €27* ✉ *Paseo de la Chopera 69, Arganzuela* ☎ *65/991–1058* 🌐 *piantao.es* 🕒 *No dinner Sun.* [M] *Legazpi.*

🍸 Nightlife

La Riviera

LIVE MUSIC | One of Madrid's largest nightlife venues, with nine bars and an outdoor terrace, La Riviera hosts big-name DJs, local and international bands, and sundown-to-sunup raves. It's a key party spot on the Madrid Pride week (early July) circuit. ✉ *Paseo Bajo de la Virgen del Puerto s/n, Arganzuela* ☎ *91/365–2415* 🌐 *salariviera.com* [M] *Puerta del Ángel.*

Chapter 9

CHAMBERÍ

Updated by
Benjamin Kemper

👁 Sights	🍴 Restaurants	🏨 Hotels	🛍 Shopping	🍸 Nightlife
★★★☆☆	★★★★★	★★★☆☆	★★☆☆☆	★★★☆☆

NEIGHBORHOOD SNAPSHOT

TOP EXPERIENCES

■ **Tapas on Calle Ponzano:** Go on a new-school tapas crawl through one of Madrid's hottest culinary corridors.

■ **Museo Sorolla:** Wander the halls of the surrealist painter's mansion-museum and see some of his boldest works.

■ **Plaza de Olavide:** Claim an outdoor table in the sun, order a round of drinks, and lose track of time on this stately circular plaza.

■ **Mercado de Vallehermoso:** Take a pulse on local food trends at this buzzy yet unpretentious gastro-market.

■ **Tortilla at Sylkar:** Sample one of Madrid's finest potato omelets at a time-honored haunt.

GETTING HERE

Covering nearly two square miles, Chamberí lies north of Malasaña and Chueca, south of Chamartín, east of Moncloa, and west of Salamanca. Its subdistricts, Trafalgar and Almagro, are where most of the action is, and they're serviced by the following metro stops: San Bernardo (Líneas 2, 4), Quevedo (Línea 2), Iglesia (Línea 1), Canal (Líneas 2, 7), Alonso Cano (Línea 7), Gregorio Marañón (Líneas 7, 10), Rubén Darío (Línea 5), and Alonso Martínez (Líneas 4, 5, 10).

There are BiciMAD bike-share ports throughout the area. As Chamberí lies outside the Madrid 360 low-emission zone, rental cars are allowed entry but parking can be tricky, especially on weekends.

PLANNING YOUR TIME

A fine itinerary would start with impressionist art at the Sorolla followed by tapas and gourmet shopping at Mercado de Vallehermoso; then, you might meander east to Plaza de Olavide for alfresco lounging and people-watching, or make a beeline to Calle de Ponzano, where you can cobble together lunch or dinner by hopping from bar to bar.

PAUSE HERE

Hiding in plain sight in the center of Chamberí is Parque de Santander, an urban oasis with tennis courts, a playground, and running track. Jog a few laps here, or let your kids loose while you rest your feet.

Until recently, Chamberí was largely dismissed as a staid and sleepy residential neighborhood with little to offer tourists. But now, it has established itself as the city's gastronomic nerve center with innovative tapas bars and fusion fine-dining restaurants springing up left and right.

Before the 19th century, Chamberí was a backwater, a desolate hodgepodge of orchards, pine groves, wheat fields, and royal forests. But as Madrid industrialized, the subdistrict of Almagro (aka the "Golden Triangle" for its shape) became the preferred residence of the aristocracy—a legacy that you can see today in opulent constructions like the Palacio de los Marqueses de Bermejillo del Rey on Paseo de Eduardo Dato, now an administrative building, and the Beti-Jai *frontón* (pelota court) on Calle del Marqués de Riscal (rarely open to the public).

◉ Sights

Andén 0 (*Platform Zero*)
OTHER MUSEUM | FAMILY | The so-called ghost station of Chamberí is now a locomotive museum managed by Metro Madrid. It occupies the grand old Chamberí Station, built in 1919 and defunct since 1966. There are vintage advertisements, old maps, and other memorabilia. Tours (free) and placards are in Spanish only. ■TIP→ Don't wait for staff to come fetch you after watching the introductory film—just head down to the platform. ⊠ *Pl. de Chamberí s/n, Chamberí* ☎ *90/044–4404* ⊕ *museosmetromadrid.es/museos/*

estacion-de-chamberi 🖾 *Free* ⊘ *Closed Mon.–Thurs.* Ⓜ *Iglesia, Bilbao.*

Calle de Ponzano
STREET | Locals will tell you that this street boasts more bars per square foot (nearly 100 in total) than anywhere else on earth. Alternative facts aside, there's a bar for every taste here, from tile-walled *tabernas* to louche cocktail lounges to newfangled fusion spots. Start with a *caña* (half-pint) or glass of vermú at a timeworn standby like El Doble (No. 58) or Fide (No. 8) before sampling traditional tapas at Taberna Alipio Ramos (No. 30) or La Máquina (No. 39). More eclectic, refined bites can be found at the tuna-centric DeAtún (No. 59), cheffy Sala de Despiece (No. 11), and modern Basque Arima (No. 51). ⊠ *Calle de Ponzano s/n, Chamberí* ⊕ *ponzaning.es* Ⓜ *Iglesia, Alonso Cano.*

★ Mercado de Vallehermoso
MARKET | Choose from made-to-order *pinsas* (ancient Roman pizzas with a cloud-like crust) at Di Buono, local craft beers at Drakkar, refined market cuisine at El 2, updated Spanish street food at Miga Cana, and high-octane Thai curries at Kitchen 154, among other flavor-packed options at this city-block-size market in the heart of Chamberí. ⊠ *Calle de Vallehermoso 36, Chamberí* ☎ *91/349–5700*

One of Madrid's most charming small museums was once home to Spain's most famous impressionist painter, Joaquín Sorolla.

🌐 *mercadovallehermoso.es* 🕒 *No dinner Sun.* [M] *Quevedo.*

Museo Geominero

SCIENCE MUSEUM | **FAMILY** | Fossils, gems, minerals, and more glitter beneath the lights at this under-the-radar museum housed in a hundred-year-old neoclassical building. ✉ *Calle de Ríos Rosas 23, Chamberí* ☎ *91/349–5700* 🌐 *www.igme.es* 🎟 *Free* [M] *Ríos Rosas.*

★ **Museo Sorolla**

ART MUSEUM | See the world through the once-in-a-generation eye of Spain's most famous impressionist painter, Joaquín Sorolla (1863–1923), who lived and worked most of his life at this home and garden that he designed and decorated. Every corner is filled with exquisite artwork—including plenty of original Sorollas—and impeccably selected furnishings, which pop against brightly colored walls that evoke the Mediterranean coast, where the painter was born. The museum can be seen as part of the Abono Cinco Palacios, a €12 pass that grants access to five mansion-museums. ✉ *Paseo del General Martínez Campos 37, Chamberí* ☎ *91/310–1584* 🌐 *museosorolla.mcu.es* 🎟 *€3 (free Sat. after 2 and Sun.)* 🕒 *Closed Mon.* [M] *Rubén Darío, Gregorio Marañón.*

🍴 Restaurants

Apartaco

$ | **SOUTH AMERICAN** | Venezuelan comfort foods draw crowds to this bar-restaurant with cheery waitstaff and a soundtrack of Latin jazz. Start with a variety platter of appetizers including *tequeños* (gooey cheese sticks), *cachapas* (cheese-stuffed corn cakes), and *tostones* (green plantain fritters); then dive into a caveman-worthy portion of *pabellón criollo* (spiced shredded beef, black beans, and rice), the house specialty. **Known for:** Venezuelan comfort food; €12 lunch prix fixe; fresh-squeezed juices. [$] *Average main: €16* ✉ *Calle de Luchana 7, Chamberí* ☎ *68/697–4916* 🌐 *www.apartaco.es* [M] *Bilbao.*

Las Tortillas de Gabino
$$$ | **TAPAS** | At this lively restaurant you'll find crowds of Spaniards gobbling up one of the city's finest, most upscale renditions of *tortilla española* (Spanish omelet) with unconventional add-ins like octopus, potato chips, and truffles. The menu also includes plenty of equally succulent non-egg choices (the rice dishes stand out). **Known for:** fancy tortillas; date-night ambience; carefully selected wines. [$] *Average main: €25* ✉ *Calle de Rafael Calvo 20, Chamberí* ☎ *91/319–7505* 🌐 *www.lastortillasdegabino.com* 🕒 *Closed Sun.* [M] *Rubén Darío.*

Perretxico Chamberí
$$ | **BASQUE** | The Madrid outpost of a legendary Vitoria-Gasteiz pintxo bar, Perretxico is known for its cocido doughnut—*cocido* being Spain's famous boiled dinner of chickpeas, various meats, and sausages. These are blended into a paste, stuffed inside a doughnut, and served alongside a demitasse of umami-packed bone broth for dunking, a wink to the classic doughnut-coffee combo. **Known for:** cocido doughnut; inventive Basque pinxtos; Chamberí hot spot. [$] *Average main: €19* ✉ *Calle de Rafael Calvo 29, Chamberí* ☎ *91/192–0069* 🌐 *perretxico.es* [M] *Rubén Darío.*

★ Restaurante Barrera
$$$ | **SPANISH** | Duck into this cozy hole-in-the-wall and be treated like family—Ana, the owner, recites the nightly menu to each table and flits around with a smile until the last guest saunters out. Barrera's famous *patatas revolconas* (paprika-spiced mashed potatoes topped with crispy pork belly), are always on offer; they might be followed by roast suckling lamb, wine-braised meatballs, or seared dayboat fish depending on the night. **Known for:** homey romantic atmosphere; terrific patatas revolconas and ensaladilla rusa; unhurried all-night dining. [$] *Average main: €29* ✉ *Calle de Alonso Cano 25, Chamberí* ☎ *91/594–1757* 🕒 *Closed Sun. No dinner Mon.* [M] *Alonso Cano.*

★ Saddle
$$$$ | **EUROPEAN** | Roast duck carved tableside, truffled pâté en croûte, flambéed Grand Marnier soufflé—Saddle does old-school opulence exceptionally well. Multi-course meals unfold in the anachronistically corporate-chic dining room (think LED backlighting and mid-century modern accents), and feature rare seasonal delicacies including *de lágrima* (tear-shaped) baby peas and buttery new potatoes flown in from the Canary Islands. **Known for:** technically impressive cooking without smoke and mirrors; Impeccable service; Madrid's most reliably superb fine-dining restaurant. [$] *Average main: €49* ✉ *Calle de Amador de los Ríos 6, Chamberí* ☎ *91/216–3936* 🌐 *www.saddle-madrid.com* 🕒 *Closed Sun.* [M] *Alonso Martínez, Colón.*

Sala de Despiece
$$$ | **SPANISH** | The opening of this ultra-trendy butcher-shop-themed restaurant spurred the revival of Calle de Ponzano as Madrid's most exciting tapas street. Feast on eye-catching, impeccably prepared dishes like carpaccio-truffle roll-ups and grilled octopus slathered in chimichurri. **Known for:** local celebrity chef; playful industrial decor; see-and-be-seen crowd. [$] *Average main: €28* ✉ *Calle de Ponzano 11, Chamberí* ☎ *91/752–6106* 🌐 *www.saladedespiece.com* [M] *Iglesia, Alonso Cano.*

★ Sylkar
$$ | **SPANISH** | **FAMILY** | Plan on a siesta after dining at this phenomenal down-home restaurant that hasn't changed a lick since opening a half-century ago. Whether you're in the boisterous downstairs bar or cozy upstairs dining room with cloth napkins and popcorn walls, you'll be blown away by Sylkar's lovingly prepared specialties including creamy ham croquettes, braised squid in ink sauce, battered hake, and the best tortilla española in Madrid for those in the runnier-the-better camp. **Known for:** legendary tortilla española; irreverent banter

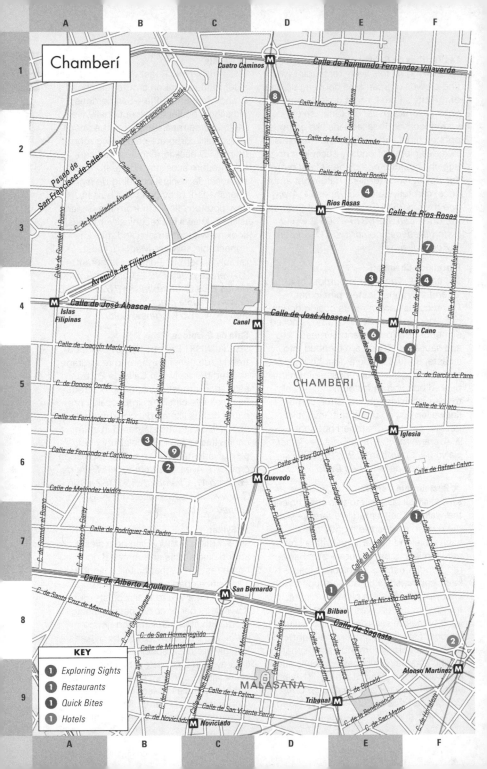

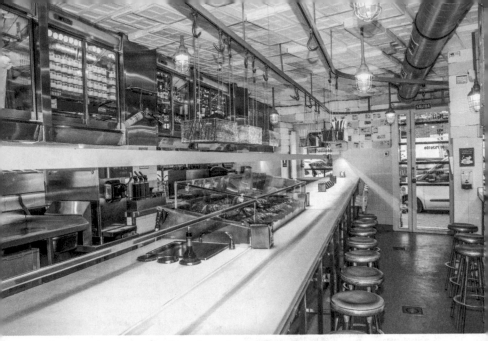

Sala de Despiece's flashy interiors and occasion-worthy fusion cuisine draw a trendy local crowd intent on sampling chef Javier Bonet's latest creations.

with the waitstaff; free tapa with every drink. $ *Average main: €24* ✉ *Calle de Espronceda 17, Chamberí* ☎ *91/554–5703* ⊕ *www.sylkarbar.com* ☉ *Closed Sun. No dinner Sat.* Ⓜ *Alonso Cano.*

Taberna San Mamés

$$$ | SPANISH | What's that fire-truck-red stew on every table in this tiny neighborhood tavern? *Callos a la madrileña,* Madrid-style tripe flavored with industrial quantities of garlic and smoky Extremaduran paprika. **Known for:** abuela-approved tripe stew; cozy traditional digs; neighborhood crowd. $ *Average main: €27* ✉ *Calle de Bravo Murillo 88, Chamberí* ☎ *91/534–5065* ⊕ *www.tabernasanmames.es* ☉ *Closed Sun. No dinner Mon.* Ⓜ *Cuatro Caminos.*

Tripea

$$$$ | FUSION | Chef Roberto Martínez Foronda turns food critics' heads with his Spanish-fusion restaurant hidden inside the Mercado de Vallehermoso, Chamberí's traditional market. The ever-changing tasting menu—a steal at €45—takes cues from *chifa* (Peruvian-Chinese) and *nikkei* (Peruvian-Japanese) culinary canons and incorporates fresh ingredients from the market. **Known for:** experimental tasting menus; Spanish-fusion cuisine; foodie buzz. $ *Average main: €45* ✉ *Mercado de Vallehermoso, Calle de Vallehermoso 36, Chamberí* ☎ *91/828–6947* ⊕ *www.tripea.es* ☉ *Closed Sun. and Mon.* Ⓜ *Quevedo.*

☕ Coffee and Quick Bites

Charnela

$$ | SEAFOOD | Welcome to mussel mecca—this Ponzano restaurant spotlights the oft-overlooked mollusk in dishes like curried moules frites; fried bechamel-stuffed tigres; and zippy ceviches and escabeches. **Known for:** good value; seafood lover's paradise; essential stop on a Ponzano tapas crawl. $ *Average main: €19* ✉ *Calle de Ponzano 8, Chamberí* ✛ *next door to Fide* ☎ *91/024–8142* ⊕ *charnelamadrid.com* ☉ *Closed Mon. No dinner Sun.* Ⓜ *Alonso Cano.*

Ciento Treinta Grados

$ | **CAFÉ** | These carb geeks cut no corners—breads here are leavened with sourdough and made with organic stone-ground flours, and the beans for their complex coffees are roasted in-house. Drop into the postage-stamp dinette for breakfast or an afternoon pick-me-up, and savor airy all-butter croissants and any range of sweet and savory pastries and breads. **Known for:** sourdough breads and pastries; house-roasted coffee beans; across from Mercado de Vallehermoso. [$] *Average main: €9* ✉ *Calle de Fernando el Católico 17, Chamberí* ☎ *91/006–7076* 🌐 *cientotreintagrados.com* [M] *Quevedo.*

Fide

$ | **SEAFOOD** | Crack open a can of pristine Spanish seafood—elvers, scallops, cockles, and more—at this veteran bar on Ponzano and you'll never think about tinned food the same way again. **Known for:** affordable high-quality conservas; old-timey steel bar; flinty Galician white wines. [$] *Average main: €14* ✉ *Calle de Ponzano 8, Chamberí* ☎ *91/446–5833.*

Mazál Bagels & Café

$ | **JEWISH DELI** | **FAMILY** | Hand-rolled New York–style bagels, made fresh daily, hit the spot when continental breakfast fatigue sets in. **Known for:** rib-sticking breakfast sandwiches; Madrid's only decent bagel; challah and other Jewish baked goods. [$] *Average main: €9* ✉ *Calle de Bretón de los Herreros 35, Chamberí* ☎ *91/936–1478* 🌐 *www.mazalmadrid.com* [M] *Ríos Rosas.*

Hotels

Hotel Orfila

$$$$ | **HOTEL** | On a leafy residential street, this 1886 town house bearing the Relais & Château fleur-de-lis feels more like a country estate than a city-center hotel. **Pros:** tranquil year-round dining terrace; old-world comfort; historical art and furniture. **Cons:** food is not up to standard; no gym; expensive room service via poorly designed app. [$] *Rooms from: €600* ✉ *Calle de Orfila 6, Chamberí* ☎ *91/702–7770* 🌐 *www.hotelorfila.com* 🛏 *32 rooms* 🍴 *No Meals* [M] *Alonso Martínez.*

Hotel Sardinero

$$ | **HOTEL** | Steps from the trendy Malasaña and gay-friendly Chueca districts and slightly off the tourist track, Hotel Sardinero occupies a turn-of-the-century palace directly above the Alonso Martínez metro stop. **Pros:** good deals on rates; two rooftop terraces; gorgeous neoclassical facade. **Cons:** some guests report plumbing issues; no restaurant; kettles and coffeemakers only available on request. [$] *Rooms from: €145* ✉ *Pl. de Alonso Martínez 3, Chamberí* ☎ *91/206–2160* 🌐 *www.hotelsardineromadrid.com* 🛏 *63 rooms* 🍴 *No Meals* [M] *Alonso Martínez.*

Intercontinental Madrid

$$$$ | **HOTEL** | Chauffeur-driven town cars snake around the block day and night at the Intercontinental Madrid, a classically decorated hotel frequented by dignitaries, diplomats, and other international bigwigs. **Pros:** dependable if starchy elegance; 24-hour gym; excellent business facilities. **Cons:** cookie-cutter business hotel decor; removed from the center; street-facing rooms can be noisy. [$] *Rooms from: €310* ✉ *Paseo de la Castellana 49, Chamberí* ☎ *91/700–7300* 🌐 *www.ihg.com/intercontinental/hotels/us/en/madrid/mddha/hoteldetail* 🛏 *302 rooms* 🍴 *No Meals* [M] *Gregorio Marañón.*

One Shot Fortuny 07

$$ | **HOTEL** | **FAMILY** | One of the better values in Madrid hotels at the moment, this modern property off the Castellana thoroughfare offers bright, streamlined rooms with starched white linens and understated furniture. **Pros:** pleasing design; tasty breakfasts on the patio (weather permitting); great price for the location. **Cons:** thin walls; inconsistent customer service; no room service or in-room coffee facilities. [$] *Rooms from:*

€179 ⊠ Calle de Fortuny 7, Chamberí ☎ 91/088–5868 ⊕ hoteloneshotfortuny07.com ⮌ 74 rooms ⦿ No Meals Ⓜ Colón, Alonso Martínez.

One Shot Luchana 22

$$ | HOTEL | Situated between Malasaña and the restaurant-lined Plaza de Olavide, this One Shot outpost has an ideal location for those looking to stay in a true-blue Madrid neighborhood with few tourists around. **Pros:** terrific value; bright airy lobby; low-key location. **Cons:** meager breakfasts; inconsistent customer service; finicky AC units. Ⓢ *Rooms from: €170 ⊠ Calle de Luchana 22, Chamberí ☎ 91/292–2940 ⊕ www.hoteloneshotluchana22.com ⮌ 43 rooms ⦿ No Meals Ⓜ Bilbao.*

The Pavilions Madrid

$$$ | HOTEL | Hitting the sweet spot between high-end luxury and state-of-the-art design, the Pavilions is a boutique hotel that stands out for its original art and sculpture by top Spanish artists, much of it available for purchase. **Pros:** swanky feel; breakfast in the solarium; indoor-outdoor pool and wellness area. **Cons:** small gym; unexciting block; entry-level rooms are cramped. Ⓢ *Rooms from: €269 ⊠ Calle de Amador de los Ríos 3, Chamberí ☎ 91/310–7500 ⊕ www.pavilionshotels.com/madrid ⮌ 29 rooms ⦿ No Meals Ⓜ Colón.*

 Nightlife

MUSIC CLUBS

Clamores

LIVE MUSIC | Jive to live jazz concerts and DJ sets until 5:30 am on weekdays and 6 am on weekends. Tickets rarely creep above €15. ⊠ *Calle de Alburquerque 14, Chamberí ☎ 91/445–5480 ⊕ www.salaclamores.es Ⓜ Bilbao.*

DANCE CLUBS

Opium

DANCE CLUBS | Sure, you can have a fancy Spanish fusion dinner in this upscale modern nightclub, but most patrons come late, when the dance floor heats up with bumping electronic and reggaeton music. ⊠ *Calle de José Abascal 56, Chamberí ☎ 91/752–5322 ⊕ opiummadrid.com Ⓜ Gregorio Marañón.*

BARS

La Alquimia Vinos Naturales

WINE BARS | The trendiest spot to sip natural wine is this cubbyhole that opened in late 2022. If you're lucky enough to snag a barstool or outdoor table (or reserve via Instagram DM—@laalquimiavinos), you'll be treated to top-notch charcuterie and hard-to-find wines ranging from effervescent *ancestrales* (pét-nats) to tinaja-fermented orange wines to chewy Spanish reds. ⊠ *Calle de Amador de los Ríos 1, Chamberí ⊘ Closed Sun. and Mon. Ⓜ Alonso Martínez.*

 Shopping

FOOD

Casa Ruiz

FOOD | For cooks on the hunt for hard-to-find Spanish ingredients, Casa Ruiz is an obligatory stop. The bulk purveyor specializes in dry ingredients, from beans to pulses to spices to chocolate, and they carry only the best. Seek out Manchegan saffron, *judiones* de La Granja (extra-large white runner beans), and Asturian *fabes* to make real-deal *fabada* (bean stew) in your home kitchen. ⊠ *Calle de Andrés Mellado 58, Chamberí ☎ 91/861–6128 ⊕ casaruizgranel.com ⊘ Closed Sun. Ⓜ Moncloa.*

Chapter 10

CHAMARTÍN AND TETUÁN

Updated by
Benjamin Kemper

◉ Sights	🍴 Restaurants	🛏 Hotels	🛍 Shopping	🍸 Nightlife
★★☆☆☆	★★★☆☆	★★★☆☆	★☆☆☆☆	★★☆☆☆

NEIGHBORHOOD SNAPSHOT

TOP EXPERIENCES

■ **Real Madrid's home turf:** Take a pilgrimage to Spanish fútbol mecca Santiago Bernabéu Stadium.

■ **DiverXO:** Settle in for a punk rock tasting menu unlike any other at Madrid's futuristic three-Michelin-star restaurant.

GETTING HERE

Chamartín and Tetuán sit directly above Salamanca and Chamberí, respectively, and clock in at a whopping 15 square km (nearly 9 square miles) in total. Chances are, if you must venture this far north, it's for a business meeting in Madrid's main financial corridor, (the northern reaches of Paseo de la Castellana) or for a soccer match at Santiago Bernabéu Stadium (metro Santiago Bernabeu, Línea 10). BiciMAD, Madrid's bike-share service, has docks scattered throughout both neighborhoods. As Chamartín and Tetuán lie outside the Madrid 360 low-emission zone, all rental cars are allowed entry. Parking is generally readily available, except for around Santiago Bernabéu Stadium on game nights.

PLANNING YOUR TIME

Chamartín and Tetuán are residential and business-oriented areas, so you'll want to make a beeline to your final destination and—unless you love wandering for the sake of wandering—move right along. The wide stately boulevards of Chamartín are well-suited to jogging and strolling but aren't particularly intriguing otherwise. Steer clear of the dodgy Bellas Vistas neighborhood of Tetuán (particularly Calle Topete), and keep your wits about you in the area around Nuevos Ministerios station.

VIEWFINDER

The most striking architecture in Chamartín can be found at Plaza de Castilla, where the Torres KIO skyscrapers lean in toward each other like a halfway-open drawbridge. They constitute the most readily identifiable silhouettes on the Madrid skyline, visible from highways entering the city and from Madrid-Barajas airport. Completed in 1996, they were an architectural novelty at the time; no inclined buildings of that size or scale had ever been constructed. Today they house the offices of various companies and are not open to the public.

Chamartín and Tetuán sprawl north of the city center, and if you have tickets to a Real Madrid match (or a business meeting on Paseo de la Castellana), you'll end up here. But don't rush out—make the most of your visit by exploring the hidden-gem food and nightlife scenes.

The historical town of Chamartín wasn't formally annexed to Madrid until 1948. During the following decades, and due to the construction of new sites such as the Chamartín Train Station and the National Auditorium of Music, it gained popularity among Madrileños as a convenient and tranquil place to live. The famous leaning "Gate of Europe" Torres KIO towers are situated here, as are many office buildings, convention centers, business hotels, and the seat of Real Madrid, Santiago Bernabéu Stadium. Tetuán is decidedly working class. On its main street, Callo de Bravo Murillo, you'll find old-school bars, kebab restaurants, pawn shops, and off-brand clothing stores. You won't find many tourists or trendy boutiques, but you will find locals enjoying an affordable and interesting food scene.

Chamartín

🍴 Restaurants

Casa Benigna

$$$ | **SPANISH** | Owner Norberto Jorge, a quirky, jolly gent, offers a produce-centric menu with painstakingly selected wines to match at this snug book-lined restaurant. Rice dishes are the house specialty, and they're cooked in extra-flat paella pans specially manufactured for the restaurant. **Known for:** fantastic paella; larger-than-life owner; homey atmosphere. [$] *Average main: €26* ✉ *Calle de Benigno Soto 9, Chamartín* ☎ *91/416–9357* 🌐 *casabenigna.com* 🕓 *No dinner Sun.* [M] *Concha Espina, Prosperidad.*

DiverXO

$$$$ | **ECLECTIC** | When you ask a Madrileño about a remarkable food experience—something that stirs the senses beyond feeding one's appetite—DiverXO is the first name you'll hear. The take-no-prisoners tasting menu incorporates a dizzying array of international ingredients and chemical processes. **Known for:** punk-rock fine dining; courses that use the whole table as a canvas; Madrid's only Michelin three-star. [$] *Average main: €365* ✉ *NH Collection Madrid Eurobuilding, Calle del Padre Damián 23, Chamartín* ☎ *91/570–0766* 🌐 *diverxo.com* 🕓 *Closed Sun.–Tues.* [M] *Cuzco.*

★ **Sacha**

$$$$ | **SPANISH** | Settle into an unhurried feast at Sacha, a cozy bistro with soul-satisfying food and hand-selected wines, and you might never want to leave—especially if you strike up a conversation with chef Sacha himself, who's quite the storyteller. The cuisine is regional Spanish—think butifarra sausages with sautéed mushrooms or razor clams with black garlic emulsion—with just enough

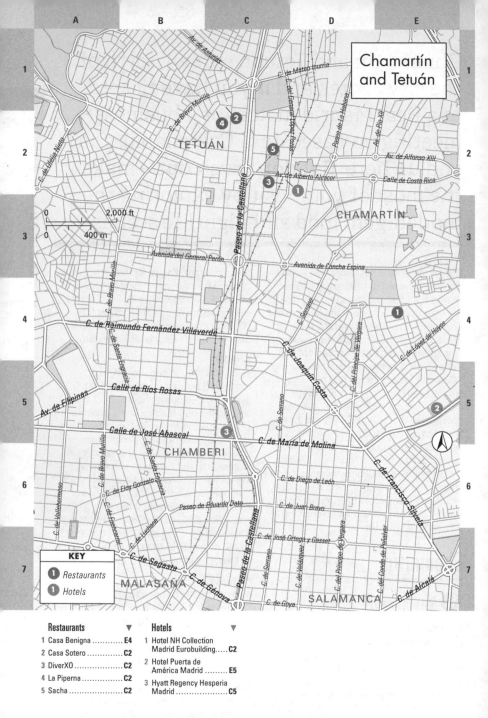

Chamartín and Tetuán

0 ——— 2,000 ft
0 ——— 400 m

imagination to make you wonder why the restaurant isn't better known. **Known for:** Spanish bistro fare; impeccable steak tartare; hard-to-find wines. $ *Average main: €32* ✉ *Calle de Juan Hurtado de Mendoza 11, Chamartín* ☎ *91/345–5952* ⊕ *www.restaurantesacha.com* ⊗ *Closed Sun.* Ⓜ *Cuzco.*

Hotels

★ **Hotel NH Collection Madrid Eurobuilding**
$$$ | HOTEL | This towering hotel, located blocks from Real Madrid's home stadium, is a state-of-the-art luxury property with large airy rooms and an enormous pool and gym complex. **Pros:** 180-degree views from some rooms; excellent gym and spa; bargain rates. **Cons:** inconsistent service; hotel can't secure bookings at DiverXO; quiet area at night. $ *Rooms from: €233* ✉ *Calle de Padre Damián 23, Chamartín* ☎ *91/353–7300* ⊕ *www.nh-hotels.com/hotel/nh-collection-madrid-eurobuilding* ⇄ *440 rooms* ⦿ *No Meals* Ⓜ *Cuzco.*

Hotel Puerta América Madrid
$$ | HOTEL | Inspired by Paul Eluard's *La Liberté*, whose verses are written across the facade, the owners of this hotel granted an unlimited budget to 19 of the world's top architects and designers. **Pros:** 12 hotel designs in one—an architectural icon; top-notch restaurant and bars; candlelit pool and steam room area. **Cons:** miles from the center; frayed at the edges; design impractical in places. $ *Rooms from: €185* ✉ *Av. de América 41, Chamartín* ☎ *91/744–5410* ⊕ *www.hotelpuertamerica.com* ⇄ *315 rooms* ⦿ *No Meals* Ⓜ *Avenida de América.*

Hyatt Regency Hesperia Madrid
$$$ | HOTEL | The legendary Hesperia hotel was bought and renovated by Hyatt Regency and is all about comfortable business stays. **Pros:** corporate-chic decor; spacious rooms; 24-hour room service. **Cons:** interior rooms can be dark; stuffy business feel; miles from the city center. $ *Rooms from: €238* ✉ *Paseo de la Castellana 57, Chamartín* ☎ *93/611–3131* ⊕ *www.hesperia.com* ⇄ *169 rooms* ⦿ *No Meals* Ⓜ *Gregorio Marañón.*

Nightlife

BARS
Domo Lounge and Terrace
COCKTAIL LOUNGES | Choose from classic cocktails and original creations at this cocktail bar with an enclosed terrace; it's run by Diego Cabrera, one of the city's top mixologists. ✉ *Calle de Padre Damián 23, Chamartín* ☎ *91/345–6160* ⊕ *www.domoeurobuilding.com* Ⓜ *Cuzco.*

Tetuán

As Madrid grew dramatically in the second half of the 19th century, rough-and-tumble barrios like Tetuán got a facelift. Today, its main artery, Calle de Bravo Murillo, divides the more developed, business-oriented eastern section from the more residential and multicultural western area of the neighborhood.

🍴 Restaurants

★ **Casa Sotero**
$ | TAPAS | Crackly fried pig ear, fat wedges of *tortilla de patata* (potato omelet), and garlicky rabbit *al ajillo* are a few of the many old-school standbys that have kept this cubbyhole bar in business since 1934. **Known for:** off-the-radar gem that's worth the hike; classic tapas and breakfasts; phenomenally affordable. $ *Average main: €10* ✉ *Calle de José Castán Tobeñas 1, Tetuán* ☎ *91/570–6481* ⊕ *casasotero.org* ⊗ *Closed Mon.* Ⓜ *Pl. de Castilla, Valdeacederas.*

La Piperna
$$ | ITALIAN | FAMILY | Tetuán is the unlikely location of this outstanding (and extremely well-priced) Italian restaurant run by a Naples native. Homemade pastas are the star of the show—try the ricotta-stuffed

¡GOOOOOOAALL!

Fútbol (or soccer) is Spain's number-one sport, and Madrid has four teams: Real Madrid, Atlético Madrid, Rayo Vallecano, and Getafe. For tickets, book online or call a week in advance to reserve and pick them up at the stadium—or, if the match isn't sold out, stand in line at the stadium of your choice. Ticket prices vary according to several factors: the importance of the rival, the seat location, the day of the week the match takes place, whether the match is aired on free TV or not, and the competition (Liga, Copa del Rey, Champions League or Europa League). Final dates and match times are often confirmed only a few days before, so it can be hard to reserve in advance. That said, Real Madrid and Atlético Madrid never play at home the same week, so there is a match every single week in the city.

Stadiums

Campo de Fútbol de Vallecas To enjoy a spirited match without the long lines and inflated price tag, step up to Rayo Vallecano's box office. The team's second-tier status doesn't make the games any less thrilling (think college ball vs. NBA), especially when you catch them on their home turf in Vallecas, which seats 14,708. You can feel good about your ticket purchase, too, since Rayo is known for its community activism. When the pandemic hit, the team's charitable foundation sewed and distributed 12,000 masks for undersupplied hospitals. ✉ *Calle del Payaso Fofó 0, Puente de Vallecas, Chamartín* ☎ *91/478–4329* 🌐 *www.rayovallecano.es* [M] *Portazgo.*

Santiago Bernabéu Stadium Home to Real Madrid, this stadium seats 85,400 and offers daytime tours of the facilities. A €590 million gut renovation is on track to be completed by early 2024, turning the stadium into a sleek UFO-like coliseum from the future; tour and game schedules may be affected, so check the website for updates. ✉ *Av. de Concha Espina 1, Chamartín* ☎ *91/398–4300* 🌐 *www.realmadrid.es* [M] *Santiago Bernabéu.*

Wanda Metropolitano Since 2017, Atlético Madrid (Real Madrid's rival team) has called this stadium in the San Blas–Canillejas district home. ✉ *Av. de Luis Aragonés 4, San Blas–Canilejas, Chamartín* 🌐 *www.atleticodemadrid.com/wandametropolitano* [M] *Estadio Metropolitano.*

On the ticket, *Puerta* is the door number that you enter, *Fila* is the row, and *Número* or № is the seat number.

tortellini alla nerano topped with fresh basil and Parmiggiano or the paccheri al ragù swimming in a 10-hour meat sauce. **Known for:** homemade regional pastas; expat Italian crowd; terrific eggplant parm. [$] *Average main: €18* ✉ *Calle de la Infanta Mercedes 98, Tetuán* ☎ *91/169–4950* 🌐 *restaurantelapiperna.com* 💳 *No credit cards* 🕒 *Closed Mon. No dinner Sun.* [M] *Valdeacederas.*

🍸 Nightlife

DANCE CLUBS

Oh My Club

DANCE CLUBS | At this hopping venue, you'll find plenty of space to dance (under the gaze of go-go girls) to hip-hop and reggaeton but also quieter nooks where you can chat. ✉ *Calle de Rosario Pino 14, Tetuán* ☎ *60/765–9705* 🌐 *ohmyclub.es* [M] *Cuzco.*

Chapter 11

CARABANCHEL, USERA, AND LATINA

11

Updated by
Benjamin Kemper

👁 **Sights**
★☆☆☆☆

🍴 **Restaurants**
★★★★☆

🛏 **Hotels**
★☆☆☆☆

🛍 **Shopping**
★★☆☆☆

🍸 **Nightlife**
★★★☆☆

NEIGHBORHOOD SNAPSHOT

TOP EXPERIENCES

■ **Tapas:** Feast on affordable no-frills bar food and drinks.

■ **Alternative Madrid:** Get a pulse on Madrid's indie art scene and bang your head at an underground rock show.

■ **Chinatown:** Devour dumplings, dim sum, and more in unsung, untouristed Usera.

■ **Puente de Toledo:** Traverse the city's most beautiful bridge.

■ **Mercado de Tirso de Molina:** Pick up culinary souvenirs and graze on budget tapas along the way.

GETTING HERE

Carabanchel, Usera, and Latina are serviced by metro lines 3, 5, 6, 10, and 11. Usera station (Línea 6) is a good jumping-off point for exploring that neighborhood while Oporto (Línea 5) is near Carabanchel's art studios and many restaurants and nightlife venues. Alternatively, access Usera by alighting at Legazpi (Línea 4); take a pleasant stroll through Madrid Río park to cross the river (15-minute walk). BiciMAD, Madrid's bikeshare service, now services these areas (though more sparsely than in the Centro). he Plaza Elíptica area is part of the "Madrid 360" low-emission zone.

PLANNING YOUR TIME

Carabanchel, Usera, and Latina are sprawling working-class barrios that are worth visiting for a handful of specific restaurants, bars, and sights, but given the area's enormous footprint and generally drab architecture, it's less suited to aimless wandering. So, pinpoint a down-home Chinese restaurant in Usera, an art gallery in Carabanchel, or a locals-only tapas bar in Latina and make a beeline. Pay special attention to your surroundings and mind your belongings, especially at night, as certain pockets of these neighborhoods can be a bit dodgy.

FUN FACT

Carabanchel is Madrid's most populous district, with nearly 250,000 inhabitants. More than any other Madrid barrio, it is synonymous with working-class Spain—humble, gritty, down-to-earth, and tightly knit. The country's most popular children's book series, *Manolito Gafotas*, is set here, which is why Spaniards the country over know its name.

As rents soar in the city center—up more than 10% in 2022 alone—Madrid's cash-strapped youth are migrating south of the Manzanares to multicultural neighborhoods like Carabanchel, Usera, and Latina. But don't expect third-wave cafés and Brooklyn-esque trendster glamour—yet. Far from being gentrified, Madrid's "left bank" combines sleepy residential areas with barren industrial ones. As these neighborhoods are relatively new, only urbanized in the second half of the 20th century, there are few historical sights and museums, which keeps tourists at bay.

Carabanchel is one of Madrid's most populous neighborhoods as well as one of its most diverse, as evidenced by streets lined with everything from arepa bars to West African groceries to rootsy Spanish taverns. For most of the year, Carabanchel sees little foot traffic beyond locals going about their business. Two festivals draw the crowds: Art Banchel and Fiestas de San Isidro Labrador (both held mid-May). The former is an alternative art event spotlighting the work of local artists, more than 300 of whom have studios in the neighborhood. The latter, centered on Parque de San Isidro, is one of Madrid's most popular *verbenas* (outdoor summer festivals), complete with traditional dance, booze-fueled partying, and bountiful *rosquillas* (anise-scented donuts), the classic fairground snack.

Usera, just east of Carabanchel, is—improbably—one of Europe's best, and newest, Chinatowns. Step off the metro and you're surrounded by Mandarin-lettered signs for markets and restaurants of countless regional styles such as Sichuan, Shanghainese, and Cantonese. Most shop owners are first-generation Chinese immigrants thanks to a diversity visa program that began some 20 years ago. (In 1980 there were barely 1,000 Chinese people in Spain; today there are over 11,000 in Usera alone.) If you happen to be in town for the Chinese

New Year, Usera is a must for its colorful parade and late-night DJ sets.

Latina, not to be confused with La Latina neighborhood in the city center, is Carabanchel's western bookend. Cross Puente de Segovia (Segovia Bridge), south of Palacio Real, and you've arrived. Like its neighbors, Latina offers a lively mix of timeworn Spanish spots and immigrant-run restaurants and stores. The subdistrict Puerta del Ángel has been newly dubbed the "Brooklyn of Madrid," thanks to an influx of photographers, graffiti artists, and the like. The rest of the neighborhood is largely in decline, however, with more shops closing than opening and homelessness on the rise. Keep an eye on this barrio in flux.

Sights

Ermita de Santa María la Antigua

CHURCH | Most Madrileños have no idea that the city's (and greater region's) oldest Mudejar church, erected in the 13th century, is located in Carabanchel. Though currently under renovation and closed to the public, it remains exceptionally well-preserved. The hermitage has a rectangular floor plan and a six-story brick-and-stone belfry with two bells (these were added in the 20th century). Note the intricate Moorish-influenced arches above the doorways and windows fashioned out of brick. If by some stroke of luck you gain entry to the church—it purportedly opens occasionally on Saturday at 11 am—you'll find colorful medieval frescoes and a well within. ⊠ *Calle de Monseñor Oscar Romero 92, Carabanchel* Ⓜ *Eugenia de Montijo.*

★ Mercado de Tirso de Molina

MARKET | Built in 1932 by Luis Bellido, the architect behind Matadero Madrid, this soaring brick market isn't found on the city-center plaza that shares its name but rather in the up-and-coming Puerta del Ángel neighborhood. After stocking up on Spanish charcuterie and pantry items (the best souvenirs!), nibble on Chinese-style tripe stew at Bar Paula, vegan huaraches at El Vegicano, and natural wine at La Desahuciada. Take note, weekenders: this is one of Madrid's only traditional markets that stays open on Sunday. ⊠ *Calle de Doña Urraca 15* ☎ *91/464–5235 for general information* ⊕ *mercadotirsodemolina.es* Ⓜ *Puerta del Ángel.*

Parque de San Isidro

CITY PARK | **FAMILY** | Spring and fall are the best times to jog, stroll, or picnic in this tranquil park with none of the tourist hustle and bustle of El Retiro. Come mid-May, Parque de San Isidro becomes party central with the arrival of the eponymous fiestas; bring family and friends and enjoy the fireworks, concerts, street food (rosquillas! chorizo hoagies!), and rides. Steer clear of this area after sunset. ⊠ *Carabanchel* ⊕ *www.esmadrid. com/agenda/sanisidro-madrid* Ⓜ *Marqués de Vadillo.*

Puente de Toledo (*Bridge of Toledo*)

BRIDGE | A masterwork in Churrigueresque (Spanish baroque) architecture, this impressive granite bridge over the Manzanares connects Arganzuela and Carabanchel. Felipe IV commissioned its construction in order to shorten the route from Madrid to Toledo in the mid-17th century (hence the bridge's name), but floods destroyed the initial structure. The bridge you can walk across today (it is pedestrian-access-only) was completed in 1732 by architect Pedro de Ribera and contains nine arches buttressed by rounded columns. At night, these are uplit and look particularly magical from below on the Madrid Río esplanade. Midway across the bridge, don't miss the niches adorned with richly carved limestone statues of Madrid's patron saints, San Isidro Labrador and Santa María de la Cabeza. ⊠ *Carabanchel* Ⓜ *Pirámides.*

Usera is one of Europe's best Chinatowns, and while it doesn't have an archway at the entrance, it does have an established Chinese community and lively Chinese New Year celebrations.

🍴 Restaurants

To discover Madrid's most soulful, unvarnished, and untouristed restaurants, you have to head south of the river. This is an intrepid foodie's paradise—uncharted even by local standards. The first thing you'll notice is a plunge in menu prices—working-class Madrid will fork over no extra euros for dainty portions or *nueva cocina* fripperies. Carábanchel and Latina are awash with old-timey bars hawking three-course €11 *menús del día* (prix fixes) and greasy-spoon tapas late into the evening, while Usera boasts a vibrant mix of decades-old neighborhood institutions and regional Chinese restaurants.

★ Aynaelda

$$ | **SPANISH** | **FAMILY** | Textbook-perfect paella in...Latina? Madrid is a notoriously disappointing city when it comes to the rice dishes popular on the Mediterranean coast, but Aynaelda slam-dunks with its sizzling paellas flavored with heady aromatics and concentrated stock. **Known for:** rice dishes up to Valencian standards;

bright airy dining room; excellent croquettes. $ *Average main: €24* ✉ *Calle de los Yébenes 38, Latina* ☎ *91/710–1051* ⊕ *aynaelda.com* ⊗ *No dinner Sun.* Ⓜ *Laguna.*

Café Astral

$ | **SPANISH** | Salt cod croquettes, fresh tomato salad, roast suckling pig—these are some of the comfort-food classics you'll find on the menu at this neighborhood haunt whose diner decor (steel bar, beige awnings, paper place mats) hasn't changed in decades. If you can snag a patio table in the summer, you've hit pay dirt. **Known for:** affordable suckling pig; generous breakfasts; hyperlocal crowd. $ *Average main: €13* ✉ *Camino Viejo de Leganés 82, Carabanchel* ☎ *91/560–0818* ⊕ *www.astralcafe.es* ⊗ *Closed Sun.* Ⓜ *Oporto.*

Lao Tou

$ | **CHINESE** | **FAMILY** | Find primal pleasure here picking the meat off a hake head served in a cauldron of gingery broth or slurping your weight of wok-charred

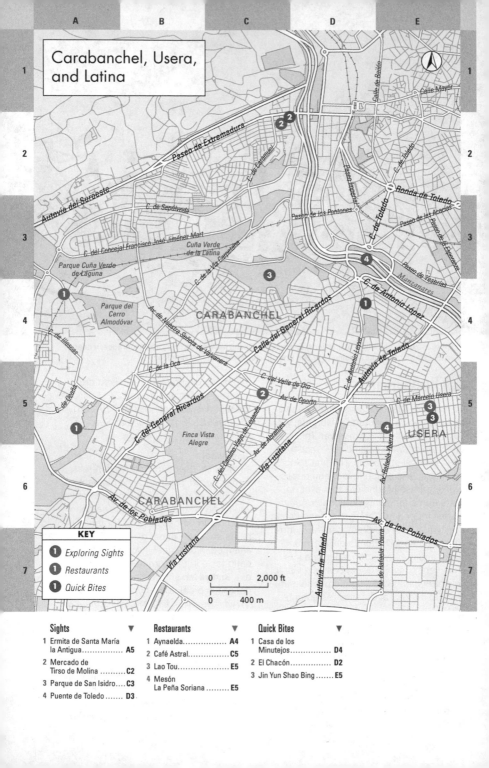

Carabanchel, Usera, and Latina

KEY

- **1** Exploring Sights
- **1** Restaurants
- **1** Quick Bites

0 ——— 2,000 ft

0 ——— 400 m

noodles tossed with chicken and seafood. Stir-fried okra, sweet-and-sour pork ribs, and shrimp soup are other perennial favorites among the mostly Chinese clientele. **Known for:** hake head soup on every table; non-Europeanized Chinese cuisine; feasting on a budget. [$] *Average main: €15* ✉ *Calle de Nicolás Sánchez 35, Usera* ☎ *65/112–1287* ⏲ *Closed Thurs.* [M] *Usera.*

★ Mesón La Peña Soriana

$ | TAPAS | Madrileños pour in from far and wide for Esther's famous *patatas bravas*, fried potato wedges cloaked in vinegary paprika-laced chili sauce. A menu brimming with snails, fried lamb intestines, pork rinds, and Castilian blood sausage confirms that you're in *el Madrid profundo.* **Known for:** killer patatas bravas; throwback interiors; Madrid-style offal dishes. [$] *Average main: €9* ✉ *Calle Fornillos 58, Usera* ☎ *64/562–6548* 🌐 *mesonlapenasoriana.wordpress.com* ⏲ *Closed Tues. and Wed.* [M] *Usera.*

Coffee and Quick Bites

★ Casa de los Minutejos

$ | TAPAS | FAMILY | Carabanchel's best-known bar, Los Minutejos, is synonymous with distressingly inhalable griddled sandwiches of crispy pig ear doused in fiery brava sauce. Tamer tapas are available for the squeamish. **Known for:** crustless "minutejo" sandwiches; ample space to spread out; no-nonsense service. [$] *Average main: €7* ✉ *Calle de Antonio de Leyva 17, Carabanchel* ☎ *91/560–6726* [M] *Marqués de Vadillo.*

★ El Chacón

$ | SPANISH | FAMILY | All the Galician greatest hits are on the menu at this Latina stalwart with an old tile floor and wooden benches. Paprika-dusted octopus, smoky *lacón* (cooked ham), and weighty slabs of *empanada gallega* (tuna pie) go down a bit too easily when accompanied by gallons of the house Albariño. **Known for:** Galician peasant food; devoted local crowd; hefty free tapa with every drink. [$] *Average main: €15* ✉ *Calle de Saavedra Fajardo 16, Latina* ☎ *91/463–1044* 🌐 *www.elchacon.com* ⏲ *Closed Wed.* [M] *Puerta del Ángel.*

Jin Yun Shao Bing

$ | NORTHERN CHINESE | FAMILY | Hot griddled flatbreads (*shao bing*) filled with soy-scented beef will set you back just €2 a pop at this hole-in-the-wall specializing in this northern Chinese delicacy. Noodle and wonton soups (average price: €5) hit the spot when it's cold out. **Known for:** addictive meat-filled flatbreads; made-to-order dumplings; shockingly affordable prices. [$] *Average main: €5* ✉ *Calle de Nicolás Sánchez 59, Usera* ☎ *91/125–3620* [M] *Usera.*

Nightlife

Gruta 77

DANCE CLUBS | This snug nightclub is all about fist-pumping rock and roll. There are live concerts most nights, and the cover rarely exceeds €10. DJs make frequent appearances as well, especially late in the evening. Beers are cheap, the music is loud, and close quarters mean you'll probably make an amigo or two. ✉ *Calle del Cuclillo 6, Carabanchel* ☎ *91/471–2370* 🌐 *gruta77.com* [M] *Oporto.*

Shopping

FOOD

Productos Zabala

FOOD | Generously stuffed empanadas—double-crusted Galician pies stuffed with any range of meats and seafood—make terrific picnic fare, and Zabala (est. 1967) makes consistently sublime ones. Take a few slabs to go and savor them under the cherry trees in the nearby Parque de la Cuña Verde de Latina. ✉ *Paseo Perales 4, Latina* ☎ *91/463–3791* 🌐 *productoszabala.com* ⏲ *Closed Sun.* [M] *Lucero.*

GALLERIES

Sabrina Amrani Gallery

ART GALLERIES | Sabrina Amrani, the Algerian-French gallerist behind this hangarlike art showroom, is also the president of Arte Madrid, the city's top art gallery association. She put Carabanchel on the contemporary art map when she opened this blindingly white space in 2011. Expect an array of experimental conceptual pieces from Europe, Asia, the Middle East, and beyond. ⊠ *Calle Sallaberry 52, Carabanchel* ☎ *91/621–7859* ⊕ *www. sabrinaamrani.com* ⊗ *Closed Sun. and Mon.* Ⓜ *Oporto, Vista Alegre.*

Veta

ART GALLERIES | The newest modern art gallery Madrileños can't stop talking about is Veta, situated in the scruffy Comillas neighborhood. Clocking in at 13,000 square feet and presided over by a young Cantabrian curator, it houses hundreds of Spanish and international works including photography, sculpture, and paintings. ⊠ *Calle de Antoñita Jiménez 37, Carabanchel* ☎ *69/719–3680* ⊕ *vetagaleria.com* ⊗ *Closed Sun. and Mon.* Ⓜ *Urgel, Opañel.*

Chapter 12

DAY TRIPS FROM MADRID

12

Updated by
Megan Lloyd

👁 Sights	🍴 Restaurants	🛏 Hotels	💼 Shopping	🍸 Nightlife
★★★★★	★★★★☆	★★★★☆	★★★★☆	★★☆☆☆

WELCOME TO DAY TRIPS FROM MADRID

TOP REASONS TO GO

★ **Fairy-tale castles and palaces:** Scurry up ancient towers and time-travel to Golden Age Spain.

★ **Castilian comfort food:** Plunge your fork into crackly roast meats and hearty game dishes.

★ **Unspoiled nature:** Embark on a scenic hike with gorgeous mountain views and birds swooping overhead.

★ **Gasp-worthy religious sights:** Ponder Spain's multicultural legacy in splendid cathedrals, synagogues, and mosques.

★ **History galore:** Uncover the secrets of Spain's rich past in towns and cities that predate Madrid.

1 **Toledo.** Discover a treasure trove of medieval art in the pre-Madrid capital of Castile.

2 **San Lorenzo de El Escorial.** Travel less than an hour outside Madrid to see Felipe II's over-the-top abode.

3 **Segovia.** Marvel at a soaring Roman aqueduct and explore the fortress said to have inspired the Disney castle.

4 **Ávila.** Walk along the ramparts of the best-preserved city walls in Europe and snack on sweet treats baked by nuns.

5 **Sepúlveda.** Descend into a medieval dungeon in a town some call the most beautiful in Spain.

6 **Sigüenza.** Tour one of Spain's best-preserved Gothic cathedrals.

7 **Cuenca.** Marvel at the Hanging Houses, then explore the Ciudad Encantada ("Enchanted City") with its alien rock formations.

8 **Almagro.** Slow things down in this quintessential Manchegan town with a vibrant evening *tapeo* (tapas scene).

9 **Salamanca.** For good luck, see if you can spot the frog on the plateresque facade of Spain's oldest university.

10 **Burgos.** Come for the stunning Gothic cathedral; stay for the nationally famous morcilla sausages.

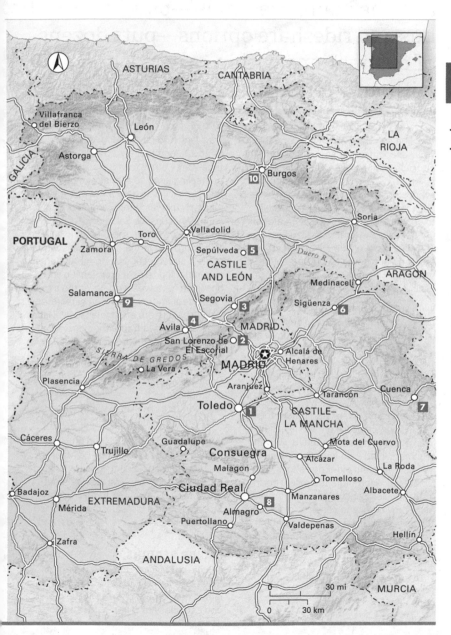

Madrid, in the center of Spain, is an excellent jumping-off point for exploring, and the high-speed train—plus bountiful bus and rideshare options—puts dozens of destinations within easy reach, even without a rental car.

You'll be surprised at how few tourists you'll encounter in many of these locales, particularly in the offseason (winter and summer), when dramatic temperature swings drive most travelers elsewhere. Their loss—having a sleepy medieval town virtually to yourself is a greater luxury than any five-star hotel can provide. The Castiles, which bracket Madrid to the north and south, and Extremadura, bordering Portugal, are filled with compelling destinations steeped in tradition.

With so many options at your fingertips, deciding where to visit outside Madrid can be daunting. Toledo and Segovia are the no-brainer picks for travelers with a day or two to spare. The former, situated an hour south of Madrid, is the seat of Old Castile, once a bustling multicultural metropolis where Jews, Muslims, and Christians cohabitated before the Inquisition. Toledo's old town is essentially an open-air museum with its warren of streets lined with ancient mosques, monasteries, and old-timey shops. Ninety-four kilometers (58 miles) north of Madrid lies Segovia, which is smaller, more provincial, and easier to digest than Toledo—you can hit the main sights (the Roman aqueduct, Gothic cathedral, and soaring "Disney" castle) in the morning and still have time for a dozy lunch of *cochinillo asado* (suckling pig), a *Segoviano* specialty.

Travelers who have already hit Toledo and Segovia—and those who relish secluded, time-warpy small towns—should consider stealing away to Almagro, Sepúlveda, El Escorial, Cuenca, or Sigüenza, each with stunning architecture and boundless country hospitality. Salamanca, Burgos, and Ávila are larger, more historic cities that flourished in the Middle Ages and contain enough captivating monuments and intriguing restaurants to keep you occupied for a weekend. Over the centuries, poets and others have characterized Castile as austere and melancholy. Gaunt mountain ranges frame the horizons; gorges and rocky outcrops break up flat expanses; and the fields around Ávila and Segovia are littered with giant boulders. Castilian villages are built predominantly of granite, and their severe, formidable look contrasts markedly with the white-washed walls of most of southern Spain.

Wherever you land in Madrid province, Castile and León, or Castile-La Mancha, it's worth dropping by the local tourist office to grab a map and inquire about the surrounding nature. In this part of Spain, you're never far from mountains, bird-watching hot spots, vineyards, and bike trails.

MAJOR REGIONS
Castile–La Mancha. Here is the land of Don Quixote, Miguel de Cervantes's chivalrous hero. Some of Spain's oldest and noblest cities are found here, steeped in

culture and legend, though many have fallen into neglect. Toledo, the pre-Madrid capital of Spain, is the main attraction, though travelers willing to venture farther afield can explore Cuenca, with its Hanging Houses, and Almagro, with its green-and-white plaza and splendid *parador*.

Castile and León. This is Spain's windswept interior, stretching from the dry plains of Castile–La Mancha to the hilly vineyards of Ribera del Duero and up to the foot of several mountain ranges: the Sierra de Gredos, Sierra de Francia, and northward toward the towering Picos de Europa. The area combines two of Spain's old kingdoms, Léon and Old Castile, each with its many treasures of palaces, castles, and cathedrals. The region's crown jewel is Segovia with its Roman aqueduct and 12th-century *alcázar* (fortress), though medieval Ávila gives it a run for its money. Farther north lies Salamanca, dominated by luminescent sandstone buildings, and the ancient capital of Burgos, an early outpost of Christianity with a jaw-dropping Gothic cathedral.

Planning

When to Go

July and August can be brutally hot, and November through February can get bitterly cold, especially in the mountains. Shoulder season, May and October, when the weather is sunny but relatively cool, are the two best months to visit—so if you plan on visiting then, be sure to book ahead.

Getting Here and Around

CAR TRAVEL
Major highways—the A1 through A6—spoke out from Madrid, putting most destinations in central Spain within an hour or two of the city. If possible, avoid returning to Madrid on major highways at the end of a weekend or a holiday. The beginning and end of August are notorious for traffic jams, as is *Semana Santa* (Holy Week), which starts on Palm Sunday and ends on Easter Sunday. National (toll-free) highways and back roads are slower but provide one of the great pleasures of driving around the Castilian countryside: surprise encounters with historical monuments and spectacular vistas.

Hotels

Many of the country's best-reviewed paradores (⊕ www.paradores.es) can be found in quiet towns such as Almagro, Ávila, Cuenca, and Sigüenza. Those in Toledo and Salamanca are more modern buildings with magnificent views. There are plenty of alternatives to paradores, such as Salamanca's Hotel Rector and Cuenca's Posada de San José, housed in a 16th-century convent.

⇨ *Hotel reviews have been shortened. For full information, visit Fodors.com.*

What It Costs in Euros			
$	$$	$$$	$$$$
FOR TWO PEOPLE			
under €125	€125–€200	€201–€300	over €300

Restaurants

This is Spain's rugged heartland, bereft of touristy hamburger joints and filled instead with the country's most traditional *tabernas* , which attract Spanish foodies from across the country. Some of the most renowned restaurants in this region are small and family-run, while a few new avant-garde spots in urban

Mileage from Madrid

Madrid to Burgos is 243 km (151 miles).

Madrid to Sepúlveda is 127 km (79 miles).

Madrid to Cuenca is 168 km (104 miles).

Madrid to Almagro is 204 km (127 miles).

Madrid to Sigüenza is 131 km (81 miles).

Madrid to Salamanca is 212 km (132 miles).

Madrid to San Lorenzo de El Escorial is 60 km (37 miles).

Madrid to Segovia is 91 km (56½ miles).

Madrid to Toledo is 88 km (55 miles).

Madrid to Ávila is 114 km (71 miles).

areas serve up modern architecture as well as experimental fusion dishes.

⇨ *Restaurant reviews have been shortened. For full information, visit Fodors.com.*

What It Costs in Euros

$	$$	$$$	$$$$
AT DINNER			
under €18	€18–€24	€25–€30	over €30

Tours

In summer the tourist offices of Segovia, Toledo, and Sigüenza organize *Trenes Turísticos* (miniature tourist trains) that glide past all the major sights; contact local tourist offices for schedules.

★ **Equiberia**

GUIDED TOURS | **FAMILY** | Horseback tours ranging 5–10 days offer a unique way to experience the gorges, fields, and forests of the Sierra de Gredos, Segovia, Ávila, and beyond; ask about their Menorca tours if you're headed to that island. ⊠ *C. Cepedamingo, Ávila ✣ in Navarredonda de Gredos* ☎ *68/934–3974* ⊕ *www.equiberia.com* ⊠ *From €1,200.*

Toledo

88 km (55 miles) southwest of Madrid.

The spiritual capital of Castile, Toledo sits atop a rocky mount surrounded on three sides by the Río Tajo (Tagus River). When the Romans arrived here in 192 BC, they built their fortress (the Alcázar) on the highest point of the rock. Later, the Visigoths remodeled the stronghold.

In the 8th century, the Moors arrived and strengthened Toledo's reputation as a center of religion and learning. Today, the Moorish legacy is evident in Toledo's strong crafts tradition, the mazelike streets, and the predominance of brick construction (rather than the stone of many of Spain's historical cities). For the Moors—an imprecise catch-all term for Islam-practicing North African settlers of the Iberian Peninsula—beauty was to be savored from within rather than displayed on the surface. Even Toledo's cathedral—one of the most richly endowed in Spain—is hard to see from the outside, largely obscured by the warren of houses around it.

Alfonso VI, aided by El Cid ("Lord Conqueror"), captured the city in 1085 and dubbed himself emperor of Toledo. Under the Christians, the town's strong intellectual life was maintained, and Toledo became famous for its school of translators, who taught Arab medicine, law, culture, and philosophy. Religious tolerance continued, and during the rule of Pedro the Cruel (so named because he allegedly had members of his own family murdered to advance his position), a Jewish banker, Samuel Levi, became the royal treasurer and one of the wealthiest men in the booming city. By the late 1400s, however, hostility toward Jews and Arabs had grown as the ruthlessly intolerant Catholic Monarchs established Toledo as a bastion of the Catholic Church.

Under Toledo's long line of cardinals—most notably Mendoza, Tavera, and Cisneros—Renaissance Toledo was a center of the humanities. Economically and politically, however, the city began to decline at the end of the 15th century. The expulsion of the Jews from Spain in 1492, as part of the Spanish Inquisition, eroded Toledo's economic and intellectual prowess. Then, when Madrid became the permanent center of the Spanish court in 1561, Toledo lost its political importance too, and the expulsion from Spain of the converted Arabs (*Moriscos*) in 1601 meant the departure of most of the city's artisans. The years the painter El Greco spent in Toledo—from 1572 to his death in 1614—were those of the city's decline, which is greatly reflected in his works. In the late 19th century, after hundreds of years of neglect, the works of El Greco came to be widely appreciated, and Toledo was transformed into a major tourist destination. Today, Toledo is conservative, prosperous, and proud—and a bit provincial (don't expect cosmopolitan luxury here). Its winding streets and steep hills can be tough to navigate, especially when you're searching for a specific sight, so take a full day (or three) to absorb the town's medieval trappings—and relish in getting lost from time to time.

GETTING HERE AND AROUND

The best way to get to Toledo from Madrid is the high-speed AVE train, which leaves from Madrid at least nine times daily from Atocha station and gets you there in 30 minutes. From the ornate neo-Mudejar train station, take a taxi, bus (L61 or L62), or walk the 1½ km (1 mile) to the city center.

ALSA buses leave Madrid every half hour from Plaza Elíptica and take 1 to 1 hour 45 minutes, depending on the route.

TOURS

★ **Toledo de la Mano**

GUIDED TOURS | Toledophile Adolfo Ferrero, author of a 200-page guidebook about the town, delves far deeper on his private tours than those run by competitors, touching on the city's multicultural history and its significance in medieval Europe. Groups of up to 55 people can be accommodated. ⊠ *Calle Nuncio Viejo 10, Toledo* ☎ *62/917–7810* ⊕ *www.toledodelamano. com* ✉ *From €150.*

Toledo Train Vision

TRAIN TOURS | **FAMILY** | This unabashedly touristy train chugs past many of Toledo's main sights, departing from the Plaza de Zocodover every hour on the hour during the week and every 30 minutes on weekends. The tour takes 45–50 minutes and has recorded information in 16 languages (including English, Spanish, and French) plus children's versions in those three languages, too. Buy tickets at the kiosk in Plaza de Zocodover. ⊠ *Pl. de Zocodover, Toledo* ☎ *62/530–1890* ⊕ *www. toledotrainvision.com* ✉ *€7.*

Sights

Alcázar

MILITARY SIGHT | Originally a Moorish citadel (*al-qasr* is Classical Arabic for "fortress"), Toledo's Alcázar is on a hill just outside the walled city, dominating the horizon. The south facade—the building's most severe—is the work of Juan de Herrera, of Escorial fame, while the

El Greco: The Titan of Toledo

"Crete gave him his life, and brushes; Toledo, a better land, where he begins with Death to attain Eternity." With these words, the Toledan poet Fray Hortensio Paravicino paid homage to his friend El Greco—and to the symbiotic connection between El Greco and his adopted city of Toledo. El Greco's intensely individual and expressionist style—elongated and often distorted figures, electric colors, and haunting mysticism—was seen as strange and disturbing, and his work remained largely underappreciated until the late 19th century, when he found wide acclaim and joined the ranks of Velázquez and Goya as a master of Spanish painting.

Born Doménikos Theotokópoulos on the island of Crete, El Greco ("the Greek") received his artistic education and training in Italy and then moved to Spain around 1577, lured in part by the prospect of painting frescoes for the royal monastery of El Escorial. King Felipe II, however, rejected El Greco's work for being too unusual. In Toledo, El Greco finally came into his own, creating many of his greatest works and honing his singular style and vision until his death in 1614. His masterpiece *The Burial of Count Orgaz*, which hangs in Toledo's Chapel of Santo Tomé, pays tribute to Toledan society. Perhaps the most famous rendering of Toledo is El Greco's dramatic *View of Toledo*, in which the cityscape crackles with a sinister energy underneath a stormy sky. El Greco's other famous landscape, *View and Plan of Toledo*, can be seen at Toledo's Museo de El Greco.

east facade incorporates a large section of battlements. The finest facade is the northern, one of many Toledan works by Miguel Covarrubias, who did more than any other architect to introduce the Renaissance style here. The building's architectural highlight is his Italianate courtyard, which, like most other parts of the building, was largely rebuilt after the Spanish Civil War, when the Alcázar was besieged by the Republicans. Though the Nationalists' ranks were depleted, they held on to the building. Dictator Francisco Franco later turned the Alcázar into a monument to Nationalist bravery. It now houses the Museo del Ejército (Military Museum), which was formerly in Madrid.

■ TIP→ **Hang onto your ticket—it's needed when you exit the museum. Check the website for any construction-related closures.** ✉ *Calle de la Union s/n, Toledo* ☎ *92/523-8800* ⊕ *www.museo.ejercito.es* 🎟 *From €5, free Sun.*

Calle del Comercio

STREET | Near Plaza de Zocodover, this is the town's narrow and busy pedestrian thoroughfare. It's lined with bars and shops and shaded in summer by awnings. It was repaved in 2021. ✉ *Calle del Comercio s/n, Toledo.*

★ Catedral Primada

CHURCH | One of the most impressive structures in all of Spain, this is a must-see on any visit to the city. The elaborate structure sits on the site of what was once Toledo's great mosque (of which only a column and the cistern remain). It owes its impressive Mozarabic chapel, with an elongated dome crowning the west facade, to El Greco's only son. The rest of the facade is mainly early 15th century. Immediately to your right is a beautifully carved plateresque doorway by Covarrubias, marking the entrance to the Treasury, which houses a small crucifixion scene by the Italian painter

Cimabue and an extraordinarily intricate late-15th-century monstrance by Juan del Arfe. The ceiling is an excellent example of Mudejar (11th- to 16th-century Moorish-influenced) workmanship. From here, walk around to the ambulatory. In addition to Italianate frescoes by Juan de Borgoña and an exemplary baroque illusionism by Narciso Tomé known as the Transparente, you'll find several El Grecos, including one version of *El Espolio* (*Christ Being Stripped of His Raiment*), the first recorded instance of the painter in Spain. ⊠ *Calle Cardenal Cisneros 1, Toledo* ☎ *92/522–2241* ⊕ *www.catedral-primada.es* ▥ *From €10.*

Convento de San Clemente

CHURCH | Founded in 1131, this is Toledo's oldest and largest convent—and it's still in use. The handful of nuns who live here produce sweet wine and marzipan. The impressive complex, a bit outside the city center, includes ruins of a mosque on which a chapel was built in the Middle Ages, those of an Islamic house and courtyard (with an ancient well and Arab baths), and those of a Jewish house from the same period. Tours, offered twice daily (though not dependably—be forewarned), might include a visit to the kitchen where the Mother Superior will let you sample some sweets if she's in a good mood. Skip the touristy marzipan shops and buy the real stuff here (sweets are sold at the entrance around the corner in Plaza Padilla). There's also an adjacent cultural center with rotating history exhibits. ⊠ *Calle San Clemente s/n, Toledo* ☎ *92/525–3080* ▥ *€6* ⊗ *Closed sporadically (call before visiting).*

Convento de Santo Domingo el Antiguo

(*Convento de Santo Domingo de Silos; Santo Domingo Convent*)
CHURCH | This 16th-century Cistercian convent houses the earliest of El Greco's Toledo paintings as well as the crypt where the artist is believed to be buried. The friendly nuns at the convent—of whom eight remain—will show you around its odd little museum, which includes decaying bone relics of little-known saints and a life-size model of John the Baptist's decapitated head. ⊠ *Pl. Santo Domingo el Antiguo s/n, Toledo* ☎ *92/522–2930* ▥ *€2.*

Hospital de Tavera (*Hospital de San Juan Bautista*)

HOSPITAL | Architect Alonso de Covarrubias's last work, this hospital lies outside the city walls, beyond Toledo's main northern gate. A fine example of Spanish Renaissance architecture, the building also houses the Museo de Duque de Lema in its southern wing. The most important work in the museum's miscellaneous collection is a painting by 17th-century artist José de Ribera. The hospital's monumental chapel holds El Greco's *Baptism of Christ* and the exquisitely carved marble tomb of Cardinal Tavera, the last work of Alonso de Berruguete. Descend into the crypt to experience some bizarre acoustical effects. A full ticket includes the hospital, museum, old pharmacy, and Renaissance patios; a partial ticket includes everything except the museum. Guided tours are available on the hour. ⊠ *Calle Duque de Lerma 2 (aka Calle Cardenal Tavera), Toledo* ☎ *92/522–0451* ⊕ *www.fundacionmedinaceli.org/monumentos/hospital* ▥ *From €5* ⊗ *Closed Mon. and Tues.*

★ Iglesia de San Ildefonso (*San Ildefonso Church, The Jesuits*)

CHURCH | Sometimes called "Los Jesuitas" for the religious order that founded it, the Iglesia de San Ildefonso is named for Toledo's patron saint, a 7th-century bishop. It was consecrated in 1718 after the baroque stone facade with twin Corinthian columns took 150 years to build. Its semispherical dome is one of the icons of Toledo's skyline. This impressive building's tower affords some of the best views over Toledo. ⊠ *Pl. Padre Juan de Mariana 1, Toledo* ☎ *92/525–1507* ⊕ *toledomonumental.com/monuments/iglesia-de-los-jesuitas* ▥ *€4.*

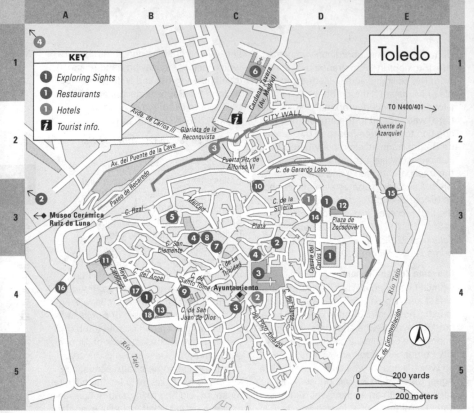

Toledo

KEY
- **1** Exploring Sights
- **1** Restaurants
- **1** Hotels
- **i** Tourist info.

Iglesia de San Román

CHURCH | Hidden in a virtually unspoiled part of Toledo, this early-13th-century Mudejar church (built on the site of an earlier Visigoth one) is now the **Museo de los Concilios y de la Cultura Visigoda** (Visigoth Museum) with exhibits of statuary, manuscript illustrations, jewelry, and an extensive collection of frescoes. The church tower is adjacent to the ruins of Roman baths. ⊠ *Calle San Román, Toledo* ☎ *92/522–7872* ⌧ *Free.*

★ Iglesia de Santo Tomé (*Santo Tomé Church*)

CHURCH | Not to be confused with the marzipan shop bearing the same name, this chapel topped with a Mudejar tower was built specially to house El Greco's most masterful painting, *The Burial of Count Orgaz.* Using vivid colors and splashes of light, it portrays the benefactor of the church being buried with the posthumous assistance of St. Augustine and St. Stephen, who have appeared at the funeral to thank the count for his donations to religious institutions named after the two saints. Though the count's burial took place in the 14th century, El Greco painted the onlookers in contemporary 16th-century costumes and included people he knew; the boy in the foreground is one of El Greco's sons, and the sixth figure on the left is said to be the artist himself. Santo Tomé is Toledo's most visited church besides the cathedral, so to avoid crowds, plan to visit as soon as the building opens. ⊠ *Pl. del Conde 4, Calle de Santo Tomé, Toledo* ☎ *92/525–6098* ⊕ *santotome.org* ⌧ *€4.*

Mezquita del Cristo de la Luz (*Mosque of Christ of the Light*)

MOSQUE | Originally a tiny Visigothic church, the mosque-chapel was transformed into a mosque during the Moorish occupation. The Islamic arches and vaulting survived, making this the most important relic of Moorish Toledo, even if a glaringly out-of-place sculpture of Jesus on the cross is the centerpiece of the building today. Legend has it that the chapel got its name when Alfonso VI's horse, striding triumphantly into Toledo in 1085, fell to its knees out front (a white stone marks the spot). It was then "discovered" that a candle had burned continuously behind the masonry the whole time the Muslims had been in power. Allegedly, the first Mass of the Reconquest was held here, and later a Mudejar apse was added. There are remnants of a Roman house in the yard nearby. ⊠ *Cuesta de Carmelitas Descalzos 10, Toledo* ☎ *92/525–4191* ⌧ *€4.*

★ Monasterio de San Juan de los Reyes

CHURCH | This convent church in western Toledo was erected by Fernando and Isabel to commemorate their victory at the Battle of Toro in 1476. (It was also intended to be their burial place, but their wish changed after Granada was recaptured from the Moors in 1492, and their actual tomb is in that city's Capilla Real.) The breathtakingly intricate building is largely the work of architect Juan Guas, who considered it his masterpiece and asked to be buried there himself. In true plateresque fashion, the white interior is covered with inscriptions and heraldic motifs. ⊠ *Calle de los Reyes Católicos 17, Toledo* ☎ *92/522–3802* ⊕ *www.sanjuandelosreyes.org* ⌧ *€4.*

Museo del Greco (*El Greco Museum*)

ART MUSEUM | This house that once belonged to Peter the Cruel's treasurer, Samuel Levi, is said to have later been El Greco's home, though historians now believe he actually lived across the street. Nevertheless, the interior of the El Greco Museum is decorated to resemble a typical house of the artist's time. The house is now incorporated into a revamped El Greco museum with several of the artist's paintings, including a panorama of Toledo with the Hospital of Tavera in the foreground, and works by several of El Greco's students (including his son) and other 16th- and 17th-century artists. Medieval caves have been excavated at

Did You Know?

The Alcázar of Toledo
has dominated the city
since at least the 3rd
century. It is the setting
for an important scene
of Franquist lore: During
the Spanish Civil War,
the Nationalist colonel
Moscardó was defend-
ing the building against
overwhelming Republican
forces. The Republicans
held his son hostage,
demanding the alcázar be
surrendered. To his son's
entreaties to "surrender
or they will shoot me,"
the father replied, "Then
commend your soul to
God and die like a hero."

the site, and there's a beautiful garden in which to take refuge from Toledo's often-scorching summer heat. ⊠ *Paseo del Tránsito s/n, Toledo* ☏ *92/588–6081* 🖥 *€3, free Sat. after 2 and Sun.* ⊘ *Closed Mon.*

Museo de Santa Cruz

ART MUSEUM | In a 16th-century Renaissance hospital with a stunning Classical-plateresque facade, this museum is open all day without a break (unlike many of Toledo's other sights). Works of art have replaced the hospital beds, and among the displays is El Greco's *Assumption* of 1613, the artist's last known work. A small archaeology museum is set in the hospital's delightful cloister. ⊠ *Calle Miguel de Cervantes 3, Toledo* ☏ *92/522–1402* 🖥 *€4, free Wed. after 4 and Sun.* ⊘ *Closed Sun. after 2:30.*

Plaza de Zocodover

PLAZA/SQUARE | Toledo's main square was built in the early 17th century as part of an unsuccessful attempt to impose a rigid geometry on the chaotic Moorish streets. Over the centuries, this tiny plaza has hosted bullfights, executions (*autos-da-fé*) of heretics during the Spanish Inquisition, and countless street fairs. Today it's home to the largest and oldest marzipan store in town, Santo Tomé. You can catch intracity buses here, and the tourist office is on the south side of the plaza. ⊠ *Pl. de Zocodover s/n, Toledo.*

Puente de Alcántara

BRIDGE | Roman in origin, this is the city's oldest bridge. Next to it is a heavily restored castle built after the Christian capture of 1085 and, above this, a vast and severe military academy, an eyesore of Francoist architecture. From the other side of the Río Tajo, the bridge offers fine views of Toledo's historic center and the Alcázar. ⊠ *Calle Gerardo Lobo s/n, Toledo.*

Puente de San Martín

BRIDGE | This pedestrian bridge on the western edge of Toledo dates to 1203

Off the Beaten Path

Museo Ruiz de Luna. Most of the region's pottery is made in Talavera de la Reina, 76 km (47 miles) west of Toledo. At this museum you can watch artisans throw local clay, then trace the development of Talavera's world-famous ceramics, chronicled through some 1,500 tiles, bowls, vases, and plates back to the 14th century. ⊠ *Pl. de San Agustín s/n, Calle San Agustín el Viejo 13, Talavera de la Reina* ☏ *92/580–0149* ⊕ *cultura.castillalamancha.es/ museos/nuestros-museos/museo-ruiz-de-luna* 🖥 *€3* ⊘ *Closed Mon.*

and has splendid horseshoe arches. At 40 meters (131 feet) long, it was one of the longest bridges in the world at the time of construction. ⊠ *Puente de San Martín s/n, Toledo.*

★ Sinagoga de Santa María La Blanca

SYNAGOGUE | Founded in 1203, Toledo's second synagogue—situated in the heart of the Jewish Quarter—is nearly two centuries older than the more elaborate Tránsito, just down the street. Santa María's white interior has a forest of columns supporting capitals with fine filigree work, a wonder of Mudejar architecture. It was a center of study and prayer until the 1355 assault on the Jewish Quarter and subsequent pogroms in 1391. ⊠ *Calle de los Reyes Católicos 4, Toledo* ☏ *92/522–7257* 🖥 *€3.*

★ Sinagoga del Tránsito (*Museo Sefardí, Sephardic Museum*)

SYNAGOGUE | This 14th-century synagogue's plain exterior belies sumptuous interior walls embellished with colorful Mudejar decoration. There are inscriptions in Hebrew and Arabic glorifying God, Peter the Cruel, and Samuel Levi (the original patron). It's a rare example of architecture reflecting Arabic as the lingua franca of medieval Spanish Jews. It's said that Levi imported cedars from Lebanon for the building's construction, echoing Solomon when he built the First Temple in Jerusalem. This is one of only three synagogues still fully standing in Spain (two in Toledo, one in Córdoba), from an era when there were hundreds—though more are in the process of being excavated. Adjoining the main hall is the **Museo Sefardí,** a small but informative museum of Jewish culture in Spain. ⊠ *Calle Samuel Levi s/n, Toledo* ☎ *92/522–3665* ⊕ *www.culturaydeporte. gob.es/msefardi/home.html* ⌖ *€3, free Sat. afternoon and Sun.*

 Restaurants

★ El Trébol

$ | SPANISH | You can't leave Toledo without indulging in one of El Trébol's famous *bombas,* fried fist-size spheres of mashed potato stuffed with spiced meat and anointed with aioli. They're best enjoyed on the twinkly outdoor patio with a locally brewed beer in hand. **Known for:** to-die-for bombas; most pleasant patio in town; local craft beers. ⓢ *Average main: €15* ⊠ *Calle de Santa Fe 1, Toledo* ☎ *92/528–1297* ⊕ *www.cerveceriatrebol. com.*

★ Restaurante Iván Cerdeño

$$$$ | SPANISH | Chef Iván Cerdeño's namesake restaurant is a beacon of Castilian *alta gastronomía*—think architectural dishes composed of foams, spherified sauces, and edible flowers served in a minimal white-tablecloth dining room. The ever-rotating tasting menus (5, 7, or 10 courses) almost always feature local game such as partridge or roe deer. **Known for:** two-Michelin-star dining; culinary hot spot; secluded location across the Tagus. ⓢ *Average main: €85* ⊠ *Cigarral del Ángel, Ctra. de la Puebla de Montalbán s/n, Toledo* ☎ *92/522–3674*

⊕ *ivancerdeno.com* ⊗ *Closed Mon. and Tues., Dinner only served Fri. and Sat.*

Taberna El Botero

$$ | SPANISH | Botero's old-school storefront draws diners into its cozy but lively tapas bar, with a solid cocktail program and global takes on the traditional, like crispy pig ear tacos with ginger and pickles. The upstairs dining room offers an extended menu and larger dishes, along with two seasonal tasting menus. **Known for:** bar open all day; global flare; flashy craft cocktails. ⓢ *Average main: €18* ⊠ *Calle Ciudad 5, Toledo* ☎ *92/528– 0967* ⊕ *tabernabotero.com* ⊗ *Closed Mon. and Tues.*

Taberna Skala

$ | SPANISH | The city's traditional smoky pork and pea stew, *carcamusas,* is a serious showstopper at this no-frills joint. Amongst the fried and boiled pig parts, also don't miss the *calentitos*—these perfectly fried mushrooms are served on crispy toast and slathered in a garlicky salsa verde. **Known for:** traditional nose-to-tail fare; fried mushrooms; hearty local pork stew. ⓢ *Average main: €10* ⊠ *Cta. Sal 5, Toledo* ⊗ *No dinner Sun.*

Coffee and Quick Bites

Tetería Dar Al-Chai

$ | MIDDLE EASTERN | FAMILY | Rest your legs at this Arabian-style tea house–bar appointed with plush couches, low tables, and colorful tapestries. Sample specially blended teas incorporating flowers, dried fruit, and spices. **Known for:** specially blended teas; delicious crepes and cakes; peaceful spot. ⓢ *Average main: €9* ⊠ *Pl. de Barrionuevo 5, Toledo* ☎ *92/522–5625* ⊕ *www.facebook.com/ teteriadaralchai.*

🛏 Hotels

★ Antídoto Rooms

$ | HOTEL | Antídoto is a breath of fresh air in Toledo's mostly staid hotel scene:

Toledo's Santa María la Blanca synagogue is a fascinating symbol of cultural cooperation: built by Islamic architects, in a Christian land, for Jewish use.

expect turquoise beamed ceilings, poured-concrete floors, and designer light fixtures. **Pros:** chic modern hotel in the heart of the old town; exceptional value; friendly staff. **Cons:** awkward room layout; in-room bathrooms with no curtains and transparent doors; sheets could be softer. [$] *Rooms from: €86* ✉ *Calle Recoletos 2, Toledo* ☎ *68/976–6605* 🌐 *www.antidotorooms.com* 🛏 *10 rooms* 🍴 *No Meals.*

Casa Palacio Rincón de la Catedral

$$ | **B&B/INN** | Tucked under the shadow of the cathedral, this 9th-century Moorish palace was reconverted into a small family-owned bed and breakfast that feels like taking a delightful step back in time. **Pros:** spot-on local recommendations; ideal location; tranquil and intimate. **Cons:** difficult to find entrance; parking is limited and expensive; some in-room bathrooms don't have doors. [$] *Rooms from: €135* ✉ *Calle Bajada Pozo Amargo 2, Toledo* ☎ *62/940–9001* 🌐 *rincondelacatedral.es* 🛏 *6 rooms* 🍴 *Free Breakfast.*

Hacienda del Cardenal

$ | **HOTEL** | Once a summer palace for Cardinal Lorenzana, who lived in the 1700s, this serene three-star hotel with a pool on the outskirts of the old town hits the sweet spot between rustic and refined. **Pros:** lovely courtyard; convenient dining; spacious rooms. **Cons:** restaurant often full; parking is pricey; stairs inconvenient for those with heavy luggage. [$] *Rooms from: €108* ✉ *Paseo de Recaredo 24, Toledo* ☎ *92/522–4900* 🌐 *www.haciendadelcardenal.com* 🛏 *27 rooms* 🍴 *Free Breakfast.*

★ Miluna

$$$$ | **HOTEL** | Taking a page from the playbook of Aire de Bardenas, Navarra's avant-garde bubble hotel, Miluna opened in 2018 on the outskirts of Toledo. **Pros:** a bubble hotel that won't break the budget; telescopes in every room; the ideal place to unplug. **Cons:** expensive and limited reservations; uncomfortable in winter and summer when temperatures are extreme; no alternate dining options in vicinity. [$] *Rooms from: €345* ✉ *C.*

de Valdecarretas, Parcela 364, Toledo
☎ *92/567–9229* ⊕ *www.miluna.es* ⤴ *12
rooms* ⦿| *Free Breakfast.*

Shopping

The Moors established silverwork, damascene (metalwork inlaid with gold or silver), pottery, embroidery, and marzipan traditions here. A turn-of-the-20th-century art school next to the Monasterio de San Juan de los Reyes keeps some of these crafts alive. For inexpensive pottery, stop at the large stores on the outskirts of town on the main road to Madrid. Many shops are closed on Sunday.

Confitería Santo Tomé

CANDY | Since 1856, Santo Tomé has been Spain's most famous maker of marzipan, a Spanish confection made from sugar, honey, and almond paste. Visit the main shop on the Plaza de Zocodover, or take a tour of the old convent-turned-factory where it's actually made at ✉ *Calle de Santo Tomé 3* (advance booking required). ✉ *Pl. de Zocodover 7, Toledo* ☎ *92/522–1168, 92/522–3763* ⊕ *mazapan.com.*

Cuartero House

FOOD | Toledo has various gourmet food stores, but this one takes the cake. Artisan cheeses, marzipan, and charcuterie are some of the mainstays, but also check out their regional olive oils and canned partridge and patés, which are easy to pack in your suitcase. ✉ *Calle Hombre de Palo 5, Toledo* ☎ *92/522–2614* ⊕ *casacuartero.com* ⊙ *Closed Sun.*

★ La Encina de Ortega

FOOD | This is a one-stop shop for local wines, olive oil, Manchego cheese, and—most notably—Ibérico pork products (ham, chorizo, dry-cured sausages) made from pigs raised on the family farm. Stick around for charcuterie boards and generously poured glasses of wine. ✉ *Calle de la Plata 22, Toledo* ☎ *92/510–2072* ⊕ *laencinadeortega.com* ⊙ *Closed Sat. afternoon and Sun.*

San Lorenzo de El Escorial

50 km (31 miles) northwest of Madrid.

An hour from Madrid, San Lorenzo de El Escorial makes for a leisurely day trip away from the hustle and bustle of the Spanish capital. The medieval town's main attraction is the Real Sitio de San Lorenzo de El Escorial, the Royal Site of San Lorenzo of El Escorial. A dozen or so trains leave daily from the Madrid Sol train station, or you can take the C3 regional line from Atocha, Chamartín, Nuevos Ministerios, or Recoletos. The journey takes about an hour, and the entrance to El Escorial is about a 15-minute walk from the train station.

Sights

★ Real Monasterio de San Lorenzo de El Escorial

CASTLE/PALACE | A UNESCO World Heritage Site and one of Spain's most visited landmarks, the imposing El Escorial palace complex was commissioned by Felipe II after the death of his father in the 1500s and remains the most complete and impressive monument of the later Renaissance in Spain. The monastery was built as an eternal memorial for his relatives, and the crypt here is the resting place of the majority of Spain's kings, from Carlos V to Alfonso XIII. A fantasy land of gilded halls, hand-painted chambers, and manicured French gardens, the gargantuan royal residence also houses an important collection of paintings by Renaissance and baroque artists donated by the crown. The library alone is worth the entry fee—its vibrant frescoes and leather-bound tomes spur the imagination. ✉ *Av. Juan de Borbón y Battemberg s/n, San Lorenzo de El Escorial* ☎ *91/890–5903* ⊕ *www.patrimonionacional.es/en/*

El Escorial's library, founded by Philip II, houses a rare collection of more than 4,700 manuscripts, many of them illuminated, and 40,000 printed books.

visita/royal-site-san-lorenzo-de-el-escorial ⛳ €12, free 3–7 on Wed. and Sun. ⊘ Closed Mon. Ⓜ El Escorial.

Segovia

91 km (56½ miles) north of Madrid.

Medieval Segovia rises on a steep ridge that juts above a stark undulating plain. It's defined by its ancient monuments, excellent cuisine, embroideries and textiles, and old-fashioned charm. An important military town in Roman times, Segovia was later established by the Moors as a major textile center. Captured by the Christians in 1085, it was enriched by a royal residence, and in 1474 the half sister of Henry IV, Isabel the Catholic (married to Fernando of Aragón), was crowned queen of Castile here. By that time Segovia was a bustling city of about 60,000 (its population hovers around 52,000 today), but its importance soon diminished as a result of its taking the losing side of the Comuneros in the popular revolt against Emperor Carlos V. Though the construction of a royal palace in nearby La Granja in the 18th century somewhat revived Segovia's fortunes, it never recovered its former vitality. Early in the 20th century, Segovia's sleepy charm came to be appreciated by artists and writers, among them painter Ignacio Zuloaga and poet Antonio Machado.

Today the streets swarm with day-trippers from Madrid—if you can, visit sometime other than in summer and spend the night to have much of the city to yourself. You'll want to hit the triumvirate of basic sights: the aqueduct, Alcázar, and cathedral. Come evening, don't miss the bustling food and nightlife scene around the Plaza Mayor.

GETTING HERE AND AROUND

High-speed AVE trains from Madrid's Chamartín station—the fastest and costliest option—take 30 minutes and drop you at the Guiomar station, about 7 km (4 miles) outside Segovia's center. Buses 11 and 12 are timed to coincide with arriving trains. Bus 11 will take you to the foot of the aqueduct after about a 15-minute ride, and Bus 12 drops you near the bus station.

La Sepulvedana buses depart Madrid (Moncloa station) for Segovia some 28 times a day. Direct routes take 1 hour 20 minutes and cost €8 each way. There are also plentiful BlaBlaCar options. (Check ⊕ www.blablacar.com or the app for details.)

Urbanos de Segovia operates the 13 inner-city bus lines and one tourist line, which are better options for getting around than struggling through the narrow streets (and problematic parking) with a car. Segovia's central bus station is a five-minute walk from the aqueduct along the car-free Paseo de Ezequiel González.

BUS CONTACTS Bus Station. ⊠ *Paseo de Ezequiel González, Segovia* ☎ *92/142–7705.* **Avanza.** ⊠ *Pl. de la Estación de Autobuses, Segovia* ⊕ *www.avanzabus.com.* **Urbanos de Segovia.** ⊠ *Segovia* ☎ *90/092–5303* ⊕ *segovia.avanzagrupo.com.*

VISITOR INFORMATION

Segovia Tourist Office. ⊠ *Pl. del Azoguejo 1, Segovia* ☎ *92/146–6720, 92/146–6721* ⊕ *www.turismodesegovia.com.*

 # Sights

★ Alcázar

CASTLE/PALACE | FAMILY | It's believed that the Walt Disney logo is modeled after the silhouette of this turreted castle. Possibly dating to Roman times, the Alcázar was expanded in the 14th century, remodeled in the 15th, altered again toward the end of the 16th, and completely reconstructed after being gutted by a fire in 1862, when it was used as an artillery school. The exterior, especially when seen below from the Ruta Panorámica, is awe-inspiring, as are the superb views from the ramparts. Inside, you can enter the throne room, chapel, and bedroom

used by Fernando and Isabel, as well as a claustrophobia-inducing winding tower. The intricate woodwork on the ceiling is marvelous, and the first room you enter, lined with knights in shining armor, is a crowd-pleaser, particularly for kids. There's also a small armory museum, included in the ticket price. ⊠ *Pl. de la Reina Victoria s/n, Segovia* ☎ *92/121–0515* ⊕ *www.alcazardesegovia.com* ⬚ *€9 for castle, tower, and museum.*

★ Aqueduct of Segovia

RUINS | Segovia's Roman aqueduct is one of the greatest surviving examples of Roman engineering and the city's main sight. Stretching from the walls of the old town to the lower slopes of the Sierra de Guadarrama, it's about 2,952 feet long and rises in two tiers to a height of 115 feet. The raised section of stonework in the center originally carried an inscription, of which only the holes for the bronze letters remain. Neither mortar nor clamps hold the massive granite blocks together, but miraculously, the aqueduct has stood since the end of the 1st century AD. ⊠ *Pl. del Azoguejo s/n, Segovia.*

★ Catedral de Segovia

CHURCH | Segovia's 16th-century cathedral was built to replace an earlier one destroyed during the revolt of the Comuneros against Carlos V. It's one of the country's last great examples of the Gothic style. The designs were drawn up by the leading late-Gothicist Juan Gil de Hontañón and executed by his son Rodrigo, in whose work you can see a transition from the Gothic to the Renaissance style. The interior, illuminated by 16th-century Flemish windows, is light and uncluttered (save for the wooden neoclassical choir). Across from the entrance, on the southern transept, is a door opening into the late-Gothic cloister, the work of architect Juan Guas. Off the cloister, a small museum of religious art, installed partly in the first-floor chapter house, has a white-and-gold 17th-century ceiling, a late example of *artesonado*

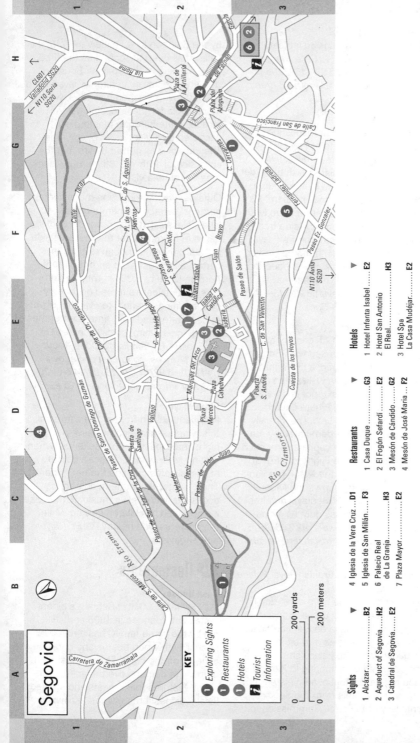

Segovia

12

Day Trips from Madrid SEGOVIA

KEY

▶ Exploring Sights
▶ Restaurants
▶ Hotels
🛈 Tourist Information

0 ———— 200 yards
0 ———— 200 meters

Sights ▶
1 Alcázar................**B2**
2 Aqueduct of Segovia....**H2**
3 Catedral de Segovia......**E2**
4 Iglesia de la Vera Cruz ...**D1**
5 Iglesia de San Millán....**F3**
6 Palacio Real
de La Granja.............**H3**
7 Plaza Mayor..............**E2**

Restaurants ▶
1 Casa Duque................**G3**
2 El Fogón Sefardí..........**E2**
3 Mesón de Cándido........**G2**
4 Mesón de José María **F2**

Hotels ▶
1 Hotel Infanta Isabel **E2**
2 Hotel San Antonio
El Real....................**H3**
3 Hotel Spa
La Casa Mudéjar..........**E2**

(a Mudéjar technique using intricately joined wooden slats). ✉ *Calle Marqués del Arco 1, Segovia* ☎ *92/146–2205* ⊕ *catedralsegovia.es* ✉ *From €3 (free Sun. Mass).*

Iglesia de la Vera Cruz

CHURCH | This isolated Romanesque church on the outskirts of town was built in 1208 for the Knights Templar. Like other buildings associated with the order, it has 12 sides, inspired by the Church of the Holy Sepulchre in Jerusalem. It's about a 45-minute walk from town (you can see this church on a cliffside from the castle windows), but the trek pays off in full when you climb the bell tower and see the Segovia skyline silhouetted against the Sierra de Guadarrama. ✉ *Ctra. de Zamarramia, Segovia* ☎ *92/143–1475* ✉ *€2.50, free Tues. 3–5pm.*

Iglesia de San Millán

CHURCH | Built in the 12th century and a model example of the Segovian Romanesque style, this church, a five-minute walk outside the town walls, is an architectural marvel. The exterior is notable for its arcaded porch, where church meetings were once held. The virtually untouched interior is dominated by massive columns, whose capitals carry such carved scenes as the Flight into Egypt and the Adoration of the Magi. The vaulting on the crossing shows the Moorish influence on Spanish medieval architecture. It opens for Mass only. ✉ *Av. del Acueducto 26, Segovia* ☎ *92/146–3876* ⊕ *www.parroquiasanmillansegovia.com* ✉ *Free.*

★ Palacio Real de La Granja (*Royal Palace of La Granja*)

CASTLE/PALACE | If you have a car, don't miss the Palacio Real de La Granja in the town of La Granja de San Ildefonso, on the northern slopes of the Sierra de Guadarrama. The palace site was once occupied by a hunting lodge and a shrine to San Ildefonso, administered by Hieronymite monks from the Segovian monastery of El Parral. Commissioned by the Bourbon king Felipe V in 1719, the palace has been described as the first great building of the Spanish Bourbon dynasty. The Italian architects Juvarra and Sachetti, who finished it in 1739, were responsible for the imposing garden facade, a late-baroque masterpiece anchored by a giant order of columns. The interior was gutted by fire, but the collection of 15th- to 18th-century tapestries warrants a visit.

Outside, walk through the magnificent gardens: terraces, ornamental ponds, lakes, classical statuary, woods, and baroque fountains dot the mountainside. Provided there is enough rainfall, on certain evenings in the summer (April–August, 12pm or 5:30–7 pm), the illuminated fountains are turned on, one by one, creating an effect to rival that of Versailles. Dates and start times sometimes change on a whim, so call ahead. ✉ *Pl. de España 15, San Ildefonso* ✛ *About 11 km (7 miles) southeast of Segovia on N601* ☎ *92/147–0019, 92/147–0020* ⊕ *www.patrimonionacional.es* ✉ *€9.*

Plaza Mayor

PLAZA/SQUARE | In front of the cathedral, this historic square comes alive every night and especially on weekends, when visiting Madrileños and locals gather at casual cafés that line the perimeter. There's a gazebo in the middle that occasionally hosts live music. (Otherwise it's occupied by children playing while their parents dine nearby.) ✉ *Pl. Mayor s/n, Segovia.*

 Restaurants

Casa Duque

$$$ | **SPANISH** | **FAMILY** | Segovia's oldest restaurant, founded in 1895 and still run by the same family, has a rustic interior with wood beams and bric-a-brac hanging on the walls. The decor suits the unfussy (if perhaps overpriced) cuisine, which features roast meats and stewed local *judiones* (broad beans). **Known for:**

Segovia's Roman aqueduct, built more than 2,000 years ago, is remarkably well preserved.

no-knife-needed cochinillo asado (roast suckling pig); genial English-language menus and service; back-in-time setting. $ *Average main: €28* ⊠ *Calle Cervantes 12, Segovia* ☎ *92/146–2487, 92/146–2486* ⊕ *restauranteduque.es.*

★ El Fogón Sefardí

$$ | SPANISH | This tavern in Segovia's historic Jewish quarter is owned by La Casa Mudéjar Hospedería hotel and has won awards for the region's best tapas. The extensive menu highlights Segovian specialties like cochinillo, as well as traditional Sephardic Jewish cuisine (though it's not a kosher kitchen), plus a variety of well-executed *raciones* (shared plates). **Known for:** Sephardic-influenced cuisine; great cochinillo; generous salads. $ *Average main: €20* ⊠ *Calle de la Judería Vieja 17, Segovia* ☎ *92/146–6250* ⊕ *www.lacasamudejar.com.*

Mesón de Cándido

$$$ | SPANISH | Beginning life as an inn in the 18th century, Cándido was declared a national monument in 1941, and today displays photos of famous patrons including Ernest Hemingway, Salvador Dalí, and Princess Grace. The cochinillo is the star; partridge stew and roast lamb are also memorable, especially on cold afternoons. ■ TIP→ **Ask for a table overlooking the aqueduct, just a few feet away, and be sure to book ahead. Known for:** wood-fired-oven-roasted cochinillo; historical building; famous former patrons like Ernest Hemingway. $ *Average main: €27* ⊠ *Pl. de Azoguejo 5, Segovia* ☎ *92/142–5911* ⊕ *mesondecandido.es.*

★ Mesón de José María

$$$$ | SPANISH | According to foodies, this old-timey *mesón* (traditional tavern-restaurant) serves the most delectable cochinillo in town, but there are plenty of lighter fresher dishes to choose from as well. Expect a boisterous mix of locals and tourists. **Known for:** best cochinillo in town; beamed dining room; local crowd (a rarity in this touristy town). $ *Average main: €30* ⊠ *Calle Cronista Lecea 11, Segovia* ✛ *off Pl. Mayor* ☎ *92/146–1111, 92/146–6017* ⊕ *www.restaurantejosemaria.com.*

Hotels

Hotel Infanta Isabel
$ | **HOTEL** | On the corner of the Plaza Mayor, this classically appointed hotel boasts cathedral views in a bustling shopping area. **Pros:** cozy lived-in ambience; central location; some rooms have balconies overlooking the plaza. **Cons:** some rooms are cramped and oddly shaped; rooms facing the plaza can be noisy on weekends; decidedly unhip decor. [$] *Rooms from: €90* ✉ *Pl. Mayor 12, Segovia* ☎ *92/146–1300* 🌐 *www.recordishotels.com/en/infanta-isabel-hotel/* 🛏 *37 rooms* 🍴 *No Meals.*

Hotel San Antonio El Real
$ | **HOTEL** | Housed in the 15th-century Monastery of San Antonio El Real (officially declared a National Monument of Segovia), this hotel is worth a visit on its own. **Pros:** tranquil outdoor spaces; centrally located; free outdoor parking. **Cons:** room decor is underwhelming; small bathrooms; walls can be thin. [$] *Rooms from: €90* ✉ *Calle San Antiono el Real s/n, Segovia* ☎ *92/143–1574* 🌐 *www.sanantonioelreal.es* 🛏 *50 rooms* 🍴 *Free Breakfast.*

Hotel Spa La Casa Mudéjar
$ | **HOTEL** | Built in the 15th century as a Mudejar palace, this historical property has spacious rooms and a well-priced spa (€35 per person; adults only) that's popular even with nonguests. **Pros:** terrific restaurant serving rare Sephardic dishes; historic building with Roman ruins; affordable spa. **Cons:** forgettable interiors; no nearby parking; beds are nothing special. [$] *Rooms from: €70* ✉ *Calle de Isabel la Católica 8, Segovia* ☎ *92/146–6250* 🌐 *www.lacasamudejar.com* 🛏 *42 rooms* 🍴 *No Meals.*

Shopping

After Toledo, the province of Segovia is Castile's most important area for traditional artisanry. Glass and crystal are specialties of La Granja, and ironwork, lace, basketry, and embroidery are famous in Segovia. You can buy good lace from the Romani vendors in Segovia's Plaza del Alcázar, but be prepared for some strenuous bargaining and never offer more than half the opening price. The area around Plaza de San Martín is a good place to buy crafts.

Montón de Trigo Montón de Paja
ART GALLERIES | This three-floor family-owned artisan shop designs and sells their own merino wool textiles, as well as leather products made from responsibly harvested materials. You'll also find a number of local paintings and prints, along with jewelry, ceramics, and numerous designs from artists around the country. The top floor of this location is actually an art gallery, but be sure to check out their second location in Plaza de Merced. ✉ *Calle Juan Bravo 21, Segovia* ☎ *92/146–2670* 🌐 *www.montondetrigomontondepaja.com.*

Plaza de San Martín
ANTIQUES & COLLECTIBLES | Several antique shops line this small plaza. Torreón de Lozoya, the 15th-century tower-mansion in the corner, hosts occasional exhibitions. ✉ *Segovia.*

Sepúlveda

58 km (36 miles) northeast of Segovia.

A walled village with a commanding position, Sepúlveda has a charming main square, but the main reasons to visit are its 11th-century Romanesque church and striking gorge with a scenic hiking trail.

GETTING HERE AND AROUND

Sepúlveda is about an hour north of Madrid on the A1. There are also several buses (and BlaBlaCar rideshares) a day from both Segovia and Madrid. The city is perched atop a hill overlooking a ravine, so you'll likely want transportation to the top. Don't park or get off the bus too soon.

Castillo de Coca

Perhaps the most famous medieval site near Segovia—worth the 52-km (32-mile) detour northwest of the city en route to Ávila or Valladolid—is the Castillo de Coca (Castle of Coca). Built in the 15th century for Archbishop Alonso de Fonseca I, the salmon-hued castle is a turreted Mudejar structure of plaster and red brick surrounded by a deep moat. It looks like a stage set for a fairy tale, and indeed, it was intended not as a fortress but as a place for the notoriously pleasure-loving archbishop to hold riotous parties. The interior, now occupied by a forestry school, has been modernized, with only fragments of the original decoration preserved. 🌐 *www.castillodecoca.com*

VISITOR INFORMATION

Sepúlveda Tourist Office. ✉ *Pl. del Trigo 6; Sepúlveda* ☎ *92/154–0425* 🌐 *sepulveda.es.*

Sights

El Salvador

CHURCH | This 11th-century wonder is the oldest Romanesque church in the province. The carvings on its capitals, probably by a Moorish convert, are quite outlandish. ✉ *Calle Subida a El Salvador 31, Sepúlveda* 🎟 *Free.*

★ Ermita de San Frutos

CHURCH | This 11th-century hermitage is in ruins, but its location—on a peninsula jutting out into a bend 100 meters above the Duratón River—is extraordinary. You'll need a car to get there, about 15 minutes' drive west of Sepúlveda. After parking, walk along the marked path—the surrounding area is a natural park and a protected nesting ground for rare vultures. Try to go at sunset; when the sun sets the monastery and river aglow. Inside the monastery, there's a small chapel and plaque describing the life of San Frutos, the patron saint of Segovia. An ancient pilgrimage route stretches 77 km (48 miles) from the monastery to Segovia's cathedral, and pilgrims still walk it each year. As an add-on to the trip, you can rent kayaks from NaturalTur to paddle the river (🌐 *www.naturaltur.com*; ☎ *92/152–1727*). ✉ *Carrascal del Río, Burgomillodo, Sepúlveda* 🎟 *Free.*

Restaurants

El Figón de Ismael

$$$ | **SPANISH** | Family owned since 1849, this iconic restaurant is tucked into a charming street and is famous for its roasted suckling lamb, cooked in a wood-burning oven. The cozy dining room is as Castilian as it gets: a stone exterior, wooden beams and finishes, and old family paintings. **Known for:** familiar and attentive service; extensive wine list; roasted suckling lamb. [$] *Average main: €28* ✉ *Calle Lope Tablada de Diego 2, Sepúlveda* ☎ *92/154–0055* 🌐 *www.elfigondeismael.com.*

Ávila

114 km (71 miles) northwest of Madrid.

On a windy plateau littered with giant boulders, with the Sierra de Gredos in the background, Ávila is a walled fairy-tale town that wouldn't look out of place in *Game of Thrones*. After it was wrested from the Moors in 1090, soaring crenelated walls were erected around its perimeter—by some 1,900 builders, who allegedly finished the task in just

Ávila's city walls, which still encircle the old city, have a perimeter of about 2½ km (1½ miles).

nine years. The walls have nine gates and 88 cylindrical towers bunched together, making them unique to Spain in form—they're quite unlike the Moorish defense architecture that the Christians adapted elsewhere. They're most striking when seen from afar; for the best views (and photos), cross the Adaja River, turn right on the Carretera de Salamanca, and walk uphill about 250 yards to a monument of pilasters surrounding a cross known as the "Four Posts."

Ávila's fame is largely due to St. Teresa. Born here in 1515 to a noble family of Jewish origin, Teresa spent much of her life in Ávila, leaving a legacy of convents and the ubiquitous *yemas* (candied egg yolks), originally distributed free to the poor and now sold for high prices to tourists. The town comes to life during the Fiestas de la Santa Teresa in October, a weeklong celebration that includes lighted decorations, parades, singing in the streets, and religious observances.

GETTING HERE AND AROUND

Jiménez Dorado (⊕ www.jimenezdorado. com) and AvilaBus serve Ávila and its surrounding villages. Twenty-three trains depart for Ávila each day from Chamartín station, and there are usually plentiful BlaBlaCar rideshares available. The city itself is easily managed on foot.

VISITOR INFORMATION

Ávila Tourist Office. ⊠ *Pl. de la Catedral, Av. de Madrid 39* ☎ *92/020–6200* ⊕ *www.turismoavila.com.*

 Sights

Basílica de San Vicente (*Basilica of St. Vincent*)

CHURCH | Where this massive Romanesque basilica stands, it's said that St. Vincent was martyred in 303 AD with his sisters, Sts. Sabina and Cristeta. Construction began in 1130, though the complex was restored in the late 19th and early 20th centuries. The west front, shielded by a vestibule, displays damaged but expressive carvings depicting the death of Lazarus and the parable of the rich man's table. The sarcophagus of St. Vincent forms the centerpiece of the interior. The extraordinary Eastern-influenced canopy above the sarcophagus is a 15th-century addition. Combined, these elements form one of Spain's most prized examples of Romanesque architecture. ⊠ *Pl. de San Vicente 6, Ávila* ☎ *92/025–5230* ⊕ *www.basilicasanvicente.es* ⊠ *€3, free Sun.*

Casa de los Deanes (*Deans' Mansion*)
HISTORIC HOME | This 15th-century building houses the cheerful **Museo Provincial de Ávila,** full of local archaeology and folklore. Part of the museum's collection is housed in the adjacent Romanesque temple of San Tomé el Viejo, a few minutes' walk east of the cathedral apse. ⊠ *Pl. de Nalvillos 3, Ávila* ☎ *92/021–1003* ⊠ *€1, free Sat. and Sun.* ⊗ *Closed Mon.*

★ Catedral de Ávila
CHURCH | The battlement apse of Ávila's cathedral forms the most impressive part of the city's walls. Entering the town gate to the right of the apse, you can reach the sculpted north portal by turning left and walking a few steps. The west portal, flanked by 18th-century towers, is notable for the crude carvings of hairy male figures on each side. Known as "wild men," these figures appear in many Castilian palaces of this period. The Transitional Gothic structure, with its granite nave, is considered to be the first Gothic cathedral in Spain. Look for the early-16th-century marble sepulchre of Bishop Alonso de Madrigal. Known as El Tostado ("the Toasted One") for his swarthy complexion, the bishop was a tiny man of enormous intellect. When on one occasion Pope Eugenius IV ordered him to stand—mistakenly thinking him to still be on his knees—the bishop pointed to the space between his eyebrows and hairline, and retorted, "A man's stature is to be measured from here to here!" ⊠ *Pl. de la Catedral s/n, Ávila* ☎ *92/021–1641* ⊕ *catedralavila.es* ⊠ *€8.*

Convento de Santa Teresa
CHURCH | This Carmelite convent was founded in the 17th century on the site of the St. Teresa's birthplace. Teresa's account of an ecstatic vision, in which an angel pierced her heart, inspired many baroque artists, most famously the Italian sculptor Giovanni Bernini. There's a small museum with creepy relics, including one of Teresa's fingers. You can also see the small and rather gloomy garden where she played as a child. ⊠ *Pl. de la Santa 2, Ávila* ☎ *92/021–1030* ⊕ *www.santateresadejesus.com* ⊠ *Church and reliquary free, museum €2* ⊗ *Museum closed Mon.*

Real Monasterio de Santo Tomás
CHURCH | In an unlikely location—among apartment blocks a good 10-minute walk from the walls—is one of the most important religious institutions in Castile. The monastery was founded by Fernando and Isabel with the backing of Inquisitor-General Tomás de Torquemada, largely responsible for the expulsion of the Jews per the Alhambra Decree, who is buried in the sacristy. Further funds were provided by the confiscated property of converted Jews who were dispossessed during the Inquisition. Three decorated cloisters lead to the church; inside, a masterful high altar (circa 1506) by Pedro Berruguete overlooks a serene marble tomb by the Italian artist Domenico Fancelli. One of the earliest examples of the Italian Renaissance style in Spain, this work was built for Prince Juan, the only son of Fernando and Isabel, who died at 19. After Juan's burial here, his heartbroken parents found themselves unable to return. ⊠ *Pl. de Granada 1, Ávila* ☎ *92/022–0400* ⊕ *www.monasteriosantotomas.com* ⊠ *€4.*

🍴 Restaurants

Las Cancelas
$$ | **SPANISH** | Locals flock to this little tavern for tapas and fat juicy steaks served in the boisterous barroom or

white-tablecloth dining area, set in a covered arcaded courtyard. There are 14 hotel rooms available, too—simple, endearingly well-worn arrangements at moderate prices. **Known for:** chuletón de Ávila (gargantuan local steak); quaint romantic dining room; good value. [$] *Average main: €21* ✉ *Calle de la Cruz Vieja 6, Ávila* ☎ *92/021–2249* 🌐 *www.lascancelas.com* 🕒 *Closed Jan.–early Feb. No dinner Sun.*

★ Restaurante El Molino de la Losa
$$$$ | **SPANISH** | **FAMILY** | At the edge of the serene Adaja River, El Molino, housed in a 15th-century mill, is one of the most idyllic restaurants in the region. Lamb, the chef's specialty, is roasted in a medieval wood oven; it's best preceded by smoky, bacon-y *revolcona* (mashed) potatoes or a bowl of stewed white beans from nearby El Barco de Ávila. **Known for:** succulent roast lamb; stunning location with views of the river and city walls; refined old-school cuisine. [$] *Average main: €30* ✉ *Calle Bajada de la Losa 12, Ávila* ☎ *92/021–1101, 92/021–1102* 🌐 *www.elmolinodelalosa.com* 🕒 *Closed Tues. No dinner Sun.–Wed.*

🛏 Hotels

Palacio de los Velada
$ | **HOTEL** | This four-star hotel occupies a beautifully restored 16th-century palace in the heart of the city next to the cathedral, an ideal spot if you like to relax between sightseeing. **Pros:** gorgeous glass-covered patio; amiable service; bountiful breakfast buffet. **Cons:** some rooms don't have views because the windows are so high; expensive off-site parking; lack of power outlets. [$] *Rooms from: €115* ✉ *Pl. de la Catedral 10, Ávila* ☎ *92/025–5100* 🌐 *www.hotelpalaciodelosvelada.com* 🛏 *144 rooms* 🍴 *No Meals.*

Parador de Ávila
$$ | **HOTEL** | **FAMILY** | Post up in a 16th-century medieval castle attached to the massive town walls at this parador whose standout feature is its lush garden containing archaeological ruins. **Pros:** gorgeous garden and views; good restaurant; family-friendly rooms and services. **Cons:** 10-minute walk to the action; interiors need a refresh; underwhelming breakfast. [$] *Rooms from: €135* ✉ *Calle del Marqués de Canales de Chozas 2, Ávila* ☎ *92/021–1340* 🌐 *paradores.es/es/parador-de-avila* 🛏 *61 rooms* 🍴 *No Meals.*

Sigüenza

132 km (82 miles) northeast of Madrid.

The ancient university town of Sigüenza dates back to Roman, Visigothic, and Moorish times and still has splendid architecture and one of the most impressive Gothic cathedrals in Castile. It's one of the rare Spanish towns that has not surrendered to modern development and sprawl. If you're coming from Madrid via the A2, the approach, through craggy hills and ravines, is dramatic. Sigüenza is an ideal base for exploring the countryside on foot or by bike, thanks to the Ruta de Don Quixote, a network of paths named for Cervantes's literary hero that passes through the town center and nearby villages.

GETTING HERE AND AROUND

There are four to five train departures daily to Sigüenza from Madrid's Chamartín station, and the journey takes about 1½ hours. Sigüenza's train station is an easy walk from the historic walled center. Buses depart from Madrid's Avenida de América station once a day and take two hours. If you arrive by car, park near the train station to avoid the narrow cobblestone streets of the city center. Rideshares, such as BlaBlaCar, are another option, provided there are trips that align with your schedule.

BICYCLE RENTAL

Neumáticos del Olmo

⊠ *Ctra. de Moratilla s/n, Nave 1, Sigüenza* ☎ *94/939–0754, 60/578–7650.*

VISITOR INFORMATION

Sigüenza Tourist Office. ⊠ *Calle Serrano Sanz 9, Sigüenza* ☎ *94/934–7007* ⊕ *www.visitasiguenza.es.*

Sights

Castillo de Sigüenza

CASTLE/PALACE | FAMILY | This enchanting castle overlooking wild hilly countryside from above Sigüenza is now a parador; non-guests can visit the dining room and common areas. The structure was founded by the Romans and rebuilt at various later periods. Most of the current building was erected in the 14th century, when it became a residence for the queen of Castile, Doña Blanca de Borbón, who was banished here by her husband, Pedro the Cruel. During the Spanish Civil War the castle was the scene of fierce battles, and much of the structure was destroyed. The lobby has an exhibit on the subsequent restoration with photographs of the bomb damage. If you have a half-hour to spare, there's a lovely walking path around the hilltop castle with a 360-degree view of the city and countryside below. ⊠ *Pl. de Castillo s/n, Sigüenza* ☎ *94/939–0100* ⊠ *Free.*

Catedral de Sigüenza

CHURCH | FAMILY | Begun around 1150 and completed in the 16th century, Sigüenza's cathedral combines Romanesque, Gothic, and Renaissance architecture. Wander from the late-Gothic cloister to a room lined with 17th-century Flemish tapestries, then onto the north transept, housing the 15th-century plateresque tomb of Dom Fadrique of Portugal. The Chapel of the Doncel (to the right of the sanctuary) contains Don Martín Vázquez de Arca's tomb, commissioned by Queen Isabel, to whom Don Martín served as *doncel* (page) before an untimely death

at the gates of Granada in 1486. In a refurbished early-19th-century house next to the cathedral's west facade, the small Diocesan Museum has a prehistoric section and religious art from the 12th to 18th century. It also runs the weekend tours of the burial chambers (catacombs) under the cathedral—a spooky favorite for kids. ⊠ *Calle Serrano Sanz 2, Sigüenza* ☎ *94/939–1023* ⊕ *catedralsiguenza.es* ⊠ *€6 including museum.*

Plaza Mayor

PLAZA/SQUARE | The south side of the cathedral overlooks this harmonious arcaded Renaissance square that hosts a medieval market on weekends. ⊠ *Plaza Mayor s/n, Sigüenza.*

Tren Medieval

TRAIN TOURS | FAMILY | Leaving from Madrid's Chamartín station, this delightful medieval-themed train service runs to Sigüenza mid-April through mid-November. The (otherwise thoroughly modern) train comes populated with minstrels, jugglers, and other entertainers, and it's a great activity for Spanish-speaking children. The ticket price includes round-trip fare, a guided visit to Sigüenza, entry to the main monuments and museums, and discounts at area restaurants. ⊠ *Estación de Sigüenza s/n, Sigüenza* ☎ *90/232–0320* ⊕ *www.renfe.com/es/es/experiencias* ⊠ *Adults €45, children over 4 €20, children under 4 free* ☉ *Closed winter.*

Restaurants

Bar Alameda

$ | TAPAS | FAMILY | This family-run bar and restaurant punches above its weight with market-driven tapas that reflect a sense of place. Spring for the stuffed foraged mushrooms or seared Sigüenza-style blood sausage. **Known for:** thoughtfully prepared tapas; local wines by the glass; family-friendly atmosphere. $ *Average main: €15* ⊠ *Calle de la Alameda 2, Sigüenza* ☎ *67/727–7773* ☉ *Closed Wed.*

Hotels

★ **Parador de Sigüenza**

$$ | HOTEL | FAMILY | This fairy-tale 12th-century castle has hosted royalty for centuries, from Fernando and Isabel right up to Spain's present king, Felipe VI. **Pros:** excellent food; sense of history and place; plenty of parking. **Cons:** much of castle is a neo-medieval replica; bland modern furniture that doesn't jibe with the space; occasionally surly service. $ *Rooms from: €140* ✉ *Pl. del Castillo, Sigüenza* ☎ *94/939–0100* ⊕ *paradores. es/es/parador-de-siguenza* 🖙 *81 rooms* ❌ *No Meals.*

Cuenca

168 km (104 miles) southeast of Madrid, 150 km (93 miles) northwest of Valencia.

Cuenca is one of the most surreal looking towns in Spain, built on a sloping escarpment whose precipitous sides plunge down to the Huécar and Júcar rivers. When real estate grew scarce a few centuries back, local builders constructed gravity-defying homes that dangle over the abyss. These Casas Colgadas ("Hanging Houses") are a unique architectural attraction. The old town's dramatic setting grants spectacular views of the surrounding countryside, and its cobblestone streets, cathedral, churches, and taverns contrast starkly with the modern town, which sprawls beyond the river gorges. Though somewhat isolated, Cuenca makes a good overnight stop if you're traveling between Madrid and Valencia, or even a worthwhile detour between Madrid and Barcelona.

GETTING HERE AND AROUND

From Madrid, buses leave for Cuenca about every two hours from Conde de Casal. From Valencia, four buses leave every four to six hours, starting at 8:30 am. A high-speed AVE train leaves Madrid approximately every two hours and stops in Cuenca (after about 55 minutes) on its way to Valencia. Slower cheaper trains also run several times daily between Cuenca and Valencia, Madrid, Albacete, and Alicante. Rideshares (such as BlaBlaCar) to and from the city are plentiful.

VISITOR INFORMATION

Cuenca Tourist Office. ✉ *Plaza Mayor 1, Cuenca* ☎ *96/924–1051* ⊕ *www.visitacuenca.es.*

 Sights

Cuenca has more than a dozen churches and two cathedrals, but visitors are allowed inside only about half of them. The best views of the city are from the square in front of a small palace at the very top of Cuenca, where the town tapers out to the narrowest of ledges. Here, gorges flank the precipice and old houses sweep down toward a distant plateau. The lower half of the old town is a maze of tiny streets, any of which will take you up to the Plaza del Carmen. From here the town narrows and a single street, Calle Alfonso VIII, continues the ascent to the Plaza Mayor, which passes under the arch of the town hall.

★ **Casas Colgadas** (*Hanging Houses*)

NOTABLE BUILDING | As if Cuenca's famous Casas Colgadas, suspended impossibly over the cliffs below, were not eye-popping enough, they also house one of Spain's finest museums, the Museo de Arte Abstracto Español (Museum of Spanish Abstract Art)—not to be confused with the adjacent Museo Municipal de Arte Moderno (Municipal Museum of Modern Art). Projecting over the town's eastern precipice, these houses originally formed a 15th-century palace, which later served as a town hall before falling into disrepair in the 19th century. In 1927 the cantilevered balconies were rebuilt, and in 1966 the painter Fernando Zóbel created the world's first museum devoted exclusively to abstract art. The works he

Cuenca's precarious Casas Colgadas are also home to the well-regarded Museo de Arte Abstracto Español.

gathered—by such renowned names as Carlos Saura, Eduardo Chillida, Lucio Muñoz, and Antoni Tàpies—are primarily by exiled Spanish artists who grew up under Franco's regime. The museum has free smartphone audio guides that can be downloaded from the website. ⊠ *Calle de los Canónigos s/n, Cuenca* ☎ *96/921–2983* ⊕ *www.march.es/arte/cuenca* 🎫 *Free* 🕐 *Closed Mon.*

Catedral de Cuenca
CHURCH | Built in the 12th century atop ruins of a conquered mosque, the cathedral, which looms over the Plaza Mayor, lost its Gothic character in the Renaissance. Inside are the tombs of the cathedral's founding bishops, an impressive portico of the Apostles, and a Byzantine reliquary. There's also a museum in the once-cellar of the Bishop's Palace containing a jewel-encrusted Byzantine diptych of the 13th century, a Crucifixion by the 15th-century Flemish artist Gerard David, a variety of carpets from the 16th through 18th centuries, and two small El Grecos. An excellent audio guide is included in the price of admission. ⊠ *Pl. Mayor s/n, Cuenca* ☎ *64/969–3600* ⊕ *www.catedralcuenca.es* 🎫 *€6.*

Ciudad Encantada (*Enchanted City*)
NATURE SIGHT | FAMILY | Not an "Enchanted City" as its name implies, Ciudad Encantada—situated 35 km (22 miles) north of Cuenca—is a series of large, fantastic mushroomlike rock formations erupting in a landscape of pines. It was formed over thousands of years by the forces of water and wind on limestone rocks, and you can see it in under two hours. See if you can spot formations named *Cara* (face), *Puente* (bridge), *Amantes* (lovers), and *Olas en el Mar* (waves in the sea). Rent a car to get here, or arrange a visit with Ecotourism Cuenca (⊕ www. ecoturismocuenca.com, ☎ 64/569–4393). ⊠ *Ciudad Encantada s/n, Cuenca* ☎ *63/490–9952* ⊕ *www.ciudadencantada.es* 🎫 *€6.*

★ Puente de San Pablo
BRIDGE | If you don't have a fear of heights, cross this narrow 16th-century footbridge to take in the vertiginous view

of the river and equally thrilling panorama of the Casas Colgadas. It's by far the best view of the city. If you've read the popular English novel *Winter in Madrid* by C. J. Sansom, you'll recognize this bridge from the final scene. ✉ *Cuenca.*

🍴 Restaurants

Much of Cuenca's cuisine is based on wild game, but farm-raised lamb, rabbit, and hen are ubiquitous on menus. Trout from the adjacent river (and, increasingly, from farms) is the fish of choice, and it turns up in entrées and soups. In almost every restaurant you'll find *morteruelo,* Cuenca's pâté of *jabalí* (wild boar), rabbit, partridge, hen, liver, pork loin, and spices, as well as *gazpacho manchego* (aka *galiano*), a meat stew thickened with dry flatbread—a remnant of the Sephardic culinary canon. For dessert, try *alajú,* a hard sugar candy containing honey, almonds, and lemon, or *torrijas,* bread slices dipped in milk, fried until custardy, and sprinkled with cinnamon-sugar.

Figón del Huécar

$$ | **SPANISH** | This family-run white-tablecloth restaurant serves updated Castilian classics in an airy dining room set in a medieval stone house overlooking the old city (ask for an outdoor table when booking). Specialty dishes include Manchegan *migas* (fried pork and bread crumbs), *ajoarriero* (pounded potatoes, garlic, bacalao, and olive oil), and veal with potatoes *al montón* (fried with garlic). **Known for:** breathtaking views; scrumptious desserts; elegant dining room. [$] *Average main: €20* ✉ *Ronda de Julián Romero 6, Cuenca* ☎ *63/259–7449* 🌐 *www.figondelhuecar.es* 🕓 *Closed Mon. No dinner Sun.*

★ La Ponderosa

$ | **TAPAS** | La Ponderosa is a quintessential yet elevated Castilian bar where locals mingle at high volume while tossing back local wine and munching on well-priced seasonal delicacies like griddled wild asparagus, suckling lamb chops, and seared wild mushrooms. It's a standing-room-only joint, so if you want to sit, you'll have to come early and find a place on the terrace. **Known for:** hidden-gem local wines; simple and delicious vegetable dishes; buzzy atmosphere. [$] *Average main: €15* ✉ *Calle de San Francisco 20, Cuenca* ☎ *96/921–3214* 🕓 *Closed Sun. and July.*

🛏 Hotels

Cueva del Fraile

$ | **HOTEL** | **FAMILY** | Surrounded by dramatic landscapes, this family-friendly three-star lodging occupies a 16th-century building on the outskirts of town. **Pros:** beautiful interior garden terrace; outdoor swimming pool and tennis courts; good value. **Cons:** location 7 km (4 miles) from town; no a/c in some rooms; interiors show their age. [$] *Rooms from: €75* ✉ *Ctra. Cuenca a Buenache, Km 7, Cuenca* ☎ *96/921–1571* 🌐 *www.hotelcuevadelfraile.com* 🕓 *Closed Jan. and Feb.* 🛏 *77 rooms* 🍴 *No Meals.*

★ Parador de Cuenca

$$ | **HOTEL** | The rooms are luxurious and serene at the exquisitely restored 16th-century convent of San Pablo, pitched on a precipice across a dramatic gorge from Cuenca's city center. **Pros:** great views of the Hanging Houses and gorge; spacious rooms; consistently good restaurant. **Cons:** expensive breakfast not always included in room rate; secure garage parking sometimes unavailable; calls to reception sometimes go unanswered. [$] *Rooms from: €180* ✉ *Subida a San Pablo s/n, Cuenca* ☎ *96/923–2320* 🌐 *paradores.es/es/parador-de-cuenca* 🛏 *63 rooms* 🍴 *No Meals.*

★ Posada de San José

$ | **B&B/INN** | **FAMILY** | This family-friendly inn, housed in a centuries-old convent, clings to the top of the Huécar gorge in Cuenca's old town. **Pros:** cozy historical rooms; stunning views of the gorge; well-prepared local food. **Cons:** built to 17th-century proportions, some doorways are low; certain rooms are cramped; sloping floors can be vertiginous when lying in bed. $ *Rooms from: €97* ✉ *Ronda de Julián Romero 4, Cuenca* ☎ *96/921–1300, 63/981–6825* ⊕ *www.posadasanjose.com* ⇆ *31 rooms* ⦿ *No Meals.*

Almagro

204 km (127 miles) south of Madrid.

The center of this noble town contains the only preserved medieval theater in Europe. It stands beside the ancient Plaza Mayor, where 85 Roman columns form two colonnades supporting green-frame 16th-century buildings. Enjoy casual tapas—such as pickled baby eggplant (*berenjenas de Almagro*), a hyperlocal specialty known the country over—and rustic Manchegan wines in the bars lining the square. Near the plaza are granite mansions emblazoned with the heraldic shields of their former owners and a splendid parador in a restored 17th-century convent.

GETTING HERE AND AROUND

Almagro can be reached by train from Madrid, with one scheduled departure per day departing from Atocha or Chamartín stations for the 2½-hour journey, but it's probably best to rent a car or book a BlaBlaCar rideshare. The drive south from the capital takes you across the plains of La Mancha, where Don Quixote's adventures unfolded.

VISITOR INFORMATION Almagro Tourist

Office. ✉ *Calle San Agustín 21, Almagro* ☎ *92/686–0717* ⊕ *almagro.es/turismo.*

 Sights

Corral de Comedias

PERFORMANCE VENUE | Appearing almost as it did in 1628 when it was built, this theater has wooden balconies on four sides and the stage at one end of the open patio. During the golden age of Spanish theater—the time of playwrights Pedro Calderón de la Barca, Cervantes, and Lope de Vega—touring actors came from all over Europe to Almagro, once a burgeoning urban center for its mercury mines and lace industry. Few such theaters stand today. Forgo the tourist-oriented spectacles unless you're thoroughly bilingual or a Spanish theater buff: poor acoustics and archaic Spanish scripts make it difficult to understand what's going on. An international classical theater festival takes place here in July. ✉ *Pl. Mayor 18, Almagro* ☎ *92/686–1539* ⊕ *www.corraldecomedias.com* 🎫 *From €5.60.*

★ Museo Etnográfico Campo de Calatrava

HISTORY MUSEUM | For a window into what agrarian life was like in this area in centuries past, pop into this tiny museum presided over by the passionate historian who amassed the antique curiosities on display. The influence of the Central European "Fúcares" families on the area is especially fascinating. A guided tour, in Spanish, takes a little less than an hour and is well worth it. ✉ *Calle Chile 6, Almagro* ☎ *65/701–0077* ⊕ *museodealmagro.com* 🎫 *€5* 🕐 *Closed Mon., morning hours are very seasonal.*

Museo Nacional del Teatro

HISTORY MUSEUM | **FAMILY** | This museum, housed in the ancestral seat of the Calatrava Order of Knights, displays models of the Roman amphitheaters in Mérida (Extremadura) and Sagunto (near Valencia), both still in use, as well as costumes, pictures, and documents relating to the history of Spanish theater. Kids love handling the antique instruments previously used for sound effects during productions. ✉ *Calle del Gran Maestre 2, Almagro* ☎ *92/626–1014, 92/626–1018* ⊕ *museoteatro.mcu.es* 🎫 *€3, free Sat. afternoon and Sun. morning* 🕐 *Closed Mon.*

Hotels

★ Parador de Almagro
$$ | HOTEL | Five minutes from the Plaza Mayor of Almagro, this parador is a finely restored 16th-century Franciscan convent with cells, cloisters, and patios. **Pros:** pretty indoor courtyards; outdoor pool; ample free parking. **Cons:** occasionally untidy public areas; double-bed rooms smaller than normal rooms; inconsistent restaurant. [$] *Rooms from: €129* ✉ *Ronda de San Francisco 31, Almagro* ☎ *92/686–0100* 🌐 *paradores.es/es/parador-de-almagro* 🛏 *54 rooms* 🍴 *No Meals.*

Salamanca

212 km (132 miles) northwest of Madrid.

Salamanca's radiant sandstone buildings, proportion-perfect Plaza Mayor, and meandering river make it one of the most majestic and beloved cities in Spain. For centuries, its eponymous university has imbued the city with an intellectual verve, a stimulating arts scene, and—in recent decades—raging nightlife to match. You'll see more foreign students here per capita than anywhere else in Spain.

If you approach from Madrid or Ávila, your first glimpse of Salamanca will be of the city rising on the northern banks of the wide and winding Tormes River. In the foreground is its sturdy 15-arch Roman bridge; soaring above it is the combined bulk of the old and new cathedrals. Piercing the skyline to the right is the Renaissance Convento de San Esteban. Behind San Esteban and the cathedrals and largely out of sight from the river, extends a stunning series of palaces, convents, and university buildings that culminates in the Plaza Mayor. Despite enduring considerable damage over the centuries, Salamanca remains one of Spain's greatest cities architecturally, a showpiece of the Spanish Renaissance.

GETTING HERE AND AROUND

You'll probably feel rushed if you try to visit Salamanca from Toledo in an out-and-back day trip. To fully enjoy its splendor, plan on an overnight. Approximately 13 trains depart Madrid for Salamanca daily, several of which are high-speed ALVIA itineraries that take just over 1½ hours. Avanza buses leave from the Estación Sur de Autobuses; BlaBlaCar rideshares (about 2 hours 15 minutes) are faster and more affordable.

Once in town, Salamanca de Transportes runs 64 municipal buses equipped with lifts for passengers with disabilities on routes throughout the city. You may opt to take a bus in order to reach the train and bus stations on the outskirts of the city.

BUS Salamanca de Transportes. ✉ *Calle Gran Vía 4, Salamanca* ☎ *92/321–2829* 🌐 *salamancadetransportes.com.*

VISITOR INFORMATION Salamanca City Tourist Office. ✉ *Pl. Mayor 32, Salamanca* ☎ *92/321–8342* 🌐 *salamanca.es.*

Sights

Casa de Las Conchas (*House of Shells*)
HISTORIC HOME | This house, whose facade is covered in scallop shell carvings, was built around 1500 for Dr. Rodrigo Maldonado de Talavera, a chancellor of the Order of St. James, whose symbol is the shell. Among the playful plateresque details are the lions over the main entrance, engaged in a fearful tug-of-war with the Talavera crest. The interior has been converted into a public library. Duck into the charming courtyard, which has an intricately carved upper balustrade that imitates basketwork. ✉ *Calle de la Compañía 2, Salamanca* ☎ *92/326–9317* 🎟 *Free.*

Salamanca's Plaza Mayor once hosted bullfights.

★ **Convento de Las Dueñas** (*Convent of the Dames*)

CHURCH | Founded in 1419, this convent hides a 16th-century cloister that is the most fantastically decorated in Salamanca, if not all of Spain. The capitals of its two superimposed Salmantine arcades are crowded with a baffling profusion of grotesques that can absorb you for hours. Don't forget to look down: the interlocking diamond pattern on the ground floor of the cloister is decorated with the knobby vertebrae of goats and sheep. It's an eerie yet perfect accompaniment to all the grinning disfigured heads sprouting from the capitals looming above you. The museum has a fascinating exhibit on Spain's little-known slavery industry. ■ **TIP→ Seek out the traditional sweets made by the nuns.** ⊠ *Pl. del Concilio de Trento s/n, Salamanca* ☎ *92/321–5442* 🖾 *€2.*

★ **Convento de San Estéban** (*Convent of St. Stephen*)

CHURCH | The convent's monks, among the most enlightened teachers at the university in medieval times, introduced Christopher Columbus to Isabel (hence his statue in the nearby Plaza de Colón, back toward Calle de San Pablo). The complex was designed by one of the monks who lived here, Juan de Álava. The west facade, a thrilling plateresque masterwork in which sculpted figures and ornamentation are piled up to a height of more than 98 feet, is a gathering spot for tired tourists and picnicking locals, but the crown jewel of the structure is a glowing golden sandstone cloister with Gothic arcading punctuated by tall spindly columns adorned with classical motifs. The church, unified and uncluttered but also dark and severe, allows the one note of color provided by the ornate and gilded high altar of 1692. An awe-inspiring baroque masterpiece by José Churriguera, it deserves five minutes of just sitting and staring. ⊠ *Pl. del Concilio de Trento 1, Salamanca* ☎ *92/321–5000* ⊕ *www.conventosanesteban.es* 🖾 *€4* ⊙ *Museum closed Mon.*

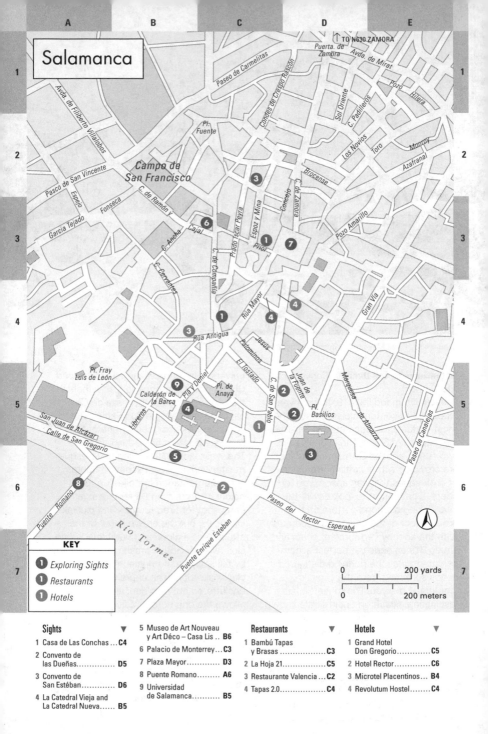

Salamanca

↑ TO N630 ZAMORA

KEY

① Exploring Sights
① Restaurants
① Hotels

| 0 | | 200 yards |
| 0 | | 200 meters |

★ **La Catedral Vieja and La Catedral Nueva**

CHURCH | Nearest the river stands the Catedral Vieja (Old Cathedral), built in the late 12th century and one of the most riveting examples of the Spanish Romanesque. Because the dome of the crossing tower has strange plumelike ribbing, it's known as the Torre del Gallo (Rooster's Tower). The much larger Catedral Nueva (New Cathedral) went up between 1513 and 1526 under the late-Gothic architect Juan Gil de Hontañón. Controversially, a 1992 restoration added an astronaut carving to the facade as a wink to the modern era—see if you can spot it. Both cathedrals are part of the same complex, though they have different visiting hours and you need to enter the New to get to the Old. ⊠ *Pl. de Anaya and Calle Cardenal Pla y Deniel, Salamanca* ☎ *92/321–7476, 92/328–1123* ⊕ *www.catedralsalamanca.org* ⊿ *€10 (includes Catedral Nueva and Catedral Vieja).*

Museo de Art Nouveau y Art Déco – Casa Lis

ART MUSEUM | Sure, the best thing about this museum is probably the stunning Moderniste building it's housed in, but the collections—comprising 19th-century paintings and glass, French and German china dolls, Viennese bronze statues, and more—are a welcome reprieve from all the churrigueresque convents and churches. ⊠ *Calle de Gibraltar 14, Salamanca* ☎ *92/312–1425* ⊕ *www.museocasalis.org* ⊿ *€5, free Thurs. 11–2.*

Palacio de Monterrey

CASTLE/PALACE | Built in the mid-16th century by Rodrigo Gil de Hontañón and one of the most stunning Renaissance palaces in Spain, this lavish abode was meant for an illegitimate son of Alonso de Fonseca I. The building, which opened to the public in 2018, is flanked by towers and has an open arcaded gallery running the length of the upper level. Such galleries—often seen on the ground floor of palaces in Italy—were intended to provide privacy for the women of the

Fonseca's Mark

Nearly all of Salamanca's outstanding Renaissance buildings bear the five-star crest of the powerful and ostentatious Fonseca family. The most famous of them, Alonso de Fonseca I, was the archbishop of Santiago and later of Seville; he was also a notorious womanizer and a patron of the Spanish Renaissance.

house and to cool the floor below during the summer. Walking the halls on either the day- or nighttime tour, feast your eyes on seldom-before-seen Titians, Coellos, and other masterpieces presided over by the Alba family. ⊠ *Pl. de Monterrey 2, Salamanca* ☎ *92/321–3020* ⊕ *www.palaciodemonterrey.com* ⊿ *From €7, free Tues. 10:30 am–11 am with prior booking* ⊘ *Closed Mon.*

★ Plaza Mayor

PLAZA/SQUARE | In the 1730s Alberto and Nicolás Churriguera built Salamanca's Plaza Mayor, one of the largest and most beautiful squares in Spain. The lavishly elegant, pinkish *ayuntamiento* (town hall) dominates its northern side. The square and its arcades are popular gathering spots for Salmantinos of all ages, and its terrazas are the perfect spot for a coffee break. At night, the plaza swarms with students meeting "under the clock" on the plaza's north side. *Tunas* (roving musicians in traditional garb) often meander among the cafés and crowds, playing for smiles, applause, and tips. ⊠ *Plaza Mayor s/n, Salamanca.*

Puente Romano (*Roman Bridge*)

BRIDGE | Next to this bridge is an Iberian stone bull, and opposite the bull is a statue commemorating the young hero of the 16th-century picaresque novel *The Life of Lazarillo de Tormes and of His Fortunes and Adversities,* a masterpiece of Spanish literature. There's also a

Did You Know?

Salamanca's "new" cathedral was built in the 16th century to help reinforce the deteriorating "old" cathedral, which dates to the 12th. Today you can see both, entering the new to get to the old.

300-meter track and a network of paths on the south side of the bridge ideal for jogging. ⊠ *Salamanca.*

Universidad de Salamanca

COLLEGE | The university's walls, like those of the cathedral and other structures in Salamanca, often bear large ocher lettering recording the names of famous university graduates. The earliest names are said to have been written in the blood of the bulls killed to celebrate the successful completion of a doctorate (call it medieval graffiti!). The elaborate facade of the Escuelas Mayores (Upper Schools) dates to the early 16th century; see if you can spy the eroded "lucky" frog that's become the symbol of the city—legend has it that students who spot it on their first try will pass all their exams. The interior of the Escuelas Mayores, drastically restored in parts, is disappointing after the splendor of the facade and not worth entering unless you're a diehard Spanish literature buff. But if you are, the lecture hall of Fray Luis de León, where Cervantes, Pedro Calderón de la Barca, and numerous other luminaries of Spain's golden age once sat, is of interest, as is the grand library. Don't miss the serene courtyard (free entry) of the Escuelas Menores (Lower Schools) that wraps around the patio in front of the Escuelas Mayores. ⊠ *Calle Libreros, Salamanca* ☎ *92/329–4400* ⊕ *www.usal.es* 🖾 *Free to view facade; €10 to enter, free Mon. morning.*

🍴 Restaurants

Bambú Tapas y Brasas

$$ | **TAPAS** | Bambú is two restaurants in one: there's a jovial basement tapas bar serving gargantuan tapas and beers, and then there's the far more sedate white-tablecloth dining room, whose *alta cocina* menu is as experimental as it is expensive. Both are worthwhile options; go with the vibe that suits you best. **Known for:** free tapas with every drink at the bar; upscale dining room;

terrific grilled meats. 🖻 *Average main: €20* ⊠ *Calle de Prior 4, Salamanca* ☎ *66/652–3523* ⊕ *www.bambubrasas. com* 🕓 *Closed Mon. and Tues.*

★ La Hoja 21

$$ | **SPANISH** | Just off the Plaza Mayor, this upscale restaurant has a glass facade, high ceilings, butter-yellow walls, and minimalist art—a welcome relief from the dime-a-dozen Castilian mésones. Savor traditional fare with a twist, such as ibérico pork ravioli and langoustine-stuffed trotters at dinner, or spring for the €20 lunch prix fixe, an absolute steal, served Tuesday through Friday midday. **Known for:** nuanced yet unpretentious modern fare; phenomenally affordable menú del día; romantic low-key atmosphere. 🖻 *Average main: €22* ⊠ *Calle San Pablo 21, Salamanca* ☎ *92/326–4028* ⊕ *lahoja21.com* 🕓 *Closed Mon. No dinner Sun.*

Restaurante Valencia

$$ | **SPANISH** | Despite its Mediterranean name, this traditional family-run restaurant serves up Castilian specialties like garlic soup, partridge salad, local river trout, white asparagus, and suckling lamb. The tiny front bar is decorated with black-and-white photos of local bullfighters and is usually packed with locals (as is the back room). **Known for:** hidden-gem local hangout; soul-warming Castilian fare; outdoor seating. 🖻 *Average main: €20* ⊠ *Calle Concejo 15, Salamanca* ☎ *92/321–7868* ⊕ *www.restaurantev-alencia.com* 🕓 *Closed Mon. and Tues. Sept.–May, Sun. and Mon. June–Aug.*

★ Tapas 2.0

$ | **TAPAS** | Decidedly modern, dependably delicious, and shockingly cheap, Tapas 2.0 might pull you back for a second meal. The cool *ensaladilla rusa* (tuna-and-potato salad) is one of the best in Spain; then there are more substantial dishes, like stewed broad beans with octopus and shrimp and saucy chicken cannelloni, all complemented by a wine list featuring unexpected pours like

German Riesling. **Known for:** award-winning ensaladilla rusa; uncommon wines; best tapas in town. 💲 *Average main: €14* ✉ *Calle Felipe Espino 10, Salamanca* ☎ *92/321–6448* ⊕ *www.tapastrespuntocero.es.*

 ## Hotels

Grand Hotel Don Gregorio

$$$ | **HOTEL** | This upscale boutique hotel has spacious contemporary rooms in a building with roots in the 15th century. **Pros:** quiet and comfortable; complimentary cava upon arrival; spa and in-room massages. **Cons:** overpriced restaurant; no outdoor space for lounging; hodgepodge passé decor. 💲 *Rooms from: €245* ✉ *Calle San Pablo 80–82, Salamanca* ☎ *92/321–7015* ⊕ *www.hoteldongregorio.com* ↪ *17 rooms* ¹⊘¹ *Free Breakfast.*

★ Hotel Rector

$$$ | **HOTEL** | From the stately entrance to the high-ceiling guest rooms, this charming 13-room hotel offers a fairy-tale European experience. **Pros:** good value for a luxury hotel; personal service; good location. **Cons:** parking costs extra; no balconies; breakfast could be more ample. 💲 *Rooms from: €245* ✉ *Paseo del Rector Esperabé 10, Salamanca* ☎ *92/321–8482* ⊕ *www.hotelrector.com* ↪ *13 rooms* ¹⊘¹ *No Meals.*

★ Microtel Placentinos

$ | **B&B/INN** | This is a cheap-and-cheerful B&B tucked down a quiet pedestrian street in Salamanca's historic center, near the Palacio de Congresos convention center and a short walk from the Plaza Mayor. **Pros:** some rooms have whirlpool baths; quirky decor; short walk to bus station. **Cons:** rooms by interior staircase can be noisy; some accommodations are cramped; boring breakfast buffet. 💲 *Rooms from: €80* ✉ *Calle Placentinos 9, Salamanca* ☎ *92/328–1531* ⊕ *microtelplacentinos.com* ↪ *9 rooms* ¹⊘¹ *Free Breakfast.*

Revolutum Hostel

$ | **HOTEL** | **FAMILY** | What some might call a "designer hostel," this is the best modern budget hotel in Salamanca. **Pros:** breakfast included; all rooms have private bathrooms; special rates for families and longer stays. **Cons:** deposit required for towels; you have to make your own bed in some rooms; small bathrooms in some rooms. 💲 *Rooms from: €55* ✉ *Calle de Sánchez Barbero 7, Salamanca* ☎ *92/321–7656* ⊕ *www.revolutumhostel.com* ↪ *20 rooms* ¹⊘¹ *Free Breakfast.*

 ## Nightlife

Particularly in summer, Salamanca sees the greatest influx of foreign students of any city in Spain: by day they study Spanish, and by night they fill Salamanca's bars and clubs.

BARS AND CAFÉS

Café Niebla Bar

COCKTAIL LOUNGES | Also known by its translated name, Mist Cocktail Bar, this award-winning mixology lab slings truly inventive cocktails with a big focus on local spirits and sherry wines. One of their most unconventional sips is laced with truffle bitters and is presented with a miniature staircase leading to the glass, and a tiny mouse figurine holding a slice of aged cheese. They also host lively jazz nights on Thursdays that start around 10 pm. ✉ *Calle de Boradores 14, Salamanca* ☎ *92/321–4530* ⊕ *cafenieblabar.com.*

★ The Doctor Cocktail

COCKTAIL LOUNGES | This petite, unpretentious coctelería off the Plaza Mayor serves an enormous breadth of drinks, from colorful tiki numbers (some with pyrotechnics) to Prohibition-era classics, until 1:30 am daily. ✉ *Calle Doctor Piñuela 5, Salamanca* ☎ *92/326–3151.*

🎭 Performing Arts

Teatro Liceo

MUSIC | This 732-seat theater, 40 yards from Plaza Mayor, is a renovated 19th-century building erected over an 18th-century convent. It hosts classic and modern performances of opera, dance, and flamenco as well as film festivals. ⊠ *Plaza de Liceo s/n, Salamanca* ☎ *92/328–1716* ⊕ *www.ciudaddecultura. org.*

🛍 Shopping

El Rastro

MARKET | This Sunday flea market—named after the larger one in Madrid—is held just outside Salamanca's historic center. It has some 400 stalls. ⊠ *Av. de Aldehuela s/n, Salamanca.*

Isisa Duende

CRAFTS | If you have a car, skip the souvenir shops in Salamanca's center and instead take a joyride 35 km (22 miles) along the SA300 road to Isisa Duende, a wooden crafts workshop run by a charming husband-and-wife team. Their music boxes, photo frames, and other items are carved and painted with local motifs. Call ahead to schedule a free tour; if you're pressed for time, you can sometimes buy their wares in the tourist office on the Plaza Mayor. ⊠ *Calle San Miguel 1, Ledesma* ☎ *62/651–0527, 62/533–6703* ⊕ *www.isisa-duende.es.*

★ Luis Méndez

JEWELRY & WATCHES | Luis and his two brothers are independent third-generation jewelers whose work is distinguished by intricate filigree. The most stunning specimens—costing more than €1,000—are fashioned out of gold and pearls, but there are more affordable options made from silver and semiprecious stones. Visit their boutique, or purchase from their online Etsy catalog. ⊠ *Calle Meléndez 8, Bajo 2, Salamanca* ☎ *92/326–0725* ⊕ *www.luismendez.net.*

★ Mercado Central

FOOD | FAMILY | At Salamanca's most historic market with more than 50 stalls, you can stock up on local gourmet specialties—such as farinato sausages, jamón ibérico, and sheep's cheeses—and round out your shopping spree with a glass of wine at any of the traditional tapas counters. ⊠ *Pl. del Mercado s/n, Salamanca* ☎ *92/321–3000* ⊕ *mercado-centralsalamanca.com* ⊗ *Closed Sun.*

Burgos

243 km (151 miles) north of Madrid.

On the banks of the Arlanzón River, this small city boasts some of Spain's most outstanding Gothic architecture. If you approach on the A1 from Madrid, the spiky twin spires of Burgos's cathedral welcome you to the city, rising above the main bridge. Burgos's second pride is its heritage as the city of El Cid, the part-historical, part-mythical hero of the so-called Reconquest of Spain. For better and for worse, the city has long been synonymous with both militarism and religion, and even today more nuns fill the streets than almost anywhere else in Spain. Burgos was born as a military camp—a fortress built in 884 on the orders of the Christian king Alfonso III, who was struggling to defend the upper reaches of Old Castile from the constant forays of the Arabs. It quickly became vital in the defense of Christian Spain, and its reputation as an early outpost of Christianity was cemented with the founding of the Monasterio de Las Huelgas in 1187. It became a place of rest and sustenance for Christian pilgrims on the Camino de Santiago. In 1938, as the Spanish Civil War raged on, soon-to-be-dictator Francisco Franco made Burgos his first seat of government, a testament to the city's conservative leanings. Today Burgos is a modern Spanish city like any other, and happily, its name is far more likely to recall its famous *queso fresco*

The small city of Burgos is famous for its magnificent Gothic cathedral.

(quark) and morcilla (blood sausage) than it is with its fraught political past.

GETTING HERE AND AROUND

Burgos can be reached by train from Madrid, with 13 departures daily from Chamartín (2½ hours on the fast ALVIA train and 4½ on the regional line) and by bus, with hourly service from various Madrid stations. There are usually several BlaBlaCar rideshares available as well. Once in town, municipal buses cover 45 routes throughout the city, many of them originating in Plaza de España.

VISITOR INFORMATION Burgos Tourist Office. ⊠ *Pl. de Alonso-Martínez 7* ☎ *94/720–3125* ⊕ *turismo.aytoburgos.es.*

 Sights

Arco de Santa María

NOTABLE BUILDING | Across the Plaza del Rey San Fernando from the cathedral, this is the city's main gate, rebuilt in the 16th century by King Carlos V. Walk through toward the river and look above

the arch at the 16th-century statues of the first Castilian judges, El Cid, King Carlos I, and Spain's patron saint, James. ⊠ *Pl. Rey San Fernando, Burgos.*

Cartuja de Miraflores (*Miraflores Charterhouse*)

CHURCH | The plain facade of this 15th-century Carthusian monastery, some 3 km (2 miles) outside the historic center, belies a richly decorated interior. There's an altarpiece by Gil de Siloe that is said to be gilded with the first gold plundered in the Americas. ⊠ *Ctra. Fuentes Blancas s/n, Burgos* ☎ *94/725–2586* ⊕ *www.cartuja.org* ☒ *Free.*

★ Catedral de Burgos

CHURCH | The cathedral contains such a wealth of art and other treasures that the local burghers lynched their civil governor in 1869 for trying to take an inventory of it, fearing that he was plotting to steal their riches. Just as opulent is the sculpted flamboyant Gothic facade. The cornerstone was laid in 1221, and the two 275-foot towers were completed in

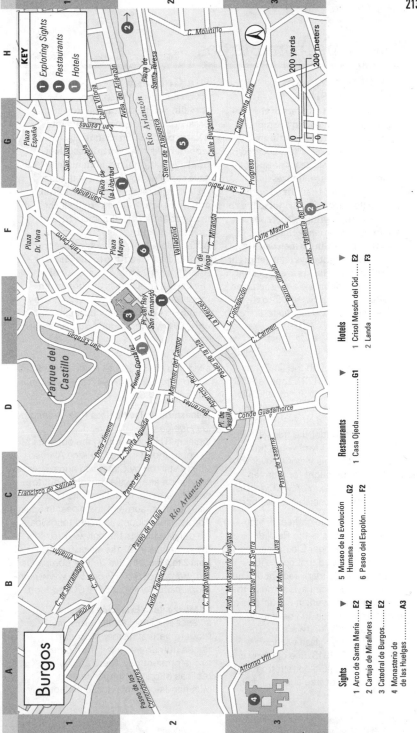

Burgos

KEY
- ① Exploring Sights
- ① Restaurants
- ① Hotels

Parque del Castillo

Río Arlanzón

200 yards
200 meters

Sights ▶
1 Arco de Santa María E2
2 Cartuja de Miraflores H2
3 Catedral de Burgos E2
4 Monasterio de
  de las Huelgas A3
5 Museo de la Evolución
  Humana G2
6 Paseo del Espolón F2

Restaurants ▶
1 Casa Ojeda G1

Hotels ▶
1 Crisol Mesón del Cid E2
2 Landa F3

Side Trips from Burgos

Monasterio de Santo Domingo de Silos

For a sojourn with masters of the Gregorian chant, head to the monastery where 1994's triple-platinum album *Chant* was recorded. Located 58 km (36 miles) southeast of Burgos, the monastery has an impressive two-story cloister that's lined with intricate Romanesque carvings. Try to drop in for an evening vespers service. It's a unique experience that's well off the tourist path. Single men can stay here for up to eight days (€50 per night with full board). Guests are expected to be present for breakfast, lunch, and dinner but are otherwise left to their own devices. ⊕ *www.abadiadesilos.es*

Ojo Guareña

If you have a day to spare or are traveling on to Cantabria, stop at this breathtaking hermitage hewn into a karst cliffside surrounded by leafy woodlands situated a mile south of Cueva. A national monument, the cave complex housing the religious structure stretches 90 km (56 miles), and there's rock art throughout the many chambers that depicts the cave as a dwelling for early humans. Archaeologists date the site's use from the Middle Paleolithic to the Middle Ages. A worthwhile guided tour of the hermitage lasts 45 minutes; even more scintillating is the tour of nearby Palomera Cave (by appointment only). ⊕ *www.merindaddesotoscueva.es*

the 14th century, though the final chapel was not finished until 1731. There are 13 chapels, the most elaborate of which is the hexagonal Condestable Chapel. You'll find the tomb of El Cid (1026–99) and his wife, Ximena, under the transept. El Cid (Rodrigo Díaz de Vivar) was a feudal warlord revered for his victories over the Moors, though he fought for them as well; the medieval *Song of My Cid* transformed him into a Spanish national hero.

At the other end of the cathedral, high above the West Door, is the Reloj de Papamoscas (Flycatcher Clock), named for the sculptured bird that opens its mouth as the hands mark each hour. The grilles around the choir have some of the finest wrought-iron work in central Spain, and the choir itself has 103 delicately carved walnut stalls, no two alike. The 13th-century stained-glass windows were destroyed in 1813, one of many cultural casualties of Napoleon's retreating troops. The excellent free audio guide has

a kid-friendly option. ✉ *Pl. de Santa María s/n, Burgos* ☎ *94/720–4712* ⊕ *catedralde-burgos.es* 🎟 *€10.*

Monasterio de las Huelgas (*Monasterio de las Huelgas*)

CHURCH | This convent on the outskirts of town, founded in 1187 by King Alfonso VIII, is still run by Cistercian nuns. There's a small on-site textile museum, but the building's main attraction is its stained-glass panels, some of the oldest in Spain. Admission includes a guided tour (Spanish only), which is the only way to view the monastery. ⚠ **The monastery closes from 2 to 4 pm.** ✉ *Calle de Los Compases s/n, Burgos* ☎ *94/720–6045* ⊕ *www.patrimonionacional.es* 🎟 *€6* 🕑 *Closed Mon.*

★ Museo de la Evolución Humana

SCIENCE MUSEUM | FAMILY | This airy modern natural history museum traces human evolution from primate to the present day. There are life-size replicas of our ancient ancestors, plus hands-on exhibits and in-depth scientific explanations (in English) that will fascinate visitors of all ages. Pair with a museum-led visit to the Atapuerca archaeological site (inquire at reception or online to arrange). ✉ *Paseo de la Sierra de Atapuerca s/n, Burgos* ☎ *94/742–1000* 🌐 *www.museoevolucionhumana.com* 🎟 *€6; free Tues., Thurs. 7–8 pm, and Wed. afternoon* 🕒 *Closed Mon.*

Paseo del Espolón

PROMENADE | The Arco de Santa María frames the city's loveliest promenade, the Espolón. Shaded with black poplars, it follows the riverbank. ✉ *Burgos.*

🍴 Restaurants

Casa Ojeda

$$$ | **SPANISH** | This restaurant—a Castilian classic—is known for refined Burgos standbys, especially *cochinillo* (suckling pig) and lamb served straight from the 200-year-old wood oven. Wines by the glass are local and reasonably priced. **Known for:** fall-off-the-bone lamb; old-school waitstaff; tried-and-true Castilian cuisine. [$] *Average main: €26* ✉ *Calle Vitoria 5, Burgos* ☎ *94/720–9052* 🌐 *restauranteojeda.com* 🕒 *Closed Mon., no dinner Sun.-Wed.*

🛏 Hotels

Crisol Mesón del Cid

$$ | **HOTEL** | Previously a 15th-century printing press and newly under the Eurostars umbrella, this hotel has bright airy guest rooms (ask for one facing the cathedral) with tile floors and exposed brick and stone walls. **Pros:** cathedral views from upgraded rooms; comfy clean digs; central location. **Cons:** parking is a tight squeeze; could use a face-lift; some rooms are noisy. [$] *Rooms from: €125* ✉ *Pl. de Santa María 8, Burgos* ☎ *94/720–8715* 🌐 *www.mesondelcid.es* 🛏 *54 rooms* 🍽 *Free Breakfast.*

El Camino de Santiago 👁

West of Burgos, the León-bound N120 crosses the ancient Camino de Santiago, or Way of St. James, revealing lovely old churches, tiny hermitages, ruined monasteries, and medieval villages across rolling fields. West of León, you can follow the well-worn Camino pilgrimage route as it approaches the giant cathedral in Santiago de Compostela.

★ Landa

$$$ | **HOTEL** | **FAMILY** | If you've ever dreamed of holing up in a luxurious castle, consider booking a room at Landa, a converted 14th-century palace some 5 km (3 miles) from the city center surrounded by lush gardens. **Pros:** stunning indoor-outdoor swimming pool; surprisingly affordable for level of luxury; beautiful lobby. **Cons:** roads to and from town are busy; car required; inconsistent food quality and unprofessional restaurant staff. [$] *Rooms from: €233* ✉ *Ctra. de Madrid a Irún, Km 235, Burgos* ☎ *94/725–7777* 🌐 *www.landa.as* 🛏 *37 rooms* 🍽 *No Meals.*

🍸 Nightlife

Due to its student population, Burgos has a lively *vida nocturna* (nightlife) in **Las Llanas,** near the cathedral. House wines and *cañas* (small glasses of beer) flow freely through the crowded tapas bars along Calles de Laín Calvo and San Juan, near the Plaza Mayor. Calle de la Puebla, a small dark street off Calle de San Juan, also gets constant revelers. When you order a drink at any Burgos bar, the bartender plunks down a free *pinchito* (small tapa)—a long-standing tradition.

Bardeblás

CAFÉS | This intimate bar stays open until 4:30 am on the weekends, inviting you to stay awhile—and you just might, thanks to its strong and affordable drinks and catchy throwback jams. ⊠ *Calle de la Puebla 29, Burgos* ☎ *94/720–1162.*

Cervecería Flandes

PUBS | With 12 beers on tap that run the gamut from Belgian ales to rare Castilian microbrews, this Burgos stalwart attracts a diverse crowd of students, travelers, and beer geeks. Just don't expect any fancy food here—potato chips, nachos, and other sundry snacks are the only grub available. ⊠ *Pl. Huerto del Rey 21, Burgos* ☎ *65/993–4813.*

🛍 Shopping

Ribera del Duero reds, bottled south of the city along the eponymous river, might not be as well known as those from Rioja, but they can be equally (if not more) sublime. You also can stock up on Burgos-style morcilla (blood sausage) and local cheese. Beyond culinary finds, keep your eye out for small artisan shops specializing in ceramics and textiles.

★ Delicatessen Ojeda

FOOD | A food-lover's paradise, this pristine, well-lit store carries all the Castilian delicacies you can imagine, from Burgos-style morcilla and cheese to roasted oil-packed peppers and top-quality dried beans and pulses. ⊠ *Calle de Vitoria 5, Burgos* ☎ *94/720–4832* ⊕ *delicatessenojeda.com* ⊗ *Closed Mon.*

Chapter 13

SEVILLE AND
AROUND

Updated by
Joanna Styles

◉ **Sights**   🍴 **Restaurants**   🛏 **Hotels**   🛍 **Shopping**   🍸 **Nightlife**
★★★★★   ★★★★★   ★★★★★   ★★★★★   ★★★★☆

WELCOME TO SEVILLE AND AROUND

TOP REASONS TO GO

★ **The Real Alcázar:** Drink in the sumptuously decorated patios and halls, the heavenly gold ceiling, ornate tile, and lush gardens dotted with pools, palms, and peacocks.

★ **Tour Catedral de Sevilla:** Tour Spain's biggest cathedral (there are 80 chapels) to see Christendom's largest altarpiece.

★ **Live and breathe flamenco:** Tune into Andalusia's soundtrack at one of Seville's many flamenco tablaos or spontaneously on any corner in Santa Cruz or Triana.

★ **Feast on tapas:** Make small plates your staples at myriad taverns, traditional and modern, where fine dining comes paired with local wines including sherry.

★ **Shop for tiles:** Learn about the history and process of making Sevillian ceramics in a former factory at the Centro de Cerámica Triana, and shop for beautiful souvenirs.

★ **Linger in the Plaza de España:** Take a leisurely stroll at this magnificent semicircular plaza located in Parque de María Luisa.

1 **Centro.** The heart of the city's commercial life.

2 **Santa Cruz.** Home to the Real Alcázar (Royal Fortress) and a glorious labyrinth of whitewashed alleys.

3 **El Arenal.** This area includes Parque María Luisa, the Torre de Oro, and picturesque taverns.

4 **La Macarena.** The city's best churches and convents, pleasant squares, and excellent restaurants are here.

5 **Triana.** Home to the main workshop for Seville's renowned tile ceramicists.

6 **Itálica.** Known for the ruins of its Roman city.

7 **Córdoba.** Home to the stunning Mezquita.

8 **Ronda.** Famous for its dramatic escarpments, views, and gorge.

9 **Around Ronda.** Caves, mountain villages, and gorges.

10 **Arcos de la Frontera.** A classic Andalusian pueblo blanco (white village).

11 **Jerez de la Frontera.** The capital of horse culture and sherry.

12 **Cádiz.** So old that Julius Caesar once held public office here.

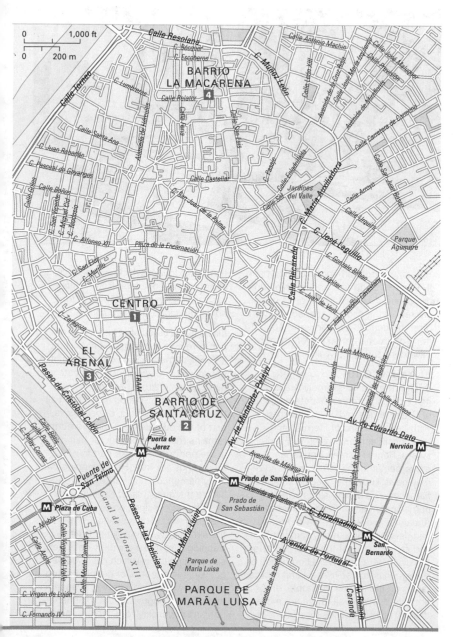

FLAMENCO

Rule one about flamenco: You don't see it. You feel it. The pain and yearning on the dancers' faces and the eerie voices are real. If the dancers manage to summon the *duende* and allow this soulful state of emotion to take over, then they have done their jobs well.

FLAMENCO 101

Origins: The music is largely Arabic in its beginnings, but you'll detect echoes of Greek dirges and Jewish chants with healthy doses of Flemish and traditional Castilian thrown in. Hindu sways, Roman mimes, and other movement informs the dance, but we may never know the specific origins of flamenco. The dance, along with the nomadic Romani, spread throughout Andalusia and within a few centuries had developed into many variations and styles, some of them named after the city where they were born (such as *malaguenas* and *sevillanas*) and others taking on the names of people, emotions, or bands. In all, there are more than 50 different styles (or *palos*) of

flamenco, four of which are the stylistic pillars others branch off from—differing mainly in rhythm and mood: *toná*, *soleá*, *fandango*, and *seguidilla*.

Clapping and castanets: The sum of its parts are awe-inspiring, but if you boil it down, flamenco is a combination of music, singing, and dance. Staccato hand-clapping almost sneaks in as a fourth part—the sounds made from all the participants' palms, or *palmas,* is part of the duende—but this element remains more of a connector that all in the performance take part in when their hands are free. Hand-clapping was likely flamenco's original key instrument before the guitar, *cajón* (wooden box used for percussion), and other instruments arrived on the scene. Perhaps the simplest way to augment the clapping is to add a uniquely designed six-string guitar, in which case you've got yourself a tablao, or people seated around a singer and clapping. Dance undoubtedly augments the experience, but isn't necessary for a tablao. These exist all throughout Andalusia and are usually private affairs with people who love flamenco. Castanets (or *palillos*) were absorbed by the Phoenician culture and adopted by the Spanish, now part of their own folklore. They accompany other traditional folk dances in Spain and are used pervasively throughout flamenco (though they are not always present in some forms of dance).

Flamenco now: Flamenco's enormous international resurgence has been building for the past few decades. Much of this revival can be attributed to pioneers like legendary singer Camarón de la Isla, guitarist Paco de Lucía, or even outsiders like Miles Davis fusing flamenco with other genres like jazz and rock. Today the most popular flamenco fusion artists include Rosalía and Dellafuente.

FLAMENCO HEAD TO TOE

Wrists rotate while hands move, articulating each finger individually, curling in and out. The trick is to have it appear like an effortless flourish. Facial expression is considered another tool for the dancer, and it's never plastered on but projected from some deeper place. For women, the hair is usually pulled back in touring flamenco performances in order to give the back row a chance to see the passionate expressions more

clearly. In smaller settings like tablaos, hair is usually let down and is supposed to better reveal the beauty of the female form overall. The dancer carries the body in an upright and proud manner: the chest is out, shoulders back. Despite this position, the body should never carry tension—it needs to remain pliable and fluid. With professional dancers, the feet can move so quickly, they blur like hummingbird wings in action. When they move slowly, you can watch the different ways a foot can strike the floor. A *planta* is when the whole foot strikes the floor, as opposed to when the ball of the foot or the heel (*taco*) hits. Each one must be a "clean" strike or the sound will be off.

An exploration of Andalusia must begin with Seville, Spain's fourth-largest city and the place where all romantic images of Andalusia—and Spain—spring vividly to life. Known for steamy-hot summers, delightfully mild winters, its operatic heroine Carmen, and stunning *Game of Thrones* settings, Seville is an enchanting city. Its fabulous food; extraordinary Mudejar, Gothic, and Renaissance architecture; and exotic flamenco rhythms never fail to seduce and charm.

Seville's whitewashed houses, bright with bougainvillea; ocher-color palaces; and baroque facades have long enchanted both Sevillanos and travelers. It's a city for the senses—the fragrance of orange blossom suffuses the air in spring, the sound of flamenco echoes through the alleyways in Triana and Santa Cruz, and views of the great Guadalquivir River accompany you at every turn. This is also a fine city for handsome people—stroll down the swankier pedestrian shopping streets and you can't fail to notice just how good looking everyone is. Aside from being blessed with even features and flashing dark eyes, Sevillanos exude a cool sophistication that seems more Catalan than Andalusian.

Like all Andalusians, Sevillanos know how to party. Highlights of the year come in the Feria de Abril, a week of colorful and musical festivities to welcome spring, quickly followed by celebrations marking Pentecost, when locals take a pilgrimage to El Rocío on the Atlantic Ocean. Religious fervor comes into its own during Semana Santa (Holy Week) when thousands of devout locals take part in some of Spain's most famous processions.

Side trips from Seville range from half-day excursions to the Roman Itálica to longer visits to some of Andalusia's finest towns and cities. Nearby Jerez, celebrated for sherry and horses, and Cádiz, a maritime jewel, are both must-sees. Ronda, one of Spain's most beautiful towns, merits a full day, as does Córdoba, whose Moorish mosque ranks as one of the country's most treasured monuments.

Planning

When to Go

Visit Seville between October and November or between April and May. It's blisteringly hot in the summer, so spend time in Los Pedroches of northern Córdoba province if you plan to visit then. Autumn catches the cities going about their business, the temperatures are moderate, and you will rarely see a line form.

December through March tends to be cool, uncrowded, and quiet, but come spring, it's fiesta time, with Seville's Semana Santa (Holy Week, between Palm Sunday and Easter) the most moving and multitudinous. April showcases whitewashed Andalusia at its floral best, with every patio and facade covered with flowers from bougainvillea to honeysuckle.

Getting Here and Around

AIR

Seville's airport is about 7 km (4 miles) east of the city. There's a bus from the airport to the center of town every half hour daily (4:30 am to midnight; €4 one-way, €6 return). Taxi fare from the airport to the city center is around €25 during the day and €28 at night and on Sunday. A number of private companies operate airport-shuttle services.

BUS

Seville has two intercity bus stations: Estación Plaza de Armas, the main one, with buses serving Córdoba, Granada, Huelva, and Málaga in Andalusia, plus Madrid and Portugal and other international destinations; and the smaller Estación del Prado de San Sebastián, serving Cádiz and nearby towns and villages.

Seville's urban bus service is efficient and covers the greater city area. Bus

Nos. C1, C2, C3, C4, and C5 run circular routes linking the main transportation terminals with the city center. The C1 goes east in a clockwise direction from the Santa Justa train station via Avenida de Carlos V, Avenida de María Luisa, Triana, the Isla de la Cartuja, and Calle de Resolana. The C2 follows the same route in reverse. The C3 runs from the Avenida de Menéndez Pelayo to the Puerta de Jerez, Triana, Plaza de Armas, and Calle de Recaredo. The C4 does that route counterclockwise. The C5 runs between Puerta de Jerez and Plaza del Duque de la Victoria. The tram (called Metro Centro) runs between the San Bernardo station and Plaza Nueva. Buses do not run within the Barrio de Santa Cruz because the streets are too narrow, though they amply serve convenient access points around the periphery of this popular tourist area.

Certain routes operate limited night service from midnight to 2 am Monday through Thursday, with services until 5 am Friday through Sunday. Single rides cost €1.40, but if you're going to be busing a lot, it's more economical to buy a rechargeable multi-travel pass (minimum charge is €7), which works out to €0.69 per ride. Special *tarjetas turísticas* (tourist passes), valid for one or three days of unlimited bus travel, cost (respectively) €5 and €10. Tickets are sold at newsstands and at the main bus station, Prado de San Sebastián.

CONTACTS Estación del Prado de San Sebastián. ☒ *Calle de Manuel Vázquez Sagastizábal s/n, El Arenal* ☎ *955/479290.* **Estación Plaza de Armas.** ☒ *Av. del Cristo de la Expiración 2, Centro* ☎ *955/038665* ⊕ *www.autobusesplazadearmas.es.*

CAR

Getting in and out of Seville by car isn't difficult, thanks to the SE30 ring road, but getting around in the city by car is problematic. We advise leaving your car at your hotel or in a lot while you're here.

TAXI

CONTACTS Radio Taxi Sevilla. ⊠ *Seville* ☎ *954/580000.*

TRAIN

Train connections include the high-speed AVE service from Madrid, with a journey time of less than 2½ hours.

CONTACTS Estación Santa Justa. ⊠ *Av. de Kansas City s/n, El Arenal* ☎ *912/320320.*

VISITOR INFORMATION

CONTACTS City of Seville. ⊠ *Paseo Alcalde Marqués de Contadero s/n, Barrio de Santa Cruz* ✛ *On waterfront, by Torre de Oro* ☎ *955/471232* ⊕ *visitasevilla.es.*

Restaurants

Eating out is an intrinsic part of the Andalusian lifestyle. Whether it's sharing some tapas with friends over a prelunch drink or a three-course à la carte meal, many Andalusians eat out at some point during the day. Unsurprisingly, there are literally thousands of bars and restaurants throughout the region catering to all budgets and tastes.

At lunchtime, check out the *menús del día* (daily menus) offered by many restaurants, usually three courses and excellent value (expect to pay €10–€15, depending on the type of restaurant and location). Roadside restaurants, known as *ventas*, usually provide good food in generous portions and at reasonable prices. Be aware that many restaurants add a service charge (*cubierto*), which can be as much as €3 per person, and some restaurant prices don't include value-added tax (*impuesto sobre el valor añadido/I.V.A.*) at 10%. Note also that restaurants with tasting menus (*menús de degustación*) usually require everyone at the table to have the menu.

Andalusians tend to eat later than their fellow Spaniards: lunch is 2–4 pm, and dinner starts at 9 pm (10 pm in the summer). In cities, many restaurants are closed Sunday night, and fish restaurants tend to close on Monday; in inland towns and cities, some restaurants close for all of August.

Restaurant reviews have been shortened. For full information, visit Fodors. com.

Hotels

Seville has grand old hotels, such as the Alfonso XIII, and a number of converted former palaces.

In Córdoba, several hotels occupy houses in the old quarter, close to the mosque. Other than during Holy Week and the Festival de los Patios in May, it's easy to find a room in Córdoba.

Rental accommodations bookable on portals such as Airbnb are popular in large towns and cities; double-check reviews before you book.

Not all hotel prices include value-added tax (I.V.A.) and the 10% surcharge may be added to your final bill. Check when you book.

Hotel reviews have been shortened. For full information, visit Fodors.com.

What It Costs in Euros			
$	$$	$$$	$$$$
RESTAURANTS			
under €18	€18–€24	€25–€30	over €30
HOTELS			
under €125	€125–€200	€201–€300	over €300

Tours

★ **annie b's Spanish Kitchen**

SPECIAL-INTEREST TOURS | Based in Vejer de la Frontera (Cádiz), Scottish-born Annie

B offers food and wine experiences, including sherry tours, tuna *almadraba* (an age-old way of trapping) trips, and cooking classes. ⊠ *Calle Viñas 11, Vejer de la Frontera* ☎ *620/560649* ⊕ *www. anniebspain.com* ✉ *From €175.*

Azahar Sevilla Tapas Tours

SPECIAL-INTEREST TOURS | Local food and wine expert and certified sherry educator Shawn Hennessey leads intimate guided tours around Seville's best tapas bars (traditional and gourmet). Choose from several different options, lunch or evening. ⊕ *azahar-sevilla.com/sevilletapas* ✉ *From €100.*

Hike & Bike The Sierras

SPECIAL-INTEREST TOURS | British-born hosts Heather and Wayne offer cycling, mountain biking, and walking day trips and tours in the countryside and pueblos blancos around Ronda for all fitness levels. ⊠ *Ronda* ☎ *638/873279* ⊕ *hike-andbikeholidays.com* ✉ *From €50.*

Sevilla Bike Tour

BICYCLE TOURS | Guided tours, leaving from the Makinline Shop on Calle Arjona at 10:30 am, take in the major sights of the city and offer interesting stories and insider information along the way. You'll cover about 10 km (6 miles) in three hours. Reservations are required on weekends and recommended on weekdays. ⊠ *Calle Arjona 8, Centro* ☎ *954/562625* ⊕ *sevillabiketour.com* ✉ *From €30.*

Sevilla Walking Tours

WALKING TOURS | Choose one of three walking tours conducted in English: the City Walking Tour, leaving Plaza Nueva from the statue of San Fernando; the Alcázar Tour, leaving Plaza del Triunfo from the central statue; and the Cathedral Tour, also leaving from the Plaza del Triunfo's central statue. ⊠ *Seville* ☎ *616/501100* ⊕ *sevillawalkingtours.com* ✉ *From €18.*

Your First Flamenco Experience

SPECIAL-INTEREST TOURS | Local dancer Eva Izquierdo from Triana teaches you how to clap in time and take your first dance steps, in authentic costume, all in an hour. ⊠ *Seville* ☎ *692/303634* ⊕ *www. ishowusevilla.com* ✉ *From €28.*

Seville

Seville offers a bewitching mosaic of flamenco, matadors, horses, refreshingly cool patios, and religious fervor. Add fine architecture (rich baroque and Renaissance monuments, colonial palaces, and the sumptuous Real Alcázar) to this mix, plus fine wining and dining, and this city brings vibrant color to any holiday.

At the top of your must-see list sit the Real Alcázar—a Mudejar delight whisking you straight to the land of Scheherazade—and the Cathedral, the largest in Spain and topped with the Giralda minaret tower. Continue your architectural feast with one of the city's splendid palaces, excellent museums, and fine churches while taking in Seville's nod to modernity in the Gaudí-style Metropol Parasol, lofty Torre Sevilla (Seville Tower), and the elegant contemporary bridges.

The layout of the historic center of Seville makes exploring easy. The Centro—the central zone around the Cathedral, Calle Sierpes, and Plaza Nueva—is splendid and monumental, but it's not where you'll find Seville's greatest charm. El Arenal, home of the Real Maestranza bullring, the Teatro de la Maestranza concert hall, and a concentration of picturesque taverns, still buzzes the way it must have when stevedores loaded and unloaded ships from the New World. Just southeast of Centro, the medieval Jewish quarter, Barrio de Santa Cruz, is home to the Real Alcázar and a lovely whitewashed tangle of alleys. The Barrio de la Macarena to the northeast is rich in sights and authentic Seville atmosphere.

The fifth and final neighborhood to explore, on the far side of the Río Guadalquivir, is in many ways the best of all: Triana, the traditional habitat for sailors, bullfighters, and flamenco artists, as well as the main workshop for Seville's renowned ceramicists.

Centro

The Centro area is the heart of Seville's commercial life. It has bustling shopping streets—several of which are pedestrianized—and leafy squares lined with bars and cafés. The residential streets contain some of the best examples of colonial architecture; noteworthy features include fine façades and roof gables topped with local ceramic tiles. Centro is also home to several of the city's most beautiful churches.

Sights

Ayuntamiento (*City Hall*)
GOVERNMENT BUILDING | This Diego de Riaño original, built between 1527 and 1564, is in the heart of Seville's commercial center. A 19th-century plateresque facade overlooks the Plaza Nueva. The other side, on the Plaza de San Francisco, is Riaño's work. Visits must be prebooked via the website. ⊠ *Pl. Nueva 1, Centro* ☎ *955/470243* ⊕ *www.sevilla.org/actualidad/visitas-casa-consistorial* ⛁ *€4, free Sat.* ⊙ *Closed Fri. and Sun.*

Calle Sierpes
STREET | This is Seville's classy main shopping street. Near the southern end, at No. 85, a plaque marks the spot where the Cárcel Real (Royal Prison) once stood. Miguel de Cervantes began writing *Don Quixote* in one of its cells. ⊠ *Calle Sierpes s/n, Centro.*

★ Catedral de Sevilla
CHURCH | Seville's cathedral can be described only in superlatives: it's the largest and highest cathedral in Spain, the largest Gothic building in the world,

and the world's third-largest church, after St. Peter's in Rome and St. Paul's in London. After Fernando III captured Seville from the Moors in 1248, the great mosque begun by Yusuf II in 1171 was reconsecrated to the Virgin Mary and used as a Christian cathedral. In 1401 the people of Seville decided to erect a new cathedral, one that would equal the glory of their great city. They pulled down the old mosque, leaving only its minaret and outer courtyard, and built the existing building in just over a century—a remarkable feat for that time.

Highlights inside include the Capilla Mayor (Main Chapel) with a magnificent altarpiece (restored in 2014), the largest in Christendom (65 feet by 43 feet) and depicting some 36 scenes from the life of Christ.

At the south end of the cathedral is the monument to Christopher Columbus: his coffin is borne aloft by the four kings representing the medieval kingdoms of Spain: Castile, León, Aragón, and Navarra. At the opposite (north) end, don't miss the Altar de Plata (Silver Altar), an 18th-century masterpiece of intricate silversmithing.

In the Sacristía de los Cálices (Sacristy of the Chalices), look for Juan Martínez Montañés's wood carving *Crucifixion, Merciful Christ*; Juan de Valdés Leal's *St. Peter Freed by an Angel*; Francisco de Zurbarán's *Virgin and Child*; and Francisco de Goya's *St. Justa and St. Rufina*. The Sacristía Mayor (Main Sacristy) holds the keys to the city, which Seville's Moors and Jews presented to their conqueror, Fernando III. Finally, in the dome of the Sala Capitular (Chapter House), in the cathedral's southeastern corner, is Bartolomé Esteban Murillo's *Immaculate Conception,* painted in 1668.

One of the cathedral's highlights, the Capilla Real (Royal Chapel) is concealed behind a ponderous curtain, but you can duck in if you're quick, quiet, and properly

Seville's cathedral is the largest and tallest cathedral in Spain, the largest Gothic building in the world, and the third-largest church in the world, after St. Peter's in Rome and St. Paul's in London.

dressed (no shorts or sleeveless tops): enter from the Puerta de los Palos on Plaza de la Virgen de los Reyes (signposted "Entrada para Culto," or "Entrance for Worship"). Along the sides of the chapel are the tombs of Beatrix of Swabia, wife of the 13th-century's Fernando III, and their son Alfonso X (the Wise); in a silver urn before the high altar rest the relics of Fernando III himself, Seville's liberator. Canonized in 1671, he was said to have died from excessive fasting.

Don't forget the Patio de los Naranjos (Courtyard of Orange Trees), on the church's northern side, where the fountain in the center was used for ablutions before people entered the original mosque.

The Christians could not bring themselves to destroy the tower when they tore down the mosque, so they incorporated it into their new cathedral. In 1565–68 they added a lantern and belfry to the old minaret and installed 24 bells, one for each of Seville's 24 parishes and

the 24 Christian knights who fought with Fernando III in the Reconquest. They also added the bronze statue of Faith, which turned as a weather vane (*el giraldillo*, or "something that turns"); thus the whole tower became known as La Giralda. With its baroque additions, the slender Giralda rises 322 feet. Inside, instead of steps, 35 sloping ramps—wide enough for two horsemen to pass abreast—climb to a viewing platform 230 feet up. Don't miss the magnificent north facade of the cathedral, housing the Puerta del Perdón (Gate of Pardon) entrance to the courtyard. Restored between 2012 and 2015, the brickwork and white plaster on the huge wall strongly reflect the original 12th-century mosque. Admission also includes a visit to the Iglesia del Salvador. ✉ *Pl. de la Virgen de los Reyes s/n, Centro* ☎ *90/209–9692* ⊕ *www.catedralde-sevilla.es* 🎫 *€11, free Thurs. from 2:45 pm if you book via the website* ☉ *Closed Sun. morning.*

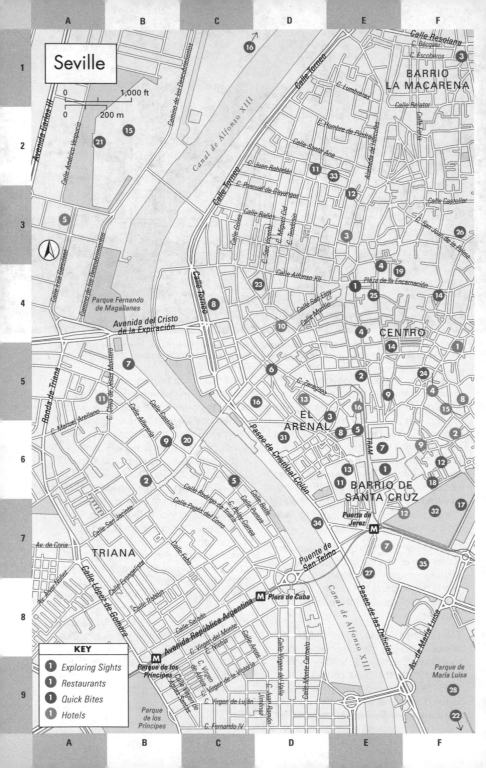

Sights ▼

1 Archivo General de Indias **E6**
2 Ayuntamiento **E5**
3 Basílica de la Macarena **F1**
4 Calle Sierpes **E4**
5 Capilla de los Marineros **C6**
6 Casa de Pilatos **G5**
7 Catedral de Sevilla **E6**
8 Centro Comercial Plaza de Armas **C4**
9 Centro de Cerámica Triana **B6**
10 Convento de Santa Paula **G3**
11 Hospital de la Caridad **E6**
12 Hospital de los Venerables **F6**
13 Iglesia de San Luis de los Franceses **G2**
14 Iglesia del Salvador **E5**
15 Isla de La Cartuja **B2**
16 Isla Mágica **C1**
17 Jardines de Murillo **F7**
18 Judería **F6**
19 Las Setas **E4**
20 Mercado de Triana **C6**
21 Monasterio de Santa María de las Cuevas **A2**
22 Museo de Artes y Costumbres Populares **F9**
23 Museo de Bellas Artes **D4**
24 Museo del Baile Flamenco **F5**
25 Palacio de la Condesa de Lebrija **E4**
26 Palacio de las Dueñas **F3**
27 Palacio de San Telmo ... **E7**
28 Parque María Luisa **F9**
29 Plaza de España **G8**
30 Plaza de los Refinadores **G6**
31 Plaza de Toros Real Maestranza........ **D6**
32 Real Alcázar **F7**
33 San Lorenzo y Jesús del Gran Poder ... **E2**
34 Torre del Oro **D7**
35 University of Seville **F7**

Restaurants ▼

1 Abantal **H5**
2 Bar Las Golondrinas **B6**
3 Bodeguita Romero **E6**
4 Cañabota **E4**
5 Casa Morales **E6**
6 Castizo **D5**
7 De la O **B5**
8 El Pimentón **E6**
9 El Pintón **E5**
10 El Rinconcillo **G4**
11 Espacio Eslava **D2**
12 La Azotea **E3**
13 La Moneda Casa Inchausti **E6**
14 Palo Cortao **F4**
15 Taberna La Sal **G6**
16 Veganitessen **D5**
17 Vineria San Telmo **G6**

Quick Bites ▼

1 La Campana **E4**

Hotels ▼

1 Aguilas 5 Sevilla Suites **F5**
2 Casa del Poeta **F6**
3 Casa Romana Hotel Boutique **E3**
4 Corral del Rey **F5**
5 Eurostars Torre Sevilla **A3**
6 Hospes Las Casas del Rey de Baeza **G4**
7 Hotel Alfonso XIII **E7**
8 Hotel Amadeus Sevilla **F5**
9 Hotel Casa 1800 .... **F6**
10 Hotel Colón Gran Meliá **D4**
11 Hotel Monte Triana **B5**
12 Legado Alcázar **E7**
13 Mercer **D5**
14 Palacio de Villapanés Hotel **G4**
15 Pensión Córdoba **F5**
16 Soho Boutique Catedral **E5**

Iglesia de San Luis de los Franceses

CHURCH | This baroque bonanza of a church, built in 1731 in honor of Louis IX of France, reopened in late 2017 after an extensive restoration. The stunning altarpiece by Pedro Duque Cornejo now gleams in all its former glory along with the ornate ceiling and side chapels. ✉ *Calle San Luis, Seville* ☎ *954/550207* 🎟 *€4, free Sun. afternoon* ⏲ *Closed Mon.*

Iglesia del Salvador

CHURCH | Built between 1671 and 1712, the Church of the Savior stands on the site of Seville's first great mosque, remains of which can be seen in its Courtyard of the Orange Trees. Also of note are the sculptures *Jesús de la Pasión* and *St. Christopher* by Juan Martínez Montañés. In 2003 archaeologists discovered an 18th-century burial site here. Walkways facilitate visits. ✉ *Pl. del Salvador s/n, Centro* ☎ *955/480426* 🎟 *€4, free with Cathedral admission* ⏲ *Closed Sun.*

Las Setas

PLAZA/SQUARE | This huge square, at the west end of Calle Cuna, is home to the world's largest wooden structure, 492 feet long by 230 feet wide. Known in the city as "Las Setas" (The Mushrooms), the piece is actually meant to represent giant trees, and walkways run through the "treetops" affording great views of the city, especially at sunset. Although it's reminiscent of Gaudí, it was built in 2011. At ground level, the Antiquarium (€2; closed Mon.) has interesting archaeological remains (mostly Roman), and there's also a large indoor food market. ✉ *Pl. de la Encarnación s/n, Centro* ☎ *606/635214* 🎟 *From €10.*

★ Palacio de la Condesa de Lebrija

CASTLE/PALACE | This lovely palace has three ornate patios—including a spectacular courtyard graced by a Roman mosaic taken from the ruins in nearby Itálica—surrounded by Moorish arches and fine *azulejos* (painted tiles). The side rooms house a collection of archaeological items. The second floor contains the family apartments, and visits are by guided tour only. **■ TIP→ It's well worth paying for the second-floor tour, which gives an interesting insight into the collections and the family.** ✉ *Calle Cuna 8, Centro* ☎ *954/227802* ✍ *reservas@palaciodelebrija.com* 🌐 *palaciodelebrija.com* 🎟 *€12.*

Palacio de las Dueñas

HISTORIC HOME | The 15th-century home and official residence of the late 18th Duchess of Alba is an oasis of peace and quiet in the bustling city. Set around an ornate patio with Mudejar arches and a central fountain, the house includes antiques and paintings, as well as memorabilia relating to the duchess. Revered in the city and one of Spain's most important noblewomen and society figures, Cayetana de Alba loved bullfighting, flamenco, and ceramics. The visit (first floor only) also includes the stables, gardens (said to have inspired some of Antonio Machado's most famous early verses), and a Gothic chapel. ✉ *Calle Dueñas 5, Centro* ☎ *954/214828* 🌐 *www.lasduenas.es* 🎟 *€12.*

🍴 Restaurants

Cañabota

$$$$ | **SPANISH** | If you fancy treating yourself to some of the best fish in town, head for this modern Michelin-star restaurant just down the road from the Palacio de la Condesa de Lebrija. Seasonal fish and seafood take center stage; you can see the catch of the day displayed in the window. **Known for:** fresh fish and seafood; daily specials like marinated sardines; efficient service. [$] *Average main: €40* ✉ *Calle Orfila 3, Centro* ☎ *954/870 298* 🌐 *canabota.es* ⏲ *Closed Sun. and Mon.*

Casa Morales

$ | **TAPAS** | Down a side street off the Avenida de la Constitución, this historic bar (formerly a wine store) takes you back to 19th-century Seville, and it is still run by descendants of the family that established it in 1850. Locals pack the place at lunchtime, when popular dishes include *menudo con garbanzos* (tripe with chickpeas) and *albóndigas de choco* (cuttlefish croquettes). **Known for:** local atmosphere; wine list; tripe with chickpeas. $ *Average main: €12* ✉ *Calle García de Vinuesa 11, Centro* ☎ *954/221242* 🕒 *No dinner Sun. and Mon. Closed Tues.*

Castizo

$ | **SPANISH** | True tradition (castizo itself) comes into its own at this busy venue serving regional dishes such as *espinacas con garbanzos* (spinach with chickpeas) alongside more modern plates like the popular *coliflor tostada con holandesa trufada* (cauliflower cheese with truffle oil), plus daily fish specials and the rice dish of the day. The open kitchen gives you a frontline view of your meal in the making. **Known for:** authentic traditional cooking; daily fish and rice specials; open kitchen. $ *Average main: €12* ✉ *Calle Zaragoza 6, Centro* ☎ *955/180562* 🌐 *www.barracastizo.es.*

El Pintón

$$ | **FUSION** | With a privileged spot a block north from the Cathedral, this central restaurant offers two dining spaces: the traditional inside patio, where wood, mirrors, and tasteful lighting create an intimate but airy space; or the pleasant terrace outside. The cuisine combines Andalusian dishes with a modern touch, with menu items such as bloody gazpacho, Idiázabal blue cheese risotto, and red tuna tartare. **Known for:** attractive interior; kitchen open all day; Mediterranean dishes. $ *Average main: €18* ✉ *Calle Francos 42, Centro* ☎ *955/075153* 🌐 *elpinton.com.*

★ Espacio Eslava

$ | **TAPAS** | The crowds gathered outside this local favorite off the Alameda de Hercules may be off-putting at first, but the creative inexpensive tapas (from €4) are well worth the wait—and so is the house specialty, the Basque dessert *sokoa*. Try delicacies like the *cigarro para Bécquer* (cuttlefish in a filo pastry cigar) and *yema sobre bizcocho de boletus* (egg atop a mushroom sponge). **Known for:** creative tapas; sokoa, a Basque dessert; vegetable strudel. $ *Average main: €14* ✉ *Calle Eslava 3, Centro* ☎ *954/906568* 🕒 *Closed Sun. and Mon.*

La Azotea

$ | **SPANISH** | With a young vibe and a vast and inventive menu (which changes seasonally), this tiny restaurant offers a welcome change from Seville's typical fried fare. The owners' haute-cuisine ambitions are reflected in excellent service and lovingly prepared food—but not in the prices. **Known for:** creative tapas; seasonal menu; local vibe. $ *Average main: €16* ✉ *Calle del Conde de Barajas 13, Centro* ☎ *955/116748.*

Coffee and Quick Bites

★ La Campana

$ | **CAFÉ** | Under the gilt-edged ceiling at Seville's most celebrated pastry outlet (founded in 1885), you can enjoy the flan-like *tocino de cielo,* or "heavenly bacon." For breakfast, enjoy a traditional feed of toasted bread with tomato and a strong coffee, served at a standing bar. Prices are reasonable despite its popularity. **Known for:** traditional atmosphere; tempting window displays; variety of pastries and desserts. $ *Average main: €5* ✉ *Calle Sierpes 1, Centro* ☎ *954/223570* 🌐 *www.confiterialacampana.com.*

Hotels

Casa Romana Hotel Boutique

$$ | **HOTEL** | Tucked away down a quiet side street in the heart of the Centro district just a 15-minute walk from the main sights, this restored 18th-century town house pays homage, decor-wise, to the Roman Emperor the street is named for. **Pros:** good location for tapas bars and restaurants; rooftop pool and cocktail bar;

classical decor. **Cons:** standard doubles on the small side; sights some distance away; rooms facing patio lack privacy. $ *Rooms from: €150* ⊠ *Calle Trajano 14, Centro* ☎ *954/915170* ⊕ *www.hotelcasa-romana.com* ⟿ *26 rooms* ⚫ *No Meals.*

Hospes Las Casas del Rey de Baeza

$$$ | HOTEL | Behind the striking white-and-ocher facade lies what was once a humble 18th-century *corrala* (corridor house), now a pretty hotel combining original features such as teal verandas with modern comforts and fine cuisine. **Pros:** pretty patios; historic touches; good food. **Cons:** rooftop views are ordinary; slightly out of town; some rooms are dark. $ *Rooms from: €250* ⊠ *Pl. de Jesús de la Redención 2, Centro* ☎ *954/561496* ⊕ *hospes.com* ⟿ *41 rooms* ⚫ *No Meals.*

★ Mercer

$$$$ | HOTEL | Housed in a 19th-century mansion, Mercer is one of the city's top boutique hotels, featuring a lofty patio with a fountain, a stunning marble staircase, and a striking geometric chandelier atop a glass gallery. **Pros:** luxury lodging; spacious rooms; rooftop terrace with plunge pool. **Cons:** pricey; a little too prim; patio rooms have no views. $ *Rooms from: €550* ⊠ *Calle de Castelar 26, Centro* ☎ *954/223004* ⊕ *www.mercersevilla.com* ⟿ *11 rooms* ⚫ *Free Breakfast.*

★ Palacio de Villapanés Hotel

$$$$ | HOTEL | This 18th-century palace with elegant updates and stylish contemporary furnishings, marble-columned patios, high ceilings, and a rooftop with terra-cotta-rooftop views, a pool, and bar is one of the most chic converted-palace accommodations in Seville. **Pros:** local off-the-beaten-path feel; oozes style and character; tall windows and high ceilings. **Cons:** not the most central location; some rooms are dark; small gym. $ *Rooms from: €400* ⊠ *Calle Santiago 31, Centro* ☎ *95/450–2063* ⊕ *coolrooms.com/palaciovillapanes/en* ⟿ *50 rooms* ⚫ *No Meals.*

Where's Columbus?

Christopher Columbus knew both triumph and disgrace, yet he found no repose—he died, bitterly disillusioned, in Valladolid in 1506. No one knows for certain where he's buried; he was reportedly laid to rest for the first time in the Dominican Republic and then moved over the years to other locations. A portion of his remains can be found in Seville's cathedral.

Soho Boutique Catedral

$$$ | HOTEL | Opened in late 2021 in the middle of Seville's pedestrian center, this modern hotel puts you at the heart of the action. **Pros:** spacious rooms; rooftop view of the Giralda; great location. **Cons:** limited breakfast; could be too functional for some; street noise in some rooms. $ *Rooms from: €220* ⊠ *Av. de la Constitución 8, Centro* ☎ *854/856059* ⊕ *www.sohohoteles.com/destinos/hotel-soho-boutique-catedral-4* ⟿ *62 rooms* ⚫ *No Meals.*

🛍 Shopping

Ángela y Adela

OTHER SPECIALTY STORE | Come to this shop for privately fitted and custom-made flamenco dresses. ⊠ *Calle Chapineros 1, Centro* ☎ *954/227186.*

Buffuna Hats

HATS & GLOVES | This shop carries handmade hats and caps for all occasions, especially sophisticated ones. ⊠ *Calle Aceituno 6, Centro* ☎ *954/537824* ⊙ *Closed weekends.*

Lola Azahares

OTHER SPECIALTY STORE | For flamenco wear, this is one of Seville's most highly regarded stores. ⊠ *Calle Cuna 31, Centro* ☎ *954/222912* ⊕ *lolaazahares.es.*

Luisa Perez y Riu

OTHER SPECIALTY STORE | Flamenco dresses and all the accessories, designed with a modern touch, are sold at this shop. ⊠ *Calle Rivero 3, Centro* ☎ *607/817624* ⊕ *luisaperezriu.com* Ⓜ *Puerta de Jerez.*

Plaza del Duque

CRAFTS | Situated a few blocks north of Plaza Nueva, Plaza del Duque holds a crafts market from Wednesday through Saturday. ⊠ *Centro.*

Barrio de Santa Cruz

The most romantic neighborhood in the city, Santa Cruz offers the visitor quintessential Seville: whitewashed houses with colorful geraniums and bougainvillea cascading down their facades, winding alleyways, and intimate squares scented with orange blossoms in the spring, all lit by old-style lamps at night. This neighborhood is also the busiest and most touristic part of Seville—so stray from the main thoroughfares and lose yourself in the side streets to discover a place where time seems to have stopped and all you hear is birdsong.

◉ Sights

Archivo General de Indias (*Archives of the Indies*)

HISTORIC SIGHT | Opened in 1785 in the former Lonja (Merchants' Exchange), this dignified Renaissance building stores a valuable archive of more than 40,000 documents, including drawings, trade documents, plans of South American towns, and even the autographs of Columbus, Magellan, and Cortés. Temporary exhibitions showcase different archives. ⊠ *Av. de la Constitución 3, Barrio de Santa Cruz* ☎ *954/500528* 🎟 *Free* ⊙ *Closed Mon.*

★ **Casa de Pilatos**

HISTORIC HOME | With its fine patio and superb azulejo decorations, this palace is a beautiful blend of Spanish Mudejar and Renaissance architecture and is considered a prototype of an Andalusian mansion. It was built in the first half of the 16th century by the dukes of Tarifa, ancestors of the present owner, the Duke of Medinaceli. It's known as Pilate's House because Don Fadrique, first marquis of Tarifa, allegedly modeled it on Pontius Pilate's house in Jerusalem, where he had gone on a pilgrimage in 1518. The upstairs apartments, which you can see on a guided tour, have frescoes, paintings, and antique furniture. Admission includes an audio guide in English. ⊠ *Pl. de Pilatos 1, Barrio de Santa Cruz* ☎ *954/225298* 🎟 *From €10.*

Hospital de los Venerables

HISTORIC SIGHT | Once a retirement home for priests, this baroque building has a splendid azulejo patio with an interesting sunken fountain (designed to cope with low water pressure) and an upstairs gallery, but the highlight is the chapel, featuring frescoes by Valdés Leal and sculptures by Pedro Roldán. The building also houses a cultural foundation that organizes on-site art exhibitions. ⊠ *Pl. de los Venerables 8, Barrio de Santa Cruz* ☎ *69/789–8659* ⊕ *hospitalvenerables.es* 🎟 *€10, includes audio guide; free Mon. 3–7 pm if you book online* ⊙ *Closed Sun. afternoon.*

Jardines de Murillo (*Murillo Gardens*)

GARDEN | From the Plaza de Santa Cruz you can stroll through these gardens, home to a statue of Christopher Columbus. In summer there's welcomed shade and refreshing fountains. ⊠ *Pl. de Santa Cruz s/n, Barrio de Santa Cruz.*

★ **Juderia**

HISTORIC DISTRICT | The twisting alleyways and traditional whitewashed houses add to the tourist charm of the Jewish Quarter. On some streets, bars alternate with antiques and souvenir shops, but most of the quarter is quiet and residential. On the Plaza de la Alianza, pause to enjoy the antiques shops and outdoor cafés. In the Plaza de Doña Elvira, with its fountain and azulejo benches, young Sevillanos gather to play guitars. Just around the corner from the hospital, at Callejón del Agua and Jope de Rueda, Gioacchino Rossini's Figaro serenaded Rosina on her Plaza Alfaro balcony. Adjoining the Plaza Alfaro, in the Plaza de Santa Cruz, flowers and orange trees surround a 17th-century filigree iron cross, which marks the site of the erstwhile church of Santa Cruz, destroyed by Napoleon's general Jean-de-Dieu Soult. ⊠ *Barrio de Santa Cruz.*

Museo del Baile Flamenco

OTHER MUSEUM | This private museum in the heart of Santa Cruz was opened in 2007 by the legendary flamenco dancer Cristina Hoyos and includes audiovisual and multimedia displays briefly explaining the history, culture, and soul of Spanish flamenco. There are also regular classes and shows. ⊠ *Calle de Manuel Rojas Marcos 3, Barrio de Santa Cruz* ☎ *954/340311* ⊕ *museodelbaileflamenco. com* ⊠ *€10 museum only; €29 museum and show.*

Plaza de los Refinadores

PLAZA/SQUARE | This shady square filled with palms and orange trees is separated from the Murillo Gardens by an iron grillwork and ringed with stately glass balconies. At its center is a monument to Don Juan Tenorio, the famous Don Juan known for his amorous conquests. ⊠ *Barrio de Santa Cruz.*

★ Real Alcázar

CASTLE/PALACE | The Plaza del Triunfo forms the entrance to the Mudejar palace, the official local residence of the king and queen, built by Pedro I (1350–69) on the site of Seville's former Moorish alcázar. Built more than 100 years after the Reconquest of Seville, this isn't a genuine Moorish palace but it's authentic enough—parts of the palace

and gardens were recreated as a Dornish palace for the final seasons of *Game of Thrones,* which filmed here in 2015 and 2018.

Entering the alcázar through the Puerta del León (Lion's Gate) and the high fortified walls, you'll first find yourself in the Patio del León (Courtyard of the Lion). Off to the left are the oldest parts of the building, the 14th-century Sala de Justicia (Hall of Justice) and, next to it, the intimate Patio del Yeso (Courtyard of Plaster), the only extant part of the original 12th-century Almohad Alcázar. Cross the Patio de la Montería (Courtyard of the Hunt) to Pedro's Mudejar palace, arranged around the beautiful Patio de las Doncellas (Court of the Damsels), resplendent with delicately carved stucco. Opening off this patio, the Salón de Embajadores (Hall of the Ambassadors), with its cedar cupola of green, red, and gold, is the most sumptuous hall in the palace. Other royal rooms include the three baths of Pedro's powerful and influential mistress, María de Padilla. María's hold on her royal lover and his courtiers was so great that legend says they all lined up to drink her bathwater. The Patio de las Muñecas (Court of the Dolls) takes its name from two tiny faces carved on the inside of one of its arches.

The Renaissance Palacio de Carlos V is endowed with a rich collection of Flemish tapestries depicting Carlos's victories at Tunis. Upstairs, the Cuarto Real Alto (Royal Chambers, where the king and queen stay when they visit) are packed with antiques. In the gardens, inhale the fragrances of jasmine and myrtle, wander among terraces and baths, and peer into the well-stocked goldfish pond. From here, a passageway leads to the Patio de las Banderas (Court of the Flags), which has a classic view of La Giralda. Allow at least two hours for your visit.

■ TIP→ **Book your ticket online to avoid long lines and at least one month in advance to avoid disappointment. If you**

Seville's grand alcázar is a UNESCO World Heritage Site and an absolute must-see.

want to see the Cuarto Real Alto, reserve as far in advance as possible and plan to arrive at least 30 minutes before your allocated time slot. ✉ *Pl. del Triunfo s/n, Santa Cruz* ☎ *95/501–0010* 🌐 *www.alcazarsevilla.org* 🎫 *€14, free for last hour of opening on Mon. if you book online; Cuarto Real €6.*

🍴 Restaurants

Abantal

$$$$ | SPANISH | Slightly off the beaten path but worth seeking, chef Julio Fernández's tasting menu takes you on a journey of the senses featuring seemingly ordinary local produce and traditional recipes elevated with unusual textures and preparations. The menu changes with the seasons, but always has nine dishes (€95) or 12 (€115) as well as extra-virgin-olive-oil menus. **Known for:** long wine list; innovative take on dishes; excellent service. [$] *Average main: €95* ✉ *Calle Alcalde José de la Bandera 7, Barrio de Santa Cruz* ☎ *954/540000* 🌐 *abantalrestaurante.es* 🕒 *Closed Sat., Sun., Wed., and Aug.*

Taberna La Sal

$ | SPANISH | This cozy restaurant offers an excellent selection of fish and meat dishes. It's renowned for its Almadraba tuna (traditionally hand-lined and caught in Zahara de los Atunes on the Cádiz coast) cooked any which way and always delicious. **Known for:** tuna dishes; sea anemone risotto; great choice of tapas. [$] *Average main: €15* ✉ *Calle Doncellas 8, Santa Cruz* ☎ *954/535846* 🌐 *www.lasalzahara.com.*

★ Vineria San Telmo

$ | SPANISH | Offering dining in a dimly lit dining room or on the street-level terrace, this popular Argentinean-owned restaurant near the touristy alcázar has a menu full of surprises. All dishes—which come as tapas, half portions, or full portions (ideal for sharing)—are superb and sophisticated, especially the eggplant stew with tomato, goat cheese, and smoked salmon; and the curried pumpkin and rocket croquettes. **Known for:** creative tapas; extensive choice of Spanish vinos; good choice of vegetarian options.

[$] *Average main: €15* ✉ *Paseo de Catalina de Ribera 4, Santa Cruz* ☎ *954/410600* 🌐 *vineriasantelmo.com/en.*

Hotels

Aguilas 5 Sevilla Suites
$$ | **HOTEL** | If you're looking for a self-catering option in the heart of Santa Cruz, you can't go wrong at this comfortable town house, originally an 18th-century mansion. **Pros:** home-away-from-home vibes; good value for families; central location. **Cons:** some rooms are dark; on pricey side for just 2 people; parking not nearby. [$] *Rooms from: €200* ✉ *Calle Águilas 5, Barrio de Santa Cruz* ☎ *658/628129* 🌐 *www.aguilas5.com* 🛏 *9 rooms* 🍴 *No Meals.*

Casa del Poeta
$$$ | **HOTEL** | Up a narrow alleyway, behind an ordinary facade, a 17th-century palace that was the haunt of Seville's poets at the end of the 19th century is now an oasis of calm. **Pros:** peaceful central location; authentic palatial atmosphere; rooftop with a view. **Cons:** difficult to reach by car (call shortly before arrival for staff to meet you); could be too traditional for some; some rooms are dark. [$] *Rooms from: €250* ✉ *Calle Don Carlos Alonso Chaparro 3, Santa Cruz* ☎ *954/213868* 🌐 *casadelpoeta.es* 🛏 *17 rooms* 🍴 *Free Breakfast.*

Corral del Rey
$$$$ | **HOTEL** | Southeast Asian and Moroccan decor fuse to perfection throughout this carefully restored 17th-century palace in the heart of Santa Cruz. **Pros:** private and peaceful setting but easy walk to sights; meticulously restored 17th-century palace with contemporary updates; rooftop terrace with plunge pool. **Cons:** no direct car access; based on both sides of small street and some guests have to cross street for breakfast; some rooms on the small side. [$] *Rooms from: €330* ✉ *Calle Corral del Rey 12, Barrio de Santa Cruz* ☎ *954/227116* 🌐 *www.corraldelrey.com* 🛏 *17 rooms* 🍴 *Free Breakfast.*

★ **Hotel Amadeus Sevilla**
$$ | **HOTEL** | With regular classical concerts, a music room off the central patio, and instruments for guests to use, including pianos in some of the soundproofed rooms, this 18th-century manor house is ideal for touring professional musicians and music fans in general. **Pros:** small but charming rooms; roof terrace; friendly service. **Cons:** no direct car access; ground-floor rooms can be dark; some rooms a little tired. [$] *Rooms from: €200* ✉ *Calle Farnesio 6, Santa Cruz* ☎ *954/501443* 🌐 *www.hotelamadeussevilla.com* 🛏 *43 rooms* 🍴 *No Meals.*

★ **Hotel Casa 1800**
$$$ | **B&B/INN** | This classy boutique hotel, located in a refurbished 19th-century mansion, is a refuge in bustling Santa Cruz. **Pros:** top-notch amenities; great service; central location. **Cons:** some rooms small; no restaurant; on noisy side street. [$] *Rooms from: €300* ✉ *Calle de Rodrigo Caro 6, Santa Cruz* ☎ *954/561800* 🌐 *www.hotelcasa1800sevilla.com* 🛏 *33 rooms* 🍴 *No Meals.*

Legado Alcázar
$$ | **HOTEL** | Nestled next to the alcázar—the monument and hotel share walls—this 17th-century noble house offers a tasteful boutique experience in a very quiet corner. **Pros:** very quiet but central location; historic features; views of the alcázar. **Cons:** no restaurant on-site; room size varies; could be too traditional for some. [$] *Rooms from: €200* ✉ *Calle Mariana de Pineda 18, Barrio de Santa Cruz* ☎ *954/091818* 🌐 *www.legadoalcazarhotel.com* 🛏 *18 rooms* 🍴 *No Meals.*

Pensión Córdoba
$ | **HOTEL** | Just a few blocks from the Cathedral, nestled in the heart of Santa Cruz, this small family-run inn is an excellent value. **Pros:** quiet central location; friendly staff; rooms have AC. **Cons:** no entry after 3 am; bathrooms need

modernizing; no elevator to second floor. $ *Rooms from: €90* ✉ *Calle Farnesio 12, Santa Cruz* ☎ *954/227498* 🌐 *pensioncordoba.com* 🛏 *11 rooms* 🍴 *No Meals.*

🍸 Nightlife

La Terraza del EME

CAFÉS | This rooftop terrace has some of the best views of the Cathedral in town. Sip your cocktail to the sound of resident DJs, who play most nights. The terrace is open daily beginning at 1 pm. ✉ *Calle Alemanes 27, Barrio de Santa Cruz* ☎ *954/560000* 🌐 *www.laterrazadeleme.com/en* [M] *Puerta de Jerez.*

🎟 Performing Arts

FLAMENCO

★ La Casa del Flamenco

FOLK/TRADITIONAL DANCE | Catch an authentic professional performance in the heart of Santa Cruz on the atmospheric patio of a 15th-century house where the excellent acoustics mean there's no need for microphones or amplifiers. Shows start daily at 7 pm in winter and 8:30 pm in summer. ✉ *Calle Ximénez de Enciso 28, Barrio de Santa Cruz* ☎ *954/029999* 🌐 *lacasadelflamencosevilla.com* 🎫 *From €27.*

Los Gallos

FOLK/TRADITIONAL DANCE | This intimate club in the heart of Santa Cruz attracts mainly tourists. Flamenco performances are entertaining and reasonably authentic. Shows at 7 pm and 8:45 pm daily. ✉ *Pl. de Santa Cruz 11, Santa Cruz* ☎ *954/216981* 🌐 *www.tablaolosgallos.com* 🎫 *€35.*

🛍 Shopping

Balcris Gallery

ART GALLERIES | Artwork by Cristóbal Donaire from nearby Jerez includes multicolored sculptures (bulls, horses, and matadors) and abstract paintings. ✉ *Calle de Placentines 1, Barrio de Santa Cruz* ☎ *954/561639* 🌐 *balcris.es* 🕒 *Closed Sun.*

Orange Tree Sevilla

FOOD | All those oranges on the trees in the city are put to good use in handmade candies, marmalades, sweetmeats, liqueurs, and beauty products. ✉ *Calle Ximénez de Enciso 22, Barrio de Santa Cruz* ☎ *954/721374* 🌐 *orangetreesevilla.com.*

El Arenal and Parque María Luisa

Parque María Luisa is part shady mid-city forestland and part monumental esplanade. El Arenal, named for its sandy riverbank soil, was originally a neighborhood of shipbuilders, stevedores, and warehouses. The heart of El Arenal lies between the Puente de San Telmo, just upstream from the Torre de Oro, and the Puente de Isabel II (Puente de Triana). El Arenal extends as far north as Calle Alfonso XII to include the Museo de Bellas Artes. Between the park and El Arenal is the university.

👁 Sights

Centro Comercial Plaza de Armas

STORE/MALL | Near the Puente del Cachorro, the old Estación de Córdoba train station has been converted into this stylish shopping center with boutiques, bars, fast-food joints, a nightclub, and a movie theater complex. ✉ *El Arenal* ✥ *Enter on Pl. de la Legión.*

Hospital de la Caridad

HISTORIC SIGHT | Behind the Teatro de la Maestranza is this former almshouse for the sick and elderly, where six paintings by Murillo (1617–82) and two gruesome works by Valdés Leal (1622–90) depicting the Triumph of Death are displayed. The baroque hospital was founded in 1674 by Seville's original Don Juan, Miguel de Mañara (1626–79). A nobleman of licentious character, Mañara was returning one night from a riotous orgy when he had a vision of a funeral procession in which the partly decomposed corpse in the coffin was his own. Accepting the apparition as a sign from God, Mañara devoted his fortune to building this hospital; he is buried before the high altar in the chapel. Admission includes an audio guide (available in English). You can also book guided tours and Gregorian chant concerts. ⊠ *Calle Temprado 3, El Arenal* ☎ *954/223232* ⊕ *www.santa-caridad.es/en* ☞ *€8, free Sun. 4:30–6:30 pm.*

Museo de Artes y Costumbres Populares (*Museum of Arts and Traditions*)
HISTORY MUSEUM | FAMILY | Among the fascinating items of mainly 19th and 20th-century Spanish folklore in this museum, located in the Mudejar pavilion opposite the Museo Arqueológico, is an impressive Díaz Velázquez collection of lace and embroidery—one of the finest in Europe. There's a reconstruction of a typical late-19th-century Sevillian house on the first floor, while upstairs, exhibits include 18th- and 19th-century court dress, stunning regional folk costumes, religious objects, and musical instruments. In the basement, you can see ceramics, pottery, furniture, and household items from bygone ages. ⊠ *Pl. de América 3, El Arenal* ☎ *954/721391* ⊕ *www.museosdeandalucia.es* ☞ *€2* ⊘ *Closed Mon.*

★ **Museo de Bellas Artes** (*Museum of Fine Arts*)
ART MUSEUM | This museum—one of Spain's finest for Spanish art—is in the former convent of La Merced Calzada, most of which dates from the 17th century. The collection includes works by Murillo (the city celebrated the 400th anniversary of his birth in 2018) and the 17th-century Seville school, as well as by Zurbarán, Diego Velázquez, Alonso Cano, Valdés Leal, and El Greco. You will also see outstanding examples of Sevillian Gothic art and baroque religious

sculptures in wood (a quintessentially Andalusian art form). In the rooms dedicated to Sevillian art of the 19th and 20th centuries, look for Gonzalo Bilbao's *Las Cigarreras,* a group portrait of Seville's famous cigar makers. An arts-and-crafts market is held outside the museum on Sunday morning. ⊠ *Pl. del Museo 9, El Arenal* ☎ *954/786498* ⊕ *www.museosdeandalucia.es/web/museodebellasartesdesevilla* ☞ *€2* ⊘ *Closed Mon.*

Palacio de San Telmo
CASTLE/PALACE | This splendid baroque palace that primarily can be viewed from the outside (guided tours are by appointment only and must be arranged in advance by phone) is largely the work of architect Leonardo de Figueroa. Built between 1682 and 1796, it was first a naval academy and then the residence of the Bourbon dukes of Montpensier, during which time it outshone Madrid's royal court for sheer brilliance. The palace gardens are now Parque María Luisa, and the building itself is the seat of the Andalusian government. The main portal, vintage 1734, is a superb example of the fanciful churrigueresque style. ⊠ *Av. de Roma s/n, El Arenal* ☎ *955/001010* ⊘ *Closed Mon.–Wed., Fri., and Sun.*

★ **Parque María Luisa**
CITY PARK | Formerly the garden of the Palacio de San Telmo, this park blends formal design and wild vegetation. In the burst of development that gripped Seville in the 1920s, it was redesigned for the 1929 World's Fair, and the impressive villas you see now are the fair's remaining pavilions, many of them consulates or schools. The old casino holds the Teatro Lope de Vega, which puts on mainly musicals. Note the Anna Huntington statue of El Cid (Rodrigo Díaz de Vivar, 1043–99), who fought both for and against the Muslim rulers during the Reconquest. The statue was presented to Seville by the Massachusetts-born sculptor for the 1929 World's Fair. ⊠ *Glorieta de San Diego s/n, Parque Maria Luisa.*

Plaza de España

PLAZA/SQUARE | **FAMILY** | This grandiose half-moon of buildings on the eastern edge of Parque María Luisa was Spain's centerpiece pavilion at the 1929 World's Fair. The brightly colored azulejo pictures represent the provinces of Spain, while the four bridges symbolize the medieval kingdoms of the Iberian Peninsula. In fine weather you can rent small boats to row along the arc-shape canal. To escape the crowds and enjoy views of the square from above, pop upstairs. ✉ *Parque Maria Luisa.*

Plaza de Toros Real Maestranza (*Royal Maestranza Bullring*)

PLAZA/SQUARE | Sevillanos have spent many a thrilling evening in this bullring, one of the oldest and loveliest *plazas de toros* in Spain, built between 1760 and 1763. The 20-minute tour (in English) takes in the empty arena, a museum with elaborate costumes and prints, and the chapel where matadors pray before the fight. Bullfights take place in the evening Thursday–Sunday from April through July and in September. Tickets can be booked online or by phone; book well in advance to be sure of a seat. ✉ *Paseo de Colón 12, El Arenal* ☎ *954/224577 for visits, 954/560759 for bullfights* 🌐 *realmaestranza.com for tours, plazadetorosdelamaestranza.com for tickets* 🎫 *Tours €10, free Wed. 3:30–7:30 pm.*

Torre del Oro (*Tower of Gold*)

HISTORIC SIGHT | Built by the Moors in 1220 to complete the city's ramparts, this 12-sided tower on the banks of the Guadalquivir served to close off the harbor when a chain was stretched across the river from its base to a tower on the opposite bank. In 1248, Admiral Ramón de Bonifaz broke through the barrier, and Fernando III captured Seville. The tower houses a small naval museum. ✉ *Paseo Alcalde Marqués de Contadero s/n, El Arenal* ☎ *954/222419* 🎫 *Free.*

University of Seville

HISTORIC SIGHT | Fans of Bizet's opera *Carmen* will want to come here, to see where the famous heroine reputedly rolled cigars on her thighs. At the far end of the Murillo Gardens, opposite Calle San Fernando, stands part of the University of Seville, in what used to be the Real Fábrica de Tabacos (Royal Tobacco Factory). Built in the mid-1700s, the factory employed some 3,000 *cigarreras* (female cigar makers) less than a century later. Free guided tours (book online only) are available on Fridays (9:30 am–12:30 pm and 4–6 pm) and Saturdays (9:30 am–12:30 pm), except in August. ✉ *Calle San Fernando 4, Parque Maria Luisa* ☎ *954/551052* 🌐 *www.us.es* 🎫 *Free* 🕒 *Closed Sun. and Mon.–Thurs. in Aug.*

🍴 Restaurants

Bodeguita Romero

$ | **SPANISH** | A couple of blocks west of the Cathedral lies one of the city's best-loved tapas venues, usually jam-packed with locals enjoying an aperitif. Established in 1939 and now in its third generation, the bar is most famous for its meat dishes including the *pringá* sandwich (slow-cooked pork, chorizo, and black pudding in a bun) and pork cheeks. **Known for:** traditional tapas; delicious house-marinated potatoes; friendly service. [$] *Average main: €12* ✉ *Calle Harinas 10, El Arenal* ☎ *954/229556* 🕒 *Closed Mon., no dinner Sun., Tues., and Wed.*

El Pimentón

$ | **MEDITERRANEAN** | A stone's throw from the Cathedral sits this undiscerning eatery famous for its signature *tortitaco* (a shrimp fritter-taco hybrid), paellas, choice of tapas, and value lunch menu (€10.50, weekdays only). The lofty ceilings and bare brick walls are functional rather than inspirational and there's no outside terrace, but the prices, deliciousness, and friendly service more than compensate. **Known for:** value; paellas; tortitaco.

$ *Average main: €14* ✉ *Calle García de Vinuesa 29, El Arenal* ☎ *954/564032.*

La Moneda Casa Inchausti

$ | SPANISH | Almost within stone's throw of the Giralda, this family-run restaurant has been making a name for itself with fresh fish dishes for over two decades. The owners hail from Sanlúcar de Barrameda downriver, and the ingredients come from their hometown and always include swordfish, sea bass, and anchovies. **Known for:** traditional soups and stews; fresh fish; value tapas. $ *Average main: €16* ✉ *Calle Tomás de Ibarra 10, El Arenal* ☎ *954/871322* ⊘ *Closed Mon. and Aug. No dinner Sun.*

Veganitessen

$ | VEGETARIAN | If you're a vegan, vegetarian, or flexitarian and finding the meat and fish scene in Seville a bit heavy, head for this bar inside the Mercado del Arenal. It started life as Spain's first vegan bakery in 2009, and since then the menu has grown to encompass breakfast and brunch, plus a long list of 100%-animal-free options to make into burgers, nachos, or wraps. **Known for:** vegan-friendly; good value daily lunch menu; cakes and pastries. $ *Average main: €10* ✉ *Calle Pastor y Landero, Mercado del Arenal, Puesto 32, El Arenal* ☎ *611/690463* ⊕ *veganitessen.es* ⊘ *Closed Sun. and Mon. No dinner.*

 Hotels

★ Hotel Alfonso XIII

$$$$ | HOTEL | Inaugurated by King Alfonso XIII in 1929 when he visited the World's Fair, this grand hotel next to the university is a splendid, historic, Mudejar-style palace, built around a central patio and surrounded by ornate brick arches. **Pros:** both stately and hip; impeccable service; historic surroundings. **Cons:** a tourist colony; expensive; too sophisticated for some. $ *Rooms from: €550* ✉ *Calle San Fernando 2, El Arenal* ☎ *954/917000* ⊕ *www.marriott.com/en-us/hotels/*

svqlc-hotel-alfonso-xiii-a-luxury-collection-hotel-seville ⤴ *148 rooms* ⊙❘ *No Meals.*

Hotel Colón Gran Meliá

$$$$ | HOTEL | Originally opened for 1929's Ibero-American Exposition, this classic hotel retains many original features, including a marble staircase leading up to a central lobby crowned by a magnificent stained-glass dome and crystal chandelier. **Pros:** good central location; excellent restaurant; some great views. **Cons:** some rooms overlook air shaft; on a busy and noisy street; pricey. $ *Rooms from: €350* ✉ *Calle Canalejas 1, El Arenal* ☎ *954/505599* ⊕ *www.melia.com/en/ hotels/spain/seville/colon-gran-melia* ⤴ *188 rooms* ⊙❘ *No Meals.*

 Performing Arts

Teatro de la Maestranza

OPERA | Long prominent in the opera world, Seville is proud of its opera house. Tickets go quickly, so book well in advance (online is best). ✉ *Paseo de Cristóbal Colón 22, El Arenal* ☎ *954/223344* ⊕ *www.teatrodelamaestranza.es.*

Teatro Lope de Vega

ARTS CENTERS | Classical music, ballet, and musicals are performed here. Tickets are best booked online. ✉ *Av. de María Luisa s/n, Parque Maria Luisa* ☎ *954/472828 for info, 955/472822 for tickets* ⊕ *www. teatrolopedevega.org.*

 Shopping

Artesanía Textil

CRAFTS | You can find blankets, shawls, and embroidered tablecloths woven by local artisans at this textile shop. Their products are also available online. ✉ *Calle García de Vinuesa 33, El Arenal* ☎ *954/215088* ⊕ *artesania-textil.com* ⊘ *Closed Sun. and Tues.*

El Postigo

CRAFTS | This permanent arts-and-crafts market just around the corner from the Cathedral has over 20 stalls and workshops. ⊠ *Calle Arfe s/n, El Arenal.*

Barrio de la Macarena

This immense neighborhood covers the entire northern half of historic Seville and deserves to be walked many times. Most of the best churches, convents, markets, and squares are concentrated around the center in an area delimited by the Arab ramparts to the north, the Alameda de Hercules to the west, the Santa Catalina church to the south, and the Convento de Santa Paula to the east. The area between the Alameda de Hercules and the Guadalquivir is known to locals as the Barrio de San Lorenzo, a section that's ideal for an evening of tapas grazing.

◉ Sights

Basílica de la Macarena

CHURCH | This church holds Seville's most revered image, the Virgin of Hope—better known as La Macarena. Bedecked with candles and carnations, her cheeks streaming with glass tears, the Macarena steals the show at the procession on Holy Thursday, the highlight of Seville's Semana Santa pageant. The patron of Romani and the protector of the matador, her charms are so great that young Sevillano bullfighter Joselito spent half his personal fortune buying her emeralds. When he was killed in the ring in 1920, La Macarena was dressed in widow's weeds for a month. The adjacent museum tells the history of Semana Santa traditions through processional and liturgical artifacts amassed by the Brotherhood of La Macarena over four centuries. ⊠ *Calle Bécquer 1, La Macarena* ☎ *954/901800* ☞ *Basilica free, museum €6.*

Fiesta Time!

Seville's color and vivacity are most intense during Semana Santa, when lacerated Christs and bejeweled weeping Mary statues are paraded through town on floats borne by often-barefoot penitents. Two weeks later, Sevillanos throw Feria de Abril, featuring midday horse parades with men in broad-brim hats and Andalusian riding gear astride prancing steeds, and women in ruffled dresses riding sidesaddle behind them. Bullfights, fireworks, and all-night singing and dancing complete the spectacle.

★ Convento de Santa Paula

CHURCH | This 15th-century Gothic convent has a fine facade and portico, with ceramic decorations by Nicolaso Pisano. The chapel has some beautiful azulejos and sculptures by Martínez Montañés. It also contains a small museum and a shop selling delicious cakes and jams made by the nuns. ⊠ *Calle Santa Paula 11, La Macarena* ☎ *954/540022* ☞ *€5* ⊗ *Closed afternoons.*

San Lorenzo y Jesús del Gran Poder

CHURCH | This 17th-century church has many fine works by artists such as Martínez Montañés and Francisco Pacheco, but its outstanding piece is Juan de Mesa y Velasco's *Jesús del Gran Poder* (*Christ Omnipotent*). ⊠ *Pl. de San Lorenzo 13, La Macarena* ☎ *954/915686* ☞ *Free.*

⑪ Restaurants

El Rinconcillo

$ | **SPANISH** | Founded in 1670, this lovely spot serves a classic selection of dishes, such as the *pavía de bacalao* (fried breaded cod), a superb *salmorejo* (a puree consisting of tomato and bread), and espinacas con garbanzos, all in generous portions. The views of Iglesia de Santa Catalina out the front window upstairs are unbeatable, and your bill is chalked up on the wooden counters as you go (tapas are attractively priced from €2.50). **Known for:** tapas; crowds of locals; views of Iglesia de Santa Catalina. $ *Average main: €14* ✉ *Calle Gerona 40, La Macarena* ☎ *954/223183* ⊕ *www.elrinconcillo.es* ⊘ *Closed Tues.*

Palo Cortao

$ | SPANISH | Down an uninspiring side street but with a very quiet terrace with views of San Pedro Church, this bar with stool seating around high tables offers tranquil dining and, most notably, one of the best sherry menus in town. Known as an *abacería* (grocer's store), it serves more than 30 finos, amontillados, and olorosos, as well as house-made vermouth on the drinks menu, and each pairs perfectly with a food choice. **Known for:** excellent sherry; pairing menu; ajoblanco (cold garlic soup). $ *Average main: €14* ✉ *Calle Mercedes de Velilla 4, La Macarena* ☎ *613/014610* ⊕ *www.palo-cortao.com* ⊘ *Closed Mon. and Tues.*

Triana

Triana used to be Seville's Romani quarter. Today, it has a tranquil, neighborly feel by day and a distinctly flamenco feel at night. Cross over to Triana via the **Puente de Isabel II,** an iron bridge built in 1852 and the first to connect the city's two sections. Start your walk in the **Plaza del Altozano,** the center of the Triana district and traditionally the meeting point for travelers from the south crossing the river to Seville. Admire the facade of the Murillo pharmacy here before walking up **Calle Jacinto.** Look out for the fine **Casa de los Mensaque** (now the district's administrative office and usually open on weekday mornings), home to some of Triana's finest potters and housing some

stunning examples of Seville ceramics. Also worth seeking out are the patios at 32, 83–87, and 138 **Calle Alfarería** and at 16 and 19 **Calle Castilla.** They aren't always open, but you can peep through the iron grills. To reach attractions in La Cartuja, take Bus C1.

Sights

Capilla de los Marineros

HISTORIC SIGHT | This seamen's chapel, built in 1759, is one of Triana's most important monuments and home to the Brotherhood of Triana, whose Semana Santa processions are among the most revered in the city. There's also a small museum dedicated to the Brotherhood. ✉ *Calle Pureza 2, Triana* ☎ *954/332645* 🎫 *Free, museum €4.*

Centro de Cerámica Triana (*Ceramics Center*)

ARTS CENTER | With none of the 40 original ceramicists remaining in Triana, this restored factory complete with its original kilns provides an interesting insight into the neighborhood's tile-making past. Downstairs, an exhibition explains the manufacturing process and the story of ceramics, while upstairs there's a selection of tiles on display. Free guided tours in English. ✉ *Calle Callao 16, Triana* ☎ *954/474293* ⊕ *ceramicatriana.com* 🎫 *€3, free with regular Alcázar ticket* ⊘ *Closed Mon.*

Isla de La Cartuja

ISLAND | Named after its 14th-century Carthusian monastery, this island in the Guadalquivir River across from northern Seville was the site of the decennial Universal Exposition (Expo) in 1992. The island has the Teatro Central, used for concerts and plays; Parque del Alamillo, Seville's largest and least-known park; and the Estadio Olímpico, a 60,000-seat covered stadium. The best way to get to La Cartuja is by walking across one or both (one each way) of the superb Santiago Calatrava bridges spanning the river.

The Puente de la Barqueta crosses to La Cartuja, and downstream the Puente del Alamillo connects the island with Seville. Buses C1 and C2 also serve La Cartuja. ✉ *Triana.*

Isla Mágica

AMUSEMENT PARK/CARNIVAL | FAMILY | The eastern shore of Isla de la Cartuja holds this theme park with more than 20 attractions, including the hair-raising Jaguar roller coaster. Discounts are available online. ✉ *Isla de la Cartuja, Av. de los Descubrimiento s/n, Triana* ☎ *954/487030* 🌐 *www.islamagica.es* 🎟 *From €25* 🕒 *Closed Nov.–Apr. and weekdays in May, Sept., and Oct.*

Mercado de Triana

MARKET | The small Triana market, which began as an improvised fish market on the banks of the Guadalquivir in the 1830s, is housed in a shiny building next to the bridge and has been given the stamp "Traditional Shopping Center." The vendors sell a colorful mix of food, flowers, cheap fashion, and costume jewelry until 3 pm every day but Sunday. The dozen or so restaurants and bars open daily till late. ✉ *Pl. del Altozano s/n, Triana* 🌐 *mercadodetrianasevilla.com.*

Monasterio de Santa María de las Cuevas (*Monasterio de La Cartuja*)

ART MUSEUM | This 14th-century monastery was regularly visited by Christopher Columbus, who was also buried here for a few years. Part of the building houses the Centro Andaluz de Arte Contemporáneo, which has an absorbing collection of contemporary art. ✉ *Isla de la Cartuja, Calle Américo Vespucio 2, Triana* ☎ *955/037070* 🎟 *€3, free Tues.–Fri. 7–9 pm and Sat.* 🕒 *Closed Mon.*

🍴 Restaurants

Bar Las Golondrinas

$ | SPANISH | Run by the same family for more than 50 years and lavishly decorated in the colorful tiles that pay tribute to the neighborhood's potters, Las Golondrinas is a fixture of Triana life. The staff never change, and neither does the menu—the recipes for the *punta de solomillo* (sliced sirloin), *chipirones* (fried baby squid), and *caballito de jamón* (ham on bread) have been honed to perfection, and they're served as tapas (€3) or *raciones* (shareable portions) that keep everyone happy. **Known for:** vibrant atmosphere; traditional tapas; good value. [$] *Average main: €14* ✉ *Calle Antillano Campos 26, Triana* ☎ *954/331626.*

De la O

$$ | SPANISH | Tucked away on the riverfront in Triana next to Puente del Cristo de la Expiración, this modern venue advocates local produce in traditional Andalusian recipes, showcased in a menu that changes on a weekly basis, along with a long wine list of Andalusian wines. The long narrow interior has striking wood-paneled walls with a verdant vertical garden in the middle, while outside dining takes in panoramic views of the river on the intimate terrace. **Known for:** quality local produce; waterfront views; dishes presented artistically. [$] *Average main: €20* ✉ *Paseo de Nuestra Señora de la O 29, Triana* ☎ *954/339000* 🌐 *delaorestaurante.com* 🕒 *Closed Mon. and Wed., no dinner Tues.*

🛏 Hotels

Eurostars Torre Sevilla

$$ | HOTEL | Andalusia's tallest building, with a 180-meter tower, designed by Cesar Pelli, rises high above the Cartuja area and makes a controversial sight on the city skyline while delivering spectacular views over Seville, Triana, and the river. **Pros:** spectacular views of the city; spacious accommodations; modern amenities. **Cons:** some distance from sights and attractions; elevator system a little confusing; indifferent service at times. [$] *Rooms from: €200* ✉ *Calle Gonzalo Jiménez de Quesada 2, Triana* ☎ *954/466022* 🌐 *www.eurostarshotels.*

com/eurostars-torre-sevilla.html 🛏 *244 rooms* 🍴 *Free Breakfast.*

Hotel Monte Triana
$$ | **HOTEL** | Comfortable, squeaky-clean facilities, and excellent value for the cost are two key reasons for choosing this hotel to the north of the heart of Triana. **Pros:** good value; private parking; friendly and helpful staff. **Cons:** 20-minute walk to city center; decor too basic for some; no on-site restaurant. [$] *Rooms from: €160* ✉ *Calle Clara de Jesús Montero 24, Triana* ☎ *954/343111* 🌐 *www.hotel-montetriana.com/en* 🛏 *114 rooms* 🍴 *No Meals.*

Performing Arts

FLAMENCO

Lola de los Reyes
FOLK/TRADITIONAL DANCE | This venue in Triana presents reasonably authentic shows and hosts "flamenco afternoons" Thursday through Saturday—check the website for details. Entrance to some shows is free, but there's a one-drink minimum; others cost from €22. Booking is advised. ✉ *Calle Pureza 107, Triana* ☎ *667/631163* 🌐 *loladelosreyes.es* [M] *Blas Infante/Parque de los Principes.*

Teatro Central
ARTS CENTERS | This modern venue on the Isla de la Cartuja stages theater, dance (including flamenco), and classical and contemporary music. Tickets can be bought online or at the ticket office. ✉ *Calle José de Gálvez 6, Triana* ☎ *955/542155 for information* 🌐 *www.juntadeandalucia.es/cultura/teatros/teatro-central.*

Shopping

Potters' District
CERAMICS | Look for traditional azulejo tiles and other ceramics in the Triana potters' district on Calles Alfarería, Antillano Campos, and Callao, such as Cerámica Triana (✉ Calle Callao 14), selling a selection of traditional ceramic items. ✉ *Triana.*

Itálica

12 km (7½ miles) north of Seville, 1 km (½ mile) beyond Santiponce.

Neighboring the small town of Santiponce, Itálica is Spain's oldest Roman site and one of its greatest, and it is well worth a visit when you're in Seville. If you're here during August, try to get tickets for the International Dance Festival (🌐 *festivalitalica.es*) held in the ruins.

GETTING HERE AND AROUND

The M170A bus route runs frequently (weekdays only, 6:40 am–2:30 am) between the Plaza de Armas bus station in Seville and Itálica. The journey time is 20–30 minutes. If you have a rental car, you could include a visit to the ruins on your way to Huelva. Allow at least two hours for your visit.

Sights

★ Itálica
RUINS | Once one of Roman Iberia's most important cities in the 2nd century, with a population of more than 10,000, Itálica today is a monument of Roman ruins. Founded by Scipio Africanus in 205 BC as a home for veteran soldiers, Itálica gave the Roman world two great emperors: Trajan (AD 52–117) and Hadrian (AD 76–138). You can find traces of city streets, cisterns, and the floor plans of several villas, some with mosaic floors, though all the best mosaics and statues have been removed to Seville's Museo Arqueológico. Itálica was abandoned and plundered as a quarry by the Visigoths, who preferred Seville. It fell into decay around AD 700. The remains include the huge elliptical amphitheater, which held 40,000 spectators; a Roman theater; and Roman baths. The finale for season 7 of *Game of Thrones* was filmed here in 2018. The small visitor center offers information on daily life in the city. ✉ *Av. Extremadura 2, Santiponce*

☎ 600/141767 ⊕ www.museosdeandalu-cia.es 🎫 €2 🕐 Closed Mon.

Córdoba

166 km (103 miles) northwest of Gra-nada, 407 km (253 miles) southwest of Madrid, 239 km (148½ miles) northeast of Cádiz, 143 km (89 miles) northeast of Seville.

Strategically located on the north bank of the Guadalquivir River, Córdoba was the Roman and Moorish capital of Spain. Its old quarter, clustered around its famous Mezquita, remains one of the country's grandest and yet most intimate examples of its Moorish heritage. Once a medieval city famed for the peaceful and prosper-ous coexistence of its three religious cultures—Islamic, Jewish, and Chris-tian—Córdoba is also a perfect analogue for the cultural history of the Iberian Peninsula.

Córdoba today, with its modest popula-tion of less than 326,000, offers a cultural depth and intensity—a direct legacy from the great emirs, caliphs, philosophers, physicians, poets, and engineers of the days of the caliphate—that far outstrips the city's current commercial and political power. Its artistic and historical treas-ures begin with the Mezquita-Catedral (mosque-cathedral), as it is generally called, and continue through the winding, whitewashed streets of the Judería (the medieval Jewish Quarter); the jasmine-, geranium-, and orange-blossom-filled patios; the Renaissance palaces; and the two dozen churches, convents, and her-mitages built by Moorish artisans directly over former mosques.

GETTING HERE AND AROUND
BIKE
Never designed to support cars, Córdo-ba's medieval layout is ideal for bicycles. There's a good network of designated bicycle tracks.

CONTACTS Rent a Bike Córdoba. ⊠ *Calle María Cristina 5, Córdoba* ☎ *957/943700* ⊕ *rentabikecordoba.com.*

BUS
Córdoba is easily reached by bus from Granada, Málaga, and Seville (lockers are available at the bus station). The city has an extensive public bus network with frequent service. Buses usually start running at 6:30 or 7 am and stop around midnight. You can buy 10-trip passes at newsstands and the bus office in Plaza de Colón. A single-trip fare is €1.30.

Córdoba has organized open-top bus tours of the city that can be booked via the tourist office.

CAR
The city's one-way system can be some-thing of a nightmare to navigate, and it's best to park in one of the signposted lots outside the old quarter.

TAXI
CONTACTS Radio Taxi. ⊠ *Córdoba* ☎ *957/764444.*

TRAIN
The city's modern train station is the hub for a comprehensive network of regional trains, with regular high-speed train ser-vice to Granada, Seville, Málaga, Madrid, and Barcelona.

CONTACTS Train Station. ⊠ *Glorie-ta de las Tres Culturas s/n, Córdoba* ☎ *912/320320.*

VISITOR INFORMATION
Tourist Office. ⊠ *Pl. de las Tendillas 5, Centro* ☎ *957/471577* ⊕ *www.turismo-decordoba.org.*

Sights

Córdoba is an easily navigable city, with twisting alleyways that hold surprises around every corner. The main city subdivisions used in this book are the **Judería** (which includes the Mezquita); **Sector Sur,** around the **Torre de la Calahorra** across the river; the area around the

Córdoba's History

The Romans invaded Córdoba in 206 BC, later making it the capital of Rome's section of Spain. Nearly 800 years later, the Visigoth king Leovigildus took control, but the tribe was soon supplanted by the Moors, whose emirs and caliphs held court here from the 8th to the early 11th century. At that point Córdoba was one of the greatest centers of art, culture, and learning in the Western world; one of its libraries had a staggering 400,000 volumes. Moors, Christians, and Jews lived together in harmony within Córdoba's walls. In that era, it was considered second in importance only to Constantinople; but in 1009, Prince Muhammad II led a rebellion that broke up the caliphate, leading to power flowing to separate Moorish kingdoms.

Córdoba remained in Moorish hands until it was conquered by King Fernando in 1236 and repopulated from the north of Spain. Later, the Catholic Monarchs used the city as a base from which to plan the conquest of Granada. In Columbus's time, the Guadalquivir was navigable as far upstream as Córdoba, and great galleons sailed its waters. Today, the river's muddy water and marshy banks evoke little of Córdoba's glorious past, but an old Arab waterfall and the city's bridge—of Roman origin, though much restored by the Arabs and successive generations, most recently in 2012—recall a far grander era.

Plaza de la Corredera, a historic gathering place for everything from horse races to bullfights; and the **Centro Comercial,** from the area around Plaza de las Tendillas to the Iglesia de Santa Marina (Santa Marina Church) and the Torre de la Malmuerta. Incidentally, the last neighborhood is much more than a succession of shops and stores. The town's real life, the everyday hustle and bustle, takes place here and the general atmosphere is very different from that of the tourist center around the Mezquita, with its plethora of souvenir shops. Some of the city's finest Mudejar churches and best taverns, as well as the Palacio de los Marqueses de Viana, are in this pivotal part of town well back from the Guadalquivir waterfront.

Some of the most characteristic and rewarding places to explore in Córdoba are the parish churches and the taverns that inevitably accompany them, where you can taste fino de Moriles, a dry, sherrylike wine from the Montilla-Moriles D.O., and *tentempiés* (tapas—literally, "keep you on your feet"). The *iglesias fernandinas* (churches named for their construction after Fernando III's conquest of Córdoba) were nearly always built over mosques with stunning horseshoe-arch doorways and Mudejar towers, and taverns tended to spring up around these populous hubs of city life. Examples are the Taberna de San Miguel (aka Casa el Pisto) next to the church of the same name, and the Bar Santa Marina (aka Casa Obispo) next to the Santa Marina Church.

■ TIP→ **Córdoba's officials frequently change the hours of the city's sights; before visiting an attraction, confirm hours with the tourist office or the sight itself.**

Alcázar de los Reyes Cristianos (*Fortress of the Christian Monarchs*)
CASTLE/PALACE | Built by Alfonso XI in 1328, the alcázar in Córdoba is a Mudejar-style palace with splendid gardens. (The original Moorish alcázar stood beside the mezquita, on the site of the present Bishop's Palace.) This is

where, in the 15th century, the Catholic Monarchs held court and launched their conquest of Granada. Boabdil was imprisoned here in 1483, and for nearly 300 years, this alcázar served as the Inquisition's base. The most important sights here are the Hall of the Mosaics and a Roman stone sarcophagus from the 2nd or 3rd century. ⊠ *Pl. Campo Santo de los Mártires s/n, Judería* ✛ *Next to Guadalquivir River* ⊕ *alcazardelosreyescristianos.cordoba.es* 🖼 *€5* ⊗ *Closed Mon.*

★ Calleja de las Flores

STREET | A few yards off the northeastern corner of the mezquita, this tiny street has the prettiest patios, many with ceramics, foliage, and iron grilles. The patios are key to Córdoba's architecture, at least in the old quarter, where life is lived behind sturdy white walls—a legacy of the Moors, who honored both the sanctity of the home and the need to shut out the fierce summer sun. Between the first and second week of May—right after the early May Cruces de Mayo (Crosses of May) competition, when neighborhoods compete at setting up elaborate crosses decorated with flowers and plants—Córdoba throws a Patio Festival, during which private patios are filled with flowers, opened to the public, and judged in a municipal competition. Córdoba's tourist office publishes an itinerary of the best patios in town (downloadable from ⊕ *patios.cordoba. es/en*); note that most are open only in the mornings on weekdays but all day on weekends. ⊠ *Judería.*

Casa de Sefarad

HISTORY MUSEUM | This private museum opposite the synagogue is dedicated to the culture of Sephardic Jews in the Mediterranean. Providing a very personal insight, the museum's director leads visitors through the five rooms of the 14th-century house, where displays cover Sephardic domestic life, music, festivities, the history of Córdoba's

Jewish Quarter, and finally a collection of contemporary paintings of the women of al-Andalus ("al-Andalus" is Arabic for "Land of the West"). ⊠ *Calle de los Judíos 17, Judería* 🖼 *957/421404* 🖼 *€5* ⊗ *Closed Sun. and Mon.*

Centro de Creación Contemporánea de Andalucía

ART MUSEUM | Located in a huge brutalist building whose intricate facade imitates the geometric shapes on the Mezquita stucco-work, this center operates primarily as a stage for live art with artists in residence and regular dance performances. It also hosts regular exhibitions by contemporary Spanish artists. Every evening at dusk, the exterior facade lights up with artwork, best viewed from the Balcón del Guadalquivir park on the north side of the river. ⊠ *Calle Carmen Olmedo Checa s/n, Sector Sur* 🖼 *697/104160* ⊕ *www.c3a.es* 🖼 *Free* ⊗ *Closed Mon.*

★ Madinat Al-Zahra (*Medina Azahara*)

RUINS | Built in the foothills of the Sierra Morena by Abd al-Rahman III (891–961) for his favorite concubine, al-Zahra (the Flower), the construction of this once-splendid summer pleasure palace was begun in 936. Historians say it took 10,000 men, 2,600 mules, and 400 camels 25 years to erect this fantasy of 4,300 columns in dazzling pink, green, and white marble and jasper brought from Carthage. A palace, a mosque, luxurious baths, fragrant gardens, fish ponds, an aviary, and a zoo stood on three terraces here; for around 70 years the Madinat was the de facto capital of al-Andalus, until, in 1013, it was sacked and destroyed by Berber mercenaries. In 1944, the Royal Apartments were rediscovered, and the throne room carefully reconstructed. The outline of the mosque has also been excavated. The only covered part of the site is the Salon de Abd al-Rahman III (due to open in mid-2023 after a decade of restoration work); the rest is a sprawl of foundations

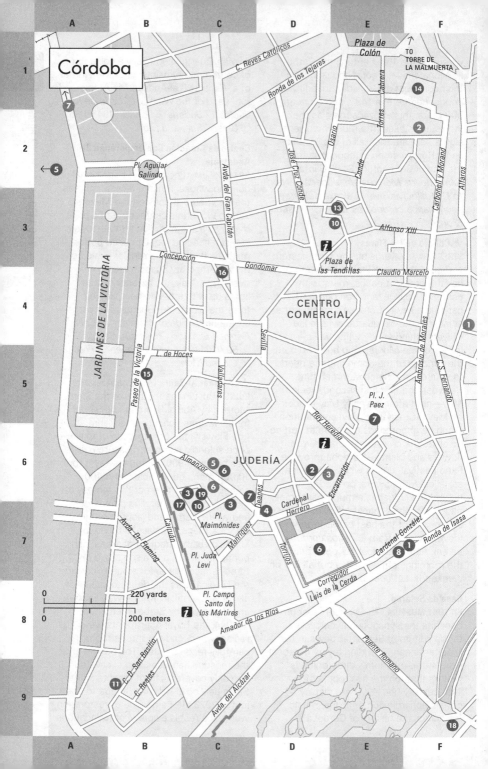

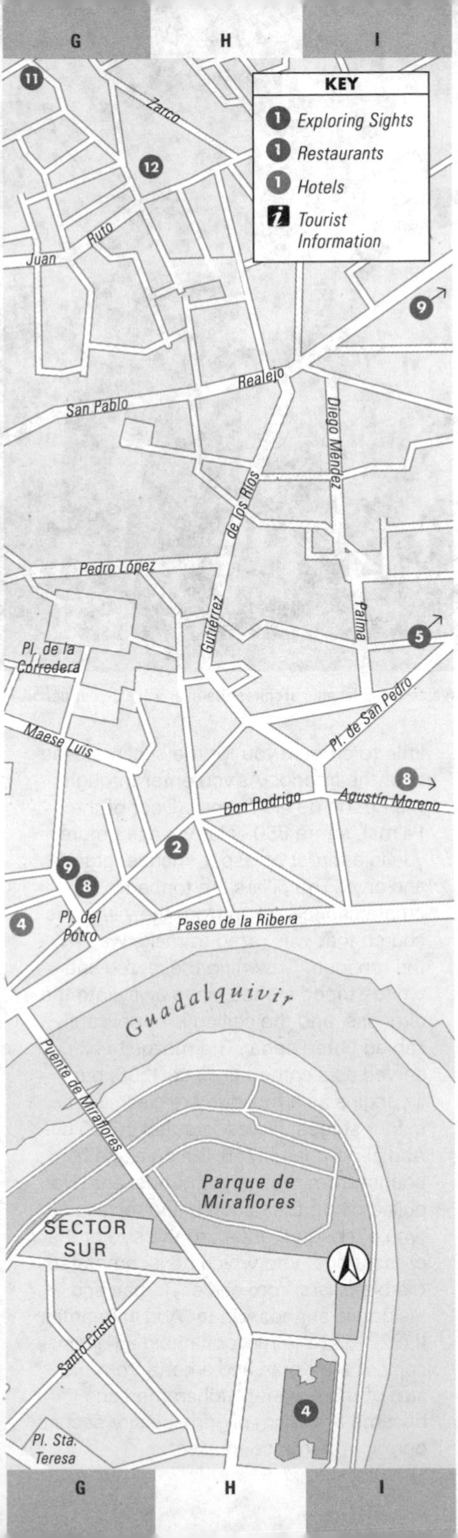

KEY

- **1** Exploring Sights
- **1** Restaurants
- **1** Hotels
- **i** Tourist Information

Sights ▼

1 Alcázar de los Reyes Cristianos.........C8
2 Calleja de las Flores.....E6
3 Casa de Sefarad.........C6
4 Centro de Creación Contemporánea de Andalucía............H9
5 Madinat Al-Zahra.......A2
6 Mezquita.................D7
7 Museo Arqueológico....E5
8 Museo de Bellas Artes.............G6
9 Museo Julio Romero de Torres.................G6
10 Museo Taurino...........C6
11 Plaza de los Dolores....G1
12 Palacio de los Marqueses de Viana...G1
13 Plaza de San Miguel....E3
14 Plaza Santa Marina.....F1
15 Puerta de Almodóvar...B5
16 San Nicolás de la Villa.................C4
17 Synagogue..............B7
18 Torre Calahorra..........F9
19 Zoco......................C6

Restaurants ▼

1 Amaltea...................F7
2 Bodegas Campos.......H6
3 Casa Mazal..............C7
4 Casa Pepe de la Judería..................D7
5 El Choco...................I4
6 El Churrasco..............C6
7 El Rincón de Carmen................C6
8 La Regadera..............E7
9 noor.......................I2
10 Taberna de San Miguel..............E3
11 Taberna La Viuda.......B9

Hotels ▼

1 Casa de los Azulejos....F4
2 Hospes Palacio del Bailío.................F2
3 Hotel Balcón de Córdoba..............E6
4 Hotel Maestre...........G6
5 La Llave de la Judería...C6
6 NH Collection Amistad Córdoba........C6
7 Parador de Córdoba....A1
8 Viento 10..................I5

Córdoba's stunning Mezquita charts the evolution of Western and Islamic architecture over a 1,300-year period.

and arches that hint at the splendor of the original city-palace. Begin at the visitor center, which provides background information and a 3D reconstruction of the city, and continue to the ruins, around 2 km (1 mile) away. You can walk, but it's uphill, so consider taking the shuttle bus (€3, or included in the €10 bus ticket from the Paseo de la Victoria in the city center). Both services run frequently. The tourist office can provide schedule details. Allow 2½ to 3 hours for your visit. You can visit the ruins at night Tuesday–Saturday between mid-June and mid-September. ⊠ *Ctra. de Palma del Río, Km 5.5, Córdoba* ✛ *8 km (5 miles) west of Córdoba on C431* ☎ *957/104933* ⊕ *www.museosdeandalucia.es/web/conjuntoarqueologicomadinatalzahra* ⊠ *€2* ⊘ *Closed Mon.*

★ Mezquita (*Mosque*)

HISTORIC SIGHT | Built between the 8th and 10th centuries, Córdoba's mosque is one of the earliest and most beautiful examples of Spanish Islamic architecture. The plain, crenellated exterior walls do little to prepare you for the sublime beauty of the interior. As you enter through the Puerta de las Palmas (Door of the Palms), some 850 columns rise before you in a forest of jasper, marble, granite, and onyx. The pillars are topped by ornate capitals taken from the Visigothic church that was razed to make way for the mosque. Crowning these, red-and-white-striped arches curve away into the dimness, and the ceiling is of delicately carved tinted cedar. The mezquita has served as a cathedral since 1236, but its origins as a mosque are clear. Built in four stages, it was founded in 785 by Abd al-Rahman I (756–88) on a site he bought from the Visigoth Christians. He pulled down their church and replaced it with a mosque, one-third the size of the present one, into which he incorporated marble pillars from earlier Roman and Visigothic shrines. Under Abd ar-Rahman II (822–52), the mezquita held an original copy of the Koran and a bone from the arm of the prophet Mohammed and became a Muslim pilgrimage site second only in importance to Mecca.

Al-Hakam II (961–76) built the beautiful mihrab (prayer niche), the mezquita's greatest jewel. Make your way over to the qibla, the south-facing wall in which this sacred prayer niche was hollowed out. (Muslim law decrees that a mihrab face east, toward Mecca, and that worshippers do likewise when they pray. Because of an error in calculation, this one faces more south than east. Al-Hakam II spent hours agonizing over a means of correcting such a serious mistake, but he was persuaded to let it be.) In front of the mihrab is the *maksoureh*, a kind of anteroom for the caliph and his court; its mosaics and plasterwork make it a masterpiece of Islamic art. A last addition to the mosque as such, the maksoureh was completed around 987 by al-Mansur, who more than doubled its size.

After the Reconquest, the Christians left the mezquita largely undisturbed, dedicating it to the Virgin Mary and using it as a place of Christian worship. The clerics did erect a wall closing off the mosque from its courtyard, which helped dim the interior and thus separate the house of worship from the world outside. In the 13th century, Christians had the Capilla de Villaviciosa (Villaviciosa Chapel) built by Moorish craftsmen, its Mudejar architecture blending with the lines of the mosque. But that was not so for the heavy, incongruous baroque structure of the cathedral, sanctioned in the very heart of the mosque by Carlos V in the 1520s. To the emperor's credit, he was supposedly horrified when he came to inspect the new construction, exclaiming to the architects: "To build something ordinary, you have destroyed something that was unique in the world" (not that this sentiment stopped him from tampering with the Alhambra to build his Palacio Carlos V). Rest up and reflect in the Patio de los Naranjos (Courtyard of the Oranges), perfumed in springtime by orange blossoms. The Puerta del Perdón (Gate of Forgiveness), so named because debtors were forgiven here on feast days, is on the north wall of the courtyard and is the formal entrance to the mosque. The Virgen de los Faroles (Virgin of the Lanterns), a small statue in a niche on the outside wall of the mosque along the north side on Calle Cardenal Herrero, is behind a lantern-hung grille, rather like a lady awaiting a serenade. The Torre del Alminar, the minaret once used to summon the Muslim faithful to prayer, has a baroque belfry that reopened to visitors in late 2014. Views from the top are well worth the climb, but be aware that it's the equivalent of 12 flights of stairs.

■ **TIP→ Allow a good hour for your visit.** ✉ *Calle Cardenal Herrero 1, Judería* ☎ *957/470512* ⊕ *mezquita-catedraldecor-doba.es/en* ✉ *Mezquita €13, free Mon.–Sat. 8:30–9:30 am, Torre del Alminar €3.*

Museo Arqueológico

HISTORY MUSEUM | In the heart of the old quarter, this museum is built around a 16th-century mansion and has finds from Córdoba's varied cultural past. You enter via the second floor, which is devoted to prehistoric, Roman, and Moorish exhibits. Highlights include a 1st-century head of Drusus (the son of Emperor Tiberius) and a marble statue of Aphrodite. The first floor shows finds from Roman and Moorish life in Córdoba including a stunning 2nd-century sculpture of Mithras killing a bull. Down in the basement you can see the ruins of a Roman theater built in the 1st century AD. The alleys and steps along Altos de Santa Ana make for great wandering. ✉ *Pl. de Jerónimo Paez s/n, Judería* ☎ *957/355517* ⊕ *www.muse-osdeandalucia.es/web/museoarqueologi-codecordoba* ✉ *€2* ⊗ *Closed Mon.*

★ Museo de Bellas Artes

ART MUSEUM | Hard to miss because of its deep-pink facade, Córdoba's Museum of Fine Arts, in a courtyard just off the Plaza del Potro, belongs to a former charity hospital. It was founded by Fernando and Isabel, who twice received Columbus here. The collection, which includes paintings by Murillo, Valdés Leal, Zurbarán, Goya, and Joaquín Sorolla y Bastida, concentrates on local artists. Highlights are altarpieces from the 14th and 15th centuries and the large collection of prints and drawings, including some by Fortuny, Goya, and Sorolla. ⊠ *Pl. del Potro 1, San Francisco* ☎ *957/103659* ⊕ *www.museosdeandalucia.es/web/ museodebellasartesdecordoba* 🎫 *€2* ◔ *Closed Mon.*

Museo Julio Romero de Torres

OTHER MUSEUM | Across the courtyard from the Museo de Bellas Artes, this museum, housed in a 19th-century palace, is devoted to the early-20th-century Córdoban artist Julio Romero de Torres (1874–1930), who specialized in mildly erotic portraits of demure, partially dressed Andalusian temptresses. Romero de Torres, who was also a flamenco *cantaor* (singer), died at the age of 56 and is one of Córdoba's greatest folk heroes. ⊠ *Pl. del Potro 1–4, San Francisco* ☎ *957/491909* ⊕ *museojulioromero. cordoba.es* 🎫 *€4 (card payment only)* ◔ *Closed Mon.*

Museo Taurino (*Museum of Bullfighting*)

OTHER MUSEUM | Two adjoining mansions on the Plaza de Maimónides (or Plaza de las Bulas) house this museum and it's worth a visit, as much for the chance to see a restored mansion as for the posters, Art Nouveau paintings, bulls' heads, suits of lights (bullfighting outfits), and memorabilia of famous Córdoban bullfighters, including the most famous of all, Manolete. To the surprise of the nation, Manolete, who was considered immortal, was killed by a bull in the ring at Linares in 1947. ⊠ *Pl. de Maimónides 1, Judería* ☎ *957/201056* 🎫 *€4 (card payment only)* ◔ *Closed Mon.*

Palacio de los Marqueses de Viana

CASTLE/PALACE | This 17th-century palace is one of Córdoba's most splendid aristocratic homes. Also known as the Museo de los Patios, it contains 12 interior patios, each one different: the patios and gardens are planted with cypresses, orange trees, and myrtles. Inside the building are a carriage museum, a library, embossed leather wall hangings, filigree silver, and grand galleries and staircases. As you enter, note that the corner column of the first patio has been removed to allow the entrance of horse-drawn carriages. ⊠ *Pl. de Don Gome 2, Centro* ☎ *957/496741* ⊕ *palaciodeviana.com* 🎫 *From €7.*

Plaza de los Dolores

PLAZA/SQUARE | The 17th-century Convento de Capuchinos surrounds this small square north of Plaza de San Miguel. The square is where you feel most deeply the city's languid pace. In its center, a statue of Cristo de los Faroles (Christ of the Lanterns) stands amid eight lanterns hanging from twisted wrought-iron brackets. ⊠ *Centro.*

Plaza de San Miguel

PLAZA/SQUARE | The square and café terraces around it—and its atmospheric tavern, Taberna San Miguel–Casa El Pisto—form one of the city's finest combinations of art, history, and gastronomy. San Miguel Church has an interesting façade with Romanesque doors built around Mudejar horseshoe arches and a Mudejar dome inside. ⊠ *Centro.*

Plaza de Santa Marina

PLAZA/SQUARE | At the edge of the Barrio de los Toreros, a quarter where many of Córdoba's famous bullfighters were born and raised, stands a statue of the famous bullfighter Manolete (1917–47) opposite the lovely church of Santa Marina de Aguas Santas (St. Marina of Holy Waters), built by Fernando III when he conquered the city in 1236. Not far from here, on the Plaza de la Lagunilla, is a bust of Manolete. ⊠ *Centro.*

Puerta de Almodóvar

HISTORIC SIGHT | Outside this old Moorish gate at the northern entrance of the Judería is a statue of Seneca, the Córdoba-born philosopher who rose to prominence in Nero's court in Rome and was forced to commit suicide at his emperor's command. The gate stands at the top of the narrow and colorful Calle San Felipe. ✉ *Judería.*

San Nicolás de la Villa

CHURCH | This classically dark Spanish church displays the Mudejar style of Islamic decoration and art forms. Córdoba's well-kept city park, the pleasant Jardines de la Victoria (Victory Gardens), with tile benches and manicured bushes, is a block west. ✉ *Calle San Felipe s/n, Centro.*

Synagogue

HISTORIC SIGHT | The only Jewish temple in Andalusia to survive the expulsion and inquisition of the Jews in 1492, Córdoba's synagogue is also one of only three ancient synagogues left in all of Spain (the other two are in Toledo). Though it no longer functions as a place of worship, it's a treasured symbol for Spain's modern Jewish communities. The outside is plain, but the inside (restored in 2018), measuring 23 feet by 21 feet, contains some exquisite Mudejar stucco tracery. Look for the fine plant motifs and the Hebrew inscription saying that the synagogue was built in 1315. The women's gallery (not open for visits) still stands, and in the east wall is the ark where the sacred scrolls of the Torah were kept. ✉ *Calle de los Judíos s/n, Judería* ☎ *957/202928* 🎟 *€1* 🕒 *Closed Mon.*

Torre Calahorra

NOTABLE BUILDING | The tower on the far side of the Puente Romano (Roman Bridge), which was restored in 2008, was built in 1369 to guard the entrance to Córdoba. It now houses the Museo Vivo de Al-Andalus (Arabic for "Land of the West"), with films and audiovisual guides (in English) on Córdoba's history. Climb the narrow staircase to the top of the tower for the view of the Roman bridge and city on the other side of the Guadalquivir. ✉ *Av. de la Confederación s/n, Sector Sur* ☎ *957/293929* 🌐 *www.torrecalahorra.es* 🎟 *€5, includes audio guide.*

Zoco

MARKET | The Spanish word for the Arab souk (*zoco*) recalls the onetime function of this courtyard near the synagogue. It's now the site of a daily crafts market, where you can see artisans at work and live music on weekends. ✉ *Calle de los Judíos 5, Judería* ☎ *957/204033* 🎟 *Free.*

🍴 Restaurants

Amaltea

$ | **INTERNATIONAL** | Satisfying vegetarians, vegans, and their meat-eating friends, this organic restaurant includes some meat and fish on the menu. There's a healthy mix of Mexican, Asian, Spanish, and Italian-influenced dishes, including salmon steamed in banana leaves, ras el hanout lamb wok, and couscous. **Known for:** vegetarian food; inviting interior with relaxed vibe; organic options. [$] *Average main: €15* ✉ *Calle Ronda de Isasa 10, Centro* ☎ *657/757598* 🕒 *No dinner Sun. Closed Sun. in summer.*

★ **Bodegas Campos**

$$ | **SPANISH** | A block east of the Plaza del Potro, this traditional old bodega with high-quality service is the epitome of all that's great about Andalusian cuisine. The dining rooms are in barrel-heavy rustic rooms and leafy traditional patios (take a look at some of the signed barrels—you may recognize a name or two, such as the former U.K. prime minister Tony Blair). **Known for:** bodega setting; regional dishes; excellent tapas bar. [$] *Average main: €22* ✉ *Calle Lineros 32, San Pedro* ☎ *957/497500* 🌐 *bodegascampos.com.*

Casa Mazal

$$ | **ECLECTIC** | In the heart of the Judería, this pretty little restaurant serves a modern interpretation of Sephardic cuisine—with organic dishes that are more exotic than the usual Andalusian fare—and a kosher menu. The many vegetarian options include gazpacho with

mango and artichoke hearts in saffron sauce; and the *siniya* (trout baked in vine leaves with pomegranate and mint) is delicious. **Known for:** traditional Sephardic cuisine; romantic ambience; vegetarian dishes. [$] *Average main: €18* ✉ *Calle Tomás Conde 3, Judería* ☎ *685/882666* ⏲ *Closed Wed.*

Casa Pepe de la Judería
$$$ | **SPANISH** | Geared toward a tourist clientele, this place is always packed, noisy, and fun, and there is live Spanish guitar music on the roof terrace most summer nights. Antiques and some wonderful old oil paintings fill this three-floor labyrinth of rooms just around the corner from the mosque, near the Judería. **Known for:** traditional Andalusian food; croquetas de jamón; live music on the roof terrace in summer. [$] *Average main: €28* ✉ *Calle Romero 1, off Deanes, Judería* ☎ *957/200744* 🌐 *restaurantecasapepedelajuderia.com.*

★ El Choco
$$$$ | **SPANISH** | The city's most exciting restaurant, which has renewed its Michelin star annually since 2012, El Choco has renowned chef Kisko Garcia at the helm whipping up innovative dishes based on his 10 Commandments to preserve good cooking. One of them is that taste always comes first, and that plays out well during a meal at this minimalist restaurant with charcoal-colored walls, glossy parquet floors, and dishes offering new sensations and amazing presentations. **Known for:** creative Andalusian cooking; good-value Michelin-star tasting menu; innovative presentation. [$] *Average main: €110* ✉ *Calle del Compositor Serrano Lucena 14, Centro* ☎ *957/264863* 🌐 *www.restaurantechoco.com* ⏲ *Closed Mon.–Wed. and Aug. No dinner Sun.*

El Churrasco
$$ | **SPANISH** | The name suggests grilled meat, but this restaurant in the heart of the Judería serves much more. In the colorful bar try tapas (from €3.50) such as the *berenjenas crujientes con salmorejo* (crispy fried eggplant slices with thick gazpacho), while in the restaurant opt for the supremely fresh grilled fish or the steak, which is the best in town, particularly the namesake *churrasco ibérico* (grilled Iberian pork, served here in a spicy tomato-based sauce). **Known for:** grilled meat; tapas; alfresco dining. [$] *Average main: €24* ✉ *Calle Romero 16, Judería* ☎ *957/290819* ⏲ *Closed Aug.*

El Rincón de Carmen
$ | **MEDITERRANEAN** | With the sights of the Judería on the doorstep, this is a good central spot for a quick bite in a typical Córdoba patio setting that's particularly pretty at night. Tapas and sharing plates make up the menu where star turns come from the *magret de pato* (duck breast) and *saquitos de bacalao con salsa dulce de pimientos* (cod pastries with sweet pepper sauce). **Known for:** attractive patio setting; generous portions; saquitos de bacalao (cod pastries). [$] *Average main: €14* ✉ *Calle Romero 4, Judería* ☎ *957/291055* 🌐 *restauranterincondecarmen.es* ⏲ *Closed Mon. and Tues.*

La Regadera
$$ | **SPANISH** | It feels as if you could be outside at this bright venue on the river whose fresh interior comes with miniature wall gardens—there's even an herb garden in the middle. Local produce takes center stage on the short menu, where you'll find a mix of traditional and modern dishes including house specials such as wild sea bass ceviche, suckling pig, and cream of lemon. **Known for:** good wine list; garden-like interior; tuna tartare. [$] *Average main: €20* ✉ *Calle Ronda de Isasa 10, Judería* ☎ *957/101400* 🌐 *www.regadera.es.*

★ noor
$$$$ | **SPANISH** | One of the few two Michelin-starred venues in Andalusia, noor offers Andalusí cuisine in three tasting menus that explore the ingredients used before the discovery of the New World as well as the fusion of the New

A typical Córdoba patio, filled with flowers

World ingredients into Spanish cooking. Local chef Paco Morales and team create in the open kitchen while diners sit at very modern tables under a dramatic Arabian nights' ceiling. **Known for:** creative authentic cuisine; destination dining; Arabian nights ambience. [$] *Average main: €95* ✉ *Calle Pablo Ruiz Picasso 8, Centro* ☎ *957/964055* 🌐 *noorrestaurant.es* 🕓 *Closed Sun.–Tues. and Jul. and Aug.*

Taberna de San Miguel

$ | **TAPAS** | Just a few minutes' walk from the Plaza de las Tendillas and opposite the lovely San Miguel Church, this popular tapas spot—also known as the Casa el Pisto (Ratatouille House)—was established in 1880. You can choose to squeeze in at the bar and dine on tapas (from €3) or spread out a little more on the patio decked with ceramics and bullfighting memorabilia, where half and full portions are served. **Known for:** tapas, including pisto; historic ambience; patio with bullfighting memorabilia. [$] *Average main: €14* ✉ *Pl. de San Miguel 1, Centro* ☎ *957/470166* 🌐 *www.casaelpisto.com* 🕓 *Closed Sun. and Mon.*

Taberna La Viuda

$ | **SPANISH** | Slightly off the beaten tourist trail and with a lively local vibe, this tavern-style venue specializes in traditional local cuisine such as salmorejo, flamenquín, and oxtail, but you'll also find creative touches on the menu in the form of tuna marinated in ginger and scrambled eggs with smoked fish and trout roe. Most dishes are available as tapas and half or full plates, and all can be paired with local wines. **Known for:** traditional local food; warm welcome; wine pairings. [$] *Average main: €12* ✉ *Calle de San Basilio 52, Judería* ☎ *957/296905.*

Hotels

Casa de los Azulejos

$ | **B&B/INN** | This 17th-century house still has original details like the majestic vaulted ceilings, and with the use of stunning tiles (azulejos)—hence the name—it mixes Andalusian and Latin American influences. **Pros:** interesting architecture; homemade breakfast; tropical central patio. **Cons:** hyperbusy interior design; limited privacy; plunge pool is open only in summer. [$] *Rooms from: €110* ✉ *Calle Fernando Colón 5, Centro* ☎ *957/470000* 🌐 *casadelosazulejos.com* 🛏 *9 rooms* 🍴 *Free Breakfast.*

★ Hospes Palacio del Bailío

$$$ | **HOTEL** | One of the city's top lodging options, this tastefully renovated 17th-century mansion is built over the ruins of a Roman house (visible beneath glass floors) in the historic center of town. **Pros:** dazzling interiors; impeccable comforts; pleasant patio gardens. **Cons:** not easy to access by car; pricey; not all rooms have views. [$] *Rooms from: €250* ✉ *Calle de Ramírez de las Casas Deza 10–12, Plaza de la Corredera* ☎ *957/498993* 🌐 *www.hospes.com/palacio-bailio* 🛏 *53 rooms* 🍴 *No Meals.*

★ Hotel Balcón de Córdoba

$$$ | **HOTEL** | In a tastefully restored 17th-century convent, this boutique hotel has spacious quiet rooms, and the mezquita is almost within arm's reach from the rooftop terrace. **Pros:** central location; historic building; rooftop views of the mezquita. **Cons:** difficult to access by car; very quiet; small breakfast area. [$] *Rooms from: €250* ✉ *Calle Encarnación 8, Judería* ☎ *957/498478* 🌐 *balcondecordoba.com* 🛏 *10 rooms* 🍴 *No Meals.*

Hotel Maestre

$ | **HOTEL** | Around the corner from the Plaza del Potro, this is an affordable hotel in which Castilian-style furniture, gleaming marble, and high-quality oil paintings add elegance to excellent value. **Pros:** good location; great value; helpful reception staff. **Cons:** lots of steps; small bathrooms; could be too basic for some. [$] *Rooms from: €90* ✉ *Calle Romero Barros 4–6, San Pedro* ☎ *957/472410* 🌐 *www.hotelmaestre.com* 🛏 *26 rooms* 🍴 *No Meals.*

★ La Llave de la Judería

$$$ | **B&B/INN** | This small hotel, occupying a collection of houses just a stone's throw from the mezquita, combines enchanting antique furnishings with modern amenities, but its greatest asset is its helpful staff. **Pros:** beautiful interiors; rooms are equipped with computers; close to the mezquita. **Cons:** street noise; direct car access is difficult; dark reception area. [$] *Rooms from: €230* ✉ *Calle Romero 38, Judería* ☎ *957/294808* 🌐 *lallavedelajuderia.es* 🛏 *8 rooms* 🍴 *No Meals.*

NH Collection Amistad Córdoba

$$$ | **HOTEL** | Two 18th-century mansions overlooking Plaza de Maimónides in the heart of the Judería have been melded into a modern business hotel with a cobblestone Mudejar courtyard, carved-wood ceilings, and a plush lounge. **Pros:** pleasant and efficient service; large rooms; central location. **Cons:** parking is difficult; not easy to find; a little impersonal. [$] *Rooms from: €240* ✉ *Pl. de Maimónides 3, Judería* ☎ *957/420335* 🌐 *www.nh-hoteles.com* 🛏 *108 rooms* 🍴 *No Meals.*

Parador de Córdoba

$$ | **HOTEL** | On the slopes of the Sierra de Córdoba, on the site of Abd al-Rahman I's 8th-century summer palace, this modern parador has sunny rooms and nice views. **Pros:** wonderful views from south-facing rooms; sleek interiors; quality traditional cuisine. **Cons:** characterless modern building; far from main sights; not all rooms have views. [$] *Rooms from: €140* ✉ *Av. de la Arruzafa 39, El Brillante* ✣ *5 km (3 miles) north of city* ☎ *957/275900* 🌐 *paradores.es/es/parador-de-cordoba* 🛏 *94 rooms* 🍴 *No Meals.*

Viento10

$$ | **HOTEL** | Tucked away to the east of the old quarter but within just 10 minutes' walk of the mezquita is a quiet romantic haven, once part of the 17th-century Sacred Martyrs Hospital and whose patio dates back to the 15th century. **Pros:**

quiet location; excellent service; Jacuzzi and sauna. **Cons:** some walking distance to the main monuments; a little plain; not easy to find. [$] *Rooms from: €130* ✉ *Calle Ronquillo Briceño 10, San Pedro* ☎ *957/764960* 🌐 *hotelviento10.es* 🛏 *8 rooms* 🍴 *No Meals.*

Nightlife

For nightlife, Córdoba locals hang out mostly in the areas of Ciudad Jardín (the old university area), Plaza de las Tendillas, and the Avenida del Gran Capitán.

Bodega Guzman
BARS | For some traditional tipple, check out this atmospheric bodega near the old synagogue. Its sherries are served straight from the barrel in a room that doubles as a bullfighting museum. ✉ *Calle de los Judíos 6, Judería.*

Café Málaga
LIVE MUSIC | A block from Plaza de las Tendillas, this is a laid-back hangout for jazz and flamenco aficionados. There's live music most days with regular flamenco nights. ✉ *Calle Málaga 3, Centro* ☎ *957/474107.*

Performing Arts

FLAMENCO

Tablao El Cardenal
FOLK/TRADITIONAL DANCE | Córdoba's most famous flamenco club offers performances by established artists on a pleasant open-air patio. Admission is €23 (including a drink), and the 90-minute shows take place Monday through Saturday at 8:30 pm from September to June and at 9:30 pm during July and August. Book by phone or the website (in Spanish only). ✉ *Calle del Buen Pastor 2, Judería* ☎ *619/217922* 🌐 *tablaocardenalnuevo.webflow.io* 🎟 *€23* 🕒 *Closed Sun.*

Flamenco!

Córdoba has a thriving flamenco scene, with the annual highlight in mid-June when the city celebrates La Noche Blanca del Flamenco, an evening and night of free concerts in squares. You can also watch free flamenco at noon on Sundays (except May) in the lovely patio at the Centro Flamenco Forforito, off Plaza del Potro. Get in line from 11 am to be sure of a seat. 🌐 centroflamencofosforito.cordoba.es.

Shopping

Córdoba's main shopping district is around Avenida del Gran Capitán, Ronda de los Tejares, and the streets leading away from Plaza de las Tendillas.

Meryan
LEATHER GOODS | This is one of Córdoba's best workshops for embossed leather. ✉ *Calleja de las Flores 2, Judería* ☎ *957/475902* 🌐 *meryancor.com.*

Ronda

147 km (91 miles) southeast of Seville, 61 km (38 miles) northwest of Marbella.

Ronda, one of the oldest towns in Spain, is known for its spectacular position and views. Secure in its mountain fastness on a rock high over the Río Guadalevín, the town was a stronghold for the legendary Andalusian bandits who held court here from the 18th to the early 20th century. Ronda's most dramatic element is its ravine (360 feet deep and 210 feet across)—known as **El Tajo**—which divides La Ciudad, the old Moorish town, from El Mercadillo, the "new town," which sprang up after the Christian Reconquest of 1485. Tour buses roll in daily with sightseers from the coast 49 km (30 miles) away, and on weekends affluent Sevillanos flock to their second homes here. Stay overnight midweek to see this noble town's true colors.

In the lowest part of town, known as El Barrio, you can see parts of the old walls, including the 13th-century Puerta de Almocábar and the 16th-century Puerta de Carlos V. From here, the main road climbs past the Iglesia del Espíritu Santo (Church of the Holy Spirit) and up into the heart of town.

GETTING HERE AND AROUND

The most attractive approach is from the south. The winding but well-maintained A376 from San Pedro de Alcántara, on the Costa del Sol, travels north up through the mountains of the Serranía de Ronda. But you can also drive here from Seville via Utrera; it's a pleasant drive of a little less than two hours. At least six daily buses run here from Marbella, five from Málaga, and five from Seville.

VISITOR INFORMATION

Ronda. ⊠ *Paseo de Blas Infante s/n, Ronda* ☎ *952/187119* ⊕ *www.turismo-deronda.es.*

 Sights

Alameda del Tajo

CITY PARK | Beyond the bullring in El Mercadillo, you can relax in these shady gardens, one of the loveliest spots in Ronda. A balcony protrudes from the face of the cliff, offering a vertigo-inducing view of the valley below. Stroll along the cliff-top walk to the Reina Victoria hotel, built by British settlers from Gibraltar at the turn of the 20th century as a fashionable rest stop on the Algeciras–Bobadilla rail line. ⊠ *Paseo de Ernest Hemingway s/n, Ronda.*

Baños Arabes (*Arab Baths*)

RUINS | The excavated remains of the Arab Baths date from Ronda's tenure as capital of a Moorish *taifa* (kingdom). The star-shape vents in the roof are an inferior imitation of the ceiling of the beautiful bathhouse in Granada's Alhambra. The baths are beneath the Puente Árabe (Arab Bridge) in a ravine below the Palacio del Marqués de Salvatierra. ⊠ *Calle San Miguel s/n, Ronda* ☎ *951/154297* ⊠ *€5.*

La Ciudad

NEIGHBORHOOD | This old Moorish town has twisting streets and white houses with birdcage balconies. Cross the Puente Nuevo to enter La Ciudad. ⊠ *Ronda.*

Palacio de Mondragón (*Palace of Mondragón*)

HISTORY MUSEUM | This stone palace with twin Mudejar towers was probably the residence of Ronda's Moorish kings. Fernando and Isabel appropriated it after their victory in 1485. Today it's the museum of Ronda, and you can wander through the patios, with their brick arches and delicate Mudejar-stucco tracery and admire the mosaics and *artesonado* (coffered) ceiling. The second floor holds a small museum with archaeological items found near Ronda, plus the reproduction of a dolmen, a prehistoric stone monument. ⊠ *Pl. Mondragón s/n, Ronda* ☎ *952/870818* ⊠ *€4.*

Plaza de Toros

SPORTS VENUE | The main sight in Ronda's commercial center, El Mercadillo, is the bullring. Pedro Romero (1754–1839), the father of modern bullfighting and Ronda's most famous native son, is said to have killed 5,600 bulls here during his career. In the museum beneath the plaza you can see posters for Ronda's very first bullfights, held here in 1785. The plaza was once owned by the late bullfighter Antonio Ordóñez, on whose nearby ranch Orson Welles's ashes were scattered—indeed, the ring has become a favorite of filmmakers. Every September, the bullring is the scene of Ronda's *corridas goyescas*, named after Francisco Goya, whose *tauromaquias* (bullfighting sketches) were inspired by Romero's skill and art. The participants and the dignitaries in the audience don the costumes of Goya's time for the occasion. ✉ *Calle Virgen de la Paz s/n, Ronda* ☎ *952/871539* ⊕ *www.rmcr.org* 🎟 *€8 for entry and museum.*

Puente Nuevo

BRIDGE | Immediately south of the Plaza de España, this is Ronda's most famous bridge, an architectural marvel built between 1755 and 1793. The bridge's lantern-lit parapet offers dizzying views of the awesome gorge. Just how many people have met their ends here nobody knows, but the architect of the Puente Nuevo fell to his own death while inspecting work on the bridge. During the civil war, hundreds of victims were hurled from it. ✉ *Ronda.*

Santa María la Mayor

CHURCH | This collegiate church, which serves as Ronda's cathedral, has roots in Moorish times: originally the Great Mosque of Ronda, the tower and adjacent galleries, built for viewing festivities in the square, retain their Islamic design. After the mosque was destroyed (when the Moors were overthrown), it was rebuilt as a church and dedicated to the Virgen de la Encarnación after the Reconquest. The naves are late Gothic, and the main altar is heavy with baroque gold leaf. A visit to the rooftop walkway offers lovely views of the town and surroundings. The church is around the corner from the remains of a mosque, Minarete Árabe (Moorish Minaret) at the end of the Marqués de Salvatierra. ✉ *Pl. Duquesa de Parcent s/n, Ronda* 🎟 *€5.*

🍽 Restaurants

★ Entre Vinos

$ | **TAPAS** | Just off the main road opposite the Hotel Colón, this small and cozy bar has established itself as one of Ronda's best for tapas, wine, and artisan beer. Local Ronda wines are a specialty here—in fact, they're the only ones available, although with more than 100 on the

wine list, you'll be spoiled for choice; ask the waiter for recommendations and which tapas to pair them with. **Known for:** Ronda wines; gourmet tapas; bodega (winery) atmosphere. 💲 *Average main: €10* ✉ *Calle Pozo 2, Ronda* ☎ *672/284146* ⊗ *Closed Sun. and Mon.*

Pedro Romero

$$ | **SPANISH** | Named for the father of modern bullfighting, this restaurant opposite the bullring is packed with bullfight paraphernalia and photos of previous diners who include Ernest Hemingway and Orson Welles. Mounted bulls' heads peer down at you as you eat *choricitos al vino blanco de Ronda* (small sausages in Ronda white wine), *rabo de toro Pedro Romero* (slow-cooked oxtail stew with herbs), or pâté de perdiz (partridge). **Known for:** traditional Ronda cooking; bullfighting decor; friendly service. 💲 *Average main: €20* ✉ *Calle Virgen de la Paz 18, Ronda* ☎ *952/871110* ⊕ *www.rpedroromero.com* ⊗ *No dinner Sun.*

Hotels

Alavera de los Baños

$ | **B&B/INN** | Fittingly, given its location next to the Moorish baths, this small, German-run hotel—which was used as a backdrop for the film *Carmen*—has an Arabian theme throughout. **Pros:** atmospheric and historic; owners speak several languages; first-floor rooms have their own terraces. **Cons:** 2-night minimum stay most weekends; steep climb into town; small bathrooms. 💲 *Rooms from: €100* ✉ *Calle Molino de Alarcón s/n, Ronda* ☎ *952/879143* ⊕ *alaveradelosbanos.com* ⊗ *Closed mid-Dec.–mid-Feb.* 🛏 *11 rooms* 🍽 *Free Breakfast.*

Hotel Montelirio

$$ | **B&B/INN** | The 18th-century mansion of the Count of Montelirio, perched over the deep plunge to El Tajo, has been carefully refurbished, maintaining some original features, but the highlight is the breathtaking view over the valley. **Pros:**

Andalusia's classic pueblos blancos look like Picasso paintings come to life.

valley views; historic building; Turkish bath and open fireplace make it great for winter. **Cons:** some rooms have windows to the street; parking limited; could be too stuffy for some. [$] *Rooms from: €170* ✉ *Calle Tenorio 8, Ronda* ☎ *952/873855* 🌐 *www.hotelmontelirio.com* 🛏 *15 rooms* 🍴 *No Meals.*

Around Ronda: Caves, Romans, and Pueblos Blancos

This area of spectacular gorges, remote mountain villages, and ancient caves is fascinating to explore and a dramatic contrast to the clamor and crowds of the nearby Costa del Sol.

Public transportation is very poor in these parts. Your best bet is to visit by car—the area is a short drive from Ronda.

Sights

★ Acinipo

RUINS | Old Ronda—20 km (12 miles) north of Ronda—is the site of this old Roman settlement, a thriving town in the 1st century AD that was abandoned for reasons that still baffle historians. Today it's a windswept hillside with piles of stones, the foundations of a few Roman houses, and what remains of a theater. Views across the Ronda plains and to the surrounding mountains are spectacular. The site's opening hours vary depending on staff availability and excavations—check with the Ronda tourist office by phone before visiting. ✉ *Ronda* ✥ *Take A376 toward Algodonales; turnoff for ruins is 9 km (5½ miles) from Ronda on MA449* ☎ *951/041452* 🎟 *Free.*

Cueva de la Pileta (*Pileta Cave*)

CAVE | At this site 20 km (12 miles) west of Ronda, a Spanish guide (who speaks some English) will hand you a paraffin lamp and lead you on a roughly 60-minute walk that reveals prehistoric wall paintings of bison, deer, and horses outlined in black, red, and ocher. One highlight is the Cámara del Pescado (Chamber of the Fish), whose drawing of a huge fish is thought to be 15,000 years old. Tours take place on the hour and last around 1 hour. To book, phone between 10 am and 1 pm only. ✉ *Benaoján* ✛ *Drive west from Ronda on A374 and take left exit for village of Benaoján from where caves are well signposted* ☎ *677/610500* ⊕ *cuevadelapileta.es* 💶 *€10.*

Olvera

TOWN | Here, 13 km (8 miles) north of Setenil, two imposing silhouettes dominate the crest of the hill: the 11th-century castle Vallehermoso, a legacy of the Moors; and the neoclassical Iglesia de Nuestra Señora de la Encarnación (Church of Our Lady of the Incarnation), reconstructed in the 19th century on the foundations of the old mosque. ✉ *Cádiz.*

Setenil de las Bodegas

TOWN | This small city, in a cleft in the rock cut by the Río Guadalporcín, is 8 km (5 miles) north of Acinipo. The streets resemble long, narrow caves, and on many houses the roof is formed by a projecting ledge of heavy rock. ✉ *Cádiz.*

Zahara de la Sierra

TOWN | A solitary watchtower dominates a crag above this village, its outline visible for miles around. The tower is all that remains of a Moorish castle where King Alfonso X once fought the emir of Morocco; the building remained a Moorish stronghold until it fell to the Christians in 1470. Along the streets you can see door knockers fashioned like the hand of Fatima: the fingers represent the five laws of the Koran and are meant to ward off evil. ✉ *Cádiz* ✛ *From Olvera, drive 21 km (13 miles) southwest to the village of Algodonales, then south on A376 for 5 km (3 miles).*

Arcos de la Frontera

31 km (19 miles) east of Jerez.

Its narrow and steep cobblestone streets, whitewashed houses, and finely crafted wrought-iron window grilles make Arcos the quintessential Andalusian pueblo blanco. Make your way to the main square, the **Plaza de España**, the highest point in the village; one side of the square is open, and a balcony at the edge of the cliff offers views of the Guadalete Valley. On the opposite end is the **Basílica de Santa María de la Asunción**, a fascinating blend of architectural styles—Romanesque, Gothic, and Mudejar—with a plateresque doorway, a Renaissance retablo, and a 17th-century baroque choir. The *ayuntamiento* (town hall) stands at the foot of the old castle walls on the northern side of the square; across is the Casa del Corregidor, onetime residence of the governor and now a parador. Arcos is the westernmost of the 19 pueblos blancos dotted around the Sierra de Cádiz.

GETTING HERE AND AROUND

Arcos is best reached by private car, but there are frequent buses from Cádiz, Jerez, and Seville on weekdays. Weekend service is less frequent.

VISITOR INFORMATION

Arcos de la Frontera. ✉ *Calle Cuesta de Belén 5, Arcos de la Frontera* ☎ *956/702264* ⊕ *www.turismoarcos. com.*

🍴 Restaurants

Gastrobar El Retablo

$ | **SPANISH** | Traditional Andalusian cuisine comes in generous portions (tapas and sharing plates) at this popular venue with a small terrace opposite the Basílica de Santa María. Stars on the menu include *carrillada de cerdo* (pork cheeks), *bacalao con puré de guisantes* (cod with pea puree), and *arroz con leche* (rice

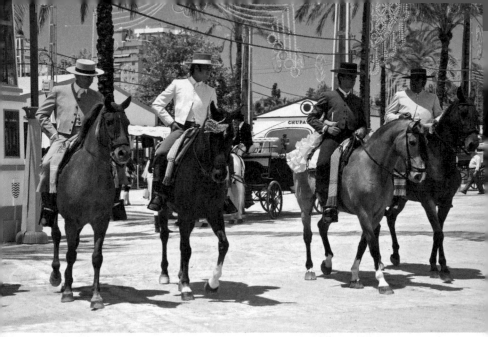

Riders fill the streets during Jerez's Feria del Caballo (Horse Fair) in early May.

pudding). **Known for:** friendly service; octopus; generous portions. $ *Average main: €14* ⊠ *Calle Dean Espinosa 6, Arcos de la Frontera* ☎ *856/041614* ⊗ *Closed Tues..*

Restaurante Aljibe

$ | **FUSION** | Local cooking meets Moroccan cuisine in one of the best fusion menus in the province at this venue with small dining spaces and an Arabian theme. White prawns, *ensalada de higos y payoyo* (fig and goat cheese salad), and *alcachofas con almejas* (artichokes with clams) sit perfectly next to *pastela* (game pie) and couscous dishes. **Known for:** Andalusian-Moroccan fusion; good service with a smile; Moroccan sweets for dessert. $ *Average main: €16* ⊠ *Calle Cuesta del Belén 10, Arcos de la Frontera* ☎ *622/836527* ⊗ *Closed Tues.*

 ## Hotels

★ El Convento

$ | **B&B/INN** | Perched atop the cliff behind the town parador, this tiny hotel in a former 17th-century convent shares the amazing view of another hotel in town, its swish neighbor (La Casa Grande). **Pros:** picturesque location; intimacy; value. **Cons:** small spaces; lots of stairs; no restaurant. $ *Rooms from: €65* ⊠ *Calle Maldonado 2, Arcos de la Frontera* ☎ *956/702333* ⊕ *www.hotelelconvento. es* ⊗ *Closed Jan. and Feb.* ☞ *13 rooms* ⊗ *No Meals.*

★ La Casa Grande

$ | **B&B/INN** | Built in 1729, this extraordinary mansion encircles a central patio with lush vegetation and is perched on the edge of the 400-foot cliff to which Arcos de la Frontera clings. **Pros:** attentive owner; impeccable aesthetics; amazing views. **Cons:** inconvenient parking; long climb to the top floor; bathrooms lack privacy. $ *Rooms from: €100* ⊠ *Calle Maldonado 10, Arcos de la Frontera* ☎ *956/703930* ⊕ *www.lacasagrande.net* ☞ *7 rooms* ⊗ *No Meals.*

Parador de Arcos de la Frontera

$$ | **HOTEL** | Expect a spectacular view from the terrace, as this parador clings to

the cliffside, overlooking the rolling valley of the Río Guadalete. **Pros:** gorgeous views from certain rooms; elegant interiors; good restaurant. **Cons:** a little tired; expensive bar and cafeteria; not all rooms have views. [$] *Rooms from: €175* ✉ *Pl. del Cabildo s/n, Arcos de la Frontera* ☎ *956/700500* 🌐 *paradores.es/es/parador-de-arcos-de-la-frontera* 🛏 *24 rooms* 🍴 *No Meals.*

Jerez de la Frontera

97 km (60 miles) south of Seville.

Jerez, world headquarters for sherry, is surrounded by vineyards of chalky soil, producing palomino and Pedro Ximénez grapes that have funded a host of churches and noble mansions. Names such as González Byass, Domecq, Harvey, and Sandeman are inextricably linked with Jerez. The word "sherry," first used in Great Britain in 1608, is an English corruption of the town's old Moorish name, Xeres. Both sherry and thoroughbred horses (the city was European Capital of Horses in 2018) are the domain of Jerez's Anglo-Spanish aristocracy, whose ancestors came here from England centuries ago. At any given time, more than half a million barrels of sherry are maturing in Jerez's vast aboveground cellars.

GETTING HERE AND AROUND

Jerez is a short way from Seville, with frequent daily trains (journey time is around 1 hour) and buses (1 hour 15 minutes), fewer on weekends. If you're traveling to the city by car, park in one of the city-center lots or at your hotel, as street parking is difficult. Jerez Airport is small and served by a number of flights to destinations in northern Europe and within Spain.

AIRPORT Jerez de la Frontera Airport. ✉ *Ctra. N-IV, Km 628.5, Jerez de la Frontera* ☎ *956/150000* 🌐 *www.aena.es.*

BUS STATION Jerez de la Frontera. ✉ *Pl. de la Estación s/n, Jerez de la Frontera* ☎ *956/149990.*

TAXI Tele Taxi. ✉ *Jerez de la Frontera* ☎ *956/344860, 956/329396.*

TRAIN STATION Jerez de la Frontera. ✉ *Pl. de la Estación s/n, off Calle Diego Fernández Herrera, Jerez de la Frontera* ☎ *912/320320.*

VISITOR INFORMATION

CONTACTS Jerez de la Frontera. ✉ *Edificio Los Arcos, Pl. del Arenal s/n, Jerez de la Frontera* ☎ *956/149863* 🌐 *www.turismojerez.com.*

👁 Sights

Alcázar

CASTLE/PALACE | Once the residence of the caliph of Seville, the 12th-century alcázar and its small octagonal mosque and baths were built for the Moorish governor's private use. The baths have three sections: the *sala fría* (cold room), the larger *sala templada* (warm room), and the *sala caliente* (hot room) for steam baths. In the midst of it all is the 17th-century Palacio de Villavicencio, built on the site of the original Moorish palace. A camera obscura, a lens-and-mirrors device that projects the outdoors onto a large indoor screen, offers a 360-degree view of Jerez. ✉ *Calle Alameda Vieja s/n, Jerez de la Frontera* ☎ *956/149955* 🎫 *€5, free Mon. (1:30–2:30 pm Oct.–June; 4:30–5:30 pm July–Sept.)* 🕒 *Closed after 2:30 pm Oct.–June.*

★ Bodegas Tradición

WINERY | Tucked away on the north side of the old quarter and founded in 1998, this is one of the city's youngest bodegas, but it has the oldest sherry. The five types sit in the casks for at least 20 years—most for longer. Visits (book in advance by phone or email) include a tour of the winery, a lesson in how to pair each sherry type, and a tour of the unique Spanish art collection that includes works by El

Greco, Zurburán, Goya, and Velázquez.
✉ *Pl. de los Cordobeses 3, Jerez de la Frontera* ☎ *956/168628* ⊕ *bodegastradicion.es* 🖾 *€50.*

Catedral de Jerez

CHURCH | Across from the alcázar and around the corner from the González Byass winery, the cathedral has an octagonal cupola and a separate bell tower, as well as Zurbarán's canvas *La Virgen Niña Meditando* (*The Virgin as a Young Girl*). ✉ *Pl. de la Encarnación s/n, Jerez de la Frontera* ☎ *956/169059* 🖾 *€7* ☉ *Closed Sun. mornings.*

González Byass

WINERY | Home of the famous Tío Pepe, with its signature logo of a sherry bottle dressed as a man with a guitar, this is one of the most commercial bodegas, dating back to 1835. The tour (in English) is well organized and includes La Concha, an open-air aging cellar designed by Gustave Eiffel. ✉ *Calle Manuel María González, Jerez de la Frontera* ☎ *956/357016* ⊕ *www.gonzalezbyass.com* 🖾 *From €20.*

Museo Arqueológico

HISTORY MUSEUM | Diving into the maze of streets that form the scruffy San Mateo neighborhood east of the town center, you come to one of Andalusia's best archaeological museums. The collection is strongest on the pre-Roman period, and the star item, found near Jerez, is a Greek helmet dating from the 7th century BC. ✉ *Pl. del Mercado s/n, Jerez de la Frontera* ☎ *956/149560* ⊕ *www.jerez.es/webs-municipales/museo-arqueologico* 🖾 *€5* ☉ *Closed Sun. and Mon.*

★ Plaza de la Asunción

PLAZA/SQUARE | Here on one of Jerez's most intimate squares you can find the Mudejar church of San Dionisio (open 10–noon, Monday–Thursday), patron saint of the city, and the ornate *cabildo municipal* (city hall) with a lovely plateresque façade dating to 1575. ✉ *Jerez de la Frontera.*

★ Real Escuela Andaluza del Arte Ecuestre

(*Royal Andalusian School of Equestrian Art*)

SPORTS VENUE | **FAMILY** | This prestigious school operates on the grounds of the Recreo de las Cadenas, a 19th-century palace. The school was masterminded by Álvaro Domecq in the 1970s. At noon every Tuesday and Thursday (Thursday only in January and February), as well as each Friday August through October, the Cartujana horses—a cross between the native Andalusian workhorse and the Arabian—and skilled riders in 18th-century riding costume demonstrate intricate dressage techniques and jumping in the spectacular show *Cómo Bailan los Caballos Andaluces* (roughly, *The Dancing Horses of Andalusia*). ■**TIP→ Reservations are essential.**

The price of admission depends on how close to the arena you sit; the first two rows are the priciest. At certain other times you can visit the museum, stables, and tack room and watch the horses being schooled. ✉ *Av. Duque de Abrantes s/n, Jerez de la Frontera* ☎ *956/319635* ⊕ *www.realescuela.org* 🖾 *From €24.*

Iglesia de San Miguel

CHURCH | One block from the Plaza del Arenal, near the alcázar, stands the church of San Miguel. Built over the 15th and 16th centuries, its interior illustrates the evolution of Gothic architecture, with various styles mixed into the design. ✉ *Pl. de San Miguel s/n, Jerez de la Frontera* ☎ *662/187511* 🖾 *Free* ☉ *Open for touring 20 mins before mass.*

Sandeman

WINERY | The Sandeman brand of sherry is known for its dashing man-in-a-cape logo. Tours of the sherry bodegas in Jerez give you some insight into his history and let you visit the cellars. Some visitors purchase tapas to have with their sherry tastings. There is also a museum and shop on-site. ✉ *Calle Pizarro 10, Jerez de la Frontera* ☎ *956/151552* ⊕ *www.*

Winery Tours in Jerez 🍴

On a bodega visit, you'll learn about the solera method of blending old wine with new and the importance of the *flor* (yeast that forms on the wine as it ages) in determining the kind of sherry.

Phone ahead for an appointment to make sure you join a group that speaks your language. Admission fees start at €12 (more for extra wine tasting or tapas); tours lasting 60–90 minutes go through the aging cellars, with their endless rows of casks. (You won't see the actual fermenting and bottling, which take place in more modern, less romantic plants outside town.) Finally, you'll be invited to sample generous amounts of pale dry fino, nutty amontillado, rich deep oloroso, and sweet Pedro Ximénez—and, of course, to purchase a few robustly priced bottles in the winery shop.

sandeman.com/visit-us/jerez/sherry-bodegas 🎟 *From €12.*

Yeguada de la Cartuja

FARM/RANCH | This farm just outside Jerez de la Frontera specializes in Carthusian horses. In the 15th century, a Carthusian monastery on this site started the breed for which Jerez and the rest of Spain are now famous. Visits are on Saturday at 11 am and include a full tour of the stables and training areas and a show (allow 2 hours). Book ahead. ✉ *Finca Fuente El Suero, Ctra. Medina Sidonia–El Portal, Km 6.5, Jerez de la Frontera* ☎ *956/162809* 🌐 *yeguadacartuja.com* 🎟 *From €19.*

🍴 Restaurants

★ Albores

$$ | SPANISH | Opposite the city hall, this busy restaurant with swift service has pleasant outdoor seating under orange trees and a modern interior with low lighting. Albores serves innovative, modern dishes with a traditional base. **Known for:** tuna cooked any which way; generous portions (sharing is encouraged; half portions also available); desserts. [$] *Average main: €18* ✉ *Calle Consistorio 12, Jerez de la Frontera* ☎ *956/320266* 🌐 *www.restaurantealbores.com.*

Atuvera

$ | FUSION | Some of the most colorful meals in Andalusia are served inside what were once the stables of a 16th-century palace. Fresh local produce is used to fuse Asian and Mexican flavors in what locals describe as a vibrant explosion of taste. **Known for:** fusion cooking; nice terrace; friendly service. [$] *Average main: €10* ✉ *Calle Ramón de Cala 13, Jerez de la Frontera* ☎ *675/548584* 🌐 *atuverajerez.com* 🕒 *No dinner Sun. Closed Mon.–Wed.*

Bar Juanito

$ | SPANISH | Traditional bars don't come more authentic than Bar Juanito, which has been serving local dishes for more than 70 years and pairs everything, of course, with sherry. You can eat standing at the bar or seated in the pleasant patio restaurant, where there's often live music on Saturday. **Known for:** wide range of sharing plates; artichoke dishes in season (early spring); pork-based stew. [$] *Average main: €14* ✉ *Calle Pescadería Vieja 8–10, Jerez de la Frontera* ☎ *956/334838* 🕒 *No dinner Sun. Closed Mon.–Sun. in July and Aug.*

★ La Carboná

$$$ | **SPANISH** | This eatery has a rustic atmosphere with arches, wooden beams, and a fireplace for winter nights. In summer you can often enjoy live music and sometimes flamenco dancing while you dine. **Known for:** multiple-course sherry-tasting menu; bodega setting; innovative dishes. [$] *Average main: €25* ✉ *Calle San Francisco de Paula 2, Jerez de la Frontera* ☎ *956/347475* 🕒 *No dinner Mon. Closed Tues. and July.*

Venta Esteban

$$ | **SPANISH** | **FAMILY** | This restaurant is slightly off the beaten track but well worth seeking out for traditional Jerez cuisine in a pleasant lively setting. Choose tapas in the bar or à la carte in the spacious and airy dining rooms. **Known for:** seafood; traditional stews; homemade custard. [$] *Average main: €20* ✉ *Calle Colonia de Caulina C.11–03, Jerez de la Frontera* ✣ *Just off Seville hwy. exit* ☎ *956/316067* 🌐 *www.restauranteventaesteban.es.*

Hotels

★ Casa Palacio Maria Luisa

$$$$ | **HOTEL** | Once home to Jerez's gentlemen's club (known as the Casino) and a symbol of the city's sherry heyday, this restored 19th-century mansion is the most comfortable luxury hotel and the only five-star grand-luxe hotel in town. **Pros:** beautifully designed, über-comfortable rooms; excellent service; lovely outside terrace. **Cons:** small pool; expensive breakfast; might be too grandiose for some. [$] *Rooms from: €340* ✉ *Calle Tornería 22, Jerez de la Frontera* ☎ *956/926263* 🌐 *casapalaciomarialuisa.com* 🛏 *21 rooms* 🍴 *No Meals.*

Hotel Doña Blanca

$ | **HOTEL** | Slightly off the main tourist route but still within easy walking distance to attractions, this traditional town-house hotel offers spacious accommodations with some of the best prices in the city. **Pros:** private terrace in some rooms; great value; generously sized rooms. **Cons:** some street noise at night; not right in the city center; might be too basic for some. [$] *Rooms from: €60* ✉ *Calle Bodegas 11, Jerez de la Frontera* ☎ *956/348761* 🌐 *www.hoteldonablanca.com* 🛏 *30 rooms* 🍴 *No Meals.*

Hotel Jerez & Spa

$ | **B&B/INN** | Tastefully furnished, this hacienda-style hotel offers luxury on the outskirts of town. **Pros:** elegant gardens; Italian restaurant on-site; saltwater swimming pool. **Cons:** outside of town center; some areas need updating; breakfast is average. [$] *Rooms from: €100* ✉ *Av. Alcalde Álvaro Domecq, 47, Jerez de la Frontera* ☎ *956/153100* 🌐 *www.hace.es* 🛏 *15 rooms* 🍴 *No Meals.*

Hotel YIT Casa Grande

$ | **HOTEL** | This cozy hotel, right in the city center with all the main attractions on its doorstep, comes complete with its original 1920s Art Nouveau design and period antiques. **Pros:** central location; personalized service; roof terrace. **Cons:** some rooms are dark; decor might not appeal to everyone; some rooms have street noise. [$] *Rooms from: €100* ✉ *Pl. de las Angustias 3, Jerez de la Frontera* ☎ *956/345070* 🌐 *www.hotelcasagrande-jerez.com* 🛏 *15 rooms* 🍴 *No Meals.*

Cádiz

32 km (20 miles) southwest of Jerez, 149 km (92½ miles) southwest of Seville.

With the Atlantic Ocean on three sides, Cádiz is a bustling town that's been shaped by a variety of cultures and has the varied architecture to prove it. Founded as Gadir by Phoenician traders in 1100 BC, Cádiz claims to be the oldest continuously inhabited city in the Western world. Hannibal lived in Cádiz for a time, Julius Caesar first held public office here, and Columbus set out from here on

Just about the whole city turns out for Jerez's Feria del Caballo, and traditional Andalusian costumes are a common sight.

his second voyage, after which the city became the home base of the Spanish fleet. In the 18th century, when the Guadalquivir silted up, Cádiz monopolized New World trade and became the wealthiest port in Western Europe. Most of its buildings—including the cathedral, built in part with wealth generated by gold and silver from the New World—date from this period. The old city is African in appearance and immensely intriguing—a cluster of narrow streets opening onto charming small squares. The golden cupola of the cathedral looms above low white houses, and the whole place has a slightly dilapidated air. Spaniards flock here in February for the Carnival celebrations, and ever more cruise ships visit the harbor, but in general it's not too touristy.

GETTING HERE AND AROUND
Every day, around 18 local trains connect Cádiz with Seville, Puerto de Santa María, and Jerez. There are buses to and from Sanlúcar de Barrameda (7 on weekdays), Arcos de la Frontera (2 daily), and the Costa del Sol (via Seville, 2 daily). A tram (services every half hour) connects Cádiz and Chiclana, and 16 ferry services run daily between the city and Puerto de Santa María. Cádiz is easy to get to and navigate by car. Once there, the old city is easily explored on foot.

BUS STATION Cádiz-Estación de Autobuses. ⊠ Av. de los Astilleros s/n, Cádiz ☏ 956/257415.

TAXI CONTACT Radiotaxi. ⊠ Cádiz ☏ 956/212121.

TRAIN STATION Cádiz. ⊠ Pl. de Sevilla s/n, Cádiz ☏ 912/320320.

VISITOR INFORMATION
CONTACTS Local Tourist Office. ⊠ Paseo de Canalejas s/n, Cádiz ☏ 956/241001 ⊕ turismo.cadiz.es. **Regional Tourist Office.** ⊠ Av. de Ramón de Carranza s/n, Cádiz ☏ 956/203191 ⊕ www.cadizturismo.com.

Cádiz's majestic cathedral, as seen from the Plaza de la Catedral

Sights

Begin your explorations in the Plaza de Mina, a large, leafy square with palm trees and plenty of benches. Look out for the ornamental facade on the Colegio de Arquitectos (College of Architects), on the west side of the square.

Cádiz Cathedral

CHURCH | Five blocks southeast of the Torre Tavira are the gold dome and baroque facade of Cádiz's cathedral, which offers views from atop the Torre del Reloj (Clock Tower) that make the climb to the top worth it. The construction of the building was begun in 1722, when the city was at the height of its power. Cádiz-born composer Manuel de Falla, who died in 1946, is buried in the crypt. The museum, on Calle Arquitecto Acero, displays gold, silver, and jewels from the New World, as well as Enrique de Arfe's processional cross, which is carried in the annual Corpus Christi parades. The cathedral is known as the "New Cathedral" because it supplanted the original neighboring 13th-century structure, which was destroyed by the British in 1592, rebuilt, then rechristened the Iglesia de la Santa Cruz (Church of the Holy Cross). ✉ *Pl. de la Catedral s/n, Cádiz* ☎ *956/286154* 💶 *€7* 🕐 *Closed Sun. morning.*

Gran Teatro Manuel de Falla

HISTORIC SIGHT | Four blocks west of Santa Inés is the Plaza Fragela, overlooked by this amazing neo-Mudejar redbrick building. The classic interior is impressive as well—try to attend a performance. ✉ *Pl. Manuel de Falla s/n, Cádiz* ☎ *956/220828.*

Museo de Cádiz (*Provincial Museum*)

HISTORY MUSEUM | On the east side of the Plaza de Mina is Cádiz's provincial museum. Notable pieces include works by Murillo and Alonso Cano, as well as the *Four Evangelists* and a set of saints by Zurbarán. The archaeological section contains two extraordinary marble Phoenician sarcophagi from the time of this ancient city's birth. ✉ *Pl. de Mina s/n, Cádiz* ☎ *856/105023* 💶 *€2* 🕐 *Closed Sun. afternoon and Mon.*

Museo de las Cortes

HISTORY MUSEUM | Next door to the Oratorio de San Felipe Neri, this small but pleasant museum has a 19th-century mural depicting the establishment of the Constitution of 1812. Its real showpiece, however, is a 1779 ivory-and-mahogany model of Cádiz, with all of the city's streets and buildings in minute detail, looking much as they do now. ⊠ *Calle Santa Inés 9, Cádiz* ☎ *956/221788* ✆ *Free* ◷ *Closed weekends.*

Oratorio de la Santa Cueva

RELIGIOUS BUILDING | A few blocks east of the Plaza de Mina, next door to the Iglesia del Rosario, this oval 18th-century chapel has three frescoes by Goya. On Good Friday, the *Sermon of the Seven Words* is read and Haydn's *Seven Last Words* played. ⊠ *Calle Rosario 10, Cádiz* ☎ *956/222262* ⊕ *cadizsacra.es* ✆ *€5, free Mon.–Thurs. 9:30–10:30 am if you book via the website* ◷ *Closed Mon.*

Oratorio de San Felipe Neri

RELIGIOUS BUILDING | A walk up Calle San José from the Plaza de Mina will bring you to this church, where Spain's first liberal constitution (known affectionately as La Pepa) was declared in 1812. It was here, too, that the Cortes (Parliament) of Cádiz met when the rest of Spain was subjected to the rule of Napoleon's brother, Joseph Bonaparte (more popularly known as Pepe Botella, for his love of the bottle). On the main altar is an *Immaculate Conception* by Murillo, the great Sevillano artist who fell to his death from a scaffold in 1682 while working on his *Mystic Marriage of St. Catherine* in Cádiz's Chapel of Santa Catalina. You can hear Mass in Latin on Sunday at noon. ⊠ *Calle Santa Inés 38, Cádiz* ☎ *956/222262* ✆ *€5* ◷ *Closed Sat. afternoon and Sun.*

Plaza San Francisco

STREET | Near the ayuntamiento is this pretty square surrounded by white-and-yellow houses and filled with orange trees and elegant street lamps. It's especially lively during the evening paseo. ⊠ *Cádiz.*

Roman Theater

RUINS | Next door to the Church of the Holy Cross are the remains of a 1st-century-BC Roman theater, one of the oldest and largest in Spain. The stage is unexcavated (it lies under nearby houses), but you can visit the entrance and large seating area as well as the visitor center. ⊠ *Calle Mesón 11–13, Barrio del Pópulo* ☎ *856/904211* ✆ *Free* ◷ *Closed weekends Oct.–Mar.*

★ Torre Tavira

NOTABLE BUILDING | **FAMILY** | At 150 feet tall, this watchtower is the highest point in the old city. More than a hundred such structures were used by Cádiz ship owners to spot their arriving fleets. A camera obscura gives a good overview of the city and its monuments. The last show is held 30 minutes before closing time. ⊠ *Calle del Marqués del Real Tesoro 10, Cádiz* ☎ *956/212910* ⊕ *www.torretavira.com/en* ✆ *€7* ⚇ *Visits by reservation only.*

Yacimiento Arqueológico Gadir

RUINS | Few Phoenician settlements have survived intact, but excavations underneath the Puppet Museum revealed some of the best-preserved ruins in Southern Europe. You can visit the 9th-century-BC remains and discover eight houses along two cobbled streets, complete with animal hoofprints encased in mud and clay. The site also has the remains of a Roman fish-preserving factory with saltwater pools. ⊠ *Calle de San Miguel 15, Cádiz* ☎ *956/226337* ✆ *Free* ◷ *Closed Sun. afternoon and Mon.*

🍽 Restaurants

★ Casa Manteca

$ | **SPANISH** | Cádiz's most quintessentially Andalusian tavern is in the neighborhood of La Viña, named for the vineyard that once grew here. *Chacina* (Iberian ham or sausage) and *chicharrones de Cádiz* (cold pork) served on waxed paper and washed down with *manzanilla* (sherry from Sanlúcar de Barrameda) are standard fare at the low wooden counter that has served bullfighters and flamenco singers, as well as dignitaries from around the world, since 1953. **Known for:** atmospheric interior; delicious cold cuts; manzanilla sherry. $ *Average main: €10* ⊠ *Calle Corralón de los Carros 66, Cádiz* ☎ *956/213603.*

Código de Barra

$$$$ | SPANISH | The only restaurant with a Michelin star in the city has chef León Griffioen at the helm, placing local produce under the Dutch microscope and creating dishes themed around the history of Cádiz. With just eight tables in minimalist surroundings, the restaurant, decked in black and gray, offers a tasting menu (€60 for 10 dishes, €70 for 13; pairing options available) that comes with several surprises, including an "olive" and "deconstructed" *tortillitas de camarones*—it's one explosion of flavor after another. **Known for:** creative take on traditional local cuisine; excellent-value tasting menus; good and long wine list (ask the staff for pairing suggestions). $ *Average main: €60* ⊠ *Calle San Francisco 7, Cádiz* ☎ *635/533303* ⊕ *restaurantecodigodebarracadiz.com* ☾ *Closed Sun.*

La Candela

$ | SPANISH | A block north of Plaza de la Candelaria and on one of Cádiz's narrow pedestrian streets, La Candela is a good place to try local fare with a modern twist. The salmorejo comes baked with pork loin tartare, the pork cheeks are melt-in-the-mouth tender, and several dishes come tempura-style or have South American touches, such as the sea bass ceviche with tiger's milk and mango. **Known for:** tapas; homemade cheesecake; Spanish-Asian fusion food. $ *Average main: €10* ⊠ *Calle Feduchy 1, Cádiz* ☎ *956/221822.*

Mercado Central de Abastos

$ | SPANISH | With over 170 stalls of fresh produce, Cádiz's main market provides an illuminating insight into the types of local fish and seafood, as well as seasonal treats. It also has a *rincón gastronómico* (gastro-corner) with several stalls serving dishes based on the produce available in the market. **Known for:** informal atmosphere; fresh produce; wide choice of quick bites. $ *Average main: €10* ⊠ *Pl. de la Libertad s/n, Cádiz* ☾ *No dinner Sun. Closed Mon.*

Hotels

Hotel Argantonio

$ | HOTEL | This small family-run hotel in the historic center of town combines traditional style and modern amenities. **Pros:** friendly and helpful staff; great location; good-size bathrooms. **Cons:** rooms in the original building are on the small side; street-facing rooms can be noisy; not easy to find. $ *Rooms from: €110* ⊠ *Calle Argantonio 3, Cádiz* ☎ *956/211640* ⊕ *www.hotelargantonio. com* ⇆ *17 rooms* ❍❙ *No Meals.*

Hotel Patagonia Sur

$$ | HOTEL | With a handy central location just two blocks from the cathedral, this modern hotel offers functional and inexpensive lodging, especially during low season. **Pros:** central location; good value; top-floor rooms have a private terrace. **Cons:** small rooms; street noise can be intrusive; two-night minimum stay in summer. $ *Rooms from: €150* ⊠ *Calle Cobos 11, Cádiz* ☎ *856/174647* ⊕ *hotelpatagoniasur.es* ⇆ *16 rooms* ❍❙ *No Meals.*

Parador de Cádiz

$$$ | HOTEL | With a privileged position overlooking the bay, this parador has spacious public areas and large modern rooms, most with balconies facing the sea. **Pros:** great views of the bay; pool; bright and cheerful. **Cons:** expensive parking; very quiet in the off-season; lacks historic appeal of other paradores. $ *Rooms from: €300* ⊠ *Av. Duque de Nájera 9, Cádiz* ☎ *956/226905* ⊕ *www. parador.es/en/parador-de-cadiz* ⇆ *124 rooms* ❍❙ *No Meals.*

GRANADA AND AROUND

Updated by
Joanna Styles

👁 **Sights**
★★★★★

🍴 **Restaurants**
★★★★☆

🛏 **Hotels**
★★★★☆

💼 **Shopping**
★★★★☆

🍸 **Nightlife**
★★★★☆

WELCOME TO GRANADA AND AROUND

TOP REASONS TO GO

★ **Be seduced by the Alhambra:** Marvel at this extraordinary Moorish delight, a fortress-palace whose patios, courtyards, halls, baths, and gardens rank among the most magnificent in the world.

★ **Lose yourself in time:** Stroll the cobbled alleyways of the Albayzín, the ancient Arab quarter, with its whitewashed façades, churches, convents, and simply stunning views of the Alhambra and the snowcapped Sierra Nevada beyond.

★ **Admire their resting places:** Visit the Capilla Real (Royal Chapel) with the tombs of Spain's greatest monarchs, Isabel and Fernando, under whose watch modern-day Spain was born and the New World was discovered.

★ **Experience the real thing:** Tour the colorful Romani caves in Sacromonte and take in a finger-clicking, foot-tapping flamenco show.

★ **Taste the tapas:** Enjoy a complimentary *tapa* with your drink at any bar in Granada, often more of a mini-meal than a mere mouthful.

Granada is compact and easy to navigate, with the exception of the Albayzín, whose charm lies in losing yourself in its maze of alleyways. Outside the center, prepare for some serious walking in hilly terrain (often on cobbled streets) or take taxis or buses.

1 La Alhambra. Perched on a verdant hill and home to Spain's greatest monument, La Alhambra stands tall over the city, offering panoramic views plus some fine hotels.

2 Realejo. Beneath La Alhambra, narrow cobbled streets and pleasant squares are home to fine palaces and mansions as well as bustling bars and restaurants.

3 Sacromonte. Hilly and riddled with caverns, Sacromonte is the heart of Granada's Romani community and its flamenco spirit.

4 Albayzín. Occupying the hillside opposite La Alhambra, the ancient Moorish quarter offers a labyrinth of whitewashed alleyways, churches, squares with panoramic views, and boutique hotels and restaurants.

5 Centro. Flat and bustling, the center houses commercial Granada with its main shopping streets, leafy squares, and fine architecture including the cathedral and Capilla Real.

6 Priego de Córdoba. An olive farming town famous for its mansions and baroque churches.

7 Baeza. One of the best-preserved old towns in Spain.

8 Úbeda. Slightly larger than Baeza, this town is known for its architecture, artisan crafts, and olive groves. Shop for all your souvenirs here.

9 The Sierra Nevada. You'll find stunning mountain views and Europe's southernmost ski resort about 45 minutes from Granada.

10 The Alpujarras. The southern slopes of the Sierra Nevada have long been loved by artists and writers for their remoteness and stunning views.

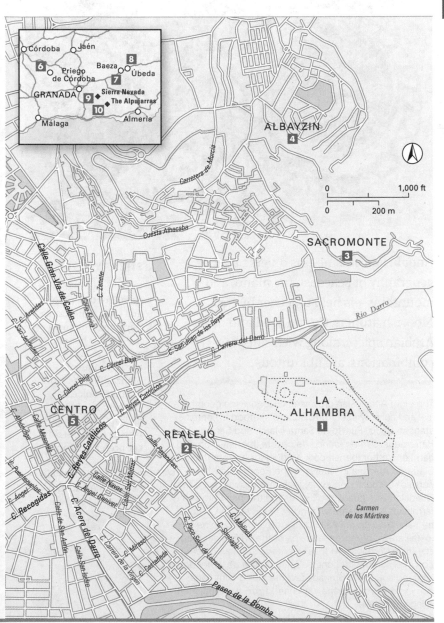

Córdoba   Jaén

6 Priego
de Córdoba   Baeza **8**
GRANADA   **7** Úbeda
9 Sierra Nevada
The Alpujarras
10
Málaga   Almería

ALBAYZIN
4

0 ———————— 1,000 ft
0 ———————— 200 m

Carretera de Murcia

Cuesta Alhacaba

SACROMONTE
3

Rio Darro

Calle Gran Vía de Colón

Calle Elvira

C. Zenete

C. Arandas

San Jerónimo

C. San Juan de los Reyes

C. Carrera del Darro

C. Cárcel Baja

C. Cárcel Baja

C. Reyes Católicos

CENTRO
5

LA
ALHAMBRA
1

C. Almireceros

C. Mesones

REALEJO
2

C. Pavaneras

C. Reyes Católicos

Calle Navas

Calle San Matías

C. Molinos

Carmen
de los Mártires

C. Ángel

C. Puentezuelas

C. Recogidas

C. Ángel Ganivet

C. Acera del Darro

Calle de San Antón

Calle San Isidro

C. Carrera de la Virgen

C. Mirasol

C. Santiago

C. Castañeda

Paseo Salón del Laberna

Paseo de la Bomba

EATING AND DRINKING WELL IN ANDALUSIA

A cool bowl of gazpacho with accompaniments

Andalusian cuisine—as diverse as the geography of seacoast, farmland, and mountains—is held together by its Moorish aromas. Cumin seed and other Arabian spices, along with salty-sweet combinations, are ubiquitous.

The eight Andalusian provinces cover a wide geographical and culinary spectrum. Superb seafood is center stage in Cádiz, Puerto de Santa María, and Sanlúcar de Barrameda. *Jamón ibérico de bellota* (Iberian acorn-fed ham) and other Iberian pork products rule from the Sierra de Aracena in Huelva to the Pedroches Mountains north of Córdoba. In Seville, look for products from the Guadalquivir estuary, the Sierra, and the rich Campiña farmland, all prepared with great creativity. In Córdoba, try *salmorejo cordobés* (a thick gazpacho), *rabo de toro* (oxtail stew), or representatives of the salty-sweet legacy from Córdoba's Moorish heritage such as *cordero con miel* (lamb with honey). Spicy *crema de almendras* (almond soup) is a Granada favorite along with *habas con jamón* (broad beans with ham) from the Alpujarran village of Trevélez.

SHERRY

Dry sherry from Jerez de la Frontera (fino) and from Sanlúcar de Barrameda (manzanilla) share honors as favorite tapas accompaniments. Manzanilla, the more popular choice, is fresher and more delicate, with a slight marine tang. Both are the preferred drinks at Andalusian *ferias* (fairs), particularly in Seville in April and Jerez de la Frontera in May.

COLD VEGETABLE SOUPS

Spain's most popular contribution to world gastronomy after paella may well be gazpacho, a simple peasant soup filled with scraps and garden ingredients and served cold. Tomatoes, cucumber, garlic, oil, bread, and chopped peppers are the ingredients, accompanied by side plates of chopped onion, peppers, garlic, tomatoes, and croutons to be added to taste. Salmorejo cordobés, a thicker cold vegetable soup with the same ingredients but a different consistency, is used to accompany tapas.

MOORISH FLAVORS

Andalusia's 781-year sojourn at the heart of Al-Andalus, the Moorish empire on the Iberian Peninsula, left as many tastes and aromas as mosques and fortresses. Cumin-laced *boquerones en adobo* (marinated anchovies) or the salty-sweet cordero con miel (lamb with honey) are two examples, along with coriander-spiked *espinacas con garbanzos* (spinach with garbanzo beans) and *perdiz con dátiles y almendras* (partridge stewed with dates and almonds). Desserts especially reflect the Moorish legacy in morsels such as *pestiños,* cylinders or twists of fried dough in anise-honey syrup.

Fried calamari with lemon

Crispy fried fish are an Andalusian delicacy.

FRIED FISH

Andalusia is famous for its fried fish, from *pescaito frito* (fried whitebait) to *calamares fritos* (fried squid rings). Andalusians are masters of deep-frying techniques using very hot olive and vegetable oils that produce peerlessly crisp, dry *frituras* (fried seafood); much of Andalusia's finest tapas repertory is known for being served piping hot and crunchy. Look for *tortillita de camarones,* a delicate lacework of tiny fried shrimp.

STEWS

Guisos are combinations of vegetables, with or without meat, cooked slowly over low heat. Rabo de toro is a favorite throughout Andalusia, though Córdoba claims the origin of this dark and delicious stew made from the tail of a fighting bull. The segments of tail are cleaned, browned, and set aside before leeks, onions, carrots, garlic, and bay leaves are stewed in the same pan. Cloves, salt, pepper, a liter of wine, and a half liter of beef broth are added to the stew with the meat, and they're all simmered for two to three hours until the meat is falling off the bone and thoroughly tenderized. *Alboronía,* also known as *pisto andaluz,* is a traditional stew of eggplant, bell peppers, and zucchini.

Nestling below the perennially snowcapped Sierra Nevada and rising majestically from a vast fertile place, Granada proudly offers visitors two jewels in Andalusia's crown: the Alhambra and the tomb of the Catholic Monarchs. The two aesthetics, Moorish and Christian, pervade the entire city in its architecture, cuisine, handicrafts, and people.

The kingdom of Granada dates back to 1013, when it was founded by the Moorish Nasrid dynasty, under whose reign the city prospered as one of the richest in Spain for over four centuries. In 1491, split by internal squabbles, Boabdil, the "Rey Chico" (Boy King) gave Fernando of Aragón his opportunity to claim Granada for Castille. Spurred by Isabel's religious fanaticism, he laid siege to the city for seven months, and on January 2, 1492, Boabdil was forced to surrender the keys of the city.

Side trips from Granada give you the chance to experience some of the finest towns in eastern Andalusia. In the rolling olive groves and high mountains, you'll find gems such as Priego de Córdoba, home to some of the region's most impressive baroque churches; Baeza and Úbeda, both with exceptional examples of Renaissance architecture; the Sierra Nevada, a paradise for mountain walkers and climbers; and the Alpujarras, one of Andalusia's most scenic mountain regions, dotted with white villages.

Planning

When to Go

The best months to go are October and November and April and May. It's blisteringly hot in the summer; if that's your only chance to come, plan on visiting Granada's Sierra Nevada to beat the heat. Autumn catches the cities going about their business, the temperatures are moderate, and you will rarely see a line form.

Getting Here and Around

AIR

Two or three daily flights connect Granada with Madrid and three connect it with Barcelona.

Aeropuerto de Granada. (*Aeropuerto Federico García Lorca*) ✉ *Granada* ☎ *902/404704.*

BUS

Granada's main bus station is at Carretera de Jaén, 3 km (2 miles) northwest of the center of town beyond the end of Avenida de Madrid. Most buses operate from here, except for buses to nearby destinations such as Fuentevaqueros, Viznar, and some buses to Sierra Nevada, which leave from the city center's Plaza del Triunfo near the RENFE station. Luggage lockers (*la consigna*) are available at the main bus and train stations, and you can also leave your luggage at City Locker (⊠ *Plaza de las Descalzas 3*) and Locker in the City (⊠ *Pasaje Conde Alcalá 1*).

Autocares Tocina operates buses between Granada and the Sierra Nevada. ALSA buses run to and from Las Alpujarras (8 times daily), Córdoba (6 times daily), Seville (7 times daily), Málaga (20 times daily), and Jaén, Baeza, Úbeda, Cazorla, Almería, Almuñécar, and Nerja (several times daily).

In Granada, airport buses (€3) run between the center of town and the airport, leaving roughly every hour from 7 am to 8 pm from the Palacio de Congresos and making a few other stops along the way to the airport. Times are listed at the bus stop.

Granada has an extensive public bus network within the city. You can buy 5-, 10-, and 20-trip discount passes on the buses and at newsstands. The single-trip fare is €1.40. Granada Cards include bus trips plus guaranteed tickets for the Alhambra and other main monuments (without having to wait in lines). The card costs from €47, saving at least a third on regular prices. You can purchase the cards online (⊕ *www.granadatur.com/granada-card*) or by phone (☎ *858/889990, daily 9 am–8 pm*) in advance of your visit; you can download them on your cell phone or print at home or at the tourist office.

ALSA. ☎ *902/422242* ⊕ *www.alsa.es.*
Granada Bus Station. ⊠ *Ctra. de Jaén s/n, Granada* ☎ *902/422242.*

CAR

With the exception of parts of the Alpujarras, most roads in this region are smooth, and touring by car is one of the most enjoyable ways to see the countryside. Local tourist offices can advise about scenic drives.

TAXI

Taxis are plentiful and may be hailed on the street or from specified taxi stands. Fares are reasonable, and meters are strictly used; the minimum fare is about €4. You are not required to tip taxi drivers, although rounding off the amount is appreciated. Uber is available in Granada and Baeza.

Expect to pay around €25–€35 for cab fare from the airport to the city center.

Taxi Genil. ⊠ *Granada* ☎ *958/132323.* **Pide Taxi Granada.** ⊠ *Granada* ☎ *958/280000.*

TRAIN

There are regular trains from Seville and Almería, as well as a thrice-daily fast service from Málaga, taking 75 minutes. A faster service to Seville (2 hours 20 minutes) is expected to come into service in mid-2023 and trains to Málaga will take 10 minutes less. There are several daily trains from Madrid, Valencia, and Barcelona.

Train Station. ⊠ *Av. de los Andaluces s/n, Granada* ☎ *912/320320.*

Restaurants

Eating out is an intrinsic part of the Andalusian lifestyle. Whether it's sharing some tapas with friends over a pre-lunch drink or a three-course à la carte meal, many Andalusians eat out at some point during the day. Unsurprisingly, there are literally thousands of bars and restaurants throughout the region catering to all budgets and tastes. Note that bars in Granada tend to serve a free tapa with every drink.

At lunchtime, check out the *menús del día* (daily menus) offered by many restaurants, usually three courses and excellent value (expect to pay €10–€15, depending on the type of restaurant and location). Roadside restaurants, known as *ventas,* usually provide good food in generous portions and at reasonable prices. Be aware that many restaurants add a service charge (*cubierto*), which can be as much as €3 per person, and some restaurant prices don't include value-added tax (*impuesto sobre el valor añadido/I.V.A.*) at 10%. Note also that restaurants with tasting menus (*menús de degustación*) usually require everyone at the table to have the menu.

Andalusians tend to eat later than their fellow Spaniards: lunch is served from 2 to 4 pm, and dinner starts at 9 pm (10 pm in the summer). In cities, many restaurants are closed Sunday nights, and fish restaurants tend to close on Mondays. In inland towns and cities, some restaurants close for all of August.

Restaurant reviews have been shortened. For full information, visit Fodors. com.

Hotels

The Parador de Granada, next to the Alhambra, is a magnificent way to enjoy Granada. Hotels on the Alhambra hill, especially the parador, must be reserved far in advance. Lodging establishments in Granada's city center, around the Puerta Real and Acera del Darro, can be unbelievably noisy, so if you're staying there, ask for a room toward the back. Though Granada has plenty of hotels, it can be difficult to find lodging during peak tourist season (Easter through late October).

Rental accommodations bookable on portals such as Airbnb are popular in large towns and cities, although quality varies—so double-check reviews before you book.

Not all hotel prices include value-added tax (I.V.A.) and the 10% surcharge may be added to your final bill. Check when you book.

Hotel reviews have been shortened. For full information, visit Fodors.com.

What It Costs in Euros			
$	$$	$$$	$$$$
RESTAURANTS			
under €18	€18–€24	€25–€30	over €30
HOTELS			
under €125	€125–€200	€201–€300	over €300

Tours

Riding Andalucia
SPECIAL-INTEREST TOURS | This is an established Alpujarras equestrian agency that organizes horseback riding in the Sierra Nevada. ⊠ *Calle Ermita 11, Bubión* 🕾 *958/763135* ⊕ *ridingandalucia.com* 🖃 *Rides from €30, tours from €945.*

Cycling Country
BICYCLE TOURS | For information about cycling tours around Granada (Andalusia and Spain) that are 1–10 days long, contact this company run by husband-and-wife team Geoff Norris and Maggi Jones in a town about 55 km (34 miles) away. ⊠ *Calle Salmerones 18, Alhama de Granada* 🕾 *958/360655* ⊕ *cyclingcountry. com* 🖃 *From €50.*

Glovento Sur
AIR EXCURSIONS | Up to five people at a time are taken on balloon trips above Granada and Guadix. ⊠ *Cuesta de San Gregorio 25, Albaicín* 🕾 *958/290316* ⊕ *www.gloventosur.com* 🖃 *From €175.*

Granada Tapas Tours
GUIDED TOURS | Long-time British resident Gayle Mackie offers a range of tapas tours lasting up to three hours. ⊠ *Granada* 🕾 *619/444984* ⊕ *www.*

granadatapastours.com ✉ *From €50, including 6 tapas.*

Nevadensis

GUIDED TOURS | Based in the Alpujarras, Nevadensis leads guided hiking, climbing, and skiing tours of the Sierra Nevada. Note that prices are per group. ✉ *Pl. de la Libertad s/n, Pampaneira* ☎ *659/109662* ⊕ *nevadensis.com* ✉ *From €120 (for two people).*

Visitor Information

Municipal Tourist Office. ✉ *Pl. del Carmen 9, Centro* ☎ *958/248280* ⊕ *www.granadatur.com.* **Provincial Tourist Office.** ✉ *Pl. de Santa Ana s/n, Centro* ☎ *958/575202* ⊕ *www.turgranada.es.*

Granada

Granada perches on three hills: the reddish Alhambra palace dominates the trio and the city skyline; on the opposite side, across the small Darro River, sprawls the Albayzín, Granada's historic Moorish quarter where time seems to have come to a standstill; and on the third hill sits the Sacromonte, studded with ancient caves and home to the city's Romani and flamenco.

All three areas are well worth exploring. The Alhambra ranks as the top must-see and merits a whole day of your visit. If your stay is longer, aim to tour the palace at night too. The Albayzín is an area best appreciated by a leisurely stroll, and Sacromonte is an interesting detour before you descend the hills to the historic center below.

The maze of streets that make up the center harbor a bustling hub of commercial activity, yet another legacy of Granada's Moorish past. The main shopping streets, centering on the Puerta Real (Royal Gate), are the Gran Vía de Colón, Reyes Católicos, Zacatín, and

Recogidas. Most antiques shops are on Cuesta de Elvira and Alcaicería—off Reyes Católicos. Cuesta de Gomérez, on the way up to the Alhambra, also has several handicrafts shops and guitar workshops. Handicrafts have a distinct Moorish air, present in the ceramics, marquetry (especially the *taraceas*, wooden boxes with inlaid tiles on their lids), woven textiles, and various wares made of silver, brass, and copper.

La Alhambra

⦿ Sights

★ **Alhambra**

CASTLE/PALACE | With more than 2.7 million visitors a year, the Alhambra is Spain's most popular attraction. The palace is an endless intricate conglomeration of patios, arches, and cupolas made from wood, plaster, and tile; lavishly colored and adorned with marquetry and ceramics in geometric patterns; and topped by delicate frothy profusions of lacelike stucco and *mocárabes* (ornamental stalactites).

Construction of the Alhambra began in 1238 by Mohammed ibn al-Ahmar, the first king of the Nasrids. The great citadel once comprised a complex of houses, schools, baths, barracks, and gardens surrounded by defense towers and seemingly impregnable walls. Today, only the Alcazaba (Citadel) and the Palacios Nazaríes, built chiefly by Yusuf I (1334–54) and his son Mohammed V (1354–91), remain.

Across from the main entrance is the original fortress, the Alcazaba. Its ruins are dominated by the Torre de la Vela (Watchtower); from its summit you can see the Albayzín to the north; to the northeast, the Sacromonte; and to the west, the cathedral. The tower's great bell was once used, by both the Moors and the Christians, to announce the

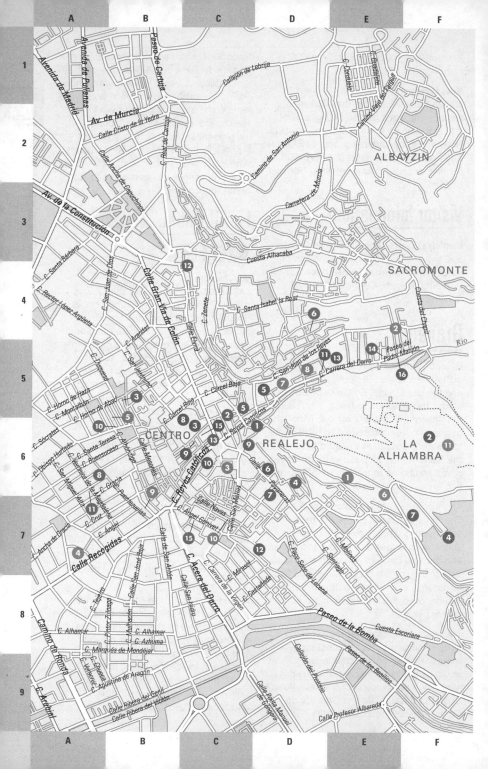

Granada

Sights ▼

1 Abadía del Sacromonte **I3**
2 Alhambra **F6**
3 Capilla Real **C6**
4 Carmen de los Mártires **F7**
5 Casa de los Pisa **D5**
6 Casa de los Tiros **D6**
7 Casa-Museo de Manuel de Falla **F7**
8 Cathedral **C6**
9 Centro José Guerrero ... **C6**
10 Corral del Carbón **C6**
11 El Bañuelo **D5**
12 El Cuarto Real **D7**
13 Museo Arqueológico **E5**
14 Museo Cuevas del Sacromonte **G3**
15 Palacio Madraza **C6**
16 Paseo del Padre Manjón **E5**

Restaurants ▼

1 Bar Los Diamantes **D6**
2 Bodegas Castañeda **C5**
3 Café Botánico **B5**
4 Damasqueros **D6**
5 El Mercader **C5**
6 El Trillo **D4**
7 hicuri **D6**
8 La Bodega de Antonio **A6**
9 La Brujidera **C6**
10 Oliver **B6**
11 Om-Kalsum **A6**
12 Paprika **C4**
13 Pastelería López-Mezquita **C6**
14 Ruta del Azafrán **E5**
15 Tinta Fina **C7**

Hotels ▼

1 Carmen de la Alcubilla del Caracol **E6**
2 Casa Morisca **F4**
3 Gar Anat Hotel Boutique **C6**
4 Hospes Palacio de los Patos **A7**
5 Hostal Rodri **B5**
6 Hotel Alhambra Palace **E6**
7 Hotel Casa 1800 .... **D5**
8 Hotel Palacio de Santa Inés **D5**
9 Hotel Párraga Siete **B7**
10 Palacio de los Navas **C7**
11 Parador de Granada **F6**

Calle Siete Cuestas

Camino del Sacromonte

Darro

0 ——————— 1,000 ft
0 ——————— 200 m

Camino de la Silla del Moro

Carmen de los Mártires

Paseo de la Sabica

Av. Santa María de la Alhambra

Paseo de las Palmas

Carretera de la Sierra

KEY

● Exploring Sights
● Restaurants
● Hotels

opening and closing of the irrigation system on Granada's great plain.

A wisteria-covered walkway leads to the heart of the Alhambra, the Palacios Nazaríes, sometimes also called the Casa Real (Royal Palace). Here, delicate apartments, lazy fountains, and tranquil pools contrast vividly with the hulking fortifications outside, and the interior walls are decorated with elaborately carved inscriptions from the Koran. The Palacios Nazaríes are divided into three sections. The first is the *mexuar,* where business, government, and palace administration were headquartered. These chambers include the Oratorio (Oratory) and the Cuarto Dorado (Golden Room); gaze down over the Albayzín and Sacromonte from their windows. The second section is the *serrallo,* a series of state rooms where the sultans held court and entertained their ambassadors. In the heart of the serallo is the Patio de los Arrayanes (Court of the Myrtles), with a long goldfish pool. At its northern end, in the Salón de Embajadores (Hall of the Ambassadors)—which has a magnificent cedar door—King Boabdil signed the terms of surrender and Queen Isabel received Christopher Columbus.

The third and final section of the Palacios Nazaríes is the harem, which in its time was entered only by the sultan, his wives, the rest of his family, and their most trusted servants, most of them eunuchs. To reach it, pass through the Sala de los Mocárabes (Hall of the Ornamental Stalactites); note the splendid, though damaged, ceiling and the elaborate stalactite-style stonework in the arches above. The Patio de los Leones (Court of the Lions) is the heart of the harem. From the fountain in the center, 12 lions, thought to represent the months or signs of the zodiac, look out at you. Four streams flow symbolically to the four corners of the cosmos and more literally to the surrounding state apartments. The lions and fountain were restored in 2012 and the Court was paved with white marble as it would originally have been.

The Sala de los Abencerrajes (Hall of the Moors), on the south side of the palace, may be the Alhambra's most beautiful gallery, with its fabulous ornate ceiling and a star-shape cupola reflected in the pool below. Here Boabdil's father is alleged to have massacred 16 members of the Abencerrajes family—whose chief was the lover of his favorite daughter, Zoraya—and piled their bloodstained heads in the font. The Sala de los Reyes (Hall of the Kings, fully restored in 2017) lies on the patio's east side, decorated with ceiling frescoes thought to be the work of a visiting Christian Spaniard and painted during the last days of the Moors' tenure. To the north, the Sala de las Dos Hermanas (Hall of the Two Sisters) was Zoraya's abode. Its stuccoed ceiling is done in an intricate honeycomb pattern. Note the symmetrically placed patterned pomegranates on the walls.

The Baño de Comares (Comares Baths, aka the Royal Baths), the Alhambra's semi-subterranean bathhouse, is where the sultans' favorites luxuriated in brightly tiled pools beneath star-shape pinpoints of light from the ceiling above. The main rooms in the baths were fully restored in 2017 but are rarely open to visitors for conservation reasons, although you can glimpse their finery from the entrance.

The Renaissance Palacio de Carlos V (Palace of Carlos V), with a perfectly square exterior but a circular interior courtyard, is where the sultans' private apartments once stood. Designed by Pedro Machuca—a pupil of Michelangelo—and begun in 1526, the palace once was the site of bullfights and mock tournaments. Today its acoustics are perfect for the summer symphony concerts held during the Festival Internacional de Música y Danza de Granada.

A part of the building houses the Museo de la Alhambra (Museum of the Alhambra), devoted to Islamic art. Upstairs is the more modest Museo de Bellas Artes (Fine Arts Museum). You can visit the Palace of Carlos V and the museums independently of the Alhambra.

Over on the Cerro del Sol (Hill of the Sun) is the Generalife, ancient summer palace of the Nasrid kings. Its name comes from the Arabic *gennat al-arif* (garden of the architect), and its terraces and promenades grant incomparable views of the city that stretch to the distant lowlands. During the summer's International Festival of Music and Dance, stately cypresses serve as the backdrop for evening ballets in the Generalife amphitheater. Between the Alhambra and Generalife is the 16th-century Convento de San Francisco, one of Spain's most luxurious paradores.

■ TIP→ Don't forget to visit the "Area of the Month"—each month one of the parts usually closed to visitors is open.

Allow a good half-day for your visit, a whole day if you have time. Note that if you book morning tickets for the Palacios Nazaríes, you must enter all parts of the Alhambra before 2 pm. If you book afternoon tickets, you'll not be able to access any part of the Alhambra (other than the museums) before 2 pm. ✉ *Cuesta de Gomérez s/n, Alhambra* ☎ *858/889002 tickets, 958/027971 information* 🌐 *tickets.alhambra-patronato.es/en* 🎫 *From €2, Museo de la Alhambra and Palacio de Carlos V free* 🕒 *Museo de Bellas Artes and Museo de la Alhambra closed Mon.*

Carmen de los Mártires
HISTORIC HOME | Up the hill from the Hotel Alhambra Palace, this turn-of-the-20th-century *carmen* (private villa) and its gardens—the only area open to tourists—are like a Generalife in miniature. ✉ *Paseo de los Mártires s/n, Alhambra* ☎ *958/849103* 🎫 *Free.*

Casa-Museo de Manuel de Falla
HISTORIC HOME | The composer Manuel de Falla (1876–1946) lived and worked for many years in this rustic house tucked into a charming hillside lane with lovely views of the Alpujarras. In 1986, Granada paid homage to him by naming its new concert hall (down the street from the Carmen de los Mártires) the Auditorio Manuel de Falla. From this institution, fittingly, you have a view of his little white house. Note the bust in the small garden: it's placed where the composer once sat to enjoy the sweeping vista. ✉ *Calle Antequeruela Alta 11, Alhambra* ☎ *958/222189* 🎫 *€3* 🕒 *Closed Mon.*

Hotels

★ Carmen de la Alcubilla del Caracol
$$ | **B&B/INN** | In a traditional Granadino villa on the slopes of the Alhambra, this privately run lodging is one of Granada's most stylish hotels. **Pros:** great views; bright airy rooms; walking distance to the Alhambra. **Cons:** difficult parking; slightly out of town; tough climb in hot weather. [$] *Rooms from: €180* ✉ *Calle Aire Alta 12, Alhambra* ☎ *958/215551* 🌐 *www.alcubilladelcaracol.com* 🕒 *Closed mid-July–Aug.* 🛏 *7 rooms* 🍴 *No Meals.*

Hotel Alhambra Palace
$$$ | **HOTEL** | Built by a local duke in 1910, this neo-Moorish hotel is on leafy grounds at the back of the Alhambra hill and has a very *Arabian Nights* interior (think orange-and-brown overtones, multicolor tiles, and Moorish-style arches and pillars). **Pros:** bird's-eye views; location near the Alhambra; historical ambiance. **Cons:** steep climb up from Granada; standard rooms on the small side; some rooms look a little tired. [$] *Rooms from: €270* ✉ *Pl. Arquitecto García de Paredes 1, Alhambra* ☎ *958/221468* 🌐 *www.h-alhambrapalace.es* 🛏 *126 rooms* 🍴 *No Meals.*

★ Parador de Granada
$$$$ | **HOTEL** | This is Spain's most expensive and most popular parador, right

within the walls of the Alhambra. **Pros:** good location for the Alhambra; lovely interiors; garden restaurant. **Cons:** no views in some rooms; removed from city life; very expensive. [$] *Rooms from: €450* ✉ *Calle Real de la Alhambra s/n, Alhambra* ☎ *958/221440* 🌐 *paradores.es/es/parador-de-granada* 🛏 *40 rooms* 🍴 *No Meals.*

Shopping

Tienda Librería de la Alhambra (*Alhambra Shop and Bookshop*)
SOUVENIRS | Packed with exquisite artisan and design objects, all Alhambra-themed, and an extensive range of history and art books, the official Alhambra shop makes a great place to shop for souvenirs and presents. Shipping service available from the shop or online. ✉ *Calle Reyes Católicos 40, Centro* 🌐 *alhambratienda.es.*

Realejo

Sights

Casa de los Tiros
HISTORIC HOME | This 16th-century palace, adorned with the coat of arms of the Grana Venegas family who owned it, was named House of the Shots for the musket barrels that protrude from its facade. The stairs to the upper-floor displays are flanked by portraits of grim Spanish royals, from Fernando and Isabel to Felipe IV. The highlight is the carved wooden ceiling in the Cuadra Dorada (Hall of Gold), adorned with gilded lettering and portraits of royals and knights. Old lithographs, engravings, and photographs show life in Granada in the 19th and early 20th centuries. ✉ *Calle Pavaneras 19, Realejo-San Matías* ☎ *600/143175* ✉ *museocasadelostiros.ccul@juntadeandalucia.es* 🎟 *€2* 🕒 *Closed Mon.*

El Cuarto Real
NOTABLE BUILDING | Just a block away from Casa de los Tiros is the beautifully restored El Cuarto Real, a 13th-century Nasrid palace which has decorations almost identical to the Alhambra. Only the fortified tower remains standing with its exquisite *qubba* (reception room) with stunning walls and ceiling motifs. The adjoining modern extension houses temporary art exhibitions, and the formal gardens make a peaceful place to rest. ✉ *Pl. de los Campos 6, Realejo-San Matías* ☎ *958/849111* 🎟 *€2* 🕒 *Closed Sun. afternoon and Mon.*

Restaurants

★ **Damasqueros**
$$$$ | **SPANISH** | The modern wood-paneled dining room and warm lighting form the perfect setting for the creative Andalusian cuisine cooked here by local chef Lola Marín, who learned her trade with some of Spain's top chefs, such as Martín Berasategui. The tasting menu changes weekly and always includes in-season produce in its six courses (cold and hot starters, fish, meat, and dessert). **Known for:** fresh local produce; wine pairing; service. [$] *Average main: €55* ✉ *Calle Damasqueros 3, Realejo-San Matías* ☎ *958/210550* 🌐 *www.damasqueros.com* 🕒 *Closed Mon. No dinner Sun.*

hicuri
$ | **VEGETARIAN** | Even if you aren't a vegan, the plant-based menu won't disappoint at this quirky restaurant, located just a block east of Casa de los Tiros. You'll find a good choice of food—there are even four types of vegan burgers with hand-cut French fries—while firm favorites with regulars include the vegetable lasagna and seitan cordon bleu. **Known for:** choice of vegan food; lunchtime menu; quirky artwork. [$] *Average main: €12* ✉ *Pl. de los Girones 4, Realejo-San Matías* ☎ *858/987473* 🌐 *www.restaurantehicuri-artvegan.com* 🕒 *Closed Sun.*

Continued on page 292

ALHAMBRA: PALACE-FORTRESS

 Floating mirage-like on its promontory overlooking Granada, the mighty and mysterious Alhambra shimmers vermilion in the clear mountain air, with the white peaks of the Sierra Nevada rising behind it. This sprawling palace-fortress, named from the Arabic for "red citadel" (*al-Qal'ah al-Hamra*), was the last bastion of the 800-year Moorish presence on the Iberian Peninsula. Composed of royal residential quarters, court chambers, baths, and gardens, surrounded by defense towers and massive walls, the Alhambra is an architectual gem where Moorish kings worked and played—and murdered their enemies.

LOOK UP

Among the stylistic elements you can see in the Alhambra are **Arabesque** geometrical designs, and elaborate **Mocárabe** arches.

Built of perishable materials, the Alhambra was meant to be forever replenished and replaced by succeeding generations. The Patio de los Leones' (above) has recently been restored to its original appearance.

INSIDE THE FORTRESS

More than 3 million annual visitors come to the Alhambra today, making it Spain's top attraction. Vistors revel in the palace's architectural wonders, most of which had to be restored after the alterations made after the Christian reconquest of southern Spain in 1492 and the damage from an 1821 earthquake. Incidentally, Napoléon's troops commandeered the site in 1812 with intent to level it but their attempts were foiled.

The courtyards, patios, and halls offer an ethereal maze of Moorish arches, columns, and domes containing intricate stucco carvings and patterned ceramic tiling. The intimate arcades, fountains, and light-reflecting pools throughout are identified in the ornamental inscriptions as physical renderings of paradise taken from the Koran and Islamic poetry. The contemporary visitor to this dreamlike space feels the fleeting embrace of a culture that brought its light to a world emerging from medieval darkness.

ARCHITECTURAL TERMS

Arabesque: An ornament or decorative style that employs flower, foliage, or fruit, and sometimes geometrical, animal, and figural outlines to produce an intricate pattern of interlaced lines.

Mocárabe: A decorative element of carved wood or plaster based on juxtaposed and hanging prisms resembling stalactites. Sometimes called *muquarna* (honeycomb vaulting), the impression is similar to a beehive and the "honey" has been described as light.

Mozárabe: Sometimes confused with Mocárabe, the term Mozárabe refers to Christians living in Moorish Spain. Thus, Christian artistic styles or recourses in Moorish architecture (such as the paintings in the Sala de los Reyes) are also identified as *mozárabe*, or, in English, mozarabic.

Mudéjar: This word refers to Moors living in Christian Spain. Moorish artistic elements in Christian architecture, such as horseshoe arches in a church, also are referred to as Mudéjar.

ALHAMBRA'S ARCHITECTURAL HIGHLIGHTS

The **columns** used in the construction of the Alhambra are unique, with extraordinarily slender cylindrical shafts, concave base moldings, and carved rings decorating the upper extremities. The capitals have simple cylindrical bases under prism-shaped heads decorated in a variety of vegetal motifs. Nearly all of these columns support false arches constructed purely for decorative purposes. The 124 columns surrounding the Patio de los Leones (Court of the Lions) are the best examples.

Court of the Lions

Cursive epigraphy is used to quote the Koran and Arabic poems. Considered the finest example of this are the Ibn-Zamrak verses that decorate the walls of the Sala de las Dos Hermanas.

Cursive epigraphy

Glazed ceramic tiles covered with geometrical patterns in primary colors cover the walls of the Alhambra with a profusion of styles and shapes. Red, blue, and yellow are the colors of magic in Sufi tradition, while green is the life-giving color of Islam.

Ceramic tiles

The **horseshoe arch**, widening before rounding off with lower ends extending around the circle until they begin to converge, was the quintessential Moorish architectural innovation, used not only for aesthetic and decorative purposes but because it allowed greater height than the classical, semicircular arch inherited from the Greeks and Romans. The horseshoe arch also had a mystical significance in recalling the shape of the *mihrab*, the prayer niche in the *qibla* wall of a mosque indicating the direction of prayer and suggesting a door to Mecca or to paradise. Horseshoe arches and arcades are found throughout the Alhambra.

Gate of Justice

The Koran describes paradise as "gardens underneath which rivers flow," and **water** is used as a practical and ornamental architectural element throughout the Alhambra. Whether used musically, as in the canals in the Patio de los Leones or visually, as in the reflecting pool of the Patio de los Arrayanes, water is used to enhance light, enlarge spaces, or provide musical background for a desert culture in love with the beauty and oasis-like properties of hydraulics in all its forms.

Alhambra fountains

The Alcazaba was built chiefly by Nasrid kings in the 1300s.

LAY OF THE LAND

The complex has three main parts: the Alcazaba, the Palacio Nazaríes (Nasrid Royal Palace), and the Generalife. Across from the main entrance is the original fortress, the **Alcazaba**. Here, the watchtower's great bell was once used to announce the opening and closing of the irrigation system on Granada's great plain.

A wisteria-covered walkway leads to the heart of the Alhambra, the **Palacios Nazaríes**. Here, delicate apartments, lazy fountains, and tranquil pools contrast vividly with the hulking fortifications outside. It is divided into three sections: the *mexuar*, where business, government, and palace administration were headquartered; the *serrallo*, a series of state rooms where the sultans held court and entertained their ambassadors; and the *harem*, which in its time was entered only by the sultan, his family, and their most trusted servants, most of them eunuchs. Nearby is the Renaissance **Palacio de Carlos V** (Palace of Charles V), featuring a perfectly square exterior but a circular interior courtyard. Designed by Pedro Machuca, a pupil of Michelangelo, it is where the sultan's private apartments once stood. Part of the building houses the free **Museo de la Alhambra**, devoted to Islamic art. Upstairs is the more modest **Museo de Bellas Artes**.

Over on Cerro del Sol (Hill of the Sun) is **Generalife**, the ancient summer palace of the Nasrid kings.

TIMELINE

1238 First Nasrid king, Ibn el-Ahmar, begins Alhambra.

1391 Nasrid Palaces is completed.

1492 Boabdil surrenders Granada to Ferdinand and Isabella, parents of King Henry VIII's first wife, Catherine of Aragon.

1524 Carlos V begins Renaissance Palace.

1812 Napoléonic troops arrive with plans to destroy Alhambra.

1814 The Duke of Wellington sojourns here to escape the pressures of the Peninsular War.

1829 Washington Irving lives on the premises and writes Tales of the *Alhambra*, reviving interest in the crumbling palace.

1862 Granada municipality begins Alhambra restoration that continues to this day.

ALHAMBRA'S PASSAGES OF TIME

From Columbus's commissioning to a bloody murder, historic events as well as everyday affairs happened between these walls.

PALACIOS NAZARÍAES (NASRID ROYAL PALACE)

Torre de Comares ❷

Torre de los Punales

Salón de Embajadores ❶

Patio de la Reja

Oratorio / Cuarto Dorado

Sala de la Barca ❸

Baño de Comares ❹

Patio de Mexuar

Patio del Cuarto Dorado

MEXUAR

SERRALLO

Patio de Machuca

Patio de los Arrayanes

← TO ALCAZABA

ENTRANCE

0 — 10 yards
0 — 10 meters

Sala de los Mocárabes

PALACIO DE CARLOS V

ROYAL CHAPEL

Tower of Comares and Patio de los Arrayanes

❶ In **El Salón de Embajadores**, Boabdil drew up his terms of surrender, and Christopher Columbus secured royal support for his historic voyage in 1492. The carved wooden ceiling is a portrayal of the seven Islamic heavens, with six rows of stars topped by a seventh-heaven cupulino or micro-cupola.

❷ **Torre de Comares**, a lookout in the corner of this hall is where Carlos V uttered his famous line, "Ill-fated the man who lost all this."

❸ Mistakenly named from the Arabic word *baraka* (divine blessing), **Sala de la Barca** has a carved wooden ceiling often described as an inverted boat.

Sala de los Reyes

7 Shhh, don't tell a secret here. In the **Sala de los Ajimeces**, a whisper in one corner can be clearly heard from the opposite corner.

8 In the **Sala de las Dos Hermanas**, twin slabs of marble embedded in the floor are the "sisters," though Washington Irving preferred the story of a pair of captive Moorish beauties.

9 In the **Patio de Los Leones** (Court of the Lions), a dozen crudely crafted lions (restored to their former glory in 2012) support the fountain at the center of this elegant courtyard, representing the signs of the zodiac sending water to the four corners.

10 In the **Sala de los Abencerrajes**, Muley Hacen (father of Boabdil) murdered the male members of the Abencerraje family in revenge for their chief's seduction of his daughter Zoraya. The rusty stains in the fountain are said to be bloodstains left by the pile of Abencerraje heads.

The star-shaped cupola, reflected in the pool, is considered the Alhambra's most beautiful example of stalactite or

honeycomb vaulting. The octagonal dome over the room is best viewed at sunset when the 16 small windows atop the dome admit sharp, low sunlight that refracts kaleidoscopically through the beehive-like prisms.

11 In the **Sala de los Reyes**, the ceiling painting depicts the first 10 Nasrid rulers. It was painted by a Christian artist since Islamic artists were not allowed to usurp divine power by creating human or animal figures.

The overhead painting of the knight rescuing his lady from a savage man portrays chivalry, a concept introduced to Europe by Arabic poets.

12 The terraces of **Generalife** grant incomparable views of the city.

Generalife gardens

Peinador de la Reina **5**

Apartamientos de Carlos V

Patio de Lindaraja

HAREM

Mirador de Daraxa **6**

Sala de las Dos Hermanas **8**

Sala de los Ajimeces **7**

Patio de los Leones **9**

Sala de los Reyes **11**

Cistern

Sala de los Abencerrajes **10**

TO JARDINES DEL PARTAL GENERALIFE **12**

4 The **Baño de Comares** is where the sultan's favorites luxuriated in brightly tiled pools beneath star-shape pinpoints of light from the ceiling above.

5 **El Peinador de la Reina**, a nine-foot-square room atop a small tower was the Sultana's boudoir. The perforated marble slab was used to

infiltrate perfumes while the queen performed her toilette. Washington Irving wrote his *Tales of the Alhambra* in this romantic tree-house-like perch.

6 Sultana Zoraya often found refuge in this charming little balcony (**Mirador de Daraxa**) overlooking the Lindaraja garden.

Hotels

Gar Anat Hotel Boutique
$$ | **HOTEL** | Once a humble hostel on the Granada leg of the Camino de Santiago pilgrimage route, this restored 17th-century palace now offers stylish boutique accommodation. **Pros:** eclectic decor; central location; generous breakfast. **Cons:** street noise can be intrusive; some rooms small and dark; slight challenge to find by car. [$] *Rooms from: €175* ✉ *Placeta de Peregrinos 1, Realejo-San Matías* ☎ *958/225528* 🌐 *www.hotelgaranat.com* 🛏 *15 rooms* 🍴 *No Meals.*

Sacromonte

The third of Granada's three hills, the Sacromonte rises behind the Albayzín and is covered with prickly pear cacti and riddled with caverns. The Sacromonte has long been notorious as a domain of Granada's Romani and thus a den of thieves and scam artists, but its reputation is largely undeserved. The quarter is more like a quiet Andalusian *pueblo* (village) than a rough neighborhood.

Many of the quarter's colorful *cuevas* (caves) have been restored as middle-class homes, and some of the old spirit lives on in a handful of *zambras* (flamenco performances in caves, which are garishly decorated with brass plates and cooking utensils). These shows differ from formal flamenco shows in that the performers mingle with you, usually dragging one or two onlookers onto the floor for an improvised dance lesson. Ask your hotel to book you a spot on a cueva tour, which usually includes a walk through the neighboring Albayzín and a drink at a tapas bar in addition to the zambra.

Sights

Abadía del Sacromonte
CAVE | The caverns on Sacromonte are thought to have sheltered early Christians. In the 15th century, treasure hunters found bones inside and assumed they belonged to San Cecilio, the city's patron saint. Thus, the hill was sanctified—*sacro monte* (holy mountain)—and this abbey was built on its summit. Audio guides are available in English. ✉ *C. del Sacromonte s/n, Sacromonte* ☎ *958/221445* 🌐 *abadiasacromonte.org* 🎫 *€5.* .

Museo Cuevas del Sacromonte
OTHER MUSEUM | This ethnographical museum shows how people lived in this area, and the rest of this interesting complex looks at Granada's flora and fauna. During the summer months, there are live flamenco concerts. Tours available in English.

⚠ **It's a steep walk to reach the center, even if you take Bus No. C2 (from Plaza Nueva) to shorten the distance.** ✉ *Barranco de los Negros s/n, Sacromonte* ☎ *958/215120* 🌐 *sacromontegranada.com* 🎫 *€5.*

Albayzín

Covering a hill of its own, across the Darro ravine from the Alhambra, this ancient Moorish neighborhood is a mix of dilapidated white houses and immaculate *carmenes* (private villas). It was founded in 1228 by the Moors who had fled Baeza after Fernando III captured the city. Full of cobblestone alleyways and secret corners, the Albayzín guards its old Moorish roots jealously, though its 30 mosques were converted to baroque churches long ago. A stretch of the Moors' original city wall runs beside the ridge called the **Cuesta de la Alhacaba.**

If you're walking—the best way to explore—you can enter the Albayzín from either the Cuesta de Elvira or the Plaza Nueva. Alternatively, on foot or by taxi (parking is impossible), begin in the Plaza de Santa Ana and follow the Carrera del Darro, Paseo del Padre Manjón, and Cuesta del Chapíz. One of the highest points in the quarter, the plaza in front of the church of San Nicolás (*€2.50*)—the **Mirador de San Nicolás**—has one of the finest views in all of Granada: on the hill opposite, the turrets and towers of the Alhambra form a dramatic silhouette against the snowy peaks of the Sierra Nevada. The sight is most magical at dawn, dusk, and on nights when the Alhambra is floodlighted. Take note of the mosque just next to the church—views of the Alhambra from the mosque gardens are just as good as those from the Mirador de San Nicolás and a lot less crowded. Interestingly, given the area's Moorish history, the two sloping narrow streets of Calderería Nueva and Calderería Vieja that meet at the top by the Iglesia de San Gregorio have developed into something of a North African bazaar, full of shops and vendors selling clothes, bags, crafts, and trinkets. The numerous little teahouses and restaurants here have a decidedly Moroccan flavor.

■ TIP→ Many of the streets are cobbled, so wear sturdy footwear with thick soles.

Sights

Casa de los Pisa
HISTORIC HOME | Originally built in 1494 for the Pisa family, the claim to fame of this house is its relationship to San Juan de Dios, who came to Granada in 1538 and founded a charity hospital to take care of the poor. Befriended by the Pisa family, he was taken into their home when he fell ill in February 1550. A month later, he died there, at the age of 55. Since that time, devotees of the saint have traveled from around the world to this house with a stone Gothic facade, now run by the Hospital Order of St. John. Inside are numerous pieces of jewelry, furniture, priceless religious works of art, and an extensive collection of paintings and sculptures depicting St. John. ✉ *Calle Convalecencia 1, Albaicín* ☎ *958/222144* 🎫 *€3* 🕒 *Closed Sun. and afternoons.*

El Bañuelo (*Little Bath House*)
HISTORIC SIGHT | These 11th-century Arab steam baths might be a little dark and dank now, but try to imagine them some 900 years ago, filled with Moorish beauties. Back then, the dull brick walls were backed by bright ceramic tiles, tapestries, and rugs. Light comes in through star-shaped vents in the ceiling, à la the bathhouse in the Alhambra. ✉ *Carrera del Darro 31, Albaicín* ☎ *958/229738* 🎫 *€7 (ticket includes admission to Dar al-Horra).*

Paseo del Padre Manjón
STREET | Lining the Río Darro, this street is also known as the Paseo de los Tristes (Promenade of the Sad Ones) because funeral processions once passed this way. The cafés and bars here are good places for a coffee break. The park, dappled with wisteria-covered pergolas, fountains, and stone walkways, has a stunning view of the Alhambra's northern side. ✉ *Albaicín.*

Restaurants

El Mercader
$$ | **INTERNATIONAL** | Eclectic decor and innovative food are on offer at this cozy venue off Plaza Nueva whose chef, Nuria de la Torre, won the local Culinary Masters competition in 2021. Her menu takes seasonal ingredients as its base while dishes combine local staples with unusual partners. **Known for:** fun decor; attentive service; innovative dishes. [$] *Average main: €22* ✉ *Calle Imprenta 4, Centro* ☎ *633/790440* 🕒 *Closed Mon. and Tues.*

★ El Trillo
$$ | **SPANISH** | Tucked away in the warren of alleyways in a restored Albayzín villa, this lovely restaurant offers what may be the best food in the area. There's a formal dining room, an outside garden with pear and quince trees, and a roof terrace with Alhambra views. **Known for:** fine dining; views of the Alhambra; rice with wild

boar. $ *Average main: €24* ⊠ *Callejón del Aljibe del Trillo 3, Albaicín* ☎ *958/225182* ⊕ *www.restaurante-eltrillo.com* ۞ *Closed Tues.*

Paprika

$ | **VEGETARIAN** | Inside a pretty brick building and with an informal terrace sprawling over the wide steps of the Cuesta de Abarqueros, Paprika offers unpretentious vegan food. Most ingredients and wines are organic, and dishes include salads, stir-fries, and curries, such as Thai curry with tofu, coconut, and green curry sauce. **Known for:** choice of vegan food; value plate of the day; organic ingredients. $ *Average main: €12* ⊠ *Cuesta de Abarqueros 3, Albaicín* ☎ *958/804785* ⊕ *paprikagranada.com* ۞ *Closed Tues.*

Ruta del Azafrán

$$ | **SPANISH** | A charming surprise nestled at the foot of the Albayzín by the Darro, this sleek contemporary space in the shadow of the Alhambra offers a selection of specialties. The diverse menu includes tuna *tataki* (a method of pounding fish in Japanese cuisine) with apple chutney and several different couscous dishes. **Known for:** international dishes; views of the Alhambra, especially at night; tasting menus. $ *Average main: €20* ⊠ *Paseo de los Tristes 1, Albaicín* ☎ *958/226882* ⊕ *rutadelazafran.com.*

 Hotels

★ **Casa Morisca**

$$ | **B&B/INN** | The architect who owns this 15th-century building transformed it into a hotel so distinctive that he received Spain's National Restoration Award for his preservation of original architectural elements, including barrel-vaulted brickwork, wooden ceilings, and the original pool. **Pros:** historic location; award-winning design; easy parking. **Cons:** stuffy interior rooms; no restaurant on-site; slightly outside the town center. $ *Rooms from: €190* ⊠ *Cuesta de la Victoria 9, Albaicín* ☎ *958/221100* ⊕ *hotelcasamorisca.com* ☝ *14 rooms* ❍ *No Meals.*

Hotel Casa 1800

$$$ | **HOTEL** | A stone's throw from the Paseo de los Tristes, this restored 17th-century mansion has a fine tiered patio. **Pros:** historic building; deluxe suite has balcony with views of the Alhambra; walking distance to most sights. **Cons:** on a street that doesn't permit cars; rooms are small (but comfortable); no bar. $ *Rooms from: €240* ⊠ *Calle Benalúa 11, Albaicín* ☎ *958/210700* ⊕ *www. hotelcasa1800granada.com* ☝ *25 rooms* ❍ *No Meals.*

Hotel Palacio de Santa Inés

$$ | **HOTEL** | It's not often you get to stay in a 16th-century palace—and this one has a stunning location in the heart of the Albayzín. **Pros:** perfect location for exploring the Albayzín; quirky interiors; some rooms have Alhambra views. **Cons:** can't get there by car; some rooms rather dark; communal areas a little tired. $ *Rooms from: €125* ⊠ *Cuesta de Santa Inés 9, Albaicín* ☎ *958/222362* ⊕ *www. palaciosantaines.es* ☝ *35 rooms* ❍ *No Meals.*

🎭 Performing Arts

FLAMENCO

Cueva de la Rocío

FOLK/TRADITIONAL DANCE | This is a good spot for authentic flamenco shows, staged nightly at 8, 9, 10, and 11 pm. ⊠ *C. del Sacromonte 70, Albaicín* ☎ *958/227129* ⊕ *cuevalarocio.es* 🎟 *From €15.*

El Tabanco

FOLK/TRADITIONAL DANCE | In the heart of the Albayzín, this small venue showcases local flamenco talent with concerts usually on Friday and Saturday nights. Book in advance to guarantee a seat. ⊠ *Cuesta de San Gregorio 24, Albaicín* ☎ *662/137046* ⊕ *eltabanco.com* 🎟 *From €10.*

El Templo del Flamenco

FOLK/TRADITIONAL DANCE | Slightly off the beaten track (take a taxi to get here) and less touristy because of it, this venue has shows at 8 and 10 pm daily. ✉ *Calle Parnaleros Alto 41, Albaicín* ☎ *622/500052 for tickets, 654/373136 for general information* ⊕ *eltemplodelflamenco.com/en* ✉ *From €15.*

Jardines de Zoraya

FOLK/TRADITIONAL DANCE | This show doesn't take place in a cave, but the music and dance are some of the most authentic available. Daily flamenco shows are at 8 and 10 pm. ✉ *Calle Panaderos 32, Albaicín* ☎ *958/206266* ⊕ *www.jardinesdezoraya.com* ✉ *From €25.*

Centro

Sights

Capilla Real (*Royal Chapel*)

RELIGIOUS BUILDING | Catholic monarchs Isabel of Castile and Fernando of Aragón are buried at this shrine. The couple originally planned to be buried in Toledo's San Juan de los Reyes, but Isabel changed her mind when the pair conquered Granada in 1492. When she died in 1504, her body was first laid to rest in the Convento de San Francisco (now a parador) on the Alhambra hill. The architect Enrique Egas began work on the Capilla Real in 1506 and completed it 15 years later, creating a masterpiece of the ornate Gothic style now known in Spain as Isabelline. In 1521, Isabel's body was transferred to a simple lead coffin in the Capilla Real crypt, where it was joined by that of her husband, Fernando, and later her unfortunate daughter, Juana la Loca (Joanna the Mad), and son-in-law, Felipe el Hermoso (Philip the Handsome). Felipe died young, and Juana had his casket borne about the peninsula with her for years, opening the lid each night to kiss her embalmed spouse good night. A small coffin to the right contains the remains of Prince Felipe of Asturias, a grandson of the Catholic Monarchs and nephew of Juana la Loca who died in his infancy. The crypt containing the five lead coffins is quite simple, but it's topped by elaborate marble tombs showing Fernando and Isabel lying side by side (commissioned by their grandson Carlos V and sculpted by Domenico Fancelli). The altarpiece, by Felipe Vigariny (1522), is comprised of 34 carved panels depicting religious and historical scenes; the bottom row shows Boabdil surrendering the keys of the city to its conquerors and the forced baptism of the defeated Moors. The sacristy holds Fernando's sword, Isabel's crown and scepter, and a fine collection of Flemish paintings once owned by Isabel. ✉ *Calle Oficios s/n, Centro* ☎ *958/227848* ⊕ *capillarealgranada.com/en* ✉ *€5.*

Cathedral

RELIGIOUS BUILDING | Carlos V commissioned the cathedral in 1521 because he considered the Capilla Real "too small for so much glory" and wanted to house his illustrious late grandparents someplace more worthy. Carlos undoubtedly had great intentions, as the cathedral was created by some of the finest architects of its time: Enrique de Egas, Diego de Siloé, Alonso Cano, and sculptor Juan de Maena. Alas, his ambitions came to little, for the cathedral is a grand and gloomy monument, not completed until 1714 and never used as the crypt for his grandparents (or parents). Enter through a small door at the back, off the Gran Vía. Old hymnals are displayed throughout, and there's a museum, which includes a 14th-century gold-and-silver monstrance given to the city by Queen Isabel. ✉ *Calle Gran Vía de Colón s/n, Centro* ☎ *958/222959* ✉ *€5 (including audio guide)* ⊘ *Closed Sun. morning.*

Centro José Guerrero

ART GALLERY | Just across a lane from the cathedral and Capilla Real, this building houses colorful modern paintings by José Guerrero. Born in Granada in 1914,

Guerrero traveled throughout Europe and lived in New York in the 1950s before returning to Spain. The center also runs excellent temporary contemporary art shows. ✉ *Calle Oficios 8, Centro* ☎ *958/225185* 🌐 *www.centroguerrero.es* 🎟 *Free* 🕒 *Closed Sun. afternoon and Mon.*

Corral del Carbón (*Coal House*)
HISTORIC SIGHT | This building was used to store coal in the 19th century, but its history is much longer. Dating to the 14th century, it was used by Moorish merchants as a lodging house and then by Christians as a theater. It's one of the oldest Moorish buildings in the city and the only Arab structure of its kind in Spain. ✉ *Calle de Mariana Pineda s/n, Centro* 🎟 *Free.*

Museo Arqueológico (*Archaeology Museum*)
HISTORY MUSEUM | Housed in the Casa de Castril with one of the finest Renaissance exteriors in the city, this small archaeological museum contains some real gems and has a stunning patio and views of the Alhambra from the second floor. The three rooms take you from prehistoric times with highlights such as raffia sandals dating from 5500 BC, through to the Iberian world whose treasures include a Greek breastplate armor (400 BC) and a white marble bull (600 BC), before reaching the Romans and Al-Andalus where you shouldn't miss the statues, ceramics, and a 15th-century astrolabe. ✉ *Carrera del Darro 41, Albaicín* ☎ *600/143141* 🎟 *€2* 🕒 *Closed Mon.*

Palacio Madraza
CASTLE/PALACE | This building conceals the Islamic seminary built in 1349 by Yusuf I. The intriguing baroque facade is elaborate; inside, across from the entrance, an octagonal room (viewable from the patio only) is crowned by a Moorish dome. It hosts occasional free art and cultural exhibitions. ✉ *Calle Zacatín s/n, Centro* ☎ *958/241299.*

🍴 Restaurants

Bar Los Diamantes
$ | TAPAS | This lively bar (with a sister branch on Plaza Nueva) is a big favorite with locals and draws crowds whatever the time of year. Specialties include fried fish and seafood—try the *surtido de pescado* (assortment of fried fish) to sample the best—as well as *sesos* (fried lambs' brains). **Known for:** fried fish; generous free tapa with first drink; busy atmosphere. [$] *Average main: €16* ✉ *Pl. de Bib-Rambla 2, Centro* ☎ *958/348255* 🌐 *www.barlosdiamantes.com.*

Bodegas Castañeda
$$ | SPANISH | A block from the cathedral across Gran Vía, this is a delightfully typical Granada bodega with low ceilings and dark wood furniture. In addition to the wines, specialties here are plates of cheese, pâté, and *embutidos* (cold meats). **Known for:** tapas; atmospheric bar; Spanish tortilla with creamy aioli. [$] *Average main: €18* ✉ *Calle Almireceros 1–3, Centro* ☎ *958/215464.*

★ Café Botánico
$$ | TAPAS | Located southeast of Granada's cathedral, this modern hot spot is a world apart from Granada's usual traditional tapas bar. It attracts an eclectic crowd of students, families, and businesspeople with a diverse international menu, including Mexican fajitas, poke bowls, and Thai cod. **Known for:** international menu; good-value lunch deal; homemade desserts. [$] *Average main: €18* ✉ *Calle Málaga 3, Centro* ☎ *958/271598* 🌐 *botanicocafe.es/en.*

La Bodega de Antonio
$ | SPANISH | Just off Calle Puentezuelas, this authentic patio complete with original pillars provides a cozy vibe. Specials include the house cod (with prawns and clams) and Galician-style octopus, best enjoyed with a *cerdito* (a "little pig" ceramic jug of sweet white wine, so named for its snout pourer). **Known for:** generous portions; choice of croquettes;

Galician-style octopus. [$] *Average main: €15* ✉ *Calle Jardines 4, Centro* ☎ *958/252275* ⏲ *Closed Wed. and Aug.*

★ La Brujidera

$ | **TAPAS** | Also known simply as Casa de Vinos (Wine House), this place, up a pedestrian street just behind Plaza Nueva, is a must for Spanish wine lovers. The cozy interior is reminiscent of a ship's cabin, with wood paneling lining the walls along with more than 150 bottles of Spanish wines. **Known for:** long wine list; meat and cheese boards; vermouth and sherries on tap. [$] *Average main: €14* ✉ *Calle Monjas del Carmen 2, Centro* ☎ *687/851507.*

Oliver

$$ | **SPANISH** | The interior may look a bit bare, but whatever this fish restaurant lacks in warmth it makes up for with the food. It serves simple but high-quality dishes like grilled mullet, dorado baked in salt, prawns with garlic, and monkfish in saffron sauce. **Known for:** tapas bar; fresh fish; migas. [$] *Average main: €20* ✉ *Pl. de la Pescadería 12, Centro* ☎ *958/262200* 🌐 *restauranteoliver.com* ⏲ *Closed Sun.*

Om-Kalsum

$ | **MOROCCAN** | The Moroccan tapas at this small and bustling venue make a pleasant change from the traditional local fare. Tagine, couscous, and kefta are all menu staples. **Known for:** Moroccan tapas; selection of tapas; lively atmosphere. [$] *Average main: €10* ✉ *Calle Jardines 17, Centro* ⏲ *Closed Sun. and no lunch Mon.*

Pastelería López-Mezquita

$ | **SPANISH** | Sweet and savory treats come into their own at this family-owned business in the city center. Top of the specialty list are *piononos* (sponge bites filled with caramel and custard) and *pastela* (Moroccan chicken pie). **Known for:** piononos; cakes and cookies; pastela. [$] *Average main: €5* ✉ *Calle Reyes Católicos 39, Centro* ☎ *958/221205* ⏲ *Closed Sun. afternoon.*

Tinta Fina

$$$ | **SPANISH** | Underneath the arches just off Puerta Real, this modern bar and restaurant has a reputation for being one of Granada's most chic venues. It's known for fresh seafood, including oysters and red shrimp, though generous portions of chargrilled steaks, steak tartare, and fresh foie gras are a hit with carnivores. **Known for:** seafood; cocktail and G&T menus; chic atmosphere. [$] *Average main: €25* ✉ *Calle Ángel Ganivet 5, Centro* ☎ *958/100041* 🌐 *tintafinarestaurante.com.*

Hotels

Hospes Palacio de los Patos

$$$ | **HOTEL** | This beautifully restored palace is unmissable, sitting proudly on its own in the middle of one of Granada's busiest shopping streets. **Pros:** central location; historic setting; great spa and restaurant. **Cons:** parking not included; some street noise; some rooms are at street level. [$] *Rooms from: €285* ✉ *Calle Solarillo de Gracia 1, Centro* ☎ *958/535790* 🌐 *www.hospes.com/en/palacio-patos* 🛏 *40 rooms* 🍴 *No Meals.*

★ Hostal Rodri

$ | **HOTEL** | This comfortable and quiet hotel lies conveniently off Plaza de la Trinidad near the cathedral and is a good option for cheaper lodging in a city with so many upscale accommodations. **Pros:** central location; clean comfortable rooms; value. **Cons:** some rooms on small side; no breakfast on-site; could be too basic for some. [$] *Rooms from: €70* ✉ *Calle Laurel de las Tablas 9, Centro* ☎ *958/288043* 🌐 *www.hostalrodri.com* 🛏 *10 rooms* 🍴 *No Meals.*

Hotel Párraga Siete

$ | **HOTEL** | This family-run hotel in the heart of the old quarter, within easy walking distance of sights and restaurants, offers excellent value and amenities superior to its official two-star rating. **Pros:** central quiet location; good on-site restaurant; easy nearby parking. **Cons:** some rooms are very small; interiors might be too sparse for some; no historic character. [$] *Rooms from: €120* ✉ *Calle Párraga 7, Centro* ☎ *958/264227* 🌐 *www.hotelparragasiete.com* 🛏 *20 rooms* 🍴 *No Meals.*

Palacio de los Navas
$$ | **B&B/INN** | Located in the center of the city, this palace was built by aristocrat Francisco Navas in the 16th century and later became the Casa de Moneda (the Mint). **Pros:** great location; peaceful oasis during the day; rooms are set around a beautiful interior patio. **Cons:** difficult parking; can be noisy at night; uninspiring breakfast. [$] *Rooms from: €130* ✉ *Calle Navas 1, Centro* ☎ *958/215760* 🌐 *www.hotelpalaciodelosnavas.com* 🛏 *19 rooms* 🍴 *No Meals.*

🍸 Nightlife

Bohemia Jazz Café
LIVE MUSIC | This atmospheric jazz bar has piano performances and occasional live bands daily. ✉ *Pl. de los Lobos 11, Centro* 🌐 *www.bohemiajazzcafe.com.*

👜 Shopping

Artesanías González
CRAFTS | Not far from La Alhambra, this is one of the best and longest-established places to buy handmade taracea chessboards, boxes, side tables, and coasters. ✉ *Cuesta de Gomérez 12, Centro* ☎ *657/987239.*

Espartería San José
CRAFTS | For wicker baskets and esparto-grass mats and rugs, head to this shop off the Plaza de la Pescadería. ✉ *Calle Jáudenes 3, Centro* ☎ *667/584875* 🌐 *esparteriasanjose.es* 🕒 *Closed Sun. and Sat. afternoon.*

Outskirts of Granada

👁 Sights

Casa-Museo Federico García Lorca
HISTORIC HOME | Granada's most famous native son, the poet Federico García Lorca, gets his due here, in the middle of a park devoted to him on the southern fringe of the city. Lorca's onetime summer home, **La Huerta de San Vicente,** is now a museum (guided tours only)—run by his niece Laura García Lorca—with such artifacts as his beloved piano and changing exhibits on specific aspects of his life. ✉ *Parque Federico García Lorca, Calle Virgen Blanca, Arabial* ☎ *958/849112* 🌐 *www.huertadesanvicente.com* 🎟 *€3, free Wed.* 🕒 *Closed Mon.*

Monasterio de la Cartuja
RELIGIOUS BUILDING | The exterior of this Carthusian monastery in northern Granada is sober and monolithic, but inside are twisted multicolor marble columns; a profusion of gold, silver, tortoiseshell, and ivory; intricate stucco; and the extravagant sacristy—it's easy to see why it has been called the Christian answer to the Alhambra. Among its wonders are the trompe l'oeil spikes, shadows and all, in the Sanchez Cotan cross over the *Last Supper* painting at the west end of the refectory. It was begun in 1506 and moved to its present site in 1516, though construction continued for the next 300 years. If you're lucky, you may see small birds attempting to land on these faux perches. You can reach it by Bus No. N7. ✉ *Paseo de Cartuja s/n, Cartuja* ☎ *958/161932* 🌐 *cartujadegranada.com* 🎟 *€5.*

Parque de las Ciencias (*Science Park*)
SCIENCE MUSEUM | **FAMILY** | Across from Granada's convention center and easily reached on Bus No. C4, this science museum is one of the most visited museums in Andalusia. It has a planetarium and interactive demonstrations

of scientific experiments. The 165-foot observation tower has views to the south and west. ✉ *Av. del Mediterráneo s/n, Zaidín* ☎ *958/131900* 🌐 *www.parqueciencias.com* 🎫 *From €7* 🕒 *Closed Mon.*

🍴 Restaurants

Restaurante Arriaga

$$$$ | **BASQUE** | Run by Basque chef Álvaro Arriaga, this restaurant sits on the top floor of the Museo de la Memoria de Andalucía just outside the city (it's well worth the taxi drive) and has panoramic views of Granada with the Sierra Nevada behind. Choose from two tasting menus (€80 for six dishes and €100 for nine dishes), both with one surprise after another and available with Andalusian wine pairing. **Known for:** tasting menus; culinary surprises (the menu starts with dessert!); panoramic views of Granada. [$] *Average main: €80* ✉ *Av. de las Ciencias 2, Armilla* ☎ *958/132619* 🌐 *www.restaurantearriaga.com* 🕒 *Closed Mon., no dinner Sun. or Tues.*

Priego de Córdoba

103 km (64 miles) southeast of Córdoba, 25 km (15½ miles) southeast of Zuheros.

The jewel of Córdoba's countryside is Priego de Córdoba, a town of 22,500 inhabitants at the foot of Monte Tinosa. Wander down Calle del Río, opposite the town hall, to see 18th-century mansions, once the homes of silk merchants. At the end of the street is the Fuente del Rey (King's Fountain), with some 130 water jets, built in 1803. Don't miss the lavish baroque churches of La Asunción and La Aurora or the Barrio de la Villa, an old Moorish quarter with a maze of narrow streets and white-walled buildings. If you plan to visit several monuments, buy the *bono turístico* (€5) to save on admission prices.

GETTING HERE AND AROUND

Priego has reasonable bus service from Córdoba (2½ hours) and Granada (1½ hours), although your best bet is to visit by car en route to either of these cities. Once there, it's perfect for pedestrian exploration.

VISITOR INFORMATION

Priego de Córdoba. ✉ *Pl. de la Constitución 3, Priego de Córdoba* ☎ *957/700625* 🌐 *www.turismodepriego.com.*

🍴 Restaurants

La Pianola (*Casa Pepe*)
$ | **SPANISH** | Expect cheap, cheerful, and lively dining at this small venue, a couple of blocks south of the castle and usually packed with locals. On the menu are usual Córdoba staples including oxtail, but the specialties here are the *saquito de boletus* (mushroom pastry) and *carrillada de cerdo* (roast pork cheek). **Known for:** value dining; good tapas; delicious French toast for dessert. [$] *Average main: €12* ✉ *Calle Obispo Caballero 6, Priego de Córdoba* ☎ *957/700409* ⏲ *Closed Mon.*

🛏 Hotels

Casa Baños de la Villa
$ | **HOTEL** | Tucked at the heart of Priego's bright white center, this boutique hotel offers an oasis of peace and quiet, plus the chance to enjoy the in-house spa pool and Turkish bath (included in the price). **Pros:** central location; friendly hosts; in-house spa. **Cons:** monotonous breakfast; some might find the decor a little brash; no exterior views from rooms. [$] *Rooms from: €100* ✉ *Calle Real 63, Priego de Córdoba* ☎ *957/547274* 🌐 *casabanosdelavilla.com* 🛏 *9 rooms* 🍴 *Free Breakfast.*

Hotel-Museo Patria Chica
$ | **HOTEL** | This charming hotel in a fully restored 19th-century mansion has so many antiques and memorabilia that the term "hotel-museum" really does live up to its name. **Pros:** central location; period furnishings; pool and restaurant on-site. **Cons:** quiet; slightly out of the town center; small bathrooms. [$] *Rooms from: €100* ✉ *Calle Carrera de las Monjas 47, Priego de Córdoba* ☎ *957/058385* 🌐 *www.hotelpatriachica.com* 🛏 *15 rooms* 🍴 *No Meals.*

Baeza

48 km (30 miles) northeast of Jaén on N321.

The historic town of Baeza, nestled between hills and olive groves, is one of the best-preserved old towns in Spain. Founded by the Romans, it later housed the Visigoths and became the capital of a Moorish taifa, one of some two dozen mini-kingdoms formed after the Ummayad Caliphate was subdivided in 1031. Fernando III captured Baeza in 1227, and for the next 200 years it stood on the frontier of the Moorish kingdom of Granada. In the 16th and 17th centuries, local nobles gave the city a wealth of Renaissance palaces.

GETTING HERE AND AROUND

Frequent buses (12 per day on weekdays, 7 per day on weekends; *ALSA* ☎ *902/422242*) connect Baeza with Jaén (45 minutes) and Úbeda, although a private car is the best option given the remoteness of the town and that you may want to explore nearby Úbeda on the same day. Baeza is small and flat, and with its sights clustered around the very center, it's very easy to explore on foot.

TOURS

Semer Guided Tours

GUIDED TOURS | Two-and-a-half-hour guided tours around Baeza (in English, minimum two people, Tuesday through Sunday) recount the history, culture, and traditions of the town. Tours of Úbeda are also available, with a discount for combined tours of both towns. ✉ *Baeza* ☎ *953/757916* 🌐 *visitasguiadasubeday-baeza.com* 🎫 *From €11.*

VISITOR INFORMATION

Baeza. ✉ *Pl. del Pópulo s/n, Baeza* ☎ *953/779982* 🌐 *turismo.baeza.net.*

Sights

Ayuntamiento (*Town Hall*)

GOVERNMENT BUILDING | Baeza's town hall was designed by cathedral master Andrés de Vandelvira. The facade is ornately decorated with a mix of religious and pagan imagery. Look between the balconies for the coats of arms of Felipe II, the city of Baeza, and the magistrate Juan de Borja. Ask at the tourist office about visits to the *salón de plenos,* a meeting hall with painted carved woodwork. ✉ *Pl. Cardenal s/n, Baeza.*

Catedral de Baeza

CHURCH | Originally begun by Fernando III on the site of a former mosque, the cathedral was largely rebuilt by Andrés de Vandelvira, architect of Jaén's cathedral, between 1570 and 1593, though the west front has architectural influences from an earlier period. A fine 14th-century rose window crowns the 13th-century Puerta de la Luna (Moon Door). Don't miss the baroque silver monstrance (a vessel in which the consecrated Host is exposed for the adoration of the faithful), which is carried in Baeza's Corpus Christi processions—the piece is kept in a concealed niche behind a painting, but you can see it in all its splendor by putting a coin in a slot to reveal the hiding place. Next to the monstrance is the entrance to the clock tower, where a small donation and a narrow spiral staircase take you to one of the best views of Baeza. The remains of the original mosque are in the cathedral's Gothic cloisters. ✉ *Pl. de Santa María s/n, Baeza* ☎ *953/744157* 🎫 *€6.*

Casa del Pópulo

HISTORIC HOME | Located in the central paseo—where the Plaza del Pópulo (or Plaza de los Leones) and Plaza de la Constitución (or Plaza del Mercado Viejo) merge to form a cobblestone square—this graceful town house was built around 1530. The first Mass of the Reconquest was supposedly celebrated on its curved balcony; it now houses Baeza's tourist office. ✉ *Pl. del Pópulo s/n, Baeza.*

Convento de San Francisco

HISTORIC SIGHT | This 16th-century convent is one of Vandelvira's religious architectural masterpieces. The building was damaged by the French army and partially destroyed by a light earthquake in the early 1800s, but you can see its restored remains. ✉ *Calle de San Francisco s/n, Baeza.*

Restaurants

Palacio de Gallego

$$ | SPANISH | Located next to the cathedral, this is one of the best restaurants in town, known for its barbecue and roasted dishes. If you're not too hungry, enjoy tapas in the bar. **Known for:** barbecue; red tuna steak; outdoor terrace. [$] *Average main: €20* ✉ *Calle de Santa Catalina s/n, Baeza* ☎ *695/117175* 🕒 *Closed Tues. No lunch Wed.*

Hotels

Hotel Puerta de la Luna

$ | HOTEL | This restored 17th-century palace, one of Baeza's best accommodation options, is centered on two patios—one with a pond and views of the cathedral tower, the other with a small pool. **Pros:**

lovely architecture; central location; good food on-site. **Cons:** difficult to find; basic breakfast; a bit too quiet. $ *Rooms from: €110* ✉ *Calle Canónigo Melgares Raya 7, Baeza* ☎ *953/747019* 🌐 *www.hotelpuertadelaluna.com* 🛏 *44 rooms* 🍴 *No Meals.*

Úbeda

9 km (5½ miles) northeast of Baeza on N321.

Úbeda's *casco antiguo* (old town) is one of the most outstanding enclaves of 16th-century architecture in Spain. It's a stunning surprise in the heart of Jaén's olive groves, set in the shadow of the wild Sierra de Cazorla mountain range. For crafts enthusiasts, this is Andalusia's capital for many kinds of artisan goods. Follow signs to the Zona Monumental, where there are countless Renaissance palaces and stately mansions, though most are closed to the public.

GETTING HERE AND AROUND

Frequent buses (12 on weekdays, 7 on weekends; *ALSA* ☎ *902/422242*) connect Úbeda with Jaén (1 hour) and Baeza, although a private car is the best option given the remoteness of the town and that you may want to explore nearby Baeza in the same day. Úbeda's sights are all within easy reach of the center, so exploring on foot is easy.

TOURS

Semer Guided Tours

GUIDED TOURS | ✉ *Calle de Juan Montilla 3, Úbeda* ☎ *953/757916* 🌐 *visitasguiadasubedaybaeza.com.*

Sights

Ayuntamiento Antiguo (*Old Town Hall*)

NOTABLE BUILDING | Begun in the early 16th century but restored as a beautiful arcaded baroque palace in 1680, the former town hall is now a conservatory of music. From the hall's upper balcony, the town council watched celebrations and *autos-da-fé* ("acts of faith"—executions of heretics sentenced by the Inquisition) in the square below. You can't enter the town hall, but on the north side you can visit the 13th-century Iglesia de San Pablo, with its Isabelline south portal. ✉ *Pl. Primero de Mayo s/n, Úbeda* ✥ *Off Calle María de Molina* ☎ *953/750637* 🎟 *Church €1* 🕒 *Closed Mon.*

Hospital de Santiago

NOTABLE BUILDING | Sometimes jokingly called the Escorial of Andalusia (in allusion to Felipe II's monolithic palace and monastery outside Madrid), this huge angular building in the modern section of town is yet another of Vandelvira's masterpieces in Úbeda. The plain facade is adorned with ceramic medallions, and over the main entrance is a carving of Santiago Matamoros (St. James the Moorslayer) in his traditional horseback pose. Inside are an arcaded patio and a grand staircase. Now a cultural center, it holds many of the events at the Festival de Ubeda, celebrating music and dance in May and June (🌐 www.festivaldeubeda.com). ✉ *Av. Cristo Rey s/n, Úbeda* ☎ *953/750842* 🎟 *Free* 🕒 *Closed Sun. in July and weekends in Aug.*

Sacra Capilla de El Salvador

RELIGIOUS BUILDING | The Plaza Vázquez de Molina, in the heart of the casco antiguo, is the site of this building, which is photographed so often that it's become the city's unofficial symbol. It was built by Vandelvira, but he based his design on several plans drafted in 1536 by Diego de Siloé, architect of Granada's cathedral. Considered one of the masterpieces of Spanish Renaissance religious art, the chapel was sacked in the frenzy of church burnings at the outbreak of the civil war, but it retains its ornate western façade and altarpiece, which has a rare Berruguete sculpture. ✉ *Pl. de Vázquez de Molina s/n, Úbeda* ☎ *609/279905* 🎟 *€5, free Tues.–Thurs. at 10–10:30 am.*

★ Sinagoga del Agua

RELIGIOUS BUILDING | This 13th-century synagogue counts among Úbeda's most amazing discoveries. Entirely underground and known as the "Water Synagogue" for the wells and natural spring under the mikvah, it comprises seven areas open to visitors, including the main area of worship, mikvah, women's gallery, and rabbi's quarters. During the summer solstice the sun's rays illuminate the stairway, providing the only natural light in the synagogue. ✉ *Calle Roque Rojas 2, Úbeda* ☎ *953/758150* 🌐 *sinagogadelagua.com* 🎟 *€5* 🕓 *Temporarily closed weekdays.*

🍴 Restaurants

Asador de Santiago

$$$ | **SPANISH** | At this adventurous restaurant just off the main street, the chef prepares both Spanish classics, like white shrimp from Huelva and slow-roasted local lamb and goat, as well as innovative dishes like *sashimi de atún rojo con ajo blanco de piñones* (red tuna with pine nut garlic soup) and *lomo de ciervo en escabeche* (venison steak in pickled sauce). The candle-filled interior is more traditional than the bar and has terra-cotta tiles, dark wood furnishings, and crisp white linens. **Known for:** fine dining; Spanish classics; roast meats. [$] *Average main: €26* ✉ *Av. Cristo Rey 2, Úbeda* ☎ *953/750463* 🌐 *asadordesantiago.com* 🕓 *No dinner Sun.*

Cantina La Estación

$$ | **SPANISH** | Meals here—one of Úbeda's top restaurants—are served in a train-carriage interior decorated with railway memorabilia, while tapas reign at an outside terrace and at the bar. This distinctive eatery serves tasting menus and always has a *guiso del día* (stew of the day) as well as creative dishes like *milhojas de cordero con boniato* (lamb millefeuille with sweet potato). **Known for:** extensive and reasonably priced wine menu; innovative dishes; fun interior. [$] *Average main: €20* ✉ *Calle Cuesta de la Rodadera 1, Úbeda* ☎ *687/777230* 🕓 *Closed Wed. No dinner Mon., Tues., and July.*

Taberna Misa de 12

$$ | **SPANISH** | Located one block from the Plaza del Ayuntamiento, this small bar has the best position on the leafy square and the pleasant outside terrace is the best place to enjoy the tapas. Despite the tiny kitchen, the menu stretches long and includes glazed artichokes, red tuna tartare, and Iberian pork cuts. **Known for:** tapas; wine list; outdoor dining. [$] *Average main: €18* ✉ *Pl. Primero de Mayo 7, Úbeda* ☎ *622/480049* 🌐 *www.misade12.com* 🕓 *Closed Mon. No dinner Sun.*

🛏 Hotels

★ Palacio de la Rambla

$$ | **B&B/INN** | In old Úbeda, this stunning 16th-century mansion has been in the same family since it was built—it still hosts the Marquesa de la Rambla when she's in town—and eight of the rooms are available for overnighters. **Pros:** central location; elegant style; all rooms have access to the garden. **Cons:** not much parking; grandiosity not for everyone; some areas are a little tired. [$] *Rooms from: €125* ✉ *Pl. del Marqués 9, Úbeda* ☎ *953/750196* 🌐 *www.palaciodelarambla.com* 🔑 *8 rooms* 🍽 *Free Breakfast.*

★ Parador de Úbeda

$$$ | **HOTEL** | This splendid parador is in a 16th-century ducal palace in a prime location on the Plaza de Vázquez de Molina, next to the Capilla del Salvador. **Pros:** elegant surroundings; perfect location; excellent restaurant. **Cons:** parking is difficult; church bells in the morning; could be too formal for some. [$] *Rooms from: €210* ✉ *Pl. de Vázquez de Molina s/n, Úbeda* ☎ *953/750345* 🌐 *paradores.es/es/parador-de-ubeda* 🔑 *36 rooms* 🍽 *No Meals.*

🛍 Shopping

Úbeda is the crafts capital of Andalusia, with workshops devoted to carpentry, basket weaving, stone carving, wrought iron, stained glass, and, above all, the city's distinctive green-glaze pottery. Calle de Valencia is the traditional potters' row, running from the bottom of town to Úbeda's general crafts center, northwest of the casco antiguo (follow signs to Calle de Valencia or Barrio de Alfareros).

Úbeda's most famous potter was Paco Tito, whose craft is carried on at three different workshops run by two of his sons, Pablo and Juan, and a son-in-law, Melchor, each of whom claims to be the sole true heir to his father's art.

Alfarería Góngora

CERAMICS | All kinds of ceramics, in both traditional and contemporary styles, are sold here. ✉ *Calle Cuesta de la Merced 32, Úbeda* ☎ *953/754605.*

Alfarería Tito

CERAMICS | The extrovert Juan Tito can often be found at the potter's wheel in his rambling shop, which is packed with ceramics of every size and shape. ✉ *Pl. del Ayuntamiento 12, Úbeda* ☎ *953/751302.*

Melchor Tito

CERAMICS | You can see classic green-glazed items—the focus of Melchor Tito's work—being made in his workshops in Calle de Valencia and Calle de la Fuente Seca 17, both of which also sell his wares. ✉ *Calle de Valencia 44, Úbeda* ☎ *953/753692.*

Pablo Tito

CERAMICS | Clay sculptures of characters from *Don Quixote,* fired by Pablo Tito in an old Moorish-style kiln, are the specialty of this studio and shop (also online). There is also a museum on the premises. ✉ *Calle de Valencia 22, Úbeda* ☎ *953/751496* ⊕ *pablotito.es/tienda.*

The Sierra Nevada

👁 Sights

Mulhacén

MOUNTAIN | To the east of Granada, the mighty Mulhacén, the highest peak in mainland Spain, soars to 11,427 feet. Legend has it that it came by its name when Boabdil, the last Moorish king of Granada, deposed his father, Abu'l-Hasan Ali, and had the body buried at the summit of the mountain so that it couldn't be desecrated. For more information on trails to the two summits, check the National Park Service's site (⊕ miteco.gob.es/en). ✉ *Sierra Nevada.*

Pico de Veleta

MOUNTAIN | Peninsular Spain's second-highest mountain is 11,125 feet high. The view from its summit across the Alpujarras to the sea at distant Motril is stunning, and on a very clear day you can see the coast of North Africa. When the snow melts (July and August) you can drive or take a minibus from the Albergue Universitario (Universitario Mountain Refuge) to within around 400 yards of the summit—a trail takes you to the top in around 45 minutes.

■ TIP→ **It's cold up there, so take a warm jacket and scarf, even if Granada is sizzling hot.** ✉ *Sierra Nevada.*

🏃 Activities

SKIING

Estación de Esquí Sierra Nevada

SNOW SPORTS | FAMILY | Europe's southernmost ski resort is one of its best equipped. At the Pradollano and Borreguiles stations, there's good skiing from December through April or May; each has a special snowboarding circuit, floodlighted night slopes, a children's ski school, and après-ski sun and swimming in the Mediterranean less than an hour away. In winter, buses to Pradollano leave Granada's bus station three times a day on weekdays and four times on weekends and holidays. Tickets are €9 round-trip. As for Borreguiles, you can get there only on skis. There's an information center (🌐 sierranevada.es/en) at Plaza de Andalucía 4. ✉ *Sierra Nevada.*

The Alpujarras

Village of Lanjarón: 46 km (28½ miles) south of Granada.

A trip to the Alpujarras, on the southern slopes of the Sierra Nevada, takes you to one of Andalusia's highest, most remote, and most scenic areas, home for decades to painters, writers, and a considerable foreign population. The Alpujarras region was originally populated by Moors fleeing the Christian Reconquest (from Seville after its fall in 1248, then from Granada after 1492).To this day, the Galicians' descendants continue the Moorish custom of weaving rugs and blankets in the traditional Alpujarran colors of red, green, black, and white, and they sell their crafts in many of the villages. Be on the lookout for handmade basketry and pottery as well.

Houses here are squat and square; they spill down the southern slopes of the Sierra Nevada, bearing a strong resemblance to the Berber homes in the Rif Mountains, just across the Mediterranean in Morocco. If you're driving, the road as far as Lanjarón and Órgiva is smooth sailing; after that come steep twisting mountain roads with few gas stations. Beyond sightseeing, the area is a haven for outdoor activities such as hiking and horseback riding. Inquire at the **Information Point** at Plaza de la Libertad in Pampaneira.

🛏 Hotels

Hotel Alcadima

$ | **HOTEL** | **FAMILY** | One of the best-value hotels in the area, this pleasant if unfancy hotel in the rustic spa town of Lanjarón makes a good base for exploring the lower part of the Alpujarras. **Pros:** swimming pool; excellent restaurant; two-bedroom suites are ideal for families. **Cons:** Lanjarón isn't the prettiest village in the area; could be too plain for some; down an unattractive side street. [$] *Rooms from: €70* ✉ *Calle Francisco Tarrega 3, Lanjarón* ☎ *958/770809* 🌐 *alcadima.com* 🛏 *45 rooms* 🍴 *No Meals.*

Los Tinaos

$ | **APARTMENT** | Located on the way to Trevélez in the pretty whitewashed village of Bubión that almost clings to the mountainside, these comfortable apartments (for two to four people) come squeaky clean, with open log fires as well as central heating and sweeping views across the valley. **Pros:** valley views; a short walk from Pitres; bar serving locally produced wine. **Cons:** apartments on the small side; could be too basic for some; steep walk down. [$] *Rooms from: €75* ✉ *Calle Parras 2, Bubión* ☎ *958/763217* 🌐 *lostinaos.com* 🛏 *10 rooms* 🍴 *No Meals.*

Index

Photo Credits

Front Cover: ImageBROKER.com GmbH & Co. KG/Alamy Stock Photo [Description: Museo Nacional Centro de Arte Reina Sofia, Museum, Madrid, Spain]. **Back cover, from left to right:** Rudy Balasko/Shutterstock. Frederic Prochasson/iStockphoto. Damlow/iStockphoto. Spine: SCStock/iStockphoto. Interior, from left to right: LouieLea/Shutterstock (1). Saiko3p/Shutterstock (2-3). David R. Frazier Photolibrary, Inc./Alamy (5). **Chapter 1: Experience Madrid:** Emperorcosar/Shutterstock (6-7). Ahkenahmed/Dreamstime (8-9). Courtesy of Álvaro López/Madrid Destination (9). César Lucas Abreu/Madrid Destination (9). Museo Nacional del Prado (10). Mr.C/ Shutterstock (10). Botin (10). Palacio de Liria (10). Álvaro López/Madrid Destination (11). JeniFoto/Shutterstock (11). Agustín Martínez/Madrid Destination (12). Agustín Martínez/Madrid Destination (12). César Lucas Abreu/ Madrid Destination (12). Paolo Giocoso/Madrid Destination (12). Paco Manzano/Flamenco Show And Restaurant Corral de la Morería (13). Josh Schuster/Mision Cafe (14). Agustín Martínez/Madrid Destination (14). César Lucas Abreu/Madrid Destination (14). Alex Segre/Shutterstock (14). Kmiragaya/Dreamstime (15). Marques/Shutterstock (15). NoirChocolate/iStockphoto (18). Alleko/iStockphoto (19). Paolo Giocoso/Madrid Visitors & Convention Bureau, S.A,2012 (20). Hiberus/Madrid Destino (20). Daniel Garcia Dominguez (20). Belén López. Foto.Jaime Massieu (21). Courtesy of Salmon Guru (21). Diego Garcia Photography/Shutterstock (22). Delpixel/Shutterstock (23). Dbdella/Dreamstime (24). Matadero Madrid (25). **Chapter 3: Sol:** LucVi/Shutterstock (51). Dobledphoto/ Dreamstime (54). Catarina Belova/Shutterstock (58). **Chapter 4: Palacio and Moncloa:** LucVi/Shutterstock (61). JeniFoto/Shutterstock (68). Karol Kozlowski/Dreamstime (70). Alex Segre/Shutterstock (73). Dimbar76/Shutterstock (74). **Chapter 5: Chueca and Malasaña:** Page Light Studios/Shutterstock (77). Bildarchiv Monheim GmbH/Alamy Stock Photo (78). Bildarchiv Monheim GmbH/Alamy Stock Photo (79). Album/Alamy (79). Raul Bal/ Shutterstock (87). **Chapter 6: Barrio de las Letras:** Alex Segre/Shutterstock (95). JJFarq/Shutterstock (99). Page Light Studios/Shutterstock (101). **Chapter 7: Retiro and Salamanca:** Saiko3p/iStockphoto (107). Yulia Grigoryeva/Shutterstock (112). Peter Barritt/Alamy (114). David R. Frazier Photolibrary, Inc./Alamy (115). Mary Evans Picture Library / Alamy (116). Public Domain (116). Public Domain (116). Public Domain (117). Public Domain (117). Public Domain (117). Public Domain (117). Public Domain (118). Peter Barritt/Alamy (118). Keystone Press/ Alamy Stock Photo (118). World History Archive/Alamy Stock Photo (118). Matej Kastelic/Shutterstock (121). Nanisimova/Shutterstock (122). JJFarq/Shutterstock (129). **Chapter 8: La Latina, Lavapiés, and Arganzuela:** Fotokon/Shutterstock (131). Sonia Bonet/Shutterstock (135). E.M. Promoción de Madrid, S.A. (Carlos Cazurro) (142). **Chapter 9: Chamberí:** Saiko3p/Shutterstock (149). Joseph Sohm/Shutterstock (152). Sala de Despiece (156). **Chapter 10: Chamartín and Tetuán:** David Monter/Dreamstime (159). **Chapter 11: Carabanchel, Usera, and Latina:** Alex Segre/Shutterstock (165). Jaime Diaz Minguez/Dreamstime (169). **Chapter 12: Day Trips from Madrid:** Emperorcosar/Shutterstock (173). Carmengabrielafilip/Dreamstime (184). Ivan Soto Cobos/ Shutterstock (187). John Silver/Shutterstock (189). Emperorcosar/Shutterstock (193). Richard Semik/Shutterstock (196). Roberaten/Shutterstock (201). Leonori/Shutterstock (205). Leonori/Shutterstock (208). Sergey Dzyuba/ Dreamstime (212). **Chapter 13: Seville and Around:** LucVi/Shutterstock (217). VicPhotoria/Shutterstock (220). KikoStock/Shutterstock (221). Pyroshot/Dreamstime (221). Sina Ettmer Photography/Shutterstock (227). Cezary Wojtkowski/Shutterstock (235). Sorincolac/iStockPhoto (250). RudiErnst/Shutterstock (255). Riverside/fodors. com member (260). Mamadela/iStockPhoto (262). Miquelito/Shutterstock (267). Fulcanelli/Shutterstock (268). **Chapter 14: Granada and Around:** Balate Dorin/Shutterstock (271). Pat_Hastings/Shutterstock (274). Carmen Martínez Banús/iStockphoto (275). AmpFotoStudio/Shutterstock (275). Botond Horvath/Shutterstock (285). Vladimir Korostyshevskiy/Shutterstock (285). Joserpizarro/Shutterstock (286). Cezary Wojtkowski/Shutterstock (287). Ivan Soto Cobos/Shutterstock (288). Arenaphotouk/Dreamstime (288). Joserpizarro/Shutterstock (288). Reimar/Shutterstock (288). Guss.95/Shutterstock (288). Leon Rafael/Shutterstock (289). Kiev.Victor/Shutterstock (290). Julian Maldonado/Shutterstock (291). Fotografiecor.nl/Shutterstock (291). About Our Writers: All photos are courtesy of the writers.

*Every effort has been made to trace the copyright holders, and we apologize in advance for any accidental errors. We would be happy to apply the corrections in the following edition of this publication.

Notes

Notes

Notes

Notes

Fodor's MADRID

Publisher: Stephen Horowitz, *General Manager*

Editorial: Douglas Stallings, *Editorial Director;* Jill Fergus, Amanda Sadlowski, *Senior Editors;* Brian Eschrich, Alexis Kelly, *Editors;* Angelique Kennedy-Chavannes, *Assistant Editor;* Yoojin Shin, *Associate Editor*

Design: Tina Malaney, *Director of Design and Production;* Jessica Gonzalez, *Senior Designer;* Jaimee Shaye, *Graphic Design Associate*

Production: Jennifer DePrima, *Editorial Production Manager;* Elyse Rozelle, *Senior Production Editor;* Monica White, *Production Editor*

Maps: Rebecca Baer, *Senior Map Editor;* Mark Stroud (Moon Street Cartography), *Cartographer*

Photography: Viviane Teles, *Senior Photo Editor;* Namrata Aggarwal, Neha Gupta, Payal Gupta, Ashok Kumar, *Photo Editors;* Jade Rodgers, *Photo Production Intern*

Business and Operations: Chuck Hoover, *Chief Marketing Officer;* Robert Ames, *Group General Manager*

Public Relations and Marketing: Joe Ewaskiw, *Senior Director of Communications and Public Relations*

Fodors.com: Jeremy Tarr, *Editorial Director;* Rachael Levitt, *Managing Editor*

Technology: Jon Atkinson, *Director of Technology;* Rudresh Teotia, *Associate Director of Technology;* Alison Lieu, *Project Manager*

Writers: Benjamin Kemper, Megan Frances Lloyd, Joanna Styles

Editor: Brian Eschrich

Production Editor: Jennifer DePrima

2nd Edition

ISBN 978-1-64097-640-5

ISSN 2691-2295

All details in this book are based on information supplied to us at press time. Always confirm information when it matters, especially if you're making a detour to visit a specific place. Fodor's expressly disclaims any liability, loss, or risk, personal or otherwise, that is incurred as a consequence of the use of any of the contents of this book.

SPECIAL SALES

This book is available at special discounts for bulk purchases for sales promotions or premiums. For more information, e-mail SpecialMarkets@fodors.com.

PRINTED IN CANADA

10 9 8 7 6 5 4 3 2 1

About Our Writers

Benjamin Kemper followed the siren song of Ibérico ham from New York to Madrid, Spain, where he writes about the places that make him hungriest. The Caucasus, Portugal, France, and—*por supuesto*—Spain are his main beats. Beyond Benjamin's frequent collaborations with Fodor's, his work has appeared in the *Wall Street Journal, Condé Nast Traveler, AFAR, Smithsonian Magazine,* and *Travel + Leisure,* among other publications. Benjamin updated the Experience Madrid, Travel Smart, and Madrid neighborhood chapters.

Megan Frances Lloyd is a food and travel writer writer based in Seville, Spain. Her work has appeared in *Condé Nast Traveler, Bon Appétit, Hemispheres Magazine , Serious Eats, Eater, PUNCH,* and *TASTE.* She also serves as the Spain correspondent for Migrants of the Mediterranean, a humanitarian storytelling organization. Megan updated the Day Trips from Madrid chapter.

Joanna Styles is a freelance writer based in Málaga, Andalusia, just about the perfect place to live. Since she first spotted orange trees in the sunshine and the snow-capped Sierra Nevada, she's been passionate about Andalusia, its people, places, and culture. Thirty years later she's still discovering hidden corners. Joanna is the author of *www.guidetomalaga.com.* Joanna updated the Seville and Granada chapters.